James McNeill Whistler

James McNeill Whistler

at the Freer Gallery of Art

David Park Curry

FREER GALLERY OF ART
Smithsonian Institution
In association with

W. W. NORTON & COMPANY
New York, London

This book was published on the occasion of the exhibition "James McNeill Whistler" at the Freer Gallery of Art, Smithsonian Institution, supported by a generous grant from American Telephone & Telegraph Company (AT&T).

Exhibition dates:
Freer Gallery of Art, Washington, D.C.,
May 11, 1984–November 5, 1984

Designed by Katy Homans, Homans/Salsgiver
Typeset by Trufont Typographers
Printed in Great Britain by Balding & Mansell

frontispiece: Peacock Room, south wall.

Library of Congress Cataloging in Publication Data

Curry, David Park.
  James McNeill Whistler.

  "Published on the occasion of the exhibition 'James McNeill Whistler' . . . exhibition dates: Freer Gallery of Art, Washington, D.C., May 11, 1984–November 5, 1984."—
  Bibliography: p.
  1. Whistler, James McNeill, 1834–1903—Exhibitions.
2. Freer Gallery of Art—Exhibitions. I. Whistler, James McNeill, 1834–1903. II. Title.
N6537.W4A4 1984   759.13   83–25525
ISBN 0-393-01847-4

W. W. Norton & Company, Inc., 500 Fifth Avenue, New York, N.Y. 10110
W. W. Norton & Company Ltd., 37 Great Russell Street, London WC1B 3NU

1 2 3 4 5 6 7 8 9 0

Contents

From our founding, we at AT&T have been dedicated to excellence in providing communications services to the public. At the same time, the company has a long history of community involvement and support of programs that enhance the quality of life across the nation, including support of the arts.

We have a particular interest in American artists, both those working today and those who have contributed to our nation's heritage.

James McNeill Whistler is surely one of our most extraordinary artistic forebears. His importance goes beyond his own genius as a painter and rests as well on his contribution to expanding America's understanding of the Orient through exposure to its art. Inspired by his own study of Asian works, Whistler advised his friend Charles Freer, who ultimately put together the Freer Collection of Oriental Art and gave it to the nation.

The opportunity to view a major portion of a single artist's work is always a special event. This extensive presentation of Whistler at the Freer provides the public with a rare look at an artist who is known more by his reputation than by the full range of his work.

We hope the show, honoring the 150th anniversary of the artist's birth, will result in a better understanding of America's cultural heritage and of the great tradition of patronage of the arts that Freer and Whistler represent.

All of us at AT&T are pleased to participate by sponsoring the exhibition and its permanent record in the catalogue.

CHARLES L. BROWN
Chairman, AT&T

Foreword

The works by James McNeill Whistler in the collection of the Freer Gallery of Art cover the full span of his creative life and represent the most extensive collection of paintings and drawings by this American artist. These holdings, integral to the history of late nineteenth- and early twentieth-century Western art, were assembled as a result of the patronage and generosity of Charles Lang Freer, the founder of the museum.

The somewhat unusual combination of Oriental and American art within one specialized museum reflects Charles Freer's enlightened connoisseurship. Whistler and Freer were close friends, and it was Whistler who in the 1880s impressed upon Freer the importance of extensive study in Oriental arts and civilization, at the time a field relatively unexplored in the West.

As Freer collected works from the Orient, he also acquired American paintings whose delicacy and refinement of tone and subject matter made them a suitable complement to his Oriental holdings. Freer perceived these American works to be a bridge by which Westerners could reach an understanding of Oriental art.

The selection of Whistler's oil and watercolor paintings, as well as the drawings and pastels, for this exhibition was made by Dr. David Park Curry, our curator of American art. It was Dr. Curry who organized the exhibition and the catalogue around four major themes, thereby giving special focus to Whistler's myriad artistic activities and contributions.

Space limitations both in the catalogue and in the exhibition galleries precluded the possibility of showing the extensive collection of Whistler etchings and prints housed at the Freer. At some future time, we hope it will be possible to highlight that exciting portion of Whistler's oeuvre.

The generous support of AT&T has enabled us to carry out the many requirements of this exhibition and to publish a richly illustrated catalogue. We are gratified by their endorsement of the project and sincerely appreciate their assistance. On the 150th anniversary of Whistler's birth, this exhibition and catalogue should reaffirm Whistler's artistic contributions to new audiences around the world. Coming as it does during the sixtieth anniversary of the public opening of the Freer Gallery, we should also express our admiration for the unique relationship between the patron, Charles Lang Freer, and the artist, James McNeill Whistler. Without the relationship the collection or, indeed, the Freer Gallery itself might never have become a reality.

THOMAS LAWTON
Director, Freer Gallery of Art

Acknowledgments

O, Atlas, they say I cannot keep a friend. My dear, I cannot afford it.
JAMES MCNEILL WHISTLER

Whistler made the above comment in *The Gentle Art of Making Enemies*. Unlike the artist, however, the art historian cannot afford to lose a friend. This volume would have been impossible without innumerable contributions by many friends and colleagues in Britain and the United States.

I am particularly indebted to the director of the Freer Gallery of Art, Dr. Thomas Lawton. He gave me free rein in a collection whose riches are a constant source of surprise and stimulation. Dr. Lawton has afforded me a rare opportunity for exciting research—the possibilities are far from exhausted in this book.

Dr. Lawton's staff facilitated many aspects of my work, from the initial outline through the preparation and publication of the manuscript. In particular I would like to acknowledge the unfailing assistance of Ellen Nollman and the library staff; and the significant contributions of Martha Smith, John Winter, Thomas Chase, and Paul Jett of the Freer Technical Laboratory; James Haden, Bernard Schopper, and the late Stanley Turek of the Photography Studio; Yoshi Shimzu, Ann Yonemura, Josephine Knapp, and Louise Cort of the curatorial staff; special assistants Martin Amt and Rocky Knorr; secretaries Peggy Dong, Jo Dugi, and Marie Heinrichs. Sarah Newmeyer-Hill and Richard Louie of the administrative staff oversaw countless details for both publication and exhibition, and secured many elusive permissions and photographs.

Part of my research travel was funded by a special grant through the office of the secretary of the Smithsonian Institution. My work on Cremorne Gardens was underwritten by a generous contribution from Willard G. Clark. The catalogue would have been impossible without lavish support from the American Telephone & Telegraph Corporation.

Friends and colleagues in other institutions were generous with time and help. I am particularly grateful to a number of Whistler scholars and curators who have generously shared insights and information. They include Susan Hobbs, Washington; and Margaret MacDonald, Glasgow; as well as Martin Hopkinson of the Hunterian Art Gallery; Nigel Thorp at the University of Glasgow Library; Lynn Bell at the University of Seskatchewan; and Robin Spencer at the University of St. Andrews.

I am also indebted to Elizabeth Broun and Marilyn Stokstad at the University of Kansas Museum of Art; Anne Farnam at the Essex Institute; Richard Field and the Print Room staff at Yale University Art Gallery; Ruth Fine at the National Gallery of Art; Deborah Gribbon at the Isabella Stewart Gardner Museum; Martha Heinz, Phoebe Peebles, Maureen Donovan, and Marjorie Cohn at the Fogg Art Museum; Kathy Lochnan at the Art Gallery of Ontario; Margaretta M. Lovell and the conservation staff at the De Young Museum; J. H. Morley at the Royal Pavilion, Brighton; the Print Room staff and Milo Naeve at the Art Institute of Chicago; Katherine Pyne and Peter Barnett at the Detroit Institute of Arts; Henry Sandon of the Dyson-Perrins Museum; Rosalind Savill at the Wallace Collection; Lawrence Smith and the staff of the British Museum Print Room; Carol Troyen, Barbara Shapiro, and Theodore Stebbins of the Museum of Fine Arts, Boston; Clive Wainwright and his staff at the Victoria and Albert Museum.

Further, I would like to thank the London dealers Jeremy Cooper, Michael Whiteway, and Peyton Skipwith; as well as Thomas Brunk, Susan Casteras, Hilarie Faberman, Molly Faries, Mary Janotta, Patricia Kane, Leah Lipton, Elizabeth Packard, Bruce Robertson, Andrew Saint, Gridley McKim Smith, Kevin Stayton, Lee Weihl, Diane Wyne of Harris and Paulson Word Systems Inc., and Susan Zilber.

The staffs of the following institutions were extraordinarily kind in locating rare books, documents, and objects for this study: the Boston Public Library Department of Prints and Drawings; the Chelsea Public Library Special Collections; the Library of Congress; the Museum of the City of London; the National Monuments Record, London; the National Gallery of Art Library, Washington; and the National Museum of American Art Library, Washington.

The ideas contained in the four essays were substantially developed within the classroom in concert with my graduate seminar on Whistler conducted at Yale University. I am deeply indebted to John Adams, Rebecca Beddell, Barbara Heins, Linda Landis, Antonia Lant, and Katherine Rubin. During the fall of 1981, they carried out research on some of the most difficult drawings in the collection, and sharply debated some of my cherished assumptions, helping to refine them. My work, on both Watteau and Cremorne Gardens was further facilitated by Miss Landis during her tenure as a Smithsonian research fellow in the summer of 1982.

For their invaluable insights and gentle criticisms, I owe particular thanks to my readers Leila Kinney, Julia Murray, Nancy Olson, George T. M. Shackelford, Marc Simpson, and Fronia Wissmann. They have saved me from myself.

This book was produced with remarkable grace by James Mairs, assisted by Jeremy Townsend, Carol Flechner, and Erica Echols at W. W. Norton & Company. Trufont Typographers set the type from almost impenetrable manuscript, and Katy Homans, John DiRe, and Eric Ceputis of Homans/Salsgiver designed the publication, bringing order out of chaos. Whistler's horror of art reproductions surely would be disarmed by the sensitive color plates printed at Balding & Mansell under the guidance of Guy Dawson.

Lewis Story and my colleagues at the Denver Art Museum have borne with patience my absences and distraction during the completion and editing of the manuscript.

Finally, a note in pink to G. Rebecca Morter.

As Whistler commented at the end of *The Gentle Art of Making Enemies*, "Atlas, we 'collect' no more."

DAVID PARK CURRY
February, 29 1984
Denver

James McNeill Whistler

Arrangement in White and Black, ca. 1876.

Artist and Patron

We live in an age of surfaces.
OSCAR WILDE

It is so difficult to choose between pearls.
CHARLES LANG FREER

IT WOULD BE HARD TO OVERESTIMATE the impact that James McNeill Whistler had upon Charles Lang Freer as a collector. While it is generally understood that Whistler had something to do with Freer's collection of American paintings, as well as his interest in Oriental art, the abstract quality of Whistler's influence has made it somewhat difficult to perceive just how great a role the artist played in the establishment of the Freer Gallery of Art. On the basis of letters and documents housed in the Freer archives, coupled with analysis of the collection's formation over time, it is now possible to state that the tastes and inclinations of the artist are as boldly stamped upon the institution as are those of the patron.

Although more difficult to assess, Whistler's impact upon Freer's preferences in Oriental art involved aestheticism of a highly refined nature and the evolution of an extremely personal yet well-educated taste on Freer's part. The formation of the collection reflects Freer's long experience as a successful negotiator in the world of business. Moreover, his friendly but firm manner was probably the key to maintaining a long-term friendship with the volatile artist. Friendship, in turn, led to the artist's cooperation and advice in putting the collection together. When Whistler was alive, prints, drawings, watercolors, and oil paintings came directly to Freer from the artist's studio. Whistler's contacts and counsel led Freer to other acquisitions. By the time Whistler died in July 1903, the artist had thoroughly imbued the patron with values that would guide Freer as he completed the collection over the next sixteen years.

Freer's evolution as a collector occurred in several overlapping stages. The lives of artist and patron span the Aesthetic Movement of the 1870s and 1880s, when popular publications emphasizing the rewards of good taste reached hitherto unequaled numbers. Central to the movement's message of aesthetic enlightenment was the ownership of works of art and the creation of beautifully appointed domestic spaces. During the late 1880s, Freer bought prints. These include etchings by Whistler, whose work was introduced to Freer by Howard Mansfield, another collector. In 1890 Freer met Whistler, following his already-established pattern of acquaintance with living American artists. A generous and supportive patron, Freer quickly gained access to the best work one of his chosen artists could offer, and Whistler, like Thomas Wilmer Dewing, Abbott Handerson Thayer, Dwight William Tryon, and others, never stinted on quality with Freer. It was also in the 1890s that Freer became interested in Oriental art, at first

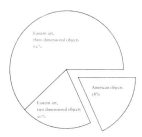

Figure 1.
Chart, Freer gift by numbers of objects.

Figure 2.
Chart, Freer gift by cost of objects.

Figure 3.
Wilson Eyre, Freer mansion, Detroit, 1893 ff. (Photograph, Freer Archive.)

Figure 4.
Variations in Flesh Color and Green: The Balcony, 1864 ff, oil on panel. Freer Gallery.

buying inexpensive Japanese prints and pottery. He made his first trip to the East in 1895. By the turn of the century, Freer's tastes had become much more sophisticated. He had narrowed his focus to include only a few American painters, Whistler the most prominent among them.[1] At the same time, he was actively expanding his Oriental collections to embrace the arts of China and other parts of the East as well as Japan.

Freer concentrated particularly upon the Whistler collection for the decade that coincided with the artist's last productive years and the first few years after his death, when speculation in Whistler paintings was at its height. Although the Oriental collections received greater emphasis in the ensuing years, Freer continued to buy the works of Whistler and other American artists. He viewed his collecting activities in a holistic sense. Virtually the last item Freer added to the collection was Whistler's *Nocturne: Cremorne Gardens No. 3*, bought in August 1919. The collector died one month later.[2]

Freer bequeathed over 11,000 objects to the Smithsonian Institution, with Eastern artworks far outnumbering American paintings. The count is based upon Freer's detailed inventory lists in which one Egyptian bead priced at 50 cents receives the same attention as Whistler's Peacock Room, which cost over $30,000. Another set of figures, based upon Freer's carefully preserved vouchers or bills of sale, gives us a more balanced impression of his goals (Figs. 1 and 2). The most general categories in the collector's own mind, apparent from the organization of his inventory lists, were Western paintings, drawings, and prints, including the Whistler collection; two-dimensional Eastern artworks, including paintings and screens; and three-dimensional Eastern pieces—jade, pottery, bronzes, and sculpture. Freer's fortune was divided among these three areas, if not equally, then at least with a certain sense of proportion. About a quarter of his fortune went for American art, the majority of these funds being spent on the Whistler collection.

Freer's interest in Whistler's paintings stemmed in part from his intention to live in grander style in the mansion he had built in Detroit in 1892 (Fig. 3).[3] Freer wanted to hang his new home with beautiful art. Although Freer remained a cautious buyer, adding only two more Whistler oils to his collection during the decade, his ambition continued to grow. During the 1890s Freer's purpose became set, and before the artist's death the patron had decided to found a museum that featured a representative sampling from every facet of Whistler's range. The collection was to bear the artist's imprimatur. Whistler wrote to Freer on July 9, 1899, "I think I may tell you without the least chance of being misunderstood, that I wish you to have a fine collection of Whistlers!!! perhaps *the* collection."[4]

An article in a Washington newspaper appeared in 1906, indicating that Whistler's collaboration with Freer was hardly a secret:

> *It is now about ten years since Mr. Freer began to inquire as to how his art collections could most effectively be presented to the American people. The matter was frequently discussed with Mr. Whistler himself, and an understanding was arrived at between the two men that Mr. Freer should have certain of the Whistler paintings on the condition either expressed or implied that ultimately they should be placed in a gallery open to the public.[5]*

Whistler's role as adviser could be compared with that of his fellow expatriate artist, Mary Cassatt, who was instrumental in the formation of the Havemeyer collection now at the Metropolitan Museum of Art. The obvious, if predictable,

Figure 5.
Nocturne: Blue and Silver—Bognor, 1871–1876, oil on canvas. Freer Gallery.

Figure 6.
Nocturne in Black and Gold: Entrance to Southampton Water, ca. 1875–1876, oil on canvas. Freer Gallery.

Figure 7.
The Thames in Ice, 1860, oil on canvas. Freer Gallery.

Figure 8.
San Biagio, etching, fourth state, K197, from "Venice," Second Series. Freer Gallery.

difference is that Whistler, unlike Cassatt, concentrated upon his own *oeuvre*.

The four Whistler oils Freer had purchased by 1901—three of them with the artist's direct aid—presage the collector's commitment to gathering a representative sample of the artist's work. When he was still negotiating for his third oil, *Nocturne: Blue and Silver—Bognor*, Freer wrote, "It is one I very much need to help balance my group of Whistler's paintings."[6] Widely divergent in style, the first four oils could be viewed as cornerstones in Freer's didactic edifice. *The Balcony* was a fine example of an Anglo-Japonesque scene, one of Whistler's important early innovations (Fig. 4). *The Thames in Ice* could be paired with either the *Bognor* or the *Nocturne in Black and Gold: Entrance to Southampton Water* to contrast Whistler's early realism with the more abstract style that typifies his later nocturnes (Figs. 5, 6, 7).

Today the Freer Gallery of Art houses major Whistler paintings, both early and late, including characteristic portraits, figure paintings, landscapes, seascapes, and genre scenes. Whistler's only surviving interior scheme, the Peacock Room, is here. Watercolors and drawings in the collection range from experimental efforts to finished exhibition pieces, while the large print collection remains an invaluable resource for studying that aspect of Whistler's *oeuvre*. When possible, Freer would purchase preparatory or related drawings for major works in his collection, and eventually he began to collect letters and documents as well. He also accumulated a large library of books, articles, and now-rare exhibition catalogues. It could be argued that Freer indeed had *the* collection of Whistlers.

Freer's early interest in prints should not be overlooked. His commitment to print collecting—one that continued until his death—casts light upon our understanding of his growth as a connoisseur and collector not only of Western but also of Eastern art. In both fields Freer proceeded from prints to paintings. The path is a logical one and not uncommon, involving issues of availability and financial as well as intellectual involvement.

By the time Freer met Whistler on March 4, 1890, the Detroit industrialist already owned more than eighty of the artist's etchings, as well as nine lithographs and a monochromatic watercolor. He possessed no oils at that time. Freer's earliest purchases suggest that he had subscribed to the then-current critical evaluation of Whistler's work. For a quarter of a century, the American expatriate had been praised for his etchings while his paintings won acceptance in inverse proportion to their degree of abstraction, the most popular being early works closely allied with the principles of mid-century realism. Although Freer was soon to widen his horizons significantly, he did not begin to acquire highly abstract oils by Whistler until patron and painter were personally acquainted.

Freer began gathering prints in about 1886.[7] His taste was by no means adventuresome, and the collection was for the most part made up of then-fashionable "painter-etchers" of the nineteenth century. Printmakers represented in Freer's collection by 1886 included familiar names like Félix-Hilaire Buhot and Johan Barthold Jongkind. They also included a number of artists who can be directly associated with Whistler.[8]

Once he had seen Howard Mansfield's collection of Whistler prints during the winter of 1886–1887, Freer became intrigued. In 1887 he inaugurated his own Whistler collection with the purchase of the "Second Venice Set" from Knoedler's in New York (Fig. 8). But the Freer-Mansfield friendship eventually cooled, and Freer's holdings soon rivaled Mansfield's. The twenty-six etchings from the "Second Venice Set" became the seed of what is now one of the two largest collections of Whistler's art in the world.[9]

Freer's print-collecting methods reveal the interests he would later pursue in other media. Not only did he become quickly enamored of a particular artist, he also had an abiding concern with issues of surface quality. Freer bought five works by Bracquemond in 1886; however, four of them were different states of the same image, *Approaching Storm*. Freer was as interested in the surface of each print, the artist's changes to the plate, and the nuances of inking as he was in subject matter.[10] Freer's early interest in the process of printmaking continued throughout his career as a collector. The Freer bequest is especially valuable for its multiple states, often rare ones, of etchings and lithographs by Whistler. The collection also includes numerous drawings related to prints, and over thirty of Whistler's original copper plates.[11] Similarly, Freer purchased not only Japanese prints, but also some of the woodblocks used to produce them.

During the 1890s, Freer still saw himself essentially as a collector of prints.[12] The impact of Freer's early print connoisseurship and the role it played in developing his eye and confidence are demonstrated in his modest choice of *Grey and Silver: The Mersey* as his first painting by Whistler (Fig. 9). Purchased in 1889, the watercolor's appearance bears a close resemblance to a heavily inked print. Freer carried on this conservatism in the purchase of Whistler oils in 1897, 1899, and 1902 (see Plates 25, 26, 27). Each is murky, monochromatic, and directly related to the subtle nuances and aesthetic impact of Whistler's print surfaces.[13]

Figure 9.
Grey and Silver: The
Mersey, watercolor, 1880s.
Freer Gallery.

The monochromatic watercolor indicates a most conservative step—it was not nearly so expensive as an oil painting. Relative cost was a factor that affected the sequence of Freer's experiences as a collector. Prints were much cheaper than the paintings, sculptures, or many of the Eastern bronzes and ceramics that Freer eventually acquired.[14] That the collector followed a similar path when forming his tastes for Oriental art is worth remarking. Freer's earliest purchases were readily obtainable ukiyo-e woodblock prints, popular in the West since the 1860s. However, as his taste and confidence expanded, Freer eventually abandoned Japanese prints and began to collect ukiyo-e paintings of approximately the same period. He later widened his scope to include Chinese paintings.

In 1900 Freer remarked, "The majority of collectors make the enormous mistake of spending the first ten or twelve years . . . gathering trash, and the balance of their life [*sic*] in getting rid of it."[15] Freer kept his collecting goals sharply focused and did not purchase his Whistlers indiscriminately. Moreover, Freer concerned himself with refining his holdings almost from the outset, a habit he maintained throughout his collecting career. As he began to focus on fewer artists, he rid himself of others.[16] The collector's aims were subject to review as his tastes developed toward the overriding concern with surface harmonies that characterizes the group of American and Oriental objects bequeathed to the nation in 1919.

Having rapidly gathered a large number of prints by Charles von Gravesand, a popular etcher of the late nineteenth century, Freer lost interest and donated them to the Detroit Institute of Art in 1905. Similarly, the Japanese woodblock prints he acquired from 1894 until 1904 were sold shortly thereafter, as Freer had decided to concentrate on Oriental paintings instead. At that point, Freer's outlay for Japanese prints was between $7,000 and $9,000, an amount close to the sum dispensed on von Gravesand's work. Print collecting was a relatively inexpensive "apprenticeship." By the time he died, Freer had spent over $3 million on his various collections.

Popular prints may have played some part in the formation of Freer's tastes. He began collecting when Art Nouveau held sway in Europe. Oriental art had

Figure 10.
Hogai (1828–1888), *Avalo-kitesvara (Hibo Kwannon)*, Japan, pigments on silk. Freer Gallery.

Figure 11.
Alphonse Mucha, poster for Job cigarette papers, color lithograph, Paris, 1896–1897. Collection Victoria and Albert Museum. (Photograph from Jiri Mucha, Marina Henderson, Aaron Scharf, *Alphonse Mucha*, rev. enl. ed. [London and New York: St. Martin's Press Academy Editions], pl. 10.) Reprinted courtesy of St. Martin's Press.

been a major contributor to the vocabulary of the "new art" which swept Europe on the heels of the Aesthetic Movement. Whistler scorned the idea of "newness," declaring that "there is no art nouveau. There is only art." This reflects his earlier elitist attitude toward the Aesthetic Movement, which was as popular in the 1870s as Art Nouveau was in the 1890s. Once the tenets of aestheticism reached the masses, Whistler declared waspishly that "art is upon the town," even though his own aesthetic battles had been a major inspiration for the movement.[17] In his gentle way, Freer was as much an elitist as Whistler. Freer evinced no interest in the Art Nouveau objects that filled London and Paris shops during the 1890s, although these items were frequently intended for domestic use and became available at the time Freer was decorating his new home. Nonetheless, an awareness of this style was unavoidable.

During his travels in the 1890s, one of the dealers Freer frequented in Paris was Samuel Bing. Although Bing's Maison de l'Art Nouveau gave the movement its most common name, he was also an established dealer in Oriental antiquities. There is ample evidence in Freer's daybook that he was on extremely good terms with Bing, from whom he purchased expensive pieces of old Near Eastern pottery.[18] Perhaps the exposure to Art Nouveau received by Freer everywhere from poster kiosks to the shelves of goods offered in Bing's shop helped to determine the patron's taste for extremely decorative Japanese paintings of the Kano school. Freer bought a bodhisattva, *Avalokitesvara (Hibo Kwannon)* by Hogai (1828–1888) in 1902 (Fig. 10). Its rich colors, gilding, and whiplash curves are echoed in the decorative arabesques of Art Nouveau masters such as Alphonse Mucha. Created in 1896, Mucha's lithograph poster for Job cigarette papers typifies the extravagant advertising art of the period, which would have confronted the Detroit industrialist from the windows of any Paris taxi (Fig. 11).

Although it is generally understood that Freer was somehow influenced by Whistler to collect Oriental as well as American art, this idea has received little thoughtful analysis, and Freer's admixture of selected American and Oriental works in a single art gallery remains something of an anomaly. Freer made frequent generalizations such as "I have aimed to gather together objects of art covering various periods of production, all of which are harmonious and allied in many ways."[19] But such harmonies and alliances were seldom discussed in specific terms that would make them self-evident today. The artist's impact upon the patron can probably be best understood in terms of abstract aesthetic relationships formulated to compare the surfaces of historically unrelated objects, including paintings, prints, and pottery.

Whether or not we recognize these harmonies now, for Freer and for close associates like the scholar Ernest Fenollosa such relationships were nothing short of cosmic. Fenollosa wrote eloquently of "complicated and unsuspected art universes, ranges of natural affinities, systems of magnetic structure" that lay under "all pure beauties of line, mass, value and color." He compared these systems to the ones "which recent science is revealing in the physical formation of what we used to call elemental atoms."[20] An element of mysticism was present in the Freer-Fenollosa aesthetic canon. Fenollosa continued, "Every reflection of light, of love, flashed from one sensitive surface to another, creates a union between the related parts, weaves a network of illuminated truths, strikes a chord into which they become merged as notes." He went on with a definition of art as "a glimpse of ultimate truth embodied in an earthly symbol; the matter of marble or pigment, or speech, intoxicated with some nameless elixir distilled from the rapture of disembodied souls."[21] Briefly stated, Freer was following a synthetic rather than an analytical aesthetic system.

Freer came to maturity during the late 1870s and early 1880s, just as the Aesthetic Movement popularized decorative arts as a path to artistic enlightenment. Advocates of this movement spread their often emotional ideals of exquisite taste from Britain to America via a flood of publications that would have been impossible to circumnavigate. Freer's comment "Unfortunately as yet the many consider art a luxury . . . they are blind to the fact that in its highest form it is really a necessity" demonstrates his sympathy with the Aesthetic Movement belief in uplifting benefits to be had from an art-filled existence.[22]

The surge in interior decoration that occurred in both England and America during this period goes a long way toward explaining a domestic quality to be found in Freer's collection. While vast in number, objects in the collection are usually fairly small in scale and were originally purchased for a domestic interior. As mentioned above, Freer's preoccupation with constructing a new home on Ferry Avenue in Detroit seems to have precipitated his activity as a serious art collector during the 1890s. Freer's collecting motives approach the concern for finely tuned spaces filled with beautiful objects that characterized the Goncourt brothers' essays into interior decoration in Paris.[23] The sociologist Walter Benjamin was later to comprehend the importance of interiors for collectors during the late nineteenth century:

> *The interior is the retreat of art. The collector is a true inmate of the interior. He makes the transfiguration of things his business. To him falls the Sisyphean task of obliterating the commodity-like character of things through his ownership of them. . . . The collector dreams that he is not only in a distant or past world but also, at the same time, a better one [where] things are free of the drudgery of being useful."*[24]

Freer as a collector was heavily influenced by personal relationships with artists. Not only Whistler, but also Frederic Edwin Church, along with Dewing, Tryon, and Thayer, helped determine Freer's personal outlook on the arts. The last three artists concerned themselves not only with painting but also with decoration that ranged from interior color schemes to mural paintings for architectural settings to the decoration of individual objects. Freer visited Tryon's studio during the spring of 1889 and commissioned seven mural-sized paintings for his reception hall. Not only did he commission numerous oils for the new house, he also relied upon his artist friends for advice concerning interior appointments.

In several letters, Freer mentioned this reliance: "Tryon is making the hall, in which his panels are hung, very beautiful. Dewing is also accomplishing very beautiful results in the little parlor which is to be hung with his paintings" (Fig. 12).[25] In another letter ordering drapery materials from a New York firm, Freer announced proudly, "Messrs. Dewing and Tryon are decorating my house and the hangings are aiding in effecting a general harmony throughout."[26] An overriding concern with aesthetic harmony, in a collection intended for a domestic space, became the hallmark of Freer's assemblage of American and Oriental works of art. This quality was recognized at the time the Freer gift was first announced in 1906:

> *Chinese and Japanese art are singular in their character and harmonize with the work of Whistler, Dewing, Tryon and Thayer, all four leading American painters. For this reason the collection is taken out*

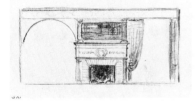

Figure 12.
D. W. Tryon, drawing for Freer's living room, depicting options for straight or arched passageway, ca. 1893. Freer Archive (letter file).

Figure 13.
Private Gallery, Freer
mansion, Detroit, 1911.
(Photograph, Freer
Archive)

Figure 14.
Interior, Freer Gallery of
Art, ca. 1980. (Photograph,
Freer Archive.)

Figure 15.
*Caprice in Purple and
Gold: The Golden Screen*,
with original frame, 1864,
oil on panel. Freer Gallery.

Figure 16.
*Arrangement in White and
Black*, ca. 1876, oil on
canvas. Freer Gallery.

Figure 17.
Attributed to Mi Fu
(1051–1107), *Mountains in
Mist*, hanging scroll, ink on
silk. Freer Gallery.

of time and belongs to all ages . . . this building will inclose a collection every object of which has perpetual harmonious esthetic interest.[27]

The scale of the Freer Gallery itself, tiny and jewellike next to the vast museum structures that line the Mall in Washington, reflects this beginning. The museum's barrel-vaulted skylit galleries are not unlike the private galleries that Freer added to his home (Figs. 13, 14).[28]

Freer made few pretensions to scholarship and relied upon the advice of scholars in the field to help him choose Oriental objects for the collection. In the case of his American objects, the artists themselves often served as the experts. Freer did not regard himself as either an artist or a historian. Rather, he was devoted to intellectual appreciation based upon personal aesthetic enjoyment.

This attitude was fostered in particular by Whistler's approach to Oriental art—one which was arbitrary and ahistorical, based upon personal taste. Whistler's painting *The Golden Screen* reveals his eclectic attitude toward objects from the East, which could be combined to suit himself without regard to historical considerations (Fig. 15). Freer followed the same line as a collector.

Among the most trusted advisers on Freer's Oriental collections was the art historian Ernest Fenollosa, in whose writings one finds the most precise enunciation of a theory of abstract relationships linking otherwise unrelated works of art from various Eastern and Western cultures.[29]

Whistler's work was viewed by Fenollosa, and consequently by Freer, as a bridge between the arts of the Orient and the Occident. This did not mean that Whistler was the only artist interested in *japonisme*, or even the first for that matter. Neither was he seen as a conscious imitator. Instead, it was believed that Whistler had gone beyond other Western painters of the 1860s and 1870s, who adopted flat color tones, local or unmodulated dark and light, angular spacing, and expressive brush work. According to Fenollosa, Whistler

was led by Japanese work much further—not only through a strengthening to solve problems already conceived, but through a suggestion of new ranges of aesthetic quality, utterly strange species of beauty, that had never been suspected, or at least fully stated, in earlier Western art. It was to explore this rich world of combinations, in their own right, that . . . became for Whistler the steady aim of his life.[30]

Whistler's importance as a bridge between East and West lay in the fact that he was "the first to grasp fully and creatively the oriental principle [i.e., aesthetic considerations distinct from subject content] in order to express occidental feeling." Thus, Whistler was forever placed "at the meeting-point of the two great continental streams; he is the nodule, the universalizer, the interpreter of East to West and West to East."[31]

Aesthetic relationships postulated by Freer that compare the surfaces of American prints or paintings with Oriental objects can clearly be seen in his own writings. About the hard-won portrait of Maud Franklin, *Arrangement in White and Black* (Fig. 16), Freer said, "It is in just such examples that Mr. Whistler approximates more closely than any other Occidental painter to the accomplishments of the masters of the Sung period."[32]

We should bear in mind that Freer's purchase of the portrait was preceded by two decades of collecting monochromatic prints, for it is surface appearance that

Figure 18.
Symphony in White, No. 2:
The Little White Girl, 1864,
oil on canvas. Tate Gallery,
London.

Figure 19.
Satsuma water bottle,
Japan, ca. 1725–1750.
Landscape painted in
underglaze blue by Tangen
(1679–1767), faïence. Freer
Gallery.

explains the relationship perceived by Freer between *Arrangement in White and Black* and Sung painting. The connection may seem obscure or arcane now. But at the turn of the twentieth century, impressionistic ink paintings, whose surfaces are close enough to those of Western etchings to seem familiar, were the first type of Chinese art of the Sung period to be admired in the West. Whistler's portrait of Maud is as evocative as a Sung painting. The figure emerges from a shadowy background like the mountains that penetrate the mist in a hanging scroll attributed to Mi Fu (1051–1107) (Fig. 17). Freer bought the scroll in 1908, only three years after acquiring *Arrangement in White and Black*.

Sometimes considered to be the final work in Whistler's series of "White Girls," the *Arrangement in White and Black* records the level of artistic sophistication that Whistler achieved a few years after his initial exposure to Japanese art. An earlier painting, *Symphony in White No. 2: The Little White Girl*, shows Whistler still making conventional use of Oriental objects as props (Fig. 18). Painted in 1864, *The Little White Girl* was the second in the series. Whistler had been an amateur collector of blue-and-white porcelain and Japanese prints during the 1860s. He gathered these objects to create pleasant domestic surroundings. He also used them as props in eclectic, obviously Western compositions. However, as he developed his style, Whistler internalized some of the principles of Oriental design, including asymmetry, subtle coloring, and evocative suggestion as a substitute for crudely stated clarity. As the last of the "White Girls," the portrait of Maud hints at an Orientalism that was conjoined with lessons Whistler absorbed from Western art. As Fenollosa had noted, Whistler was using Oriental principle to express Occidental feeling.

It is important to remember that subject matter has *not* been eliminated. However, it would have been secondary in the eyes of Freer and Fenollosa when they evaluated Whistler's painting. Fenollosa wrote:

> *Subject, indeed, is not . . . lost; but rather absorbed by, or translated into the beauty of form—quite as the thought of a lyric poem becomes transfigured in its graceful garb of words. Now it remained for Whistler, not quite to discover this important truth, but to suspect and sound the incredible vastness and variety implicit in this frankly accepted lyrical world of vision.*[33]

Whistler's eye had developed partially through close association—literally living with—Oriental works of art. His expanding awareness of the artistic possibilities inherent in Oriental art foreshadows Freer's own experience as a collector who surrounded himself with beautiful objects while his appreciation continued to grow.

Whistler's art had a discernible impact upon Freer's way of perceiving art by others. The patron posited relationships that linked objects differing by medium as well as by culture, and Whistlerian terminology was sometimes applied. In preparing inventory lists for the eventual transfer of the collection to Washington, Freer described pottery in his care. He characterized a Satsuma water bottle purchased in 1892 as "Hexagonal. White cracked glaze; Whistlerian landscape in blackish blue underglaze" (Fig. 19).[34] The collector compared pottery to paintings by other Americans as well. A parallel could be drawn either from East to West or vice versa. Freer wrote to Tryon about his painting *May Morning*: "I think when you put the finishing touches to the sky you must have had in mind the pink flush on the big white bowl."[35] Freer was referring to a Japanese pottery piece owned by Tryon. Indeed, the patron often gave Oriental pottery or bronzes to his favorite artists as gifts. Many artists besides Whistler owned Oriental art during this period. Two pieces now in the Freer collection were purchased at the sale of John La Farge's estate in 1908. They were a Shidoro water bottle and a Korean tea bowl.[36] La Farge was one of the earliest American artists to write about Oriental art and his own painting often contained japonesque elements.

The books on the East that Freer is known to have bought earliest were those read by Transcendentalists. He also read Kakuzo Okakura's *Ideals of the East*, one of the first histories of Oriental art.[37] Eventually, Freer's knowledge of Oriental art history increased. But even though he continued to study, gradually building up a large library of books on Oriental art, Freer still understood his objects primarily on the basis of their physical appearance. Regarding his own misidentification of a Kenzan box, Freer wrote his friend Rufus E. Moore, "I still hold to my original conviction concerning the box. What you say concerning signatures is altogether right from a scientific point of view, but I find greater personal satisfaction in depending upon the art feeling expressed."[38] Trying to make a decision on a potential acquisition, he wrote one dealer, "If you will describe the shape and colours of the pieces of pottery mentioned, I can form a better idea of them."[39]

He tended to relate to objects in terms of already-familiar material, notably the vocabulary of landscape and seasonal change. Freer's inventory describes a Chinese bowl from the Sung period as "covered with softly luminous celadon glaze, the hue a delicate grayish sea-green, suggesting in consistency the sea in its churning shallows, lightened by minute air bubbles." Freer summed up a Shigaraki tea bowl as "reddish brown covered inside and outside with very fine glaze of autumn tones. Mixed with the glaze are many small particles of opaque white resembling a shower of fine hail stones."[40]

It should be recalled that Freer was collecting Oriental pottery during the height of the American art-pottery collecting craze. The popular arts again mirror Freer's more erudite collecting passions, just as Art Nouveau posters appeared on the streets at the time he was buying Edo paintings. The central issue in American art pottery was the development of glaze formulas. These were jealously guarded by various competing firms. The shapes of the pottery were of secondary importance. American art pots were seldom thrown by the person who decorated them. Similarly, many of the pottery pieces Freer acquired had beautiful glazes but not very exciting shapes. For example, a modern scholar has described the Shigaraki tea bowl that Freer admired for its glaze as "odd" in form, an "amateur potter's first brave attempt."[41]

Freer did go so far as to acquire the work of one American art potter. His collection includes about thirty pieces of Pewabic pottery by Mary Chase Perry Stratton. Her work is more remarkable for iridescent glazes than for its frequently clumsy shapes. Stratton had access to Freer's collection of Eastern pottery, and she drew inspiration for some of her glazes and forms from pieces she saw at Freer's home on Ferry Avenue. A comparison of Stratton's bottle, made sometime between 1910 and 1917, with a Japanese jar makes this clear (Fig. 20). Although modern scholars date the Japanese jar to the Meiji period (1868–1911), it was once thought to be an old Karatsu piece from the sixteenth century, and Freer himself considered the jar "very fine." The Pewabic bottle has an iridescent reddish glaze over which pronounced rivulets of purplish blue have been allowed to drip. The colors and drip patterns are remarkably similar to the voluptuous glazes on the Meiji jar. That the two objects are chronologically close underscores Freer's reliance upon the connoisseur's argument of the eye.

Freer's occupation with the aesthetic nuances of surface and color pervaded

Figure 20.
Left: Jar, Japan, Meiji period (1868–1911). Freer Gallery. Right: Mary Chase Perry Stratton, American (1867–1961), Bottle, ca. 1910–1917, impressed mark: "Pewabic, Detroit." Freer Gallery.

Figure 21.
Armchair, Davenport and
Company, Boston, commis-
sioned 1892, oak frame
with silver glaze, rush seat.
Freer Gallery.

Figure 22.
*Symphony in Grey: Early
Morning—Thames*, 1871,
oil on canvas. Freer Gallery.

Figure 23.
Detail of Figure 21.

Figure 24.
Detail of Figure 22.

Figure 25.
Maruyama Okyo
(1733–1795), *Geese over a
Beach*, Japan, ink-on-paper
screen. Freer Gallery.

his life, extending to the very stone walls that fenced his Detroit mansion. He noted, "The colours of the stone are purple, blue and gray. About fifteen to twenty percent of the stone shows surface rust and stain, which adds greatly to the appearance of the wall."[42]

Within the mansion, this same emphasis upon understated color received great attention, particularly in the special gray wood stain developed by Freer himself for the paneled walls of several rooms. Freer told Dewing, "Before you put any color on the interior wood-work of the roof, I would like the effect I have produced in the 'Den' of my house which is now a beautiful pale silvery smoke color."[43]

Several chairs made by Davenport and Company of Boston to match Freer's paneling are now at the Freer Gallery of Art (Fig. 21). Each chair is a touchstone for the various elements that fed into Freer's aesthetic sensitivities: a slender form and rush seat evoke the "art furniture" of the 1870s and 1880s, particularly the "Sussex" chairs manufactured by William Morris and beloved of Aesthetic Movement advocates. Thinly applied lacquer reveals the underlying oak grain as if to illustrate the Arts-and-Crafts principle of truth to materials.

But the elegant lacquered surface, itself both Oriental and Whistlerian in inspiration, also testifies to Freer's love for monochromatic color schemes, first evidenced in his collection of prints, later in many of his Western oils and Eastern ink paintings. Whistler's *Symphony in Grey: Early Morning—Thames* celebrates the sensuality of the artist's materials with thinly brushed silvery pigments (Fig. 22). In one of his most evocative Oriental compositions, Whistler allowed the pebbly surface of the fine canvas to break through clouds of shimmering gray, just as the oak grain underlies the silver lacquer on each chair (Figs. 23 and 24).

Fenollosa responded to the sensuous nature of Whistler's grays, noting that the artist was "the first occidental to express . . . in almost flat planes, pearly films of grays so subtly differentiated that, without blending, each seems to vibrate and deliquesce into its neighbor."[44] The Davenport chair and the Whistler oil painting could be displayed next to an Edo-period ink-on-paper screen, *Geese over a Beach* by Maruyama Okyo, as a testament to Freer's never-ending commitment to visual harmony (Fig. 25). Infinite combinations were possible. Fenollosa noted, "A mural painting by Kano Yeitoku, a tea-bowl by Kenzan, and an oil sea-scape by Whistler achieve similar delicious tone-effects."[45]

A central purpose of the Freer collection as a group was to offer the raw material for making fruitful artistic syntheses. Fenollosa averred:

> *Things are not related to one another solely in series, or classified and enumerated groups. Several things, thoughts, or feelings may be so related as mutually to modify one another.*[46]

When a balanced amount of modification took place—neither too much nor too little—art was the result, and "all cases of such synthesis are cases of esthetic beauty." This type of synthesis could only be discerned by a select few. "It can only be revealed to the trained synthetic faculty of a choice soul." Clearly, then, the artist was no average person. "It is not enough for the artist to be an individual, he must be an individual *seer*. He must consecrate himself that he be made worthy to receive the transcendent gift of synthesis."[47] Fenollosa's reasoning sounds, as we may expect, quite close to Whistler's *Ten o'Clock Lecture*, which presented the artist as one chosen by the gods:

Figure 26.
Charles Adams Platt (1861–1933) *The Mountain*, ca. 1918, oil on canvas. Freer Gallery.

Figure 27.
Painting Gallery, Whistler Memorial Exhibition, Copley Hall, Boston, 1904. Courtesy of the Library of Congress, Pennell collection.

Figure 28.
Print Gallery, Whistler Memorial Exhibition, Copley Hall, Boston, 1904. Courtesy of the Library of Congress, Pennell collection.

Figure 29.
Symphony in Green and Violet, ca. 1868, oil on panel. Freer Gallery.

Through [the artist's] brain, as through the last alembic, is distilled the refined essence of that thought which began with the Gods, and which they left him to carry out. Set apart by them to complete their works he produces that wonderous thing called the masterpiece, which surpasses in perfection all that they have contrived in what is called Nature.[48]

Freer believed that the arts he collected were interchangeable. This is made clear in a letter to the architect Charles Adams Platt, who was designing the gallery that would eventually house the patron's enormous holdings. Freer invited Platt to his home, noting that "there are a number of objects in the collection I think it important for you to see, and some of the paintings contain suggestions for furniture."[49] Freer even lent Platt some Oriental paintings during the planning of the museum, and Platt eventually responded by painting a gray mountain landscape with Oriental overtones (Fig. 26).

An aesthetically pleasing mix also was the goal when Freer undertook an exhibition design. Asked to share objects from his collection at the St. Louis World's Fair in 1904, he sent a small group of pastels by Whistler, Tryon, and Dewing. They were carefully selected, "paying particular attention to quality and harmony." After some thought, Freer decided to add a group of Japanese wood carvings as decorative embellishments to the exhibition. Freer traveled to New York, and with the painter Dewing in attendance he visited Yamanaka and Company to choose "a group of beautiful, neutral-toned, ancient wood-carvings to hang above the line of pastels." Freer noted that both Dewing and Tryon approved of the idea, and he went on to explain, "Inasmuch as the pastels need to be hung on a line of easy vision, we felt that the space above would appear to better advantage if it were hung with these wood carvings. We also feel that you will delight in seeing them there." Freer concluded that the room would be "one of the most refined" at the fair.[50]

In fact, the concept was too refined to admit any alteration. Freer later voiced strong opposition to the suggestion that three-dimensional bronze objects be introduced into the room.[51] He had already orchestrated the colors, and his arrangement was intended to display only two-dimensional objects where delicate surface interplay could take place.

Although no photographs of the exhibition have yet been located, one may gain some sense of the effect Freer achieved by looking at installation shots from the Whistler Memorial Exhibition held in Boston just before the St. Louis fair. Oriental objects were used as decorations, interspersed with Whistler's paintings and drawings (Fig. 27). Some of the wood carvings in the Boston exhibition were gilded. Wood carvings were also installed over the doorways to the rooms containing prints. Large blue-and-white vases with distinct linear patterns were placed in several spots to compliment the black etched or lithographed lines on white grounds in Whistler's graphics (Fig. 28).

According to Freer, the art historian Fenollosa believed that Whistler's *Symphony in Green and Violet* "outsesshued Sesshu" (Fig. 29). One combination of objects that Freer considered aesthetically pleasing is documented in a rare autochrome made by Alvin Langdon Coburn in about 1909. Freer is posed with a pastel by Whistler entitled *Resting*. The pastel is flanked by small statuettes from the Orient (Fig. 30). It is likely that the purpose of such a combination would have been to demonstrate how various artists had attenuated or stylized the human figure. These artists acted at different times, independent of one another. Fenollosa wrote:

Figure 30.
Alvin Langdon Coburn,
portrait of Freer with his
collection, autochrome, ca.
1909. Freer Archive.

Figure 31.
Freer comparing Whistler's
Venus Rising from the Sea
with a large Oriental jar,
photograph, ca. 1915. Freer
Archive.

Figure 32.
Ceramic jar. Chinese, Yüan
dynasty (1280–1368).
Freer Gallery.

Figure 33.
Nocturne: San Giorgio,
1879, pastel. Freer Gallery.

In the wide play of his experimenting with absolute beauty,
[Whistler] struck again and again, without conscious imitation . . .
the characteristic beauties of the most remote masters, both Western
and Eastern. And it is this modern centrality in which Mr. Freer
discerns his supreme importance.[52]

Such was the "artistic truth" derived from aesthetics that Freer aimed to discover through his comparative collecting.

A posed snapshot shows the patron comparing Whistler's oil painting, *Venus Rising from the Sea*, with a large Babylonian pottery jar (Fig. 31). The point would have been to study the harmonious nuances between the glazed pottery and the surface of the oil painting. But synthetic comparisons between ancient pottery and Whistler's pastel drawings are perhaps easier to grasp. Fenollosa wrote that Freer eschewed porcelain because the tones achieved in the glazes were obvious and hard. Freer preferred the "softer and rougher grounds of pottery," which were "more like the old, coarse tinted papers, on which both old and modern masters have loved to try their suggestive sketches." Fenollosa went on, "Here is revealed the first kinship between Whistler's painting, and warmly glazed ceramics—that he himself sought for old paper sheets, ancient Dutch and Flemish hand-laid textures, over which to throw his pigments like translucent enamels."[53] Reasoning based solely on aesthetics permitted Freer and Fenollosa to compare the pottery with Whistler's drawings and paintings:

If now, we examine more minutely the mysteries of light-play in the
composition of these tones [on pottery], we shall see the secret chord
that pulls Whistler's painting into their harmonic scheme. The under-
clays—gray, yellow, olive, brick-red, or stone-brown—which I have
already compared to old papers, are full of the dissolved light of
opaque surfaces, a diffused luminosity almost peachy and down-like.
And it is this sort of cool depth which Whistler, even in his oil work,
loved to prepare upon the tea-jar grounds of his canvases.[54]

Fenollosa concluded that Whistler's use of thin layers of shadowy, evocative color were half-concealing, half-revealing, like the endless depths of glazed ceramic surfaces. He wrote, "Small wonder that [Whistler's] landscapes and portraits, set beside a Persian jar, the vortex of a Chinese saucer, or a muffled Kioto cup, are seen so perfectly to balance that the two ranges of harmony become identical" (Figs. 32 and 33).[55]

Recognizing the collection's importance as a rich repository of material for making instructive aesthetic abstractions, Fenollosa warned that "it may take years and generations for the exotic flower of synthesis to become naturalized in its new American home."[56] But the purpose of Freer's museum collection, which, after all, coincided with various other reform missions of the late nineteenth and early twentieth centuries, aimed at nothing short of counteracting what the patron perceived as the evils of deadening realism in art. The aesthetic lessons of the Freer Gallery were intended as much for the budding artist as the would-be scholar, and it is not in the least surprising that the museum's potential could be described in terms of temperance. Fenollosa warned, "We have debauched our aesthetic faculty by intemperate draughts at the bar of realism."[57]

Freer himself was anything but intemperate. Fiscal awareness and discretion mark Freer's relations with both artists and dealers. His businesslike approach to collecting provides the key for our understanding of an industrialist turned art patron.

Freer had made his fortune through a series of calculated business decisions. He tended to proceed logically toward any desired goal. The most important of these was a merger he engineered among numerous railroad supply companies in about 1900. This transaction made him independently wealthy.[58] Freer's approach also involved a good dose of common sense. While others battled over transcontinental railroad rights, Freer and his business partner Frank Hecker realized that by becoming suppliers of rolling stock they would make profits no matter which entrepreneur undertook the construction and management of the country's railroads.

The formation of Freer's art collection reflects the same businesslike methodology, for the industrialist saw collecting as the logical outgrowth of fortune.[59] Freer's offer of his art collection to the Smithsonian Institution was accepted in 1906, following some debate and the direct intervention of President Theodore Roosevelt.[60] Freer retained a life interest during which time he would build and refine the collection. In 1906 he began making methodical inventory lists of his holdings, and from that time forward he collected new objects and reviewed previous acquisitions with an eye toward the eventual opening of the Freer Gallery of Art.[61]

The friendship that Freer began with Whistler in London in 1890 lasted until the artist's demise in July 1903. Durable accord with any patron was an unusual event for Whistler; again we have evidence that Freer carried his levelheaded business practices over into his endeavors as a collector. Freer had already demonstrated his ability to handle difficult personalities in the railroad-car plants. Advising a business associate not to fire a subordinate, he wrote, "Genius is always erratic." He recognized that such men combined volatile sensitivity with ambition. The practical Freer urged toleration for "a future result . . . which would be of enormous value to all parties concerned." Freer's perception could easily extend to Whistler and suggests how the patron was able to get on so well with the artist.[62]

Freer avoided pressuring his artists to complete commissions, although he often had paid for them several years earlier. In Whistler's case this meant that numerous works owned by the patron were still in the studio at the time of the artist's death. Some were left unfinished, including Freer's own portrait (Fig. 34).

Freer was obliged to exercise patience with Whistler from the outset.[63] Only once did Freer collect an overdue painting (Fig. 35). In typical fashion, Whistler sold it enthusiastically to Freer but kept it in the studio. Later the artist wrote, "The Little Lady of Soho! I am glad you have chosen her. . . . I think before she is packed, I know of a touch I must add. And then she can follow you in the next steamer."[64] Several steamers later Whistler wrote, "I am having sent to you a photogravure they have just done of the Little Lady Sophie—to keep her in your mind, in case she remains with me for another couple of steamers."[65] She did. Freer still had not received the picture the following year. After yet another request for a reprieve, apparently made by Whistler through the London dealer William Marchant, Freer wrote firmly:

> I would . . . be delighted to accommodate Mr. Whistler and consent to his keeping for exhibition purposes The Little Lady Sophie of Soho were it not for the fact that the receipt of the picture has already been delayed one whole year. . . . I would like very much indeed to have the picture with me during the winter months, and to loan it to an important exhibition of Mr. Whistler's work which is to be made in Boston early next spring.[66]

Figure 34.
Portrait of Charles Lang Freer, 1902–1903, oil on panel. Freer Gallery.

Figure 35.
Rose and Gold: The Little Lady Sophie of Soho, 1898–1899, oil on canvas. Freer Gallery.

Figure 36.
D. W. Tryon, *Springtime*,
1892, oil on canvas. Freer
Gallery.

Figure 37.
*Harmony in Blue and Gold:
The Little Blue Girl*, 1894–
1903, oil on canvas. Freer
Gallery.

Figure 38
Attributed to Beatrix
Godwin Whistler,
*Caricature of Charles Lang
Freer*, ink. Hunterian Art
Gallery, University of
Glasgow.

The exhibition seems not to have taken place, but the temptation of favorable publicity may have been the lever that pried the painting out of Whistler's hands at last.

Freer did not try to control Whistler through carefully defined commissions. He learned early in their relationship that such control was impossible. In 1894 he commissioned a "spring" picture, probably having in mind something that was vaguely like the landscapes related to the four seasons painted by Dwight William Tryon for the Detroit mansion (Fig. 36). Eventually Whistler produced *Harmony in Blue and Gold: The Little Blue Girl*, which is related to spring only tangentially (Fig. 37). It depicts a young girl, and there is a budding flower at her feet. The painting was still in the studio in 1903. Freer occasionally visited Whistler and would have seen the work progressing under the artist's hand. Wise enough to let the commission take its course, Freer finally received a work of art that was both highly personal in content and aesthetically pleasing to him.

The tact with which Freer handled Whistler reflected his years as a successful negotiator of business mergers. In return for his openhandedness, Freer enjoyed not only Whistler's respect, but also his continuing assistance in forming the collection. Further, a genuine friendship developed over the years. Although both men maintained a dignified reserve, the strength of their bond sometimes shines on a page from the ordinarily staid Freer-Whistler correspondence.[67] Freer thoroughly enjoyed his association with Whistler and did not fret about the havoc the artist at times visited upon his own plans.[68]

Freer's enlightened patronage involved high-minded ideas of stewardship typical of late nineteenth-century museum founders. Freer was clearly not a speculator, and his collecting was governed by an advanced policy concerning the rights of living artists, which he applied to all the painters he supported: "It seems to me that the possessor of a work of art by a living artist is practically a caretaker, and in all matters pertaining to exhibitions he should be governed not so much by his own desires as he should be by those of the creator of the work" (Fig. 38).[69] Freer also demanded reproductions that did justice to the paintings. He completely sympathized with Whistler's horror of cheap reproductions that missed the subtlety of the art, and he joined with Rosalind Birnie Philip, executrix of Whistler's will, in trying to fend off opportunists who descended in a cloud around "the ladies of the family." In the years just before and after Whistler's death, Freer provided aid and legal counsel, witnessed Whistler's will, and advised Miss Birnie Philip on her rights in several publication disputes.

The channels through which Freer acquired his Whistler holdings were many. He entered into negotiations with dealers, private collectors, and close friends, but always maintained the position of a judicious businessman.[70] The most obvious channel was Freer's direct access to Whistler's studio. In 1890 Freer set up a standing order with Whistler for any new prints he might execute, and Whistler also sent Freer selected proofs from earlier works. Freer's second Whistler oil was purchased directly out of the artist's studio (see Plate 27). Others would follow. Buying directly from the artist was an important avenue of access, for Whistler was unwilling to sell his works to every would-be customer; and as the problem over dispatching *The Little Lady Sophie of Soho* demonstrated, even the patient Freer had a certain amount of difficulty in getting the artist to part with works still in his control.

Major oils which came to Freer from other collections tended to be ones that bore Whistler's stamp of approval. In 1899, Freer bought his third oil, the *Bognor Nocturne*, from Whistler's old friend Alfred Chapman. Of his sea pieces, Whistler considered the *Bognor* "one of my very finest, perhaps the most brilliant." In 1892 Whistler had complained to the Goupil Gallery that their album of photographs of his paintings excluded the *Bognor*, "which surely was one of the most important of the whole collection of pictures," according to the artist himself.[71]

Freer's acquisition of *The Thames in Ice* illustrates Whistler's willingness to intervene with other collectors and dealers to help Freer. The artist's aid may have been stimulated in part by his reluctance to part with objects still in his own hands. Whistler advised Freer that J. J. Cowan was about to sell some Whistler paintings late in 1901:

> *As they are what you really ought to have I am writing to him to try and hold in until he shall have heard from you. I certainly advise you to secure these things, or in any case . . .* The Thames in Ice, *and the water colour picture of Mrs. Whibley . . . take my advice and buy them "in a poke."*[72]

Figure 39.
The Shell, 1890s, fabricated chalks on gray-brown paper. Freer Gallery.

Freer acted with alacrity to secure the work.

Just as paintings from the studio continued to enter Freer's collection after Whistler's death, so, too, were tips concerning available pictures, such as *The Shell* (Fig. 39), passed on by Whistler's heir, Rosalind Birnie Philip.[73] Like Whistler himself, Birnie Philip was able to sway Freer's judgment. Although Freer originally intended to purchase only the shutters and south wall panel from the Peacock Room, Birnie Philip and her sister Mrs. Whibley were instrumental in persuading him to preserve the entire interior.

Dealers also played a major role in building the collection. When Freer acquired *The Balcony* in 1892, he first asked Howard Mansfield to look at the painting in Paris, where it was in the hands of Durand-Ruel, a French dealership. Mansfield was enthusiastic, and later that year Freer purchased the painting through E. G. Kennedy at the Wunderlich Gallery in New York.[74] The purchase reveals Freer's reliance upon a fellow collector as adviser, as well as the international cooperation between dealers that was often part of a transaction. Freer bought at auction only occasionally. He rarely purchased items sight unseen and would do so only upon recommendation by the most trusted friends and associates, Whistler prominent among them.

Seeking out reputable dealers with whom he could establish long-term relationships, Freer acquired objects both singly and in lots. He negotiated most often for Whistler's works with firms that had retained the artist's good will.[75] One of these was William Marchant, a London dealer. Freer hoped to buy *Caprice in Purple and Gold: The Golden Screen*, a painting that Whistler wanted to see in Freer's keeping (see Fig. 15).[76] For two years Freer's negotiations were conducted through Marchant, but when the owner was finally ready to sell, Freer found that the painting was too costly. He wisely left the matter in the dealer's hands:

> *The valuation placed by Lord Battersea on his picture is one which . . . exceeds the sum that I feel disposed to appropriate. This being the case, I am in doubt as to what course to pursue. I do not for a moment wish to even suggest that Lord Battersea's price is too high [but] I feel it only just that you should know these facts. Now, whether or not it would be proper to submit these conditions to Lord Battersea, I question in my own mind. However, I am inclined to leave the matter entirely to your own discretion—so, if you deem it*

Figure 40.
At the Piano, 1858–1859,
oil on canvas. The Taft
Museum, Cincinnati,
Louise Taft Semple Bequest.

Figure 41.
Nocturne: Blue and Gold—
Valparaiso, 1866, oil on
canvas. Freer Gallery.

Figure 42.
Arrangement in Black, No.
3: Sir Henry Irving as Philip
II of Spain in Tennyson's
Queen Mary, 1876–1885,
oil on canvas. All rights
reserved. The Metropolitan
Museum of Art, Rogers
Fund.

proper, you may show this letter to Lord Battersea, or, if you prefer
to suppress the letter, you may do so.[77]

We do not know exactly how Marchant handled Lord Battersea, but he was able to come to a satisfactory agreement, maintaining the £3,000 limit set by Freer.

Freer's negotiations did not always end in success. A number of important Whistler paintings did not enter the collection because Freer balked at prices he considered excessive. He wrote Marchant:

> *You know, I think how fond I am of Davis' Piano Picture, but when I*
> *talked £3000 to [D. C.] Thompson [the London dealer] he laughed,*
> *and refused to submit so small an offer. I then said to Mr.*
> *Thompson, "Very well, that is as high as I care to bid for it." He*
> *urged me to offer £4000, but I declined. If you can obtain it for*
> *£3000, I should like to have it.*[78]

At the Piano was then in the collection of Sir Edmund Davis (Fig. 40). Freer's offer through Marchant was not accepted. Unfortunately for Freer, his interest was just a bit too late. *At the Piano* had been sold by Francis Seymour Haden, Whistler's brother-in-law, to Alexander Reid, the Glasgow dealer, early in 1897. This occurred after E. G. Kennedy of Wunderlich's in New York failed to negotiate the purchase. Reid sold it in March 1897 to J. J. Cowan, an Edinburgh dealer and collector. But while Kennedy, Reid, and Cowan were all sympathetic to Freer's collecting aspirations, by the time Freer wanted to purchase the painting in 1899, Cowan had already sold it to Edmund Davis for £2,800. D. C. Thompson acted as an agent for Agnew, London dealers, in the transaction. From then on the painting fell outside of both Freer's price range and his circle of dealer friends.[79]

Freer did not forgive Thompson entirely. When searching for a suitable epithet to label Louise Kinsella, who had sat for Whistler and then tried to sell her portrait, Freer commented, "Her methods suggest those of Thompson."[80] But ever the good businessman, Freer did not formally break relations with the dealer, who later was associated with the French Gallery. Hence, a few works did enter the Freer collection under Thompson's aegis, including one important painting, *Nocturne: Blue and Gold—Valparaiso*, purchased in 1909 (Fig. 41).

Freer did not like speculating in pictures much more than Whistler himself. He was well aware of sharply rising prices after the artist's death but maintained his levelheaded approach. In 1904 Messrs. Dowdeswell and Dowdeswell, Ltd., another London firm, cabled him:

> *Can sell you Whistler's famous full-length portrait of Irving as Philip*
> *of Spain, six thousand pounds here Please cable if you want it.*

Freer replied coolly, "It is, of course, a beautiful work of art, but not one that I should care to add to my collection" (Fig. 42). Freer mailed a copy of the Dowdeswell telegram to his friend and fellow collector Richard Canfield in New York, commenting, "Things are still moving on the other side. Witness the cablegram enclosed herewith. . . . The British dealers must think we are a lot of fools. . . . Of course, I have declined the picture, with very slight comments."[81] Earlier that year Freer told Canfield of an offer for *Connie Gilchrist* at $30,000. Freer noted, "The price asked is a pointer to the future."[82]

As a participant in the somewhat speculative market for Whistler paintings at

Figure 43.
Blue and Silver: Trouville,
1865, oil on canvas. Freer
Gallery.

Figure 44.
*Nocturne: Blue and
Silver—Battersea Reach,*
1870–1875, oil on canvas.
Freer Gallery.

Figure 45.
*Harmony in Grey and
Green: Miss Cicely
Alexander,* 1872–1873, oil
on canvas. The Tate
Gallery, London.

Figure 46.
Succès d'Ernest à Cologne,
1858, pencil. Freer Gallery.

the turn of the century, Freer realized that travel and carefully nurtured personal contacts were necessary for ferreting out some of the best objects. Freer followed this policy in collecting Eastern as well as Western art, having previously engaged in extensive travel during his successful business career. As a collector Freer was constantly on the road. He visited museums to refine his already discriminating eye. He called on artists in their studios, and on private collectors in their homes, encountering works of art that later entered his keeping.

The collector relished his active quest. On the eve of his departure for Europe in April 1902, he wrote, "I have stirred up the matter so thoroughly in London that I am sure to be shown whatever of Mr. Whistler's work is at all likely to be purchasable."[83] In another note Freer reported progress on a painting of Trouville, "which I have been following up for some time. . . . I hope to scull it in." *Blue and Silver: Trouville* was added to the collection in July 1902, after an international arrangement that involved the previous owner and two dealers (Fig. 43).[84]

Freer's daybook covering his 1902 trip to England documents the energy he devoted to visiting museums and private collections. Among the collectors he visited were H. R. Newberry, Sir Edmund Davis, Alexander Hannay, Lord Battersea, G. N. Stevens, T. R. Way, W. C. Alexander, J. Martin White, Lady Valerie Meux, and Mrs. Watney. Mrs. Watney owned the Peacock Room. The other collectors together held most of the important Whistler paintings then in private hands, and some of their holdings eventually belonged to Freer.

In some cases a dealer was responsible for gaining Freer entry into a private collection. Freer wrote to Marchant in February 1902, "My hunger for the Whistler *Nocturne* owned by Mr. Rawlinson which you and I had the pleasure of seeing together in his residence still continues."[85] Freer acquired the painting through Marchant later that year (Fig. 44). Although many works that Freer saw on his visits were later added to the collection, others were never to be had. Either the cost was too dear, as in the case of Davis's *At the Piano*, or the owner would not sell at any price. This was what happened with *Harmony in Grey and Green: Miss Cicely Alexander*, an important portrait commissioned by the sitter's father (Fig. 45). In a letter written in 1913, Freer stated:

> *I have told Mr. Alexander more than once that the portrait in white, of his daughter, is in my opinion Whistler's greatest figure painting and I still think so. Its artistic value is very great and its financial value is not easily estimated. I should like to see it cared for in the future, by the American National Gallery at Washington, and if Mr. Alexander is willing to sell it to me for the sum of . . . £10,000 . . . I will . . . present it to the U.S. Government along with the other collections now in my care, but already the property of the American Nation.*[86]

Freer's bid failed. Had he acquired the picture, *Miss Alexander* would have been the single most expensive work in his entire collection of Eastern and Western art.

On a few occasions Freer managed to secure an entire collection intact. He had already purchased Seymour Haden's substantial group of Whistler drawings and prints by 1899. That purchase included early sketches and rare states of some of Whistler's etchings (Fig. 46). In 1902 Freer acquired the collection of small oil paintings, watercolors, and drawings owned by H. S. Theobald of London. Theobald had bought many of these works from the London dealer

Figure 47.
Chelsea Shops, early 1880s,
oil on panel. Freer Gallery.

Figure 48.
*The White Symphony:
Three Girls*, ca. 1868 ff., oil
on panel. Freer Gallery.

Figure 49.
Venus Rising from the Sea,
ca. 1869–1870, oil on
canvas. Freer Gallery.

Dowdeswell after Whistler's 1884 exhibition. Freer's first visit with Theobald took place on May 16, 1902. Freer's daybook reads, "Mr. H. S. Theobald. 46 Hyde Park Square during Morning. Mr. Whistler Chelsea Studio in afternoon."[87] There is little doubt that Whistler counseled Freer to buy. Freer visited Theobald twice more before completing the single transaction that accounts for nearly a quarter of the Whistler oils in his collection (Fig. 47).[88]

Several case histories of particular acquisitions will shed further light upon Freer's methods of collecting. The artist's influence on the patron's collection extended beyond the choice of items from the studio or advice on paintings available through dealers or friends.

Whistler led Freer to cultivate a fruitful relationship with the Way family, even though Whistler was no longer on speaking terms with the two London printers who had played a significant part in his career as a lithographer. Whistler had quarreled with them over publication of a catalogue of lithographs in 1896. At the time of Whistler's bankruptcy in 1879, Way, Sr., was one of the chief creditors, and he was awarded thirty paintings during the proceedings.[89] Some of these were returned to Whistler at various junctures during the 1880s and 1890s. It seems that in 1881 Way had returned five of the "Six Projects," a group of figure paintings intended for interior decoration. Having lost them once, Whistler was reluctant to sell any to Freer. However, *The White Symphony: Three Girls*, which the artist considered one of his most important conceptions, still remained in Way's hands (Fig. 48). Whistler gave Freer sound advice, and the collector obtained *The White Symphony* later that summer.[90] The other five "Projects" remained with Whistler. Freer finally bought them from Miss Birnie Philip, literally days after the artist died.

In dealing with the father, Freer must have gained the confidence of the son. T. R. Way, Jr., contacted Freer on July 1, 1902. Way, Sr., had given his son several pictures after the Whistler bankruptcy in 1879. These, consequently, had not been returned by Way, Sr., to Whistler in 1896 as part of the settling of accounts over the lithography-catalogue quarrel. Way, Jr., proposed that Freer purchase *Cremorne No. 2*, one of the two principal pictures in his possession, saying, "You will understand that it has never been offered to anyone before, indeed I have always said that I would . . . give it to our National Gallery, and have never allowed any bids to be made. But 'circumstances alter cases'." Evidently Way was painfully aware of his distance from the estranged master. He made the following request as part of the proposed transaction, "I will ask you £1,250 for the picture, and if you agree to give me this sum for it, I will ask you as a favour to purchase for me from Mr. Whistler himself etchings or drypoints to the value of £150 not mentioning my name in the matter." Way concluded his plaintive missive with, "The other picture, the girl with the blue sea and pink blossom I shall certainly not part with, if you take the Cremorne—but shall some day do with it what I had intended doing with the latter."[91] We do not know whether Freer risked Whistler's ire to supply Way with any prints. However, he did not purchase the *Cremorne No. 2* which is now at the Metropolitan Museum of Art. Instead, by July 29, 1903, Freer convinced Way to part with "the other picture," and *Venus Rising from the Sea* entered the Freer collection in November (Fig. 49).

Freer's dealings with the Ways suggest that Whistler's personal opinions regarding his own work colored Freer's tastes, and that Whistler's battles to some extent became Freer's as well. *Venus Rising from the Sea* represents a subject dear to Whistler's heart. He frequently treated the theme over the years, most notably in this painting and in the *Venus* for the "Six Projects." Way, Sr., had

Figure 50.
Grey and Silver: Pier,
Southend, early 1880s,
watercolor. Freer Gallery.

Figure 51.
Annabel Lee, ca. 1870,
fabricated chalks on brown
paper. Freer Gallery.

Figure 52.
Rose et Vert, L'Iris: Portrait
of Miss Kinsella, 1893–
1902, oil on canvas. Terra
Museum of American Art,
Daniel J. Terra collection.
(Photograph courtesy Davis
and Long Company, Inc.,
New York.)

obtained both versions during the 1879 bankruptcy sale. After the printer returned the *Venus* of the "Six Projects" to Whistler, the artist kept it in his apartment. Freer could have seen the painting at 110 Rue du Bac during the 1890s.[92] It is not surprising that Whistler might want Freer to have the other *Venus.* His "Six Projects," we recall, remained in the artist's possession until his death, with the single exception of the *White Symphony,* which the artist helped the patron to acquire.

Cremorne No. 2, which Freer did not buy, is thought to have been a factor in the rupture between the printers and the artist in 1896. Seeing the picture in T. R. Way's rooms, Whistler apparently tried to repossess it, arguing that "I have never had any [financial] consideration for the picture." According to Way, Whistler "probably knew where he could place [it] at a big price."[93] Freer might well have decided not to risk offending Whistler in the matter. Later the collector demonstrated interest in buying a different Cremorne picture, *Nocturne: Black and Gold—the Fire Wheel,* which Whistler said "has always been one of my favourite pictures."[94] But that painting eventually went to the Tate Gallery in London. Freer did not satisfy his longing for one of the series until he bought *Nocturne: Cremorne Gardens, No. 3,* shortly before his death in 1919.

Freer continued to cultivate Way, Jr. Having purchased a few watercolors (Fig. 50), Freer boldly indicated his interest in another work still owned by the Way family:

> I am tempted to make the amount of the draft £500 instead of £300, and ask you to send for the additional remittance the pastel drawing of a single figure which hangs over your father's desk—I mean the one in the center of the wall, the subject being a girl standing against a railing. But I must not be too selfish so I refrain. Should you, in the future, desire to dispose of the other examples of Mr. Whistler's work now in your father's collection, I will be very pleased to have you write me frankly your views on the subject.[95]

Freer's hint must have been well received, for the pastel, probably *Annabel Lee,* entered the collection the following year (Fig. 51). Freer made the majority of his purchases from the Way family in 1905. He bought an oil sketch, the frame for *The Golden Screen,* ten watercolors, and twenty-five drawings.

On occasion, personal animosities of Whistler and the surviving "ladies of the family," Rosalind Birnie Philip and Ethel Whibley, prevented paintings from entering the Freer collection. This problem arose in connection with portraits of individuals with whom Whistler had quarreled. Freer decided not to acquire *Rose et Vert: L'Iris—Portrait of Miss Kinsella* because it was thus tainted (Fig. 52).

Freer would have encountered *Rose et Vert* in Whistler's studios, where it was worked upon from June 1894 until the artist's death. Considered unfinished when it was exhibited in Paris in 1904, the portrait had the type of evocative sketchiness that Freer greatly admired in Whistler's work. The painting was offered to Freer through Mrs. Bernard Berenson. Fearing that "delay on my part might result in having the picture fall into the hands of . . . some . . . fiendish dealer," Freer entered into negotiations immediately. However, he then learned from Birnie Philip that the portrait had never actually been delivered to Louise Kinsella and was still unpaid for—it was still part of the Whistler estate. Freer told Birnie Philip, "I regret my haste. But what is to be done?" He promised to return the picture to the estate were it to come into his possession.[96]

Further information was forthcoming from Birnie Philip, and Freer replied:

> *The particulars you wrote concerning the status of affairs with Miss Kinsella are really impressive. There is no question in my mind that she has turned dealer. . . . It is a comfort to feel that you have understood her motives from the first. I trust you may defeat her schemes to get possession of the portrait. No further word has come to me from Mrs. Berenson. Should she write me again, I shall, of course, advise you.*[97]

Birnie Philip finally delivered the painting to the sitter's sister, probably in 1905. After another unsuccessful effort to sell it in 1907, this time to the National Gallery in London, the sitter's family kept the portrait until 1972.[98] Whistler's contempt for sitters who tried to sell their own portraits for profit was the central issue in this incident.

Any desire to acquire a portrait sketch of Walter Sickert, Whistler's estranged pupil, was similarly dampened by correspondence from Birnie Philip. She wrote to advise Freer, presumably about either the Pennell-Sickert quarrel over the use of transfer paper in the making of lithographs or the Whistler-Eden quarrel over Lady Eden's portrait.[99] After refusing Sickert's offer, Freer wrote Birnie Philip, "Thank you for suggestions concerning the Sickert portrait. Now that I know of his bad behavior, I should feel very unhappy with a portrait of him in my home. I shall decline any further advances."[100] Freer did obtain other items from Sickert's holdings, but they came through the London dealer Obach, not directly from Sickert himself.

When good relations prevailed, Freer sought the aid of fellow collectors to acquire significant paintings. He was particularly friendly with the racy Richard Canfield, who was notorious as a gambler and a Wall Street operator as well as a connoisseur of fine art.[101] While it never rivaled Freer's collection, Canfield's holdings included major Whistler oils like *Arrangement in Brown and Black: Portrait of Miss Rosa Corder* and *Arrangement in Black and Gold: Comte Robert de Montesquiou-Fezensac.* The two collectors were frequent collaborators who clearly recognized the special nature of their friendship.[102]

Figure 53.
Symphony in Grey and Green: The Ocean, with original frame, 1866, oil on canvas. Copyright the Frick Collection, New York.

Canfield was always respectful of Freer's wishes. In 1903, at a time when Freer was aggressively adding to his Whistler holdings, Canfield wired from London, advising Freer that he had withdrawn from negotiations for paintings owned by Arthur Studd "for fear [of] innocently interfering" with Freer's plans. Canfield continued, "Should much like to acquire couple pictures other than portraits. Does trial for *Ocean* conflict. If so, will withdraw." There was no conflict. Freer bowed to Canfield's wish to own *Symphony in Grey and Green: The Ocean* (Fig. 53). Canfield's trial offer was accepted, and the oil in its magnificent frame, decorated by Whistler, entered the gambler's collection shortly after this exchange.[103]

In one unusually exciting and well-documented instance, Freer cooperated with Canfield to acquire *Arrangement in White and Black*, a portrait of Whistler's mistress Maud Franklin (see Fig. 16). Enough correspondence survives to reconstruct the process and to reveal the heady atmosphere of speculation that surrounded important Whistler oils in the years immediately following the artist's death.[104] The owner of the painting at the time Freer became involved was a Dr. Linde of Lübeck, Germany. He had purchased the *Arrangement* from Colnaghi, London dealers, in March 1897, for £900. During the intervening seven years the painting tripled in price and passed through the hands of several short-term owner-speculators before reaching Freer's collection in Detroit.[105]

Canfield learned of the picture's availability from a friend named Spier, who sent him a photograph in January 1904, along with the comment "The picture belongs to a German lawyer [Linde] and is not in the hands of the trade."[106] On February 2, Freer wrote to Canfield, "You are very kind to offer to give me a chance at its purchase, but I could not think of doing such a thing until you had first decided whether or not you would like it." Freer urged Canfield to have Spier get the painting to London for inspection, suggesting William Marchant as the dealer to authenticate it. Freer added that Marchant "has seen enough of the best of Mr. Whistler's work to tell the difference between one of high rank and another of lesser importance." The collector concluded that they might send Marchant to Germany to look at the painting if it were not possible to borrow it on approval.[107] A few days later, having received further word from Canfield, Freer suggested to Canfield that they exclude Marchant from the negotiations.[108] At the end of the month, Freer wrote Canfield again, to say that he had received a description of the painting drafted by Spier. He added, "The plot thickens, and, of course, grows all the more interesting."[109]

Freer communicated with Birnie Philip, informing her that Canfield had sent him a photograph of *Arrangement in Black and White*. Although he found the photograph "wretchedly bad," it gave him "a strong desire to see the picture."[110] Freer also sent Spier's written description on to Birnie Philip for her advice and comment. These exchanges, courtesies, and requests for opinion cost a certain amount of time.

The two collectors had decided to outmaneuver the London dealer Marchant, but they were themselves being outmaneuvered. On March 20, Freer received the following terse telegram from his secretary in Detroit: "Canfield, Hotel Bristol, Paris, cables—Duret has picture. Will wire later." Spier had received correspondence indicating that Théodore Duret, the French art critic and sometime dealer, had purchased the picture from Linde, probably for resale. Spier forwarded this bad news to Canfield, commenting, "The only question is whether Duret and Dr. Linde are doing this business together."[111]

After his cablegram to Freer on March 20, Canfield sent two letters, now lost, that must have told Freer to expect a note from Duret himself. Duret's communication arrived on April 7, accompanied by both a good photograph and a heliogravure of *Arrangement in White and Black*, made for Duret's forthcoming biography on Whistler. Duret wrote, "A most important picture by Whistler has come to Paris. . . . [It was] exhibited by Whistler at the Grosvenor Gallery in 1878. It has remained concealed for many years far away, in the collection of Dr. Linde, in Luebeck . . . unknown to the present generation." At this juncture in the negotiations, the painting was all too well known to Freer. Duret offered to "arrange with the people who own the picture now, not to sell it before you could see it, if I knew that you were coming to Paris this Spring."[112]

Freer lamented to Canfield, "Yea, verily, we did make a mistake in not having snapped up the picture at the time of the arrival of the original photograph [from Spier]. You will remember how I then felt about it, and how seriously you and I discussed the matter at our meeting that evening in Delmonico's." Canfield's famous gambling club was at 5 East Forty-fourth Street, next door to the restaurant. Freer went on, "Well, if our intuitions were always right, and if we never made mistakes, we would, indeed, be worth while." Freer concluded philosophically, "[Duret] has certainly gotten in ahead of us, and, while we naturally feel disappointed that he should have done so, and hate to go down in our pockets to pay him for interfering to our disadvantage, isn't it perhaps a contingency to be viewed in rather a broad manner?"[113]

Figure 54.
*Arrangement in Black:
Portrait of Federick
Richards Leyland*, 1870–
1873, oil on canvas. Freer
Gallery.

Figure 55.
Dwight William Tryon, *The
Rising Moon, Autumn*,
1889, oil on panel. Freer
Gallery.

Figure 56.
*Nocturne: Cremorne
Gardens, No. 3*, 1872–
1877, oil on canvas. Freer
Gallery.

Freer offered to drop negotiations with Duret if they would be offensive to Canfield. But Canfield evidently did not oppose the deal, for Freer traveled to Paris in the spring and bought the painting from Duret.[114] In thanking Freer for his bank draft, Duret commented, "I have handed it to Messrs. Bernheim, the owners of the picture." G. Bernheim was a Paris dealer with whom Whistler had had lamentable relations.[115] It was probably Bernheim who advanced the funds to Duret for acquisition of the painting from Linde.

Later that year Freer took the opportunity to criticize Duret's biography of Whistler. Freer found the book "lacking in important facts" and complained, "Duret has fallen into the error of nearly all hackney art writers, and has treated his subject in an altogether too conventional way." However, when the painting finally arrived in Detroit on June 28, Freer told Canfield simply, "It delights me."[116]

Canfield again helped Freer when *Arrangement in Black: Portrait of Frederick Richards Leyland* was available (Fig. 54). In 1892 this painting had passed from Leyland to his daughter Florence, who had married the artist Val Prinsep. It was featured in the London Memorial Exhibition of 1905, an exhibition that Freer neither approved of nor lent to because he felt that it opposed Whistler's intentions as well as Birnie Philip's expressed reservations. The exhibition was organized by people that Freer, Canfield, and Birnie Philip scornfully labeled "the busy ones," including Joseph and Elizabeth Pennell, Whistler's biographers. Nonetheless, Canfield managed to secure the painting, certainly one of the most important of Whistler's male portraits. Canfield cabled, "Have bought Prinsep's full length portrait of Leyland three thousand for you if you want it."[117] This time, the dealer Marchant was brought in, and the actual payment was made to him.[118] Whistler was dead and couldn't discourage Freer from owning the likeness of a man with whom the artist had quarreled violently. Moreover, Freer's own portrait had never been finished. It must have been a pleasure to acquire the evocative canvas that records the only other patron to play as significant a role in Whistler's career as had Freer himself.

In 1914, Canfield's collection was offered for sale by the Knoedler Gallery in New York. Prior to the sale, Canfield had given Freer first choice of his paintings, but Freer did not buy, citing financial obligations. By 1914, Freer's most active days of collecting Whistler's work were over. While he continued to add to that part of his collection, the building of the Oriental holdings by means of extensive trips to the East had become his major occupation.

But even though the Whistler collection was almost complete, the artist's impact upon the patron's taste still lingered. Freer considered the harmonious blend of objects to be a priority in his collecting long after Whistler had died. He regaled Miss Birnie Philip with tales of his success in acquiring Chinese art treasures on his travels, remarking that they would "harmonize with the Master's work with which they are to keep company hereafter."[119]

Stylistic differences between the first and last American oils in the collection set the limits of Freer's taste, developed over thirty years of collecting. Dwight William Tryon's *Rising Moon, Autumn* (Fig. 55), purchased in 1889, is wedded to the lessons of the Barbizon school which were absorbed by both American painters and conservative collectors of the late nineteenth century. Whistler's *Nocturne: Cremorne Gardens, No. 3* (Fig. 56), was bought in August 1919, just one month before Freer died. This pleasure-garden scene typifies the broad abstractions that Freer came to prefer. He had departed from the paintings in the familiar manner of the Barbizon school to explore uncharted territory where he sought the previously undiscovered treasures of the Orient.

Yet, during his long search, at the core of Freer's unusual art collection were a number of American works of art. The abstraction and decorative qualities encountered in exotic Eastern art were put in perspective by the presence of abstract decorative works in the Western genres of landscape and figure painting. Moreover, these works were selected with the reassuring assistance of the artists themselves.

Writing to a friend, Freer emphasized the spiritual nature of the associations he discerned between objects, and he asserted yet again that "Mr. Whistler does unite the art of the Occident with that of the Orient."[120] What Whistler had done as an artist, Freer set out to do as a collector.

In the *Ten o'Clock Lecture*, Whistler cast Art in the role of a mistress generously sharing her secrets with the artist alone. Having implied that the universal bridge linking great works of art was an undefinable sensual pleasure, Whistler concluded, "The story of the beautiful is already complete—hewn in the marbles of the Parthenon—and broidered, with the birds, upon the fan of Hokusai—at the foot of Fusi-yama."[121] Freer's contribution was to gather together works of art united by the aesthetic harmony of their beautiful surface textures and colors. As the collector noted, "It is so difficult to choose between pearls."[122]

Symphony in White, No. 1:
The White Girl, 1862, oil
on canvas, 214.8 × 108 cm.
National Gallery of Art,
Washington, Harris
Whittemore Collection.

Artist and Model

Influence creates nothing. It awakens.
ANDRÉ GIDE
Why drag in Velásquez?
JAMES MCNEILL WHISTLER

Figure 57.
Copy after François
Boucher's *Diane au bain*,
late 1850s, whereabouts
unknown. From Andrew
Mclaren Young *et al. The
Paintings of James McNeill
Whistler*, 2 vols. (New
Haven and London, 1980),
Reprinted courtesy of The
Library of Congress,
Pennell collection.

WITH THE POSSIBLE EXCEPTION of a modest text by Camille Mauclair entitled *De Watteau à Whistler* (1905), little or nothing has been written to suggest a connection between the art of James McNeill Whistler and Jean-Antoine Watteau.

Paintings and drawings which provide important nonverbal information about Whistler's sources have been far less accessible than the written word. Among Whistler's earliest works are now-lost copies of paintings by Boucher and Greuze (Fig. 57).[1] The copies signal an interest in eighteenth-century France, yet this facet of Whistler's highly synthetic art has been virtually ignored, and the painter himself did not discuss the issue in print.

Whistler's French connection should not surprise us. Although he carefully maintained a romantic public posture as a creative genius, his work was closely related to both the artistic events of his own generation and the rich heritage of western Europe. In histories organized along nationalistic lines, it is somewhat difficult to place the peripatetic American-born painter. But most of his formal training was French, and his professional concerns were to a large extent those of the French modernists of the 1860s. They wanted to depict contemporary life, but also intended to align themselves closely with tradition. His biographers noted, "Whistler believed that to carry on tradition was the artist's business." [2]

Like his contemporary, the French poet and critic Charles Baudelaire, Whistler had an "extraordinary gift for taking already-existing concepts and reanimating them so that they are still recognizable, but, in an essential sense, fresh and surprising." [3] Moreover, at the time Whistler lived and worked, interest in early eighteenth-century French art was ubiquitous and, therefore, not newsworthy.[4] Yet, even though no texts treating Whistler's involvement with rococo art come readily to hand, there can be no question that he felt the beneficial impact of eighteenth-century French art and decoration in a variety of ways which will be explored below with particular reference to the *oeuvre* of Jean-Antoine Watteau.

At the time Whistler adopted his model, Watteau's reputation had just been renovated. Writers like Edmond and Jules de Goncourt elevated Watteau in the ranks of art history from a merely pleasing to a "serious" artist—indeed, the major font of eighteenth-century French painting. In about 1865, Théophile Gautier, Watteau's champion since the 1830s, described his grace, elegance, and unconstrained freedom. Gautier added that Watteau's "art is serious if his genre might seem frivolous."[5] Whistler drank deeply at the font—but he reanimated the lessons learned there with other interests and stimuli, producing his own unique synthesis.

Watteau's reputation underwent its curious reworking from about 1830 to 1860.[6] While writers of the eighteenth and early nineteenth centuries differentiated between Watteau's melancholic personality and his paintings, which were seen as charming and even happy, writers and painters imbued with romanticism began to conflate the man and his imagery. His art became synonymous with the past elegance of the *ancien régime*. During the Restoration and July Monarchy, dispossessed aristocrats perceived that mediocrity was characteristic of the newly powerful bourgeoisie. It became increasingly evident that the elegance of the eighteenth century was now but a dream. Founded upon the romantic notion that melancholy and suffering were the basis for great art, a subjective, poetic interpretation of Watteau's *oeuvre* was furthered by the work of the critic Gautier and the painter Émile Deroy. The new assessment was almost indelibly stamped upon the history of art by the Goncourts, whose essay "La Philosophie de Watteau" for *L'Artiste* (1856) reappeared four years later in *L'Art du XVIIIe Siècle.*

Watteau's revamped reputation crystallized as Whistler arrived in Paris, a student, determined to become a fashionable artist, afloat on the froth of society. It is thus significant that the reinterpretation of Watteau was firmly linked to fashion, decoration, and the desire on the part of returning French émigrés to divorce themselves from styles that reflected bourgeois attitudes. Associated with the *grande luxe* of the *ancien régime*, Watteau's *oeuvre* was taken up by the fashionable world during the 1830s.[7] Gautier and his friends hosted fancy dress balls whose costumes and decorations evoked Watteau's imaginary landscapes populated with elegant merrymakers, and they hung copies of his works in their apartments. Watteau's art appealed to their most refined and aesthetic sensibilities. Whistler subsumed such values as cornerstones of his own artistic creed. Moreover, because the new interpretation of Watteau was actually a conflation of biographical information with a preconceived interpretation of the paintings, it was marked by a certain evasive or abstract quality: the sense of melancholy in Watteau's work was a question of veiled poetry, not of something obvious. One had to *feel* Watteau's melancholy as a type of invisible music that pervaded his work; it did not reveal itself easily to the eye; neither did it rely upon overt subject matter.[8] Whistler's later emphasis upon poetic vision as well as his musical analogies are well known. Further, Whistler divorced himself as completely as possible from bourgeois behavior. The bohemian artist could mirror the aristocrat in his freedom from conventional mores.

Perhaps most important here is the Goncourts' achievement in solidifying Watteau's new position as a serious artist in the pantheon of French painters. The freshly enthroned Watteau offered the young painter a paradigm whose work encompassed the kind of decorative aesthetic decisions that Whistler would consistently make for the length of his career.

By 1855, the year Whistler came to Paris, works of art inspired by Watteau were already *de rigueur* at the Salon exhibitions. That year the *Journal des Arts* praised a screen executed in pastel. It paraphrased Watteau's famous painting *The Departure for Cythera*, Watteau's *morceau de réception* which had hung in the Louvre since the preceding century (Fig. 58). The imitation was bigger, if not better, than its model: "The same richness, the same touch of brilliance characterizes *The Apotheosis of Watteau*, another piece of grand decoration. Here is a

Figure 58.
Jean-Antoine Watteau,
Pèlerinage à l'île de Cythère, oil on canvas.
Musées Nationaux de France.

résumé of the work of the first eighteenth-century *peintre galante*, somewhat enlarged to be visible from a distance."[9]

It would have been virtually impossible for Whistler to overlook Watteau. Accessible European collections, from Russia to Great Britain, held many of Watteau's delicate chalk drawings and small oils as well as major works. From 1843 to 1849, Whistler divided his time between St. Petersburg and London. The Whistler family was in the habit of visiting the galleries and would have had ample opportunity to see paintings by Watteau. During his brief sojourn at West Point from 1851 to 1854, Whistler's studies with Robert Weir included copying from nineteenth-century printmakers, including Gavarni, who is not without his eighteenth-century affinities.[10] Once Whistler returned to the French capital as a serious art student, he would have continuing access to collections that included Watteau.

Much of Watteau's *oeuvre* had already been gathered together and published as engravings during the 1720s and 1730s. Other publications appeared in the 1740s and 1750s.[11] Watteau had been so widely collected in England during the eighteenth century that Horace Walpole praised him in *Anecdotes of Painting in England* (1762) as "an original and engaging painter" who "described a kind of impossible pastoral." Walpole found Watteau's shepherdesses "coquet" yet "genteel," and his nymphs "as much below the forbidding majesty of goddesses as they are above the hoyden awkwardness of country girls."[12] These refined qualities were to have great appeal as Whistler took up his brush a century later in an era of aesthetic dandyism.[13]

Watteau's popularity outlasted Whistler's student days and became part of the French artistic climate for the remainder of Whistler's life. In 1860 Watteau's paintings were included in a large exhibition of eighteenth-century art in Paris. The La Caze collection, which included nine Watteau paintings, was donated to the Louvre in 1869. Meanwhile the stream of books and magazine articles continued unabated. From 1860 to 1899, years that roughly span Whistler's productive artistic career, at least twenty-five books concerning Watteau were published.[14]

Efforts to celebrate the popular eighteenth-century painter took several forms. One was a series of drives for commemorative monuments. In 1852 efforts to refurbish Watteau's burial place at Nogent-sur-Marne commenced. Valenciennes, Watteau's birthplace, lagged behind, but in 1884 its citizens could read in their local paper "Ce grand artist a sa statue, voilà le point essentiel." Yet another Watteau monument was dedicated in the Luxembourg Gardens of Paris on November 18, 1896. A number of prominent artists took part in this project, including Félix Bracquemond, Carolus Duran, and Pierre Puvis de Chavannes.[15]

Despite all this, however, the impact of the eighteenth-century Frenchman goes unremarked in the Whistler literature. Since Whistler's death in 1903, the most frequently trodden path into his art has been paved with print. Whistler's own theories, his voluminous correspondence, his much publicized quarrels, as well as prodigious biographies and reams of reminiscences by both friend and foe have provided written guides to the wellsprings of Whistler's creativity. These writings have alerted us to art that was of interest to Whistler as he formed his own style—the contributions of Hogarth or Velásquez or the arts of Japan are well recorded.

Although the specific connection has not been drawn, writers have responded in a similar manner to the work of both Watteau and Whistler for over a century. Parallel responses provide a substantial body of evidence for deducing a connec-

Figure 59.
Symphony in White, No. 1:
The White Girl, 1862, oil
on canvas. The National
Gallery of Art, Washington,
Harris Whittenmore
collection.

Figure 60.
Jean-Antoine Watteau, *Le*
Grand Gilles, 1717–1719,
oil on canvas. Musées
Nationaux de France.

tion between the two artists. The connection is borne out by visual evidence that includes paintings, drawings, prints, and interior decorations.

Whistler's student Mortimer Menpes noted, "When the Master saw a good thing, he accepted it."[16] A comparison of *Symphony in White No. 1: The White Girl* (1862) with Watteau's *Gilles* (1717–1719) indicates that when Whistler encountered Watteau, he saw a good thing (Figs. 59 and 60).[17] Possibly *Gilles* was originally intended to be a signboard advertising the Commedia dell'Arte's new theater in Paris. The subject of the painting is a "parade," the free presentation made outside the theater to attract patronage.[18] The purpose of the Salon exhibitions was to allow artists to catch the attention of the art establishment. *The White Girl* was, among other things, a signboard advertising Whistler's talents. It was not hung with the officially approved paintings. Instead, Whistler's work joined Manet's *Déjeuner sur l'herbe* as a *succès de scandale* at the 1863 Salon des Réfusés.[19] Both Manet and Whistler hungered for official recognition. Like Manet, Whistler painted a modern work that was consciously tied to past art. In each, what was stylistically unfamiliar to Salon visitors and critics obscured aspects of the painting that refer to earlier works by recognized masters.[20]

The White Girl depicts Whistler's mistress, Jo Hiffernan. However, it also records Whistler's heretofore clandestine liaison with the art of Watteau. The single most striking parallel between the two paintings is their almost identical visual impact: each artist created a curiously lonely figure, somewhat flattened and uncomfortably silhouetted against its background. Each artist staged a tour de force that captured the nuances of light playing over a model clad in white. Excited by the challenge of an all-white palette, Whistler told George du Maurier that "the picture, barring the red hair, is one gorgeous mass of brilliant white."[21] Fantin-Latour assured Whistler:

> *We find the whites excellent; they are superb, and at a distance*
> *(that's the real test) they look first class. Courbet calls your picture*
> *an apparition. . . . Baudelaire finds it charming, exquisite, absolutely*
> *delicate. Legros, Manet, Bracquemond, De Balleroy, and myself, we*
> *all think it admirable.*[22]

During Whistler's lifetime, critics expressed similar reactions to Watteau's handling of white pigments. In 1902 Edgcumbe Staley called *Gilles* "a sartorial lighthouse—the explosion of white light is quite remarkable." With *fin de siècle* elegance, Staley described Watteau's "pearly, creamy white, like an opal taking reflections from all around."[23] Claude Phillips, another of Whistler's contemporaries, also admired Watteau's realization of a white costume with delicate transparent shadows. *Gilles* was seen as a testament to Watteau's "supreme mastery of a technical difficulty," an achievement that would have been immediately apparent to Whistler, inspiring the expatriate American to attempt such a feat himself. Whistler consciously recalled the eighteenth-century master's painting while creating a masterwork of his own.[24]

Although Whistler turned his model slightly, her shoulders are set similarly to Gilles's and her hands fall in essentially the same pose. Jo's hair frames her face in a dark halo, just as Gilles's shadowed round hat sets off his visage. Each figure has a heavy-browed gaze that is somehow both direct and glazed, and each has a full-lipped, sensuous mouth. Details of Jo's pleated white bodice repeat the vertical frills of Gilles's ruff, while her puffed and pleated sleeves echo the sharp folds that seem to pin the clown by the elbows so that he cannot escape.

Figure 61.
Jean-Antoine Watteau,
Italian Comedians, 1720,
oil on canvas. National
Gallery of Art, Washington,
Samuel H. Kress collection.

Whistler changed the setting from a stagey landscape to a studio interior, but he retained the arrested moment of a *tableau vivant*. Instead of an androgynous male, we are given an alluring female. The trees that frame Gilles's stage are reduced by Whistler to vague vegetal patterns in Victorian lace curtains. There are no faces at Jo's feet; the colors in Watteau's Commedia dell'Arte figures reappear only in scattered flowers, which also recall the garland of roses strewn on the steps in front of Gilles in another Watteau painting (Fig. 61). Whistler transposed the donkey's head into a bear's, replacing both the dumb animal and the human figures in *Gilles*.

Whistler has carried the white-on-white color scheme much further than Watteau. Yet, despite Whistler's elimination of anecdotal detail, the melancholy, ambiguous presence of the two figures is similar. Both Gilles and Jo are exhibited at center stage, caught in bright light. Each stands without shelter, isolated, exposed to the spectator's relentless contemplation.

The critic Paul Mantz came closest to understanding Whistler's historicism in his review of the 1863 Salon for the *Gazette des Beaux-Arts*:

> *We would indeed reveal our ignorance of the history of painting if we dared to pretend that Mr. Whistler is an eccentric when, on the contrary, he has precedents and a tradition that one should not ignore, especially in France. . . . Whistler could have learned that [Jean-Baptiste Oudry] . . . sought on many occasions to group . . . objects of different whites and that he exhibited at the Salon of 1753 a large painting representing against a white background diverse white objects, including a white duck, a napkin of damask linen, porcelain, cream, a candle, a chandelier of silver, a paper. These associations of analogous nuances were understood a hundred years ago by everyone, and the difficulty which would baffle more than one master today passed then for child's play. In searching for a similar effect Mr. Whistler continues therefore in the French tradition.*[25]

Mantz was talking about *The White Duck*, painted by Oudry in 1753 (Fig. 62). Whistler could have seen it in the large exhibition of eighteenth-century French paintings held in Paris in 1860.[26]

Mention of *The White Duck* does shed light upon Whistler's academic ambition, as well as his eighteenth-century orientation. When it was first shown in 1753, Oudry's painting was recognized as an academic exercise, based upon a paper which he had presented in 1744 to the Academy.[27] Criticism at that time made much of the painting as a splendid performance. One critic wrote:

> *Oudry's white backgrounds are quite successful. This year there is a new type—one which is instructive. It shows us that objects of quite similar appearance can only be differentiated by their characteristic nuances. Without question, it takes a great deal of artistry to separate objects of the same color. Such paintings rarely achieve grand effects, but they always reveal the great talents of the artist.*[28]

Figure 62.
Jean-Baptiste Oudry, *The White Duck*, 1753, oil on canvas. Collection of the Marchioness of Cholomondeley. From Hal N. Opperman, *Jean-Baptiste Oudry, 1686–1755* (exh. cat.) (Fort Worth: Kimball Art Museum, 1983), fig. 113. Reprinted courtesy of the Kimball Art Museum.

On the other hand, Watteau's *Gilles* was not just an academic exercise, and Watteau had certainly understood the concept of white-on-white painting several decades before Oudry created his *White Duck*. A century later, although

Figure 63.
Thomas Couture, *Chaque fête à son lendemain*, ca. 1855, oil on canvas. Vancouver Art Gallery, (Photograph, Jim Gorman, Vancouver Art Gallery).

Figure 64.
Gavarni, *(Air: Larifla! . . .)*, *Nos femm' sont cou-cou!*, 1847, lithograph. Private collection.

Figure 65.
Dancing Clowns, ca. 1855–1859, drawing after Gavarni, pencil. Freer Gallery.

Gilles was included in the 1860 exhibition and was even engraved that year for the *Gazette des Beaux-Arts*, Mantz made no comment regarding its relationship to Whistler's work. This is particularly surprising given Whistler's close approximation of Watteau's composition.

To understand why Whistler borrowed Watteau's white clown and in what a meaningful manner he disguised the loan, we must first acknowledge the ubiquitous presence of Pierrot images in mid-nineteenth-century France. The interpretation of Watteau's clown as a melancholy figure occurred at this period and coincides with the general reinterpretation of Watteau's *oeuvre*.[29]

That Whistler might attempt a veiled reference to the white clown is not unusual. Pierrot figures appeared in works by Gérôme, Couture, and Manet among others. Couture's clown (Fig. 63) was even reproduced as an elaborate wallpaper for the International Exhibition held in London in 1862. But Whistler differs in having captured the ethos of Watteau's painting without overtly using a white clown.

The White Girl addressed the sensitivities of French critics at about the same time that the Goncourts were praising Watteau's painting as "une création de poème et de rêve." In 1863 Michelet constructed a melodramatic scenario for *Gilles* that remarked specifically upon the tragic yet sublime aspect of the painting: "For a moment the clown has forgotten the stage. In the middle of the crowd he dreams (so many things!—he sees life in a flash)—he dreams, he is overwhelmed . . . 'Salut, people, I am going to die.' "[30] Although no specific connection with the Watteau painting was made, some critics immediately perceived the poetic melancholy of Whistler's enigmatic figure in white. Ernest Chesneau used language suspiciously close to the Goncourts', praising *The White Girl* for its revelation of "a romantic imagination of dreams and poetry."[31] Fernand Desnoyers also was touched by the painting's haunting presence. He wrote that it was the portrait of a spiritualist or a medium.[32] An evocative comment made by the Goncourts about Watteau's equally evocative canvases could be appropriately extended to Whistler's *Symphony in White No. 1*: "C'est l'amour, mais c'est l'amour poétique, l'amour qui songe et qui pense, l'amour moderne, avec ses aspirations et sa couronne de mélancolie."[33]

Whistler may have intended to recast an old theme, creating an allegory of modern love clad in contemporary dress. The wistful quality of *The White Girl* and its fairly evident sexual overtones point toward the Pierrot images of Gavarni, another artist who presented *l'amour poétique* in nineteenth-century terms. As a student, Whistler had copied some of Gavarni's lithographs, including the vigorous *Air: Larifla!*, where two men clad in clown costumes give themselves over to wild dancing at a public ball (Figs. 64 and 65). Popular in the eighteenth century, clown costumes were still favorites at masked lenten balls of the mid-nineteenth century. Many of Gavarni's carnival lithographs show the intrigue and assignations that were arranged in the semianonymous free atmosphere of costumed parties.[34] In a sense the white clowns were seen as figures for social study as well as amusement. In 1851 Gavarni published a group of lithographs entitled *L'École des Pierrots*. In a typical scene, *Le Sommeil de l'Innocence*, a young girl dressed as a sailor receives a *billet-doux* from an unseen admirer. Meanwhile, clad in his Pierrot costume, her aging escort remains unaware of the transaction. The somnolent man is doubtless soon to be a cuckold.[35]

In light of the above, the sexual interpretation of Whistler's *White Girl* conjured up by the critic Jules-Antoine Castagnary takes on added significance.

Castagnary read Whistler's *Symphony* as a song of lost innocence with eighteenth-century precedents. The wilting lily in Jo's hand indicated her loss, but Castagnary hastened to assure his readers that this loss had occurred within the bounds of matrimony. He challenged Whistler:

> *Does a tour-de-force in painting consist of putting white on white?!
> I think not. Permit me to see something higher in your work:* the
> bride's morning after, *that troubling moment when a young woman
> reflects on the absence of yesterday's virginity. . . . There are white
> curtains at a closed alcove. Behind them the* other one *is doubtless
> still sleeping. You recall* la Cruche cassée *or* la Jeune fille pleurant son
> oiseau mort, *the playful subjects beloved by Greuze. Whistler's inter-
> pretation is graver, more severe, more English. His* White Girl *is
> evidently married: the night she has just passed was legitimate, ap-
> proved by the Church and the world . . . but ask the wilting flower
> she holds in her hand. This is the continuation of the allegory begun
> with the broken pitcher and the little dead bird.*[36]

Figure 66.
Jean Baptiste Greuze, *La
Cruche cassée*. Musées
Nationaux de France.

Whistler copied Greuze's allegory of lost innocence, *La Cruche cassée*, at the Louvre in 1857 (Fig. 66).[37]

During the eighteenth century, ambiguous, sexually charged role playing was already emphasized in engravings after Watteau's many images of Gilles. These were published with accompanying rhymes that stressed the Commedia dell'Arte stage as a mirror for contemporary life. Pierrot and his fellow players could be seen laughing at human folly.[38] In Watteau's Italian comedy pictures, the role of the androgynous Gilles is never clear. Sometimes he is a lover, but more often the butt of a joke or the observer of another's amours (Fig. 67). He is never to be depended upon:

Figure 67.
Charles Nicolas Cochin
after Jean-Antoine
Watteau, *Pour Garder
l'Honneur d'une belle*,
eighteenth century,
engraving. Reproduced in
Emil Dacier and Albert
Vuaflart, *Jean de Jullienne
et les graveurs de Watteau*
(Paris, 1921).

> *Pour garder l'honneur d'une belle
> Veillez et la nuit et le jour
> Contre tes pièges de l'amour
> C'est trop peu de Pierrot pour faire sentinelle.*[39]

Sexual innuendo was still associated with Pierrot in the nineteenth century. Gavarni's white clowns, indebted to images by Watteau, frequently are accompanied by legends that have to do with the intrigues of lovers.[40]

The staged quality of Whistler's *White Girl* reflects not only the prints of Watteau and Gavarni, but also the continuing theater tradition of the white clown that informs all of these two-dimensional images. Plays and pantomimes featuring Pierrot had been presented throughout the 1800s. During the 1820s and 1830s, Gaston Debureau interpreted Pierrot as a villain rather than a childish fool. His version of the white clown was "capable of all vices and all crimes, sardonic, solitary, and silent . . . his white mask showed no emotion: it became the terrifying outward symbol of an inner corruption."[41]

Figure 68.
Adrien Tournachon
(Nadar), *Charles Debureau
as Gilles*, ca. 1858. From
Nigel Gosling, *Nadar*
(London: Secker and
Warburg, 1976), p. 38.
Reprinted courtesy of
Martin Secker and
Warburg, Ltd.

Coincident with the Goncourts' interpretation of Watteau's melancholy, which they deduced partially from the painter's images of Gilles, Gaston Debureau's son Charles created a new, elegant, and wistful character (Fig. 68). The popular clown remained good theater.[42] Whistler could easily have seen some of the pantomimes featuring Pierrot before he painted his *White Girl*. Such pantomimes were offered in cabarets, theaters, and pleasure gardens in both Paris

Figure 69.
Adrien Tournachon
(Nadar), *Sarah Bernhardt
as Gilles*, ca. 1870s,
photograph. From Gosling,
p. 259. Reprinted courtesy
of Martin Secker and
Warburg, Ltd.

Figure 70.
Gavarni, *Dieu! mes
amours, comme mon
seigneur et maître est une
chose dont je me fiche pas
mal ce soir!*, ca. 1840,
lithograph. Private
collection.

and London. But the resonances between live stage presentations and static images were felt in both directions. Even Sarah Bernhardt appeared in a Pierrot costume, carefully positioned to resemble Watteau's iconic *Gilles* (Fig. 69). Years later, in 1956, Thelma Niklaus wrote of the theater's "modern" Pierrot as "the haunting and poetic symbol of man's perpetual frustration. The pallor of his wistful face [expresses] unbearable sorrow. He is the seeker of dreams."[43] The romantic conception made popular by the Goncourts has taken root.

Jo's trancelike state, however suggestive of the seeker of dreams, remains a barrier precluding any single interpretation of the painting. Whistler does not commit himself, but provides his enigmatic subject with several attributes. Even these are ambiguous, however. Some of the flowers scattered at her feet cannot be identified. Recognizable flowers include not only the lily, emblematic of purity and sweetness, but also white lilac for youthful innocence. The purple and yellow pansies symbolize thoughts but not necessarily regrets.[44]

There is no agreement as to whether Jo stands upon a bearskin or a wolfskin.[45] Both the wolf and the bear figured as costumes in Gavarni's carnival prints and were seen in conjunction with Pierrot figures. The pointed black mask, commonly worn with the Pierrot outfit, was actually a wolf mask (Fig. 70). Gavarni also depicted several bear costumes worn at the balls. The connotations of each of these prints was sexual.[46] Bears also figured in plays Whistler could have witnessed at urban pleasure gardens. A visitor to London's Cremorne Gardens, two blocks from Whistler's residence in Cheyne Walk, reported seeing "a farce acted by Pierrots, harlequins, policemen and field-marshals. There were waterfalls, snow-capped mountains and polar bears in white cotton trousers."[47]

The bear seems to be the most likely interpretation of Whistler's animal skin since its ears are rounded. The bear can be associated with luxury and with the combat between virtue and vice, as well as with anger and greed. The greedy, honey-eating bear was especially popular in Russian tradition, learned by Whistler during his childhood. It was also associated with either demonic activities or with those of a fool, like the ass. Whistler replaced Watteau's donkey head with the bear rug. In several stories a bear consorts with a beautiful woman, and in one Norwegian legend, a hero disguised as a bear becomes a handsome young man at night.[48] And possibly the rug symbolized Whistler himself.

We know that Whistler's relationship with Jo was a stormy one. Jo is placed in a dominant position upon the flattened animal skin. Hers is the position of power, with its compositional reference to medieval saints or perhaps the Virgin, standing upon an allegorical animal. This pose with its message of dominance survived in the nineteenth century, even in photographs, like one of Queen Mary on a tiger rug.[49] In the *White Girl* Whistler added dark red pigment, like dried blood, around the edges of the fur rug. Even that passage is ambiguous, for at first it appears to be a bit of undergrounding showing through. Whistler's *Symphony in White, No. 1* remains an inaccessible riddle; the artist refused to spin out a transparent narrative.

In short, while Whistler was inspired by both the composition and the content of Watteau's *Gilles*, the use he made of that image serves as something of a warning against simplistic source hunting in so complex an artist's work. Whistler saw the eighteenth-century white clown through the eyes of his own period. In synthesizing this with other interests, such as the Pre-Raphaelite *femme fatale*, Whistler produced not an ill-digested admixture, but a haunting canvas with lasting enigmatic appeal.

Of all Whistler's major paintings from his early period, *Symphony in White*

Figure 71.
Arangement in White and
Black, ca. 1876, oil on
canvas. Freer Gallery.

No. 1: The White Girl most closely approaches a specific painting by Watteau. Later paintings from the "White Girl" series demonstrate greater concern with other issues. In about 1876, Whistler completed the last of his "White Girls" with *Arrangement in White and Black* (Fig. 71). Whistler has banished almost all detail, and confines himself to mysterious shadows half perceived through juxtaposition of light and dark tones. Whistler shows us a new mistress—Maud Franklin had replaced Jo Hiffernan. There is nothing of the wistful Gilles about Maud; her face emerges from the darkness with almost startling candor. The only trace of Watteau's impact here is found in Whistler's affection for beautiful women and their fashionable costumes recorded in paint, as sensuous in its own way as the original garments must have been. Yet the painting exhibits Whistler's confidence in his commitment to decorative issues explored fourteen years earlier in the *Symphony in White No. 1*.

Shortly after Whistler's death, another American painter, Kenyon Cox, recognized *The White Girl* as a tentative effort, but one which pointed the direction toward sophisticated, abstract decorative surfaces that Whistler was to take:

> *It is somewhat timid and awkward as yet, but in its reliance for artistic effect upon the decorative division of space, on grace of line, and on the delicate opposition of nicely discriminated tones, it is already . . . characteristic. The artist has found the road he was destined to tread, and henceforth steps aside from it but seldom.*[50]

For years Whistler was undervalued by scholars and critics as a "decorative" painter of works without content, a painter whose abilities were at best minor.[51] Whistler's early association with French modernists involved him in aspirations toward breaking the bounds of traditional easel painting, and he was not the only artist to stress the primacy of aesthetic decisions.[52] During the 1870s, Whistler mastered design principles of Oriental art that furthered the decorative nature of his own work. Unfortunately for Whistler, as his art became less easily read it was increasingly suspect by a conservative audience conditioned to expect narrative painting. Even at the end of his career, when Whistler finally gained public acceptance, his aesthetic emphasis was subject to attack. Reviewing Whistler's important exhibition at Goupil's in 1892, one critic commented:

> *There are two ways in which it is perfectly fair for the non-artistic world to regard fine art; artists have but one way. If we consider the last only—that is to say, if we exclusively regard the technical dexterity, the brush-system, the executive characterization—then it is difficult not to speak with what seems like exaggeration of Mr. Whistler's best paintings. His colour is so exquisite, his actual method of producing the effect he desires by means of his brush so masterly, and all this adroit technique is so completely part of a very fine and a very peculiar personal temperament, that we are not much surprised that those who enjoy these things sincerely—a limited company—use to express their pleasure language which savours of extravagance. . . . But there is the other mode, and the moment comes when we see that, exquisite and invaluable as this emotional workmanship is . . . art cannot confine itself to such manifestations; when this consideration asserts itself underneath the flutter of nervous pleasure, we realize that a world of nocturnes and arrangements would be as tedious as an eternal soufflé.*[53]

Figure 73.
Symphony in Green and Violet, from the "Six Projects," ca. 1868, oil on panel. Freer Gallery.

Figure 74.
Symphony in Blue and Pink, from the "Six Projects," ca. 1868, oil on panel. Freer Gallery.

Figure 75.
Symphony in White and Red, from the "Six Projects," ca. 1868, oil on panel. Freer Gallery.

Shortly after the artist's death in 1903, the concept of "ornament as crime" in architectural circles began an inexorable march toward the puristic atmosphere of postwar Europe, an atmosphere in which Whistler's exquisite canvases failed to excite great scholarly interest. Only in the past few years has a serious reassessment of his contribution begun.

The standard pejorative applied to his work—*decorative*—has seldom been clearly defined, yet it still provides an important avenue of access to Whistler's art. Herein lies a major link to the eighteenth century in general and to Watteau in particular. Whistler's debt to Japanese art was remarked upon by the 1860s. However, it has not been observed that Whistler's *japonisme* followed a European model. Moreover, the model was not easel painting but architectural decoration. The eclectic chinoiserie of eighteenth-century France served Whistler well as he absorbed what he needed out of Eastern art, gradually learning to express Occidental ideas with Oriental feeling. Watteau was involved in the creation of decorative interior schemes, particularly after his association with Claude Audran.[54] These essays into chinoiserie link Watteau to Whistler. Whistler's quintessential japonesque project was the famous Peacock Room of 1876–1877. Upon examination, the Peacock Room proves full of French rococo elements. It was, after all, conceived and executed during the rococo revival.

Architects, painters, and designers all poured their talents into the decorative masterpieces of the rococo period. Their work was still being reinterpreted more than a century later. Ornate furniture and interiors, labeled Louis XIV, Louis XV, or rococo revival, dominated Whistler's youth, flourishing in Europe and America, not to mention Czarist Russia, from the 1830s through the 1850s and 1860s.[55]

Since Whistler's primary artistic interests have always been recognized, if not appreciated, as decorative, his reputation has been tainted by the same suspicion of frivolity that tinges assessments of rococo revival interiors, dismissed as the work of decorators and unworthy of the rigorously minded architect or serious painter.

At least one Whistler interior design has been hidden for years. It was recently discovered on the back of a framed watercolor in the Freer collection (Fig. 72). Whistler combined a feather motif, which he also used in the Peacock Room, with a rococo cartouche filled with flowers on a trellis. Probably coeval with the Peacock Room, the watercolor also includes single blossoms lazily distributed along the dado.

The "Six Projects" comprise an earlier scheme, better known and more elaborate, intended to result in architectural decoration modeled along the lines of eighteenth-century French tradition. Whistler began his group of figural oil

Figure 72.
Design for a wall decoration, late 1870s, watercolor. Freer Gallery.

Figure 76.
Variations in Blue and Green, from the "Six Projects," ca. 1868, oil on panel. Freer Gallery.

Figure 77.
The White Symphony: Three Girls, from the "Six Projects," ca. 1868, oil on panel. Freer Gallery.

Figure 78.
Venus, from the "Six Projects," ca. 1868, oil on panel. Freer Gallery.

Figure 79.
Woman with Parasol, ca. 1868, black and white chalk on gray-brown paper. Freer Gallery.

Figure 80.
Étienne Jeaurat after Jean-Antoine Watteau, *Oriental Figure* (Fille du Royaume d'Ava), eighteenth century, engraving. Reproduced in Dacier and Vuaflart, pl. 250, planche 42.

sketches in 1868, and his lavish palette of soft salmons, tender turquoise-greens, reticent yellows, creamy pinks, and pale mauves can only be termed rococo (Figs. 73–78). The "Six Projects" recall the evanescent colors of Watteau's palette, which were considered idiosyncratic at the time. The Goncourt brothers asked in 1856, "From what school do Watteau's pictures come? They are painted with an unprecedented originality of color. Watteau's fantasy of tones seems to seek something more than colored matter."[56] In Watteau, Whistler could have seen a precedent for the ethereal hues that characterize much of his own work when he painted.

When he painted the "Six Projects," Whistler might have had in mind his own version of Watteau's famous *Departure for Cythera* (see Fig. 58). The decorative scheme Whistler so tantalizingly outlined was never brought to completion, and the architectural space scheduled to receive the decorations is completely unknown. The intended order of the paintings is not recorded. Given its unfinished abstract nature, the series is open to more than one interpretation. Nevertheless, it is possible to propose that the "Projects" were programmatic and that they suggested a journey. Perhaps the women progress from the light-filled interior of the *White Symphony: Three Girls* outdoors onto the balcony of *Variations in Blue and Green* where they gaze out to sea. In *Symphony in White and Red* they are on a pier, and one figure descends stairs to enter a boat. The *Symphony in Blue and Pink* shows the women together again on a windswept beach. Possibly they seek Venus. She appears alone in a panel where the beach seems to be a continuation in color and form of the preceding painting. Billowing drapery gives Venus the air of having just arrived. Whether or not the women are looking for Venus or she for them, the "Six Projects" eloquently record Whistler's personal search for an abstract, synthetic beauty.

Whistler's decorative ideas were not limited to interior schemes. He also created designs for screens and fans, as Watteau had done. Moreover, he used a French rococo-inspired eclecticism in some of his japonesque drawings and paintings. A small chalk study for the woman with a parasol can be compared to one of the "diverse figures chinoises" designed by Watteau. (Figs. 79 and 80).[57] Nobody would mistake one of Watteau's little coquettes for an Oriental woman. In 1895 Watteau's "femme Bonze" from the decorations at the Château de la Muette, was admired for her "piquant charm, which notwithstanding the more or less Chinese get-up, is not Pekinese, but wholly Parisian of the 18th century." Equally eclectic, Whistler conflated Grecian drapery with an Oriental umbrella in his chalk study. The result is much closer to a contemporary fashion print than to any figure in Hokusai's *Manga*,[58] the type of Japanese source Whistler is most likely to have consulted. Like Watteau, Whistler displays an overriding

Figure 81.
La Princesse du Pays de la Porcelaine, 1863–1864, oil on canvas. Freer Gallery.

Figure 82.
Study for a Portrait of Mrs. Leyland, 1871 ff., fabricated chalks on brown paper. Freer Gallery.

Figure 83.
Study for a Portrait of Mrs. Leyland, 1871 ff., fabricated chalks on brown paper. Freer Gallery.

Figure 84.
Study for a Portrait of Mrs. Leyland, 1871 ff., fabricated chalks on brown paper. Freer Gallery.

Figure 85.
Symphony in Flesh Colour and Pink: Portrait of Mrs. Frances Leyland, 1871–1874, oil on canvas. Copyright the Frick collection, New York.

Figure 86.
Jean-Antoine Watteau, *Gersaint's Signboard*, 1721, oil on canvas. Collection Schloss Charlottenburg.

sense of fashion and creates a fundamentally Western image that has incorporated Eastern elements.

Japonesque paintings that Whistler brought to completion also relate clearly to current fashion, as do some of his sketches. In *Rose and Silver: La Princesse du Pays de la Porcelain*, 1864, Christine Spartali strikes the exaggerated pose of a fashion model. Her gown is splendid, but it is not worn in an Oriental manner. The mélange of Japanese garments, a Japanese screen and fan, and a Chinese rug and vase again recalls the fashionable eclecticism of more than a hundred years earlier (Fig. 81).

From about 1865 until the turn of the century Watteau's elegant ladies were imitated in popular fashions. Magazines like *Revue de la Mode, Gazette de la Famille*, and *L'Art et la Mode* were filled with items of women's wear associated with Watteau. The *Revue de la Mode* reported in 1884 that "Women especially must love Watteau. He created a type, a style for them. He is the magician who taught them how to be beautiful. His name remains synonymous with exquisite elegance, utter charm." Hats, dresses, even buttons bore Watteau's stamp.[59]

Whistler's designs for the dress worn by the subject of his *Symphony in Flesh Colour and Pink: Portrait of Mrs. Frances Leyland* (1871–1874) leave no doubt that Whistler was well acquainted with the fashion for clothing derived from Watteau's paintings (Figs. 82 and 83). The Watteau dress remained popular for such a long time because it conferred "elegance to an ordinary figure."[60] Studies by Whistler of Mrs. Leyland's bound sleeve, along with his numerous drawings of rosettes, evoke a statement regarding Watteau: "The fold in a cloak, the tuck in a corsage, the slashing of a sleeve, and the rosette on a shoe, are matters of as much importance as the features and the pose of the whole figure" (Fig. 84).[61] The oft-scraped surface of Whistler's *Symphony* shows that the artist repositioned rosettes. Seen from the back, the regal Mrs. Leyland is flattered immensely by the elegant sweep of her train with its "pli Watteau" (Fig. 85). Not only the cut of the dress, but also the portrait's peach-pink color scheme recalls a lavish dress in Watteau's painting, *Gersaint's Signboard* (Fig. 86).[62]

Compositions with complicated interrelationships reveal Whistler as an artist who mined his own imagery in the manner of Degas. Continuing exploration of a self-referential set of ideas is another trait that Whistler shared not only with contemporary French modernists, but also with Watteau: "The repetition of figures from different paintings is one of the attractions of Watteau's elusive art, it endows the fantasy of his creations with a sense of continuity and serves as a touchstone for the memory."[63] Continuity drawn from within his own *oeuvre* is another way in which the modernist carries on the working methods of past centuries. Turning and inflecting familiar poses, Whistler incorporated a variety of fresh insights to create ever-new variations upon his favorite themes.

Weary, an etching of 1863, is an early example of such a theme—the general concept of a woman in an armchair intrigued Whistler throughout his career, as it did many artists of both the eighteenth and nineteenth centuries. The etching depicts Jo, her head gently tilted, the enveloping curve of the chairback echoed in the graceful spread of her gown (Fig. 87). During the 1870s, Whistler explored the idea further in several drawings and prints. Whistler's lithotint of 1878, entitled *Study*, recalls the earlier image of Jo. However, the artist changed his vantage point to a more severely frontal view, and the model now rests her head on her hand. Again, the chairback forms a supporting space that encompasses the semireclining figure (Fig. 88).

At some point in the sequence of seated women, Whistler must have looked very closely at Watteau's *Dame étendue sur une chaise longue* (Fig. 89). The

Figure 87.
Weary, 1863, etching, K92,
second state. Freer Gallery.

Figure 88.
Study, 1878, lithograph,
K3. Freer Gallery.

Figure 89.
Jean-Antoine Watteau,
*Dame étendue sur une
chaise longue*, chalk.
Reproduced in *Watteau et
sa génération* (Paris, 1968),

no. 42. Reprinted courtesy
of Galerie Cailleux and
Fondation Custodia (coll.
F. Lugt), Institut Néer-
landais, Paris.

Figure 90.
The Two Sisters, 1894,
lithograph, K71. Freer
Gallery.

Figure 91.
La Belle Dame paresseuse,
1894, lithograph, K62.
Freer Gallery.

Figure 92.
Venus, 1859, etching, K59,
second state. Freer Gallery.

drawing had been in England since the mid-eighteenth century. Auctioned in London in 1881, it became part of the collection of J. P. Heseltine, a trustee of the British National Gallery of Art as well as a supporter of Whistler. Heseltine was the man responsible for trying to raise money to pay Whistler's court costs after the financially ruinous Ruskin trial. Whistler certainly would have had access to the *Dame étendue* once it entered Heseltine's possession, if not before.[64]

The image by Whistler that most closely replicates the *Dame étendue* was made in 1894, considerably after Heseltine bought the drawing. *The Two Sisters*, a lithograph, involves direct quotation from the French drawing of 1715–1716. Beatrix Whistler is supported in an angular armchair whose placement and large blank spaces derive from the Watteau drawing (Fig. 90). The general arrangement of the figure is also derivative. However, as usual, Whistler varied the pose he borrowed from Watteau.[65]

Watteau's drawing is characterized by the sketchy application of chalks with minimal shading and virtually no stumping. For his print Whistler chose a lithographic crayon, whose greasy texture more closely approximates the appearance of chalk than the sharp point of an etcher's needle can. Whistler's handling of the crayon is heavier than Watteau's use of the chalk, but in both works the linear quality is dominant.

The relaxed pose of Watteau's figure is gently peaceful. The fatigued aspect of Whistler's sitter departs from Watteau's example and embodies the Victorian concept of the Pre-Raphaelite female. Whistler grafted her aesthetic ennui onto his French example. An Anglo-French blending here parallels the similar conflation in the *White Girl* decades earlier. Whistler's women in armchairs consistently evoke the idea of lassitude; the visual content is emphasized by the artist's selection of titles that refer to sleeping or laziness: *La Belle Dame endormie* or *La Belle Dame parresseuse*, for example (Fig. 91). In these prints, Whistler explored the seated figure from different angles.

As certain images revolved in the artist's mind, he created other images based upon them. Since we don't know exactly when Whistler saw the Watteau drawing, we cannot state its role precisely, but we may surmise that it complimented Whistler's investigation of a theme already embarked upon. Perhaps he returned to a model artwork, just as he might return to a live model, in order to refocus his thinking about a particular problem. More than once Whistler hired someone to pose nude long after a painting was begun. He made belated use of "Fosco," studying the young man's anatomy in order to improve the stance of Frederick Leyland's legs in the partially completed *Arrangement in Black: Portrait of F. R. Leyland*.[66] The female model hired for work on *The White Symphony: Three Girls* was posing for Whistler seven years after he completed the oil sketch that is now part of the "Six Projects."[67]

The "Six Projects" indicate that Whistler, like Watteau, was interested in the myth of Venus. Indeed, images of her continued to recur in Whistler's work for four decades. The earliest is an etching dated 1859. *Venus* alludes to Watteau's *Reclining Nude* of 1714–1715 (Figs. 92 and 93). Whistler's goddess is asleep, not

Figure 93.
Jean-Antoine Watteau,
Reclining Nude, ca.
1713–1715, oil on panel.
Norton Simon Foundation,
Pasadena, California.
(Photograph, A. E. Dolinski
Photographic.)

Figure 94.
Venus Rising from the Sea,
ca. 1869–1870, oil on
canvas. Freer Gallery.

Figure 96.
Study, 1895, lithograph,
K77. Freer Gallery.

Figure 95.
Jean-Antoine Watteau,
Jugement de Paris, ca. 1721,
oil. Musées Nationaux de
France.

Figure 97.
The Purple Cap, 1890s,
fabricated chalks on gray-
brown paper. Freer Gallery.

Figure 98.
Jean-Antoine Watteau,
*Study of Seated Woman
with Children,* chalks.
Trustees of the British
Museum.

Figure 99.
Venus and Cupid, Tanagra
figurine, from Ionides
collection, photograph
from Whistler's album.
Hunterian Art Gallery,
University of Glasgow,
Birnie Philip Bequest.

awake; but the way she lies in the rumpled sheets, uncovered to the knees, emphasizes her voluptuous figure, suggesting that Whistler might have known Watteau's image.[68] Shortly after he painted the "Six Projects," Whistler created another image of the goddess, *Venus Rising from the Sea,* using the same rococo-inspired palette of pale pinks and blue-greens (Fig. 94).[69]

Whistler probably borrowed several poses directly from Watteau when creating the little nudes of his late career. In Watteau's *Judgment of Paris,* which entered the Louvre in 1869 with the La Caze collection, a nude figure lifts her garment over her head (Fig. 95). The pose is adopted almost verbatim in Whistler's *Study,* a lithograph of 1895 (Fig. 96). Whistler used the pose a number of times from different vantage points in a manner consistent with his treatment of women in armchairs. The model in Watteau's painting is probably Venus, who was chosen by Paris as the winner in an ancient mythical beauty contest. In repeatedly treating the theme of the young female nude, Whistler himself seems to have engaged in a sort of personal "judgment of Paris." He wrote of a favorite model from this period, "She is one of my latest pets—and of a rare type of beauty."[70]

Whistler and Watteau shared an interest in gentle eroticism. It was, in each case, an eroticism that could almost be overlooked. In 1895, Claude Phillips discussed passion in Watteau's work:

> *Watteau is rarely if ever dramatic in the stricter sense of the word. He can wrap his personages round with an indefinable unity of senti-ment . . . but he cannot connect them with that invisible wire which makes all the personages of the dramatic painter at the given mo-ment of representation thrill together, whether with the attraction of sympathy or the clash of opposing passion.*[71]

A disembodied quality characterizes Whistler's figures of the 1890s. Denys Sutton has called them "unsubstantial." He comments:

> *As far as his art is concerned, [Whistler] was rarely seized by that overwhelming passion for life which impels a painter to involve himself with themes of a richly sensuous nature. An element of fear seems to mark his attitude to flesh painting as if the animal quality of the female form, which is superbly voluptuous when rendered by a Titian or a Courbet was too much for him.*[72]

It is unlikely that the fleshy nude was "too much" for Whistler; rather it probably was not subtle enough. Sutton's comment, written seven decades after Phillips's, is close in its perception of an artist's work somewhat devalued for the avoidance of weighty corporeality.

In defense of Watteau's figure drawing, Donald Poesner has observed, "The drawings do not aim to articulate the structure and mechanics of bone and muscle, but attempt to capture the voluptuousness of the female body."[73] A similar argument may be made for Whistler, who communicated sensuality not only through mass and line but also through color.

If seated women with children were popular eighteenth-century French subjects, so were Venus and Cupid.[74] In many of his late works of the 1890s, Whistler seems to have commingled the chaste mother and child with more suggestive mythological content. *The Purple Cap* typifies Whistler's group of exquisite pastels, watercolors, etchings, and lithographs that seem, at first, to recall eighteenth-century pictures of mothers and children (Figs. 97 and 98).[75]

Figure 100.
Mother and Child: The Pearl, 1880s–1890s, fabricated chalks on gray-brown paper. Freer Gallery.

Figure 101.
Venus Nursing Eros, Tanagra figurine, from Ionides collection, photograph from Whistler's album, ca. 1880. Hunterian Art Gallery, University of Glasgow, Birnie Philip Bequest.

Figure 102.
Tintoretto, *The Birth of the Milky Way*, 1582, photograph from Whistler's studio. University of Glasgow Library special collections.

Figure 103.
Jean-Antoine Watteau, *Gilles and his Family*, ca. 1716, oil on panel. Reproduced by permission of the Trustees, the Wallace collection, London.

But the scantily clad figures are closer in spirit to eighteenth-century pictures of the goddess of love.[76] Whistler absorbed other sources as well, for *The Purple Cap* also makes reference to ancient classical art (Fig. 99). Whistler owned a group of photographs showing Tanagra figurines, many of which were in the collection of his friend Lucas Ionides. Figure 99 is taken from the album. Another pastel in this vein, *Mother and Child: The Pearl* (Fig. 100), relates to similar Tanagra figurines such as *Venus Nursing Eros* (Fig. 101), also from Whistler's photo album.

Popular with collectors during the 1870s and 1880s, Tanagra figurines were admired for their roughened surfaces. Vestiges of powdery color in pastel shades clung to the weathered clay, bespeaking great age. Whistler could easily transpose the effect of delicately colored, flaking clay surfaces to the flat plane of his rough pastel paper. Patches of color on the figurines may have suggested Whistler's use of pastel sticks to create discrete clouds of evanescent color that seem to hover over the surfaces of his drawings. Tanagra may also have had an impact on his use of the sticks to draw brief colored lines, for the thickest paint clings to incised furrows and indented hollows in the clay. Moreover, his tinted papers echo the warm color of terra cotta showing through aged paint.

Whistler's drawing of *Mother and Child: The Pearl* recalls not only Watteau's *Reclining Nude* but also a Venus figure borrowed from a painting by Tintoretto, *The Birth of the Milky Way*. Whistler kept a large photograph of the Venetian painter's canvas in his studio (Fig. 102). By arranging living models in poses based upon composites of other works of art, Whistler blurred the act of conflation while producing an aesthetically pleasing and convincing entity.

Whistler's ability to synthesize should not obscure the impact that Watteau might have had upon his pastel technique, which was somewhat unorthodox by nineteenth-century standards. Whistler's chalk drawings date from the 1860s on, and during his trip to Venice he established himself as an early participant in the pastel revival, a movement heavily indebted to eighteenth-century French precedent.[77] Unlike many fellow revivalists, however, Whistler's work in pastel remained closer to drawing than to painting. He seldom stumped or blended his chalks, and he relied upon a substructure of clear black lines to carry each composition. Watteau's chalk drawings were usually rendered in some combination of red, black, and white without a great deal of stumping or shading.[78]

Baudelaire had pointed out that a work of art was actually an evocation, one which worked its magic through the fusion of color and line.[79] Whistler seems to have taken this concept to heart, and Watteau's smallest oils would have provided easily understood examples for Whistler's handling of pastel (Fig. 103). In his minute oils, Watteau created figures with pencil-thin lines of color, applied with a tiny brush. Whistler handled his chalks in a like manner as he attempted to create a sense of volume and tried to master color with line.[80] Moreover, the use of tinted papers follows eighteenth-century French practice. The critic Paul Mantz described Watteau's lightness of touch, an often-remarked characteristic, as "the almost imperceptible brush of the petals of a flower caused by an alighting butterfly."[81] Whistler drew with Watteau's precious linear sensuality. He signed *The Purple Cap* with his accustomed butterfly, having deftly laid gossamer films of turquoise and violet over black lines that define the model's silken draperies. The colors so lightly touch the surface that in places they are nearly imperceptible.

The languid, almost lazy fluidity of Whistler's drawing leads us to the discussion of yet another contribution made by Watteau to the development of Whistler's art. We associate Whistler's anguish over his drawing ability with his self-proclaimed desire for Ingres's tutelage. But how Ingres's use of line relates to Watteau's and what implications there may be for Whistler have not been mentioned.

In August 1867, the year of an enormous retrospective exhibition of Ingres in Paris, Whistler wrote an emotional letter to his friend Fantin-Latour, summarizing his dilemma over color versus design or drawing—one of the fundamental issues in nineteenth-century academic art. In the letter Whistler stated his strong rejection of Courbet's realism and voiced the wish that he had learned to draw under Ingres, an artist whom he had copied directly by 1857.[82] Already charged by Whistler's emotionalism, the issue was further polarized by the partisan Pennells, Whistler's indefatigable biographers. They called his letter "an absurd piece of modesty for he drew better than Ingres, as his etchings prove."[83] Although there is no point in pitting Whistler against Ingres, numerous drawings show that Whistler drew a perfectly acceptable figure when that was his intention. However, as I mentioned above, more than one series of artworks pinpoints Whistler's use of the live model late in his working sequence, after color harmonies were established.

Whistler's classicizing phase in association with Albert Moore is also well known. Significantly, Moore has been called "the greatest Ingriste in England."[84] Whistler's interest in Ingres, and to some extent also in Moore, was based on his desire to improve his drawing—his ability to render line. It is interesting that Ingres himself had copied Watteau. Ingres drew from prints of Watteau's work in order to study composition through linear means: "These brief sketches, despite their spontaneity, reveal the artist's appreciation of lines that form or sustain the mystery of equilibrium."[85] It was precisely this sense of precarious balance, established by a sensuous linearity touched with color, that came to characterize Whistler's mature pastel drawings. The pastels reflect Whistler's lasting struggle to control color with line.

Whistler must have had recourse to the Elgin Marbles while he was associated with Albert Moore. The antique architectural decorations had been newly installed at the British Museum in 1865. While it is not my purpose to discuss the marbles at length here, I want to emphasize the thread running through artworks sought out by Whistler as models. Decoration provided the common denominator that made it possible for Whistler to blend his interest in Oriental art with that of classical Greece and rococo France.[86]

The clouds of broken color, largely derived from the surface appearance of Tanagra figurines, are combined with a controlling network of lines—the "mystery of equilibrium" found in Watteau's drawing. Together they allowed Whistler to achieve a distinctive balance of color and line that separates his pastel drawings from those of his contemporaries.

In *Blue and Rose: the Open Fan*, Whistler captured a lissome figure's general presence while summarizing her features (Fig. 104).[87] In this drawing, color is used *as* line. Whistler draws with long strokes of robin's egg and marine blue, interwoven with the black chalk lines that establish the figure on the page. Where color is blended at all, it is thinly applied, and seems to lose rather than gain substance. It becomes the fugitive shimmer of light upon diaphanous silk. Of all Whistler's late figure studies in various media, the pastels are perhaps the most successful. While oil paintings like *Phryne the Superb!—Builder of Temples* have an overworked quality (Fig. 105), pastels like *The Open Fan* retain their fresh quality. Tiny scale and elegant jewellike surfaces were appropriate for the *fin de siècle*, and other artists in Paris were pursuing similar themes while varying their erotic content.[88]

Figure 104.
Blue and Rose: the Open Fan, 1890s, fabricated chalks on brown paper. Freer Gallery.

Figure 105. *Purple and Gold: Phryne the Superb! Builder of Temples*, 1898 ff., oil on panel. Freer Gallery.

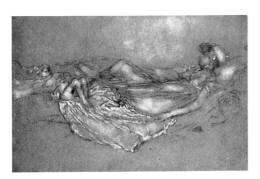

Figure 106.
The Shell, 1890s, fabricated chalks on gray-brown paper. Freer Gallery.

Certainly in *The Shell* Whistler ravished the senses with color rather than concrete form. Two reproductions of this pastel dramatically demonstrate how Whistler's masterful balance between line and color is lost in a black and white photograph (Fig. 106, Plate 296). That such colorless glimpses of his work have had a deleterious effect on the artist's reputation is obvious.

Whistler's small drawing measures only about seven by eleven inches, yet he included more than twenty different colors. His method of application ranged from tiny dots and strokes to longer, thicker lines, all made with the pointed ends of the pastel sticks. There are also shimmering areas where he brushed the flat side of a chalk ever so lightly over the surface of the paper. But each color remains individual—there is almost no blending, even in areas where Whistler superimposed one tiny dot of color upon another. Sensuality is also presented by the erotic pose of the two figures. The woman and her child are set like precious stones in the draperies. The whole comprises a shell-like form that gives the pastel its title.

Finely tuned to color's sensual possibilities, Whistler remained primarily an expressive colorist, despite his desire for the controlled linearity of an *Ingriste.* From the outset, when Whistler wrote about color, it was in sensual terms. In the famous letter to Fantin-Latour, Whistler exposed his lifelong passionate attachment to color:

> *Truly color is vice! Of course, it can be, and has the right to be one of the finest virtues. Controlled by the strong hand and careful guidance of her Master drawing, color is a splendid Mistress, with a mate worthy of herself, her lover, but her Master likewise, the most magnificent Mistress possible, and the result is evident in all the glorious things that spring from their union.*[89]

At about the same time the Goncourts were exclaiming over Watteau's sensual use of red and black chalks. They admired Watteau's

> *trifles and felicities of art which are everything—a whole quantity of little effects full of verve and inspiration . . . it is a red chalk shot with purple, a black crayon of incomparable smoothness, and chalk added with all the artist's wit and skill, to form upon the paper the colour of chamois, the pink and white of flesh.*[90]

Whistler made no such exclamations about Watteau. Jo Hiffernan, whose appearance in *Symphony in White No. 1* offers the most compelling evidence for borrowings from Watteau, eventually joined the ranks of Whistler's cast-off mistresses. But at least one liaison was enduring, for the artist was faithful to color, and the relationship did not remain illegitimate. Whistler gained mastery, leaving behind many beautiful paintings and drawings now in the Freer collection, objects that silently—yet eloquently—acknowledge his debt to an eighteenth-century model.

The Peacock Room.

Artist and Architect

*The Decorative Arts arise from, and should properly
be attendant upon, Architecture.*
OWEN JONES

Figure 107.
Peacock Room, north wall,
with *La Princesse du Pays
de la Porcelain*, 1876–1877.
Freer Gallery.

Figure 108.
Peacock Room, south and
west walls.

THE PEACOCK ROOM, executed in 1876–1877, is Whistler's most important essay into decorative art. It was a dining room conceived for the artist's first significant patron, the self-made shipping baron Frederick Richards Leyland. As the only Whistler interior left to us, the Peacock Room is crucial for understanding the role of decoration in the development of his abstract painting style. This, in turn, is linked to our perception of the room as a traditional collaboration between artist and architect, in which Whistler's role was a two-dimensional one. It is by recognizing the artist-architect relationship for what it was, and by separating out the contributions that each man made to this particular interior, that we can gain a general understanding of the function of the decorative arts in Whistler's *oeuvre*.

By the mid-nineteenth century it was common for painters in Britain to involve themselves in the creation of decorative art. Sir Henry Cole managed the Summerly Art Manufactures from 1849 to 1851, giving painters the opportunity to work with others who were experienced in making actual three-dimensional objects and spaces rather than in capturing the illusion of depth upon a two-dimensional piece of canvas.[1]

Although we instantly associate the Peacock Room with Whistler, it was actually a collaboration between the artist and the now-little-known architect Thomas Jeckyll. Jeckyll was among Britain's earliest advocates of *japonisme*. Motifs inspired by the arts of Japan captured European imaginations during the 1860s, 1870s, and 1880s, having a forceful impact upon both painting and decoration. Jeckyll remodeled the dining room at 49 Prince's Gate to receive Leyland's extensive collection of blue and white china, along with the large canvas, *La Princesse du Pays de la Porcelaine*, painted by Whistler in 1863–1864 and acquired by Leyland several years later. During the early months of 1876 Jeckyll completed the three-dimensional volume in which Whistler would work his two-dimensional magic. Whistler eventually rethought the entire interior in ways completely related to his goals as a painter of flat canvases.[2]

Beginning in April 1876, the room underwent a year-long transformation, changing at Whistler's hands from a rather fussy Anglo-Dutch porcelain cabinet with dark leather walls and spindly walnut shelves carved with Oriental motifs to a carefully balanced chamber shimmering with gold and turquoise paint, unified by repeated color and pattern. The originality of Whistler's unusual synthesis was recognized immediately.[3] The room still stands today as one of the most exciting interiors of the British Aesthetic Movement (Figs. 107 and 108).

But a juicy scandal erupted between artist and patron in the spring of 1877, and what should have been the high point of generous patronage on Leyland's part became instead a notorious yet fascinating quarrel that ended in a permanent break between the irascible artist and his first important supporter. Whistler's transformation had completely exceeded the authority granted by Leyland's commission. The fight was fueled by Leyland's anger that Whistler had hidden his prized antique leather hangings under layers of paint.

Today, it is not only the leather hangings that are obscure. Jeckyll's contributions to the room, while not unknown, have received scant attention. How Jeckyll's work affected Whistler's remains a virtually unexplored issue. From the time of the quarrel Whistler indulged in little sins of omission and commission that incorporated the Peacock Room into his personal myth of genius. Leyland was the artist's intended victim. Jeckyll was probably an unintended casualty. The unfortunate architect died in August 1881 after several years' bout with mental illness. Jeckyll was already unbalanced by the time Whistler was painting the Peacock Room. This is clear in a letter to Whistler, dated November 11, 1876, in which Jeckyll mentioned that God had been helping him with working drawings and that the letter itself was valuable because God had written it.[4]

Neither of Jeckyll's two obituaries makes any mention of his work on the Peacock Room. This may have been partially because Jeckyll's remodeling had not been considered particularly good architecture.[5] But it may also reflect collegial respect for Jeckyll and an unwillingness to stir up the controversy one more time. Perhaps Jeckyll's mental stability was damaged by Whistler's actions in the Peacock Room, although to date no concrete evidence substantiates this. Instead, we have the Pennells' lurid report that Jeckyll's final visit to the Peacock Room "had a tragic end. When he saw what had been done with his work, he hurried home, gilded his floor, and forgot his grief in a mad-house."[6] Such sensationalism typifies the atmosphere that has always surrounded the Peacock Room.

Before the Whistler-Leyland quarrel, the painter had taken pains to ensure that newspaper coverage mentioned the architect's contribution alongside his own. Following one-sided praise of his work on the Peacock Room, Whistler wrote to the *Academy* in gracious acknowledgment of Jeckyll's architecture, "If there be any quality whatever in my decoration, it is doubtless due to the inspiration I have received from the graceful proportions and lovely lines of Mr. Jeckyll's work about me."[7] With the exception of the chastised *Academy*, newspapers seldom brought up Jeckyll's name in discussions of the room during the late winter and early spring of 1877. By that time Whistler was actively engaged in his quarrel with Leyland. He made no effort to correct such misstatements as the *Builder's* assertion that "the whole work . . . has been executed by the Artist's own hand."[8]

Anecdote clouds the events of 1876–1877 at Prince's Gate. The deaths of the principal characters brought no new unbiased evaluation. By 1904, Leyland, Jeckyll, and Whistler were dead. The room had been moved from London to Detroit after its purchase by Charles Lang Freer, the second major patron in Whistler's long career.[9] Until it was brought to Washington after Freer's death in 1919, the room occupied a wing in the collector's home, where it received few visitors.

Writings about the Peacock Room, particularly about the quarrel, quickly became more accessible than the room itself. Over time, this printed material has developed a self-generating life of its own, apart from the artifact it supposedly concerns. Studies of the Peacock Room suffer from the general problem that affects Whistler scholarship: the literature is riddled with mythology and re-peated, often-inflected anecdotes which are sometimes, but not always, traceable to the artist himself. As we shall shortly see, Whistler was an Ur-source for the Peacock Room's mythology. To see just how Jeckyll was victimized along with Leyland, we must dip into the quarrel yet again, bearing in mind that in the long run Whistler helped to trivialize the event, thereby penalizing himself with re-gard to later historians' assessment of his work.

Near the end of an acrimonious exchange of letters, Whistler drafted an illustrated note to Leyland: "I refer you to the Cartoon opposite you at dinner, known to all London as l'Art et l'Argent, or the Story of the Room" (Fig. 109).[10] The scandal that amused London society during the spring and summer of 1877 has continued to entertain both scholars and the public. Investigations of the Peacock Room have stalled on the question of "L'Art et l'Argent." There are endless, ever-varying accounts of the quarrel that telescope and garble the de-tails. At the lowest level of scholarship it is still possible to read that the entire south wall panel, which measures nearly six feet by fifteen feet, was rapidly executed without the patron's knowledge after the falling-out:

Figure 109.
Fighting Peacocks, drawing after south panel of Peacock Room, 1877, pencil. Hunterian Art Gallery, University of Glasgow Library.

> *The shipping magnate . . . hired an interior designer to turn one room of his home into the proper setting for a collection of blue and white porcelain. Whistler heard about the designer's plan and de-cided to redecorate the room on his own. While the owner was out of town, Whistler slipped into the house and covered the antique Span-ish leather walls with blue paint and golden peacocks . . . the de-signer went mad, and the shipping magnate refused to pay Whistler's fee. But the artist had the last laugh. When the shipping magnate was out of town at another time, Whistler went into the house once again and added another pair of peacocks to the room—The Rich Peacock, representing his ungrateful patron, and The Poor Peacock, depicting none other than Whistler himself.*[11]

This preposterous passage, printed in 1980, stands as a prime example of the mythology of the room handed down to us.

Whistler cultivated a public posture of artistic genius, but his hard labor was performed in private. While fellow artists recognized his twin personalities, others, including early biographers, were mesmerized by claims of artistic spon-taneity. For the artist to foster a romantic image of himself, he had to diminish the architect's importance. Whistler accomplished this purpose by neglect, whereas he conscientiously worked to build the story of Leyland's cupidity.

Any notion of the room's spontaneous evolution is completely compromised by a full-scale cartoon pounced for transfer to the south-wall panel (Fig. 110). Found in Whistler's studio after his death, the cartoon is executed in watercolors and gouache on paper.[12] The formal elements of what was later construed as an iconographic confrontation between artist and patron were clearly there from the start. By November 29, 1876, the cartoon had served its purpose. On that day Whistler's friend Alan Cole went to Prince's Gate, where he saw "golden peacocks at the end of the room." On December 4, Cole noted that the golden peacocks were "superb" but one cannot conclude that the south wall panel was complete at that point.[13]

Figure 110.
Pounced cartoon for *Fighting Peacocks*, 1876, pencil, watercolor, and gouache. Hunterian Art Gallery, University of Glasgow.

As Cole's diary demonstrates, Whistler was not averse to showing works in progress. However, under ordinary circumstances, neither Leyland's house nor his collection was available for public visitation.[14] Whistler had received prominent guests in the Peacock Room as early as the summer of 1876.[15] This can only have happened with the family's knowledge. When a newspaper reporter misspelled Leyland's name, Whistler's reaction suggests that he was worried about his patron's reaction to journalistic exposure.[16] Nonetheless, Whistler hosted a major press viewing on February 9, 1877. The flurry of newspaper publicity prompted by interest in the decorations at Prince's Gate was probably a major factor in the breach between artist and patron.[17]

Concurrent with the February viewing, the artist published a broadside, giving the Peacock Room its official title: *Harmony in Blue and Gold*. Neither the broadside nor the multiple newspaper accounts of February 1877 make any mention of the color silver, just as Cole made no comment on silver in his December diary entries. But the color silver can be found today in the south wall panel.

Circular shapes can be seen at the feet of the so-called "angry" peacock in the pounced cartoon. They can be read as fallen feathers. Some have been highlighted with a thin white wash—but so have feathers on various other parts of the two birds. The cartoon proves that these circular forms were always part of the composition. Various shades of black, gray, and white articulate the peacocks in the cartoon. The finished birds in the south panel are rendered in two shades of gold paint: a warm orange-gold and a cooler greenish shade. What, then, about the silver? Whistler was permitted to continue working on the room until at least March 1877.[18] And at some point silver-colored paint appeared—but *only* in the south panel. Silver was used for the crest feathers on the head of the docile peacock, and for some circular breast feathers in the angry peacock. The little feathers projecting from the angry peacock's neck are silver, and more circular silver forms are scattered at his feet (Fig. 111).

As noted above, the composition is popularly believed to depict the quarrel. The rich peacock representing Leyland is variously reported to clutch shillings or shekels in his greedy claws.[19] Whistler, cast in the unlikely role of a mild peacock, stands aloof from venal considerations. This standard interpretation was once recognized as anecdotal, but it was fixed in print by the time of Leyland's death sale in 1892. The sale catalogue repeated the story, adding:

> *This cryptic panel was the painter's vengeance, but its hidden meaning is so discretely concealed that it would remain forever lost in the spirited charm of the whole, had not anecdotic memories treasured up the souvenir of the artist's wrath and of its ingenious manifestation.*[20]

Yet the entire composition, with the exception of the silver-colored paint, predates the quarrel, which did not occur until after the February press viewing and subsequent publicity.

The erect feathers on the angry peacock's neck are regularly interpreted as a slur upon the self-made Leyland's preference for fancy frilled shirts. However, the little tufts were part of the original design and can be seen in the pounced cartoon. One of Whistler's most stinging insults was hurled at Leyland late in the summer of 1877: "Whom the gods intend to be ridiculous they furnish with a frill."[21]

Whistler purposefully furnished Leyland with a frill in a satirical piece sardonically entitled *The Gold Scab: Eruption in Frilthy Lucre* (Fig. 112). The thinly painted oil sketch contains direct quotations from the Peacock Room, including the turquoise color and the feather motifs. Although no metallic pigment was

Figure 111.
Peacock Room, south panel, detail of three silver coins at *Angry Peacock*'s feet. (Photograph, Freer Technical Laboratory.)

Figure 112.
The Gold Scab: An Eruption in Frilthy Lucre, after 1877, oil on canvas. Permission of the Fine Arts Museums of San Francisco, gift of Mrs. Alma de Bretteville Spreckels through the Patrons of Art and Music.

Figure 113.
Caricature of F. R. Leyland, ca. 1877, ink. Hunterian Art Gallery, University of Glasgow, Birnie Philip Bequest.

Figure 114.
Peacock Room, detail, south panel, crest feathers on *Docile Peacock*. (Photograph, Freer Technical Laboratory.)

Even in this black and white shot, one can see that the gold paint was not completely covered by silver, especially at the bottom of each feather.

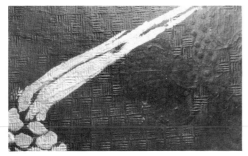

Figure 115.
Peacock Room, detail, south panel, a single silver coin-feather (center) among the gold in peacock's plumage. (Photograph, Freer Technical Laboratory.)

Figure 116.
Peacock Room, detail, south panel, passage of silver paint (center) quickly applied over gold and partially obliterating gold diagonal strokes underneath. (Photograph, Freer Technical Laboratory.)

used, *The Gold Scab* graphically identifies Leyland with greed. His face and the nearest money bag are rendered in odious ochre pigment. In *The Gold Scab* Leyland is shown as a devil peacock, wearing starched shirt frills. Whistler borrowed neck feathers from the angry peacock's neck and placed them on a similarly shaped bass note on the sheet music. Any viewer unable to make the connection was assisted by feathers that fringe the capital F of "Frilthy." The work of an artist devoted to subtle suggestion, this pugnacious pun could only be termed strident.

Whistler's well-composed satire was on view at the White House in Tite Street before the 1879 sale of the bankrupt artist's possessions. The beauty of the canvas "exudes like the scent of a poisonous flower," according to one report.[22] *The Gold Scab* was one of several paintings and drawings in which Whistler emphasized frills to annoy the unlucky patron (Fig. 113).[23] There can be no question that *The Gold Scab* was a postquarrel conception.[24] In the late 1890s, when Leyland was already dead, Whistler deliberately let George Jacomb-Hood, the painting's owner at the time, believe that *The Gold Scab* was actually intended to hang in the Peacock Room. Jacomb-Hood's misapprehension eventually found its way into print.[25]

But the unexpected appearance of silver-colored paint suggests that even before Whistler painted *The Gold Scab*, he made changes to the Peacock Room that would give substance to the legend he intended to foment. To determine the exact nature of these changes, a technical examination was undertaken. The examination was confined to the south wall panel, the only portion of the room where silver-colored paint is found.[26]

Whistler covered gold with platinum for the crest feathers on the docile peacock's head (Fig. 114). This can be seen with the naked eye, as the gold was not completely covered. Cross sections of the paint layers reveal that Whistler laid platinum directly over the bole, which has a brownish-gold color in this case, in the breast feathers of the angry peacock as well as on the circular forms at his feet (Fig. 115).[27] Examination also indicates that the silver paint was added hastily and that it slops over onto gold in several places (Fig. 116). Whistler used platinum, for it does not tarnish as silver would have done.

It is particularly significant that *all* of the circular forms at the feet of the angry peacock are colored silver. Whistler changed them from fallen feathers to scattered coins. Once he had taken permanent umbrage against his patron, the artist distinguished between gentlemen's transactions in guineas worth twenty-one shillings, and tradesmen's dealings in pounds worth twenty shillings. No guineas were minted in Britain after 1820. Gold one-pound coins were circulated thereafter. The shilling, on the other hand, was made of silver.

Surviving letters indicate that there was an altercation about the artist's fee, but that it occurred months before the explosive quarrel.[28] On October 30, 1876, Leyland paid Whistler six hundred pounds. Coupled with the four hundred pounds he had already tendered, this sum was to serve as Whistler's fee for the decorations at Prince's Gate.[29] The work was by no means complete, and Leyland was essentially paying in advance, as he had done for earlier commissions. Moreover, the artist tacitly consented not to charge more. He wrote to Leyland, "We agreed to bear alike the disaster of the decoration. I pay my thousand guineas as my share in the dining room, and you pay yours."[30]

Any charge of venality probably should be laid at Whistler's door rather than Leyland's. Although Whistler did complain of the change from guineas to pounds, his central concern would seem to have been the loss of an additional fifty pounds revenue. He wrote to Leyland: "I have enfin received your cheque—

for six hundred pounds. Shorn of my shillings I perceive!—another fifty pounds off—Well I suppose that will do—upon the principle that anything will do." Whistler crossly remonstrated, "The work just created *alone* remains the fact— and that it happened in the house of this one or that one is merely anecdote—so that in some future dull Vasari you also may go down to posterity like the man who paid Correggio in pennies!"[31]

Whistler's reference to Correggio's pennies suggests that the artist believed he was receiving too little for the work, but it is doubtful that the patron's method of payment was either intended or perceived as an insult at that time. Whistler's missive understandably miffed Leyland, and the patron responded, "I am more surprised than I can tell you that you should think fit to write me in such a tone. The work is not yet finished."[32] Whistler's attitude at this stage was conciliatory. He immediately replied, "Your right to change the guinea of tradition to the current sovereign I don't dispute—I merely notice it . . . forgive the tone if you find it flippant."[33] However, once relations between artist and patron had broken down, he changed his mind. At that time Whistler must have changed the fallen feathers to scattered coins.

On the basis of technical evidence, we can conclude that the silver-colored paint was a last-minute addition, made by Whistler himself for vengeful purposes. The artist was capable of sending a hapless critic a caustic response by return post. He would certainly have had both the wit and the time to edit the south wall slightly in order to gall his patron. We can accept the popular iconography of the south wall as a quarrel between artist and patron, so long as we qualify it as an "editorial change" to a nearly complete, previously thought-out composition.[34]

As far as "the story of the room" is concerned, it is clear that the artist was not above embroidering the truth. Whistler made another misleading statement about the Peacock Room in a letter to the *World* on December 31, 1884: "I secreted the noble bird." The comment was republished in *The Gentle Art of Making Enemies* in 1890 and has deceived many scholars since.[35] What the artist actually hid was his substitution of shillings for feathers.

In the furor over parsimonious patronage the Peacock Room's complicated architectural heritage has gone begging for scholarship.[36] Hidden under unnumbered versions of the quarrel is still more of the story of the room, and of the relation between artist and architect.

The Peacock Room is demonstrably close to architectural tradition. Despite E. W. Godwin's reasoned article on the room's eclectic nature, the interior was, from the outset, a controversial explosion so exciting that its traditional aspects have been almost completely disregarded in the literature to date.[37] Actually the entire concept feeds not only on the relatively new stream of *japonisme*, which was strong in Europe by the early 1860s, but also on an older admixture of European chinoiserie and the rococo as well as an interest in Dutch art. When the room was erected at 49 Prince's Gate, the mansion was undergoing renovation, first at Jeckyll's hands, later under the guidance of Richard Norman Shaw.[38] It should be emphasized that the Peacock Room was built and decorated just after the crest of the rococo revival, as the Queen Anne style was becoming established. The room as we know it today owes something to Jeckyll's "Pont Street Dutch" architecture and to both Jeckyll's and Whistler's comingled visions of Edo and Cathay. In short, the creators of the Peacock Room looked for antecedents.

During the seventeenth century a Dutch monopoly controlled the steady stream of Eastern goods to Western markets. The so-called China trade, which

Figure 117.
Cabinet, black and gold lacquer, Japan, seventeenth or eighteenth century, on black japanned stand, England, third quarter eighteenth century. Victoria and Albert Museum.

Figure 118.
Edmond Goldschmidt, autochrome from *Série chinoise*, Paris, ca. 1895–1898. Reprinted courtesy of Madame H. Millet.

increased during the eighteenth century, was mainly in small transportable decorative arts, including porcelains and lacquer wares.

There was always confusion—or perhaps simply disregard—for the sources of supply. China contributed its name to ceramics, while Japan gave its name to the process for imitating lacquers. Together these form a somewhat jumbled amalgam of stylistic influences from the East.

A late seventeenth-century chest on stand, now at the Victoria and Albert Museum, is representative of objects made for the Western market (Fig. 117). The lacquer chest is based on an Occidental form—the vargueno—which had been imported to the Orient by traders. It was put on its richly carved stand after coming to Britain.[39]

A young model surrounded by various trappings was photographed by Edmond Goldschmidt as part of his *Série chinoise* of 1895–1890 (Fig. 118). Goldschmidt used Louis Mante's autochrome color process.[40] He combined assorted objects from China and elsewhere into a new artwork with an exotic and bizarre effect. What carries over from the seventeenth century to the nineteenth is the creative process of making something new out of something old. The stimulus to Western art was that of Oriental objects seen out of context.

Because they created something exciting and fresh, Whistler and Jeckyll can be credited with an enduring monument. However, we can naturally expect to find architectural and artistic precedent for the Peacock Room in previous centuries even though Whistler might have preferred us to think otherwise:

> Well, you know, I just painted as I went on, without design or sketch—it grew as I painted. And towards the end I reached such a point of perfection—putting in every touch with such freedom—that when I came round to the corner where I had started, why, I had to paint part of it over again, or the difference would have been too marked. And the harmony in blue and gold developing, you know, I forgot everything in my joy in it.[41]

Notwithstanding Whistler's airy comment, the Peacock Room is related in general to many fanciful architectural schemes of the eighteenth and nineteenth centuries. They include early examples of European chinoiserie like the Chinese House at Sans Souci in Potsdam, and the Chinese Room erected for Sir Thomas Robinson at Claydon House (Fig. 119). The former went up in 1754, the latter in 1769 as the style spread from royalty to landed gentry. Nineteenth-century designers carried on in the vein of picturesque exoticism, notably with Nash's Royal Pavilion at Brighton, begun in 1815. Among the many splendid interiors crowded into this orientalizing confection was the Music Room decorated by Crace and Sons (Fig. 120).[42] The Peacock Room forwards an established architectural tradition of nonrigorous stylistic eclecticism in which the main purpose was to achieve a striking and exotic impact.

The Jeckyll-Whistler collaboration is functionally as well as stylistically tied to tradition. The Peacock Room is a major component in a string of porcelain display rooms that began in the late seventeenth century. Cabinet designs were widely circulated through prints like Daniel Marot's *Chinese Room*, engraved in about 1700 (Fig. 121). *Porzellanzimmer* were immensely popular during the baroque and rococo periods, especially in Germany. It must be remembered that England's artistic ties with Germany were particularly strong in the mid-nineteenth century—that is, during and immediately after the rule of Prince Albert.

One of the earliest porcelain cabinets was built just outside of Berlin for

Figure 119.
Chinese Room, Claydon House, 1769. Reproduced in Hugh Honour, *Chinoiserie* (London, 1961), pl. 87b. Reprinted courtesy of *The Connoisseur*.

Figure 120.
The Music Room, Royal Pavilion, Brighton, decorated by Crace and Sons after 1815. (Photograph courtesy the Royal Pavilion Art Gallery and Museums, Brighton.)

Figure 121.
Daniel Marot, *Design for a Chinese Room*, engraving, ca. 1700. Reproduced in *Transactions of the Oriental Ceramic Society* 25 (1949–1950):pl. 6, btwn. pp. 22 and 23. Reprinted courtesy of the Oriental Ceramic Society.

Figure 122.
J. B. Broeber, engraving after Andreas Schluter's design for *Porzellanzimmer* at Oranienburg (ca. 1688–1695). Reproduced in *Transactions of the Oriental Ceramic Society* 25 (1949–1950):pl. 5, opp. p. 22. Reprinted courtesy of the Oriental Ceramic Society.

Figure 123.
George du Maurier, Aesthetic Movement cartoon. From *Punch* (1880).

Figure 124.
Murray Marks's trade card. Reproduced in George C. Williamson, *Murray Marks and His Friends* (London and New York: Bodley Head, 1919), opp. p. 14.

Friedrich III of Brandenburg. Designed by Andreas Schluter, the *Porzellanzimmer* at Oranienburg was described in 1695 as a room in which every excrescence on the walls supported porcelain (Fig. 122).[43] Little cups were fixed in the fluting of the Corinthian columns, one hundred sixty per flute. Five pyramid-shaped pedestals on the floor supported yet more porcelain. The multitude was multiplied by looking glasses placed behind the pedestals. On the ceilings were painted allegories of Asia presenting porcelain to Europe.

The description of Oranienburg lays out the characteristic elements that were to become standard in porcelain cabinets. These include pots on elaborate shelving, ornately framed paintings, mirrors, built-in furniture, and complicated lighting fixtures. All these elements appeared over one hundred fifty years later in the Peacock Room.

It is not surprising that the Peacock Room would have such a strong generic root. Queen Mary had introduced the porcelain cabinet to England when she came to Hampton Court from Holland in the late seventeenth century. Certainly before Whistler painted the peacocks, the room at Prince's Gate had a decidedly Dutch flavor, imparted by dark leather walls and walnut shelves filled with blue and white pots. As the eighteenth century went on, many great houses had porcelain cabinets of various styles, in which the splendor of architectural decoration vied with, and sometimes even defeated the prized porcelains. The cabinets at Nymphenberg and Schönbrunn are well-known examples.

Merchant princes and prominent establishment artists of the mid-nineteenth century lost no opportunity to align themselves symbolically with powerful families of past centuries. They frequently adopted royal architectural forms and practices. Leyland's intention in fixing up 49 Prince's Gate was clearly stated in an article which described his mansion for the readers of *Harper's New Monthly Magazine* in 1890. It was "the place where [Leyland] realizes his dream of living the life of an old Venetian merchant in modern London."[44]

During the nineteenth century, the Dutch continued to supply English customers with pieces of blue and white china. Both Leyland and Whistler were caught up in the fashion for blue and white during the 1860s and 1870s.[45] As the blue and white craze spread to the middle class, it became the subject of ridicule. A *Punch* cartoon appeared in 1880 entitled *The Six Mark Teapot*, a pun upon the title of one of Whistler's japonesque paintings (Fig. 123):

> Aesthetic Bridegroom: *"It is quite consumate is it not?"*
> Intense Bride: *"It is indeed! Oh, Algernon! Let us live up to it!"*[46]

Despite the cartoon, however, it cannot be gainsaid that major collectors commissioned ornate schemes like the Peacock Room in order to live up to their blue and white china.

The London dealer Murray Marks assembled Leyland's blue and white collection before the Peacock Room was built. Marks's trade card, bearing a Chinese jar with a peacock feather in it, exemplifies the vogue for such decorative arts among London's fashionable set (Fig. 124). According to contemporary reports, Marks "often ran over to Holland where blue-and-white was quite common and still cheap."[47] Not only did Marks gather porcelains for Leyland, he also chose the antique cordova leather hangings for the room. He even may have been the man who brought the architect Jeckyll into the renovation project at Prince's Gate.[48]

Jeckyll mounted the leather on wood panels. Because there was not quite enough leather to cover the high walls of the room, brown canvas was installed

Figure 125.
The *Owl Cabinet*, from
Whistler's rooms.
Reproduced in E. R.
Pennell, *The Whistler
Journal* (Philadelphia,
1921), facing p. 63.
Reprinted courtesy of J. B.
Lippincott Company.

Figure 126.
Porcelain stand,
Oranienburg. Reproduced
in *Transactions of the
Oriental Ceramic Society*
25 (1949–1950):pl. 7-c,
btwn. pp. 22 and 23.
Reprinted courtesy of the
Oriental Ceramic Society.

Figure 127.
Bedford Lamere, Peacock
Room, 1892. (Photograph,
National Monuments
Record, London.)

Figure 128.
Peacock Room in Detroit,
ca. 1909. (Photograph,
Freer Archive.)

in a register that circles the chamber just above the wooden dado. Jeckyll built his intricate shelving system over the panels. He also built the large sideboard at the end of the room. Hundreds of blue and white pots were then installed. With the shelves crowded full of porcelain and set against the dark leather, the room would have looked Dutch—somber and sumptuous, an impression exaggerated by heavy pendant light fixtures designed by the architect and based upon Jacobean or Elizabethan ceiling drops.

A collector himself, Whistler respected the way in which Jeckyll's architectural interior functioned as a porcelain cabinet. Whistler's "Owl Cabinet," a piece of Chinese export furniture which he kept stocked with porcelains in his own apartment, is curiously close in appearance to one of the baroque porcelain stands from Oranienburg (Figs. 125 and 126). But by gilding Jeckyll's shelves and painting out the dark leather in favor of his own lightsome scheme of brilliant birds and plumage, Whistler aligned the room more closely with rococo predecessors whose flavor leaned toward vaporous Oriental exoticism rather than heavier Dutch baroque forms. An artist with a strong sense of history, Whistler was thoroughly acquainted with eighteenth century French art. His pastels on tinted papers demonstrate his knowledge of revived eighteenth century techniques. The lyrical color combinations he favored in many of his oils reflect his love for French artists like Jean-Antoine Watteau and François Boucher. Whistler's treatment of the Peacock Room is another facet of his participation in the rococo revival.

It is well known that Whistler's painting out of the antique leather helped to provoke the famous quarrel which has done so much to conceal the room's history. However, Frederick Leyland was not the only aggrieved party. Murray Marks was also mortally offended, and his lasting rancor has added to the confusion over what actually happened in 1876–1877 at Prince's Gate. The London dealer and decorator was referred to in the press as "a man of exquisite taste." Whistler dared to cross that taste in favor of his own artistic predilections. After Whistler painted the room, it was reported that Marks "was bitterly disappointed, because he considered the background unsuitable for the exhibition of the blue-and-white china or at least less so than had been the simple Cordova leather which *he* had put up."[49] Unfortunately our information about Marks comes from a worshipful biography, frankly subtitled "a tribute of regard." The biographer's statement that Marks and Leyland together "removed a very large portion of the blue porcelain after Whistler had completed his work" is probably not to be trusted.[50]

Marks did continue to advise Leyland on matters of decoration when Richard Norman Shaw was brought in to replace Jeckyll, who died after the Whistler-Leyland quarrel but before the mansion was completely renovated. However, Leyland's porcelain collection was not dispersed until he died in 1892, fifteen years after Whistler painted the Peacock Room.[51] Marks's campaign to discourage the use of porcelain in the room must be countered with several telling items of information. First, the Leyland children had the entire mansion photographed in 1892, shortly after their father's death, in order to preserve their memories before the collections were auctioned.[52] The room was full of blue and white at that time (Fig. 127). Second, the London dealer Obach borrowed another collection of blue and white to fill the shelves when the room was displayed to the public in 1904.[53] Finally, when Freer brought the room to Detroit, he used it to display pottery from the Near and Far East (Fig. 128). The Leyland family, Obach, and Freer all recognized the room's importance as a functional porcelain cabinet over a quarter of a century after the quarrel. In a letter written

Figure 129.
The Colonel Waltz, 1881, lithographed sheet music cover. Collection Victoria and Albert Museum.

Figure 130.
Lewis Day, shelf clock, ca. 1878, walnut case, hand-painted blue and white tile face. Private collection.

Figure 131.
Thomas Jeckyll, "Japanese Pavilion" for Philadelphia Centennial Exhibition, 1876, iron, cast by Barnard, Bishop and Barnards, Norwich. From *British Architect* (November 1878).

Figure 132.
Thomas Jeckyll, bracket panel for "Japanese Pavilion," 1876, pencil and blue wash on paper, 55.8 × 42.4 cm. Spencer Museum of Art, University of Kansas, museum purchase: Letha Churchill Walker Fund.

Figure 133.
Thomas Jeckyll, sunflower andiron, ca. 1876, cast by Barnard, Bishop and Barnards, Norwich. Freer Gallery.

shortly before his death, Freer expressed his intention that the Whistler-Jeckyll collaboration would continue to be used as a *Porzellanzimmer*, describing to Rosalind Birnie Philip "the Peacock Room in which, on the original shelves, beautiful pieces of Oriental or other harmonizing pottery will stand."[54]

Artistic harmony, thoroughly understood and espoused by Freer, was a guiding principle of the Aesthetic Movement. The artist and the architect each contributed one of the two important motifs that link the Peacock Room firmly to that movement. Jeckyll utilized the sunflower, and Whistler added the peacock. A sheet music cover from 1881 indicates that the two motifs were popularly paired (Fig. 129). Each motif had symbolic importance in both the East and the West, and each symbol was featured in Anglo-Dutch as well as Anglo-Japanese decorative arts. The bird and the flower were appropriate symbols for the Aesthetic Movement, which associated itself with both renewal and enlightenment.

The peacock had long been a symbol connected with the sun. From India, where it was used in sun worship, the peacock spread east to China and Japan, and west through Persia and Greece to Europe. When Christianity adopted the peacock, it was as a symbol of resurrection. Moreover, its gorgeous plumage made it a bird suitable for potentates and kings, and eventually for self-made millionaires of Leyland's stamp.[55]

As Oscar Wilde had observed, the sunflower was already stylized by nature. It was perfect for use as a decorative motif, and was common in the Aesthetic homes of the day, both within and without.[56] The sunflower frequently embellished "Pont Street Dutch" or Queen Anne architecture.[57] There were multiple wallpaper versions of the blossom, and it also decorated small objects ranging from timepieces to beer mugs. A shelf clock, designed by Lewis Day in about 1878, combines hand-painted sunflowers on a tile face with incised sunflowers on the case (Fig. 130). The tile is blue and white, reminding us of the "Chinamania" of the period. The busily turned legs recall the intricate spindly shelving supports designed by Jeckyll to hold Leyland's porcelain collection in the Peacock Room.

The sunflower was also used in japonesque designs like a pavilion for the Philadelphia Centennial in 1876 (Fig. 131). Jeckyll was the designer of the sunflower pavilion, and it is probable that Whistler advised him on colors to paint parts of the structure.[58] Jeckyll's drawing for a bracket on the pavilion, when compared to one of his andirons for the Peacock Room, show how easily the stylized blossom could be transferred from one decorative use to the next (Figs. 132 and 133).

Jeckyll's sunflowers remind us that he was among the first to adopt orientalizing designs during the 1860s, once the Japanese became regular exhibitors at the great international fairs. At least two rooms by Jeckyll precede the Peacock Room and experiment with japonesque schemes. These were designed for Alexander Ionides. The rooms were executed by Jeckyll in 1870 and described by Lewis Day twenty years later. A sitting room, fitted up with exotic porcelains, was called "the prototype of that étagère in the famous Peacock Room."[59] Day discussed the room's overmantle as a framework with

> *panels in it consisting of old Japanese lacquer of the carved coral kind, admirably suited for a background to the rare red and white Nankin vases, which form its principle ornament. In the deep green marble of the mantlepiece are embedded a number of blue-and-white Nankin saucers. . . . The main colour of the walls is a low-toned green.*[60]

Figure 134.
Thomas Jeckyll, overmantle incorporating Oriental lacquer and ceramic pieces, Kent Hill, Norfolk. Reproduced in Mark

Girouard, *The Victorian Country House* (New Haven and London, 1979), p. 369. Reprinted courtesy of Country Life Books.

Figure 135.
Thomas Jeckyll, design for billiard room, 1871. From Lewis Day, "A Kensington Interior," *Art Journal* (London) (May 1893):142.

Figure 136.
Sketch for staircase decoration, 49 Prince's Gate, ca. 1876, pencil. Hunterian Art Gallery, University of Glasgow.

Figure 137.
Panel for staircase dado, 1876, oils and gold leaf on wood. Freer Gallery.

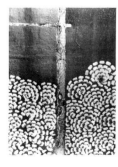

Figure 138.
Peacock Room, detail showing original antique decorated leather under Whistler's layers of paint. (Photograph, Freer Archive.)

A similar mantlepiece is now in a private collection in Britain. It includes a circular mirror in the center, Japanese ceramics at the bottom, and lacquer panels at the top (Fig. 134).[61]

Jeckyll designed for the Ionides family a billiard room framed in oak (Fig. 135). According to Day:

> The oak is relieved throughout by panels of red lacquer. Hundreds of Japanese trays must have been slaughtered to supply them. . . . Immediately under the cornice is again a band of these lacquer panels and another occurs just above the dado. The wall space . . . is divided up by oak framing . . . filled with fine old Japanese prints [and] Japanese paintings on silk . . . the effect is very much as though the frames were window frames, and one were looking out of them.[62]

In Jeckyll's designs, Japanese objects have been taken out of context. The window-wall idea is Western, related to mural painting. Moreover, just as eighteenth-century French cabinetmakers had cut up lacquer wares to make inlaid cabinets and screens, nineteenth-century British designers ignored the integrity of Chinese and Japanese art to rework it into a European format. Such an attitude governed Jeckyll as he designed a carved and ebonized étagère with shelves that evoke the structure of the Peacock Room. An Oriental ceramic panel was incorporated into the back. Its white ground and bright red and green ornamentation contrast sharply with the black wood, reminding us that one of the main features sought by the British designers who gathered Oriental objects was color.[63]

Like Jeckyll, Whistler was among the earliest devotees of Japanese design. And it was *japonisme* that provided Whistler's entrée into the Leyland ménage at Prince's Gate. Whistler's first work there, completed in March 1876, was to decorate a set of staircase dado panels. His designs complimented an old staircase removed from a demolished house and inserted into Leyland's front hall (Fig. 136).[64]

The project allowed Whistler to perfect techniques used some months later in the Peacock Room. At the same time it forced the artist to design around previously existing architectural elements. During the course of the staircase decoration, Whistler exercised his ability to work within complex spatial restrictions, creating sophisticated surface relationships. Whistler chose decorative motifs that were inspired by the arts of both Japan and the West (Fig. 137).

In April 1876, Leyland asked Whistler to help his friend Jeckyll to select colors for the dining room.[65] The antique leather was already decorated with scattered flowers of bright red, yellow, and blue. The cordova leather's original colors are known since the shelving system was built over them, and Whistler did not remove the shelves when he painted the walls a solid turquoise blue (Fig. 138). Embossed patterns which further enriched the leather in its original state are still visible under Whistler's layers of paint (Fig. 139). A large panel of untouched original leather was preserved behind Whistler's painting of the *Princesse* for some time, although it is no longer there (Fig. 140).[66]

Initially Whistler tried to adjust the color effects of the leather, lightening them with touches of primrose yellow and blue. At the same time he would have painted the double dado around the room and possibly the canvas material which had been inserted behind the lowest register of shelves (see Fig. 159). Apparently Whistler complained that the red flowers on the leather, as well as the red border of Leyland's Oriental carpet, clashed with the reds in Whistler's

Figure 139.
Peacock Room, detail showing embossed and painted patterns on original leather. (Photograph, Freer Archive.)

Figure 140.
Peacock Room, north wall, showing original leather in niche ordinarily occupied by *La Princesse du Pays de la Porcelaine*, photograph, ca. 1890. Freer Archive.

Figure 141.
Harmony in Green and Rose: The Music Room, 1860–1861, oil on canvas. Freer Gallery.

Figure 142.
La Princesse du Pays de la Porcelaine, 1863–1864, oil on canvas. Freer Gallery.

Figure 143.
Interior of a room in Whistler's first house in Lindsey Row, Chelsea, 1860s, photograph. Reproduced in Elizabeth Pennell. Reprinted courtesy of J. B. Lippincott Company.

painting, *La Princesse du Pays de la Porcelaine*.[67] In an undated letter written to Leyland sometime that fall, Whistler said:

> *Your walls are finished—They are to receive their last coat of varnish tomorrow—(indeed the men promised to do part this afternoon)— and on Friday you can put up the pots—the blue which I tried as an experiment was quite injurious on the tone of this leather—and so I have carefully erased all trace of it—retouching the small yellow flowers wherever required—leaving the whole work perfect and complete—The wave pattern above and below—on the gold ground—will alone be painted in blue—and this I shall come and do on Friday—without at all interfering with the pots on the leather.*[68]

Whistler was not satisfied with the color harmonies he tried to establish. He complained that the yellow paint and gilding "swore" at the yellow tone of the leather—they were not in harmony.[69]

Eventually Whistler painted the room as we know it today. Even the floor was blue. At some point, the offending rug was removed and replaced with a machine-woven blue or turquoise carpet. The blue carpet is mentioned in a number of the newspaper reviews during the winter of 1877, and Whistler's own broadside mentions the "blue floor."[70] A machine-made rug is visible in some of the nineteenth-century photographs of the room (see Fig. 127).

Whistler's disgust with the incompatible yellows and golds remind us that he surveyed the dining-room space with a painter's eye. The relationship between the architect and the artist was typical for its time, and Whistler's contribution remains that of a painter used to thinking in terms of two-dimensional planes. His concern about the correspondence between the rug and the *Princesse* is essentially a tale of two surfaces—flat planes with color upon them. When Whistler left it, the room was comprised of six carefully balanced and related color planes.

Whistler's interest in decorative surface appears in his earliest paintings, before he became enamoured of Japanese art. *The Music Room*, 1860–1861, is an early work demonstrating the artist's strong emphasis upon pictorial devices that reiterate the surface of the canvas (Fig. 141). Whistler continually restates the picture plane, creating an illogical space through seemingly logical means. Patterns are used to flatten the viewer's sense of deep space. The woman in black forms a strong shape arbitrarily placed at a juncture in the wall. She obscures the angle that would chart the space in a logical sense. Rhythmic triads such as the three women and the three picture frames cut off at the top emphasize the artist's compositional choice making. They tend to bring the background forward, flattening it and reminding us that *The Music Room* is not a glimpse of reality, but a two-dimensional work of art with its own integrity. Whistler was easily able to transfer this formula of decorative patterned surface to japonesque works such as *La Princesse du Pays de la Porcelain* (Fig. 142).

Both the painting and the room that houses it belong to the earliest phase of Whistler's *japonisme*, when eclecticism was the ruling principle. The *Princesse* wears Japanese garments but stands upon a Chinese rug, a testament to the disinterest in historical precision that carried over from the 1700s to the 1860s and 1870s.

Many of the Oriental objects that appear in Whistler's early japonesque paintings also filled his house in Cheney Walk (Fig. 143). It is clear that Whistler derived not only pleasure, but also artistic inspiration from the decorative ob-

Figure 144.
Nampa Jhoshi, *Birds and Blossoms*, 1867, Japan, watercolor on silk; mounted as verso of Whistler's only surviving screen, *Blue and Silver: Screen, with Old Battersea Bridge*; photograph prior to restoration. Hunterian Art Gallery, University of Glasgow.

Figure 145.
Paired peacocks, from George Ashdown Audsley and James Lord Bowes, *The Keramic Art of Japan* (London: H. Sotheran and Company, 1881).

Figure 146.
Peacock Room, south panel, *Fighting Peacocks*.

jects with which he chose to surround himself. Whistler's furnishings were dispersed at a number of sales following his bankruptcy in 1879, hindering connections between specific objects and the artworks they might have influenced. However, the paintings, fans, screens, ceramics, and furniture visible in Whistler's rooms offer a general record of his taste. One Japanese work is dated 1867, indicating that Whistler's collection included modern Oriental objects made for export (Fig. 144).[71]

A number of potential sources for the Peacock Room decorations can be cited, although they by no means exhaust the possibilities. The paired peacocks on the south wall bear some resemblance to an image reproduced in *The Keramic Art of Japan*, a book written by Audsley and Bowes in 1875 (Figs. 145 and 146). The golden shutters bearing languid blue peacocks with impossibly long tails reflect the stylized birds in woodblock prints by Hiroshige and others (Figs. 147 and 148). There is no proof that Whistler owned this particular print, but he would have had ample opportunity to see similar images found anywhere from ceramics to paintings. From any such object he might have learned the graceful Oriental manner of depicting birds (Fig. 149). On the shutters, painted images silhouetted against a gold-leaf ground echo the appearance of Japanese screens from the Momoyama and Edo periods. As far as wall decoration is concerned, peacocks had long been featured in both Chinese hand-painted wallpapers and derivative European copies "in the Chinese taste" during the eighteenth century. Whistler's friend, the architect E. W. Godwin, carried on the motif in his japonesque peacock wallpaper designed in 1873 (Fig. 150). The central point to remember is that while the peacock was prevalent during the 1870s in Britain, Whistler used it to fashion something unique.

Whistler and Jeckyll probably shared some of the same sources. Both the incised shelving by Jeckyll and the carved frame for the *Princesse*, executed to Whistler's design, have drawn upon patterns from Owen Jones's influential *Grammar of Ornament*, published at least seven times and in three languages between 1856 and the year the Peacock Room got under way. Patterns on Jeckyll's shelves are Chinese and Persian (Figs. 151–154). Whistler's frame alter-

Figure 147.
Hiroshige, *Peacock*, nineteenth century, woodblock print. (Photograph, Freer Archive.)

Figure 148.
Peacock Room, central shutter, oils and gold leaf on wood. Freer Gallery.

Figure 149.
Satsuma faïence tray, from Audsley and Bowes, pl. XV.

Figure 150.
E. W. Godwin, "Peacock" wallpaper, 1873, handprinted by Jeffrey & Co. Collection of the Public Records Office, London. Reproduced in Aslin, pl. 73. Reprinted courtesy of Bookthrift of Simon and Schuster, Inc.

Figure 151.
Thomas Jeckyll, detail of incised shelving, Peacock Room.

Figure 152.
Owen Jones, "Chinese No. 2," Plate XL, fig. 16, in Jones, *The Grammar of Ornament* (London, 1856). Private collection.

Figure 153.
Thomas Jeckyll, detail of incised shelving, Peacock Room.

Figure 154.
Owen Jones, "Nineveah & Persia No. 2," Plate XIII, fig. 23, *The Grammar of Ornament*.

Figure 155.
Whistler-designed frame for *La Princesse du Pays de la Porcelain*, detail.

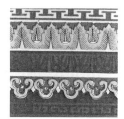

Figure 156.
Owen Jones, "Chinese No. 2," Plate XL, fig. 10, *The Grammar of Ornament.*

Figure 157.
Owen Jones, "Egyptian No. 7," Plate X, fig. 20, *The Grammar of Ornament.*

Figure 158.
Owen Jones, "Chinese No. 1," Plate LIX, fig. 7, *The Grammar of Ornament.*

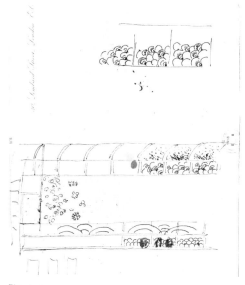

Figure 159.
Peacock Room, drawing for decorations before the Spanish leather was painted out, ink. British Museum.

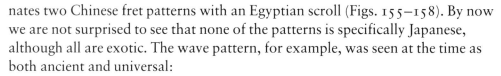

nates two Chinese fret patterns with an Egyptian scroll (Figs. 155–158). By now we are not surprised to see that none of the patterns is specifically Japanese, although all are exotic. The wave pattern, for example, was seen at the time as both ancient and universal:

> *That alternation of semicircles . . . may be equally well described as the scale pattern or the feather pattern, but [it] also might just as well have been evolved from a wave or a flower. Features like this belong to no particular country, no particular style.*[72]

Whistler said that the patterns he added to the room were based upon the peacock feather. However, he clearly drew upon the ancient wave patterns in the *Grammar of Ornament*, several of which are even reproduced in the blue and turquoise color combination that dominates the Peacock Room. Whistler had also seen the fish-scale motifs in *The Keramic Art of Japan* (Figs. 159–161). More importantly, Whistler was inspired by patterns that Jeckyll had already used in the Peacock Room. The pattern in Jeckyll's leaded glass door reappeared on some of Whistler's dado panels (Figs. 162 and 163).

As has been noted above, the relationship between Whistler and Jeckyll was not fundamentally different from other such artist-architect combinations during the late nineteenth century. Ordinarily the architect created a three-dimensional form upon which the artist painted. The *Saint George Cabinet* was designed by Philip Webb and painted by William Morris in 1862 (Fig. 164). Similarly, the architect Godwin designed the *Butterfly Cabinet*, which Whistler then painted the year after the Peacock Room was completed (Fig. 165).

A careful scrutiny of the *Butterfly Cabinet* is helpful for understanding Whistler's priorities and purposes in his decoration of the Peacock Room. Whistler depended upon the reflective qualities of shiny gilding to break up and lighten the cabinet's otherwise ponderous form, which was originally designed as a fireplace surround, part of William Watt's furniture display stand for the Exposition Universelle in Paris in 1878. Whistler gilded and then painted the back of the cabinet on the central section which divides the upper and lower segments (Fig. 166). He also gilded the interior of the glassed-in portion at the top. These were the areas that would have been in deepest shadow, and Whistler considerably increased the amount of light in each space. The two panels at the bottom, with their patterns reminiscent of the Peacock Room, were originally used as dado panels that flanked the cabinet, helping to balance Godwin's

Figure 160.
Owen Jones, "Chinese No. 1," Plate LIX, fig. 26, *The Grammar of Ornament.*

Figure 161.
Fish-scale patterns, from Audsley and Bowes, pl. IV, figs. 4 and 5.

Figure 162.
Thomas Jeckyll, detail of leaded glass door, Peacock Room, west wall.

Figure 163.
Peacock Room, west wall, detail, oils and metallic paint.

Figure 166.
Butterfly Cabinet, detail.
(Photograph, Pennell
collection. Courtesy of the
Library of Congress.)

Figure 165.
E. W. Godwin and J. McN.
Whistler, *Butterfly Cabinet*,
1878. Hunterian Art
Gallery, University of
Glasgow.

Figure 164.
Philip Webb and William
Morris, *Saint George
Cabinet*, 1862. Victoria and
Albert Museum.

Figure 167.
Kaga bowl, from Audsley
and Bowes, pl. XXI.

Figure 168.
Design for the coloring of a
room, 1870s–1880s, pencil
and watercolor. Freer
Gallery.

unmodulated yellow tiles at the bottom of the piece. Elsewhere on the mahogany surface, Whistler sprinkled little touches of gold paint that add sparkle to the rich, somber surfaces of the mahogany. Whistler's decoration helped move the eye across the piece horizontally, countering the decided upward thrust of the strongly tectonic form with its vertical elements and towering broken pediment.

The *Butterfly Cabinet* was described in 1878 as "A Harmony in Yellow and Gold [made] of light yellow mahogany . . . with gilt bars below the shelf and cornice, inclosing tiles of pale sulpher . . . [it holds] bits of Kaga porcelain, chosen for the yellowishness of the red which is a characteristic of that ware."[73] This is a highly aesthetic program of delicate color harmonies.

The Kaga ware bowl illustrated here was prized for "the deep red only met with in the finest quality of Kaga ware . . . richly wrought with gold" (Fig. 167).[74] What interested the writer was the bowl's color. Whistler also chose Kaga pieces for the color, finding it harmonious with the wood and paint of the *Butterfly Cabinet*. This is an important clue for our understanding of the Peacock Room not only as a porcelain chamber, but also as six carefully related color planes where the blue and white pottery functioned in harmony with Whistler's chosen palette. As usual, Whistler had historical precedent behind him, this time in the baroque *Porzellanzimmer* at Dresden, where the Emperor Augustus planned to house his collection of over twenty thousand porcelains in sumptuous rooms, each devoted to pieces of a single color.

Whistler was indeed a consumate colorist, and he made few distinctions between the conception of a wall plane and the flat surface of a painting. While no other Whistler interiors survive, we do know that in simpler schemes he actually prepared his walls as he would a canvas, in colored layers. Whistler's biographers described his use of delicate flushes of color as similar to eighteenth-century distemper. His walls were conceived like paintings, even when no figurative pattern appeared:

> In the houses he decorated for his friends he was as restrained as in his own and as careful to mix his colors, ever distrustful of the British workman. "Why on earth should the workmen think for themselves?" he once asked. . . . With two coats of yellow on white they [had] made the walls crude and glaring though he had ordered one coat of yellow on grey, knowing that the result . . . "would have been . . . soft and sweet."[75]

His method can still be seen in surviving projects, like this watercolor scheme for an unidentified room (Fig. 168). Whistler's wall treatments also can be seen in the backgrounds of some of his portraits.

Figure 169.
Peacock Room, northwest corner, nineteenth-century photograph. Freer Archive.

Figure 170.
Peacock Room, south wall.

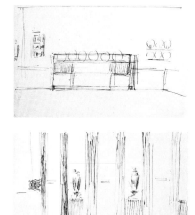

Figure 171.
Drawings for installations of porcelain, 1870s, ink. Trustees of the British Museum.

Like his simple distempered walls, Whistler conceived the Peacock Room as a series of colored layers, analogous to layers on a canvas. And like the yellow and gray interior described by the Pennells, Whistler allowed one color to break through another in the Peacock Room. As he had done consistently in paintings since *The Music Room*, Whistler tried to keep the viewer's eye upon the surface of the walls.

In the manner of the *Butterfly Cabinet*, Whistler capitalized upon the reflective surfaces of Dutch Metal and gilt paint to lighten the dark, potentially gloomy dining room at Prince's Gate. At the same time, Whistler's endless gold peacock feathers engulf the surfaces of the room. The very thickness of the paint picked up the light as would a faceted jewel, enriching the room's surfaces at the same time that their sheer multiplicity overwhelmed the viewer with a sense of repeated pattern that tends to flatten all surface planes.

Gilding Jeckyll's dark walnut shelving, Whistler brought out the incised linear patterns—he exaggerated the contrasted light between flat and cut surface. Before they were gilt, the many carved patterns were almost invisible, as Whistler later pointed out to the architect's brother.[76] Caught in the glare of a nineteenth-century photographer's flash, Jeckyll's many carved patterns appear with a vibrance that reveals the wisdom of Whistler's decision (Fig. 169).

By painting Jeckyll's sideboard in the same patterns that he used on the dado, Whistler foreshortened it—he pulled the ill-proportioned form back against the wall (Fig. 170). At the other end of the room, Whistler gilded Jeckyll's black cast-iron sunflower andirons. Once they reflected the light instead of absorbing it, the sunflowers became two strong golden discs that carried the eye over the cavernous inky space of the fireplace. The viewer's eye stays on the surface, skipping from the gold decorations on the dado straight across the faces of the two andirons and back to the dado in a continuous horizontal line that helped to form a visual support for the large, heavily framed oil painting hanging above the mantle. All of Whistler's gilding reveals the decision-making process of a painter dealing in flat surfaces.

The walls of the Peacock Room are seductive layers of color. The deepest layers are the opaque blue-green paint that covers the leather and parts of the dado, and the metal leaf that covers wooden doors and shutters, and some dado panels. Daubs of gold paint float above the blue-green. Blue and green glazes cloud the metal leaf, and opaque blue and green strokes float above the glazes. The golden shelves crisscross the blue and green with strong vertical and horizontal strokes. Whistler depended on the blue and white porcelain to create a lively layer of color and movement, interwoven with the glittering grid of the shelving. As gaslight flickered across their rounded surfaces, the pots would have formed a shimmering glaze of broken blue and white tones, glossy enough to balance the bright gold along the dado. The repetitious pots would have moved the eye across the wall surface just as sparkling daubs of gold skip over the surface of the dado panels. Only by standing in the room can the strength and beauty of Whistler's design be completely understood. If ever a work of art defied the photographer's ability to convey its aesthetic impact, it must be the Peacock Room.

As both a collector and an artist, Whistler would have been sensitive to the somewhat flattened graphic shapes created by the porcelains, especially by large-scale pieces whose figure decoration could be read at quite a distance in the dim light. Several drawings associated with projects for W. C. Alexander depict pottery arranged by Whistler as groups of regular related shapes (Fig. 171).

Similarly, Whistler used circles in the form of additional moldings to reg-

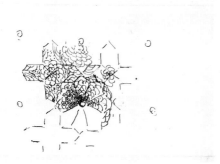

Figure 172.
Drawings for Peacock
Room ceiling and dado
panels, 1876, ink. Trustees
of the British Museum.

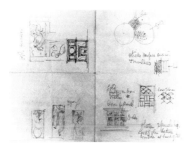

Figure 173.
E. W. Godwin, sketches of
Peacock Room details,
February 1877, ink on
leaflet. Hunterian Art
Gallery, University of
Glasgow Library, Birnie
Philip Bequest.

Figure 174.
Bedford Lamere, *The
Peacock Room*, 1892,
photograph. Royal
Commission on Historical
Monuments (England),
National Monuments
Record, London.

ularize the star shapes created by the woodwork for Jeckyll's pendant lights. He further flattened the ceiling by using contrasting shades of blue. These design decisions were recorded by E. W. Godwin when he visited the room before writing his article for the *Architect* in 1877. Godwin made sketches of Whistler's room on a copy of the Peacock Room broadside of 1877 (Figs. 172 and 173). In his article, Godwin affirms Whistler's desire to smooth out the ceiling surface:

> *We find the fussy ceiling broadened by enclosing the stars in circles, within which the feather or scale pattern . . . is ranged in irregular or broken rings, the spandrils or spaces between the meeting points of our circles being filled with a feather pattern much darker in effect.*[77]

The ceiling bore several of the same motifs that decorated the dado, tying the ceiling and wall surfaces together. Mirrors and gilt shelving were complimented by a blue table-cover set with a gilt table service.[78] Even the floor covering in this room was blue. The Peacock Room is surely one of the earliest modern *Gesamt-kunstwerke* that were to dominate the decorative arts of the early twentieth century.

Yet the magnificence of this interior space is firmly based upon tradition. Over all, a richly garbed Princess and her majestic peacocks preside in a splendor not far removed from the most elaborate royal porcelain cabinets of Germany and France (Fig. 174).

In 1867 P. G. Hamerton made the mistake of criticizing Whistler's *Symphony in White No. 3*. Hamerton complained that the painting was

> *not precisely a symphony in white. One lady has a yellowish dress and brown hair and a bit of blue ribbon, the other has a red fan. . . . There is a girl in white on a white sofa, but even this girl has reddish hair, and of course there is the flesh colour of the complexions.*[79]

Whistler's response was acid. "Bon Dieu! did this wise person expect white hair and chalked faces? And does he then, in his astounding consequence, believe that a symphony in F contains no other note, but shall be a continued repetition of F.F.F.—Fool!"[80]

The color notes of the Peacock Room—or the *Harmony in Blue and Gold*—range from deep blues through pungent greens to bright yellow-gold and pure white. This was not a one-note composition. Neither was it a one-man band. We cannot forget the supporting member of the duet: Thomas Jeckyll. Our evaluation of the room must be guided by the perception that it is a traditional collaboration between artist and architect. Together Whistler and Jeckyll scaled preciously refined heights to create a splendid statement of the Aesthetic Movement grounded upon the bedrock of architectural precedent.

*Nocturne in Black and
Gold: The Falling Rocket*,
1874, oil on canvas,
53.5 × 75.5 cm. Institute
of Art, Detroit, Michigan.

Artist and Site

As music is the poetry of sound, so is painting the poetry of sight, and the subject-matter has nothing to do with harmony of sound or of color
JAMES MCNEILL WHISTLER

Who now remembers gay Cremorne?
THOMAS HARDY

THE LITERATURE OF ART HISTORY IS ENRICHED with artists' statements which frequently serve as the building blocks for later critical theories and interpretations. And perhaps it is in the nature of the artist as stylist to create—with or without intention—verbal reflections of his own art objects when he attempts to discuss them through the spoken or written word.[1] The Goncourt brothers, in their acute commentary on the artistic community in Paris during the 1860s and 1870s, were fascinated by the conversation of Constantin Guys, singled out by Baudelaire as "the painter of modern life." According to the Goncourts, Guys was "always holding you under the thrall of his highly-coloured, almost visible utterance."[2] Similarly, Whistler's writing, like his painting, demonstrates self-conscious facture, or art making. His remarks upon art theory have a vivid, imagistic quality that could be labeled "decorative." On occasion, he captured with his pen the verbal equivalent of his painting style, which is marked by the primacy of sensitive color:

> *In the citron wing of the pale butterfly, with its dainty spots of orange, he sees before him the stately halls of fair gold, with their slender saffron pillars, and is taught how the delicate drawing high upon the walls shall be traced in tender tones of orpiment, and repeated by the base in notes of graver hue.*[3]

Whistler studded his prose with colorful metaphors and sprinkled witticisms and clever puns on the page, just as he touched little bits of color to pastel drawings that were mostly black and white. When an artist manages to replicate his visual work through his verbal statements, he takes the risk that his words will be no better understood than his pictures.

An accomplished literary stylist, Whistler had little sympathy for the difficulties experienced by critics who struggled to communicate visual information—paintings—through a verbal medium—the written word.[4] In print as well as in paint, he attacked the received opinion of the day, which held that art's highest achievement was to convey some sort of story, the nobler the better. Whistler's infrequent, sometimes intemperate remarks on art theory were part of his endless battle against a long-established literary approach to painting. Whistler sharply denounced the art critic as a "middleman" largely responsible for public misconception of the purpose of art:

For him a picture is more or less a hieroglyph or symbol of a story. Apart from a few technical terms, for the display of which he finds an occasion, the work is considered absolutely from a literary point of view; indeed, from what other can he consider it? And in his essays he deals with it as with a novel—a history—or an anecdote. He fails entirely and most naturally to see its excellences, or de-merits—artistic—and so degrades Art, by supposing it a method of bringing about a literary climax. . . . He finds poetry where he would feel it were he himself transcribing the event, invention in the intricacy of the mise en scène, *and noble philosophy in some detail of philanthropy, courage, modesty, or virtue, suggested to him by the occurrence. . . . Meanwhile the* painter's *poetry is quite lost to him—the amazing invention that shall have put form and color into such perfect harmony, that exquisiteness is the result.*

Whistler was indignant that any work of art could be thus co-opted by a critic: "As he goes on with his translation from canvas to paper, the work becomes his own."[5]

Proud of his own individuality and creativity, Whistler viewed subject matter, or "Nature" as it was called in the common parlance, as nothing more than the springboard from which the artist made his inspired leap into the realm of art. By focusing upon phenomenon rather than treatment, critics were apt to lose or ignore the artist's contribution, for Nature alone was not art: "To say to the painter, that Nature is to be taken as she is, is to say to the player, that he may sit on the piano." But the artist could read Nature's secrets and translate them into art:

He looks at her flower, not with the enlarging lens, that he may gather facts for the botanist, but with the light of the one who sees in her choice selection of brilliant tones and delicate tints, suggestions of future harmonies . . . in the long curve of the narrow leaf, corrected by the straight tall stem, he learns how grace is wedded to dignity, how strength enhances sweetness, that elegance shall be the result. . . . In all that is dainty and lovable he finds hints for his own combinations, and thus is Nature ever his resource and always at his service.[6]

The historian of Oriental art, Ernest Fenollosa, correctly grasped the synthesizing character of Whistler's creative process. "It was to explore this rich world of combinations in their own right, that . . . became for Whistler the steady aim of his life."[7] Like Baudelaire, Whistler rejected realism as a negation of the imagination which was able to "see all in one synoptic glance."[8]

For Whistler, then, the creative act held precedence over the artist's chosen subject matter. "Take the picture of my mother, exhibited at the Royal Academy as an *Arrangement in Grey and Black,*" he wrote. "Now that is what it is. To me it is interesting as a picture of my mother; but what can or ought the public to care about the identity of the portrait?" (Fig. 175). Algernon Swinburne immediately criticized Whistler's comment, claiming that the inconsistency of the polemic invalidated it. Swinburne avowed that the painter had denied subject matter, yet could not escape it. He detected in the *Arrangement in Grey and Black* "an expression of living character, an intensity of pathetic power, which gives to that noble work something of the impressiveness proper to a tragic or elegiac poem."[9] Once again we find the analogy between painting and writing employed by a critic in an effort to make himself comprehensible to the reader,

Figure 175.
Arrangement in Grey and Black: Portrait of the Painter's Mother, 1871, oil on canvas. Musées Nationaux de France, Louvre (Musée d'Orsay). (Photograph: Musées Nationaux de France.)

72

who was used to receiving information through print rather than visual image. We may also add that Swinburne's reaction to the portrait was almost as personal as Whistler's. The poet had been very close to Mrs. Whistler during the years she resided with her son in Chelsea.[10]

Whistler replied caustically in "Et Tu, Brute!" and the issue of facture versus content in Whistler's work was polarized.[11] Today, it is probable that the majority of the public would recognize *Whistler's Mother* as an important painting. Yet most people would find it hard to describe the gray and black harmony upon which the portrait is based. Ironically, while this particular painting is famous solely for its subject, Whistler's art in general has long been dismissed as "decorative" and therefore frivolous, largely because of his insistence upon his aesthetic decisions. Whistler's flamboyant personality, not his subtle works of art, made him a household name.

What we have here is a case not of "either-or" but of "both-and," if I may apply a concept from architectural criticism to a problem in painting.[12] What Robert Venturi terms "orthodox modern" architects scorned decoration, and the impact of their opprobrium was felt not only in painting circles but also in the history of art. The tradition of "either-or" has certainly clouded art-historical judgment to an extent. Perhaps the key word in Venturi's phrase is "orthodox." Whistler was hardly that, yet nowhere does he actually deny the presence of subject matter. Whistler is a practitioner of "both-and."

A careful reading of Whistler's theory indicates that the artist acknowledged the existence of the subject, though he did not elevate it. "The picture should have *its own* merit, and not depend upon dramatic, or legendary, or local interest," he argued.[13] Fenollosa's assessment of Whistler's art, already quoted in an earlier essay, bears repeating: "Subject, indeed, is not . . . lost; but rather absorbed by, or translated into the beauty of form—quite as the thought of a lyric poem becomes transfigured in its graceful garb of words."[14] The metaphor is literary, as we might expect. Baudelaire noted, "The best account of a picture may well be a sonnet or an elegy."[15]

In recent years we have come to appreciate that French avant-garde artists of the 1860s and 1870s sought contemporary themes that would capture the spirit of their own era. Their revolutionary stylistic innovations in no way obviate this deliberate focus upon such major issues as urban change—change that brought problems, but also new leisure time for the bourgeoisie—change that built the race track, dance hall, and city park. In response to these developments Baudelaire published "The Painter of Modern Life" in the magazine *Figaro* in 1863. By modernity, Baudelaire meant "the ephemeral, the fugitive, the contingent, the half of art whose other half is the eternal and the immutable."[16] The painter of modern life "makes it his business to extract from fashion whatever element it may contain of poetry within history, to distill the eternal from the transitory," because, according to Baudelaire, beauty fused the two. Beauty resulted from the "changing modes of feeling characteristic of different ages." Baudelaire told his readers that "every age had its own gait, glance and gesture."[17]

The expatriate Whistler, shuttling back and forth from Paris to London, was part of the circle of French painters who answered Baudelaire's call. Whistler's concerns are to a large extent those of Manet, Monet, Degas, and other artists who were once narrowly perceived in the "either-or" terms of formalism as painters bent upon capturing their impressions of light and air.

While he maintained his ties with France, the peripatetic American painter moved to the first of several Chelsea residences in 1862, after numerous visits to that section of London. Filled with dramatic, legendary, and local interest,

Figure 176.
Thomas Rowlandson,
Cheyne Walk, Chelsea, ca.
1810–1815, pen, inks, and
watercolor over pencil.
Museum of London.

Figure 177.
Cheyne Walk, ca. 1850,
photograph. Courtesy of
the Royal Borough of
Kensington and Chelsea
Libraries and Art Service.

Figure 178.
James Hedderly, *Chelsea
Embankment under
Construction*, mid-1870s,
photograph. Royal
Borough of Kensington and
Chelsea Libraries and Art
Service.

Figure 179.
Trees of Cremorne Gardens
and landing pier, taken
from tower of Old Church
Chelsea, ca. 1860–1870,
postcard. Royal Borough of
Kensington and Chelsea
Libraries and Art Service.

Chelsea offered London's closest equivalent to *la vie de bohème* of the Latin Quarter in Paris. For over a century Chelsea had been a riverside enclave of artists and writers. It boasted such famous residents as Thomas Carlyle, who had been in the quarter since 1834. By the time Whistler arrived, Carlyle was a living legend, receiving such distinguished visitors as John Stuart Mill, Alfred Lord Tennyson, Charles Darwin, John Ruskin, and Charles Dickens. Whistler's portrait of Carlyle recalls the appeal of history painting, however unorthodox the results.

Although he was as reclusive as Carlyle was receptive, J. M. W. Turner, in whose work Whistler had more than a passing interest, had also spent some years as a resident of Chelsea. Once Dante Gabriel Rossetti moved to Cheyne Walk in 1863, other Pre-Raphaelite artists, including William Morris, Edward Burne-Jones, and John Everett Millais, began to frequent the neighborhood. Whistler became Rossetti's neighbor in March of 1863, taking an apartment at No. 7 Lindsey Row. Thereafter the poet Algernon Swinburne divided his time between the houses of Rossetti and Whistler. Eventually Oscar Wilde, the aesthete indebted to Whistler, took up residence in Chelsea too.[18]

Whistler's decisions to paint sites in Chelsea parallel the choices of his associates in Paris. Physically, Chelsea had changed little since the preceding century (Figs. 176 and 177). But during the late 1870s, it would be substantially altered by the building of embankments along the Thames River (Fig. 178). The embankments held railroad tracks and sewer systems, hallmarks of urban change that suggest a parallel between Whistler's riverfront neighborhood and Paris as the Impressionists knew it during the Haussmann reconstructions.[19]

Before it disappeared in 1877 under a grid of narrow, new little streets, Chelsea's Cremorne was the last of the London pleasure gardens, resorts on the city's outskirts to which Londoners rushed to "get away from bricks and mortar," according to a visitor of 1856.[20] Pressure for additional housing space played a major role in the destruction of Cremorne Gardens: "The most heinous offence of Cremorne has really been that it is a large open space in the midst of a neighborhood long since built over or laid out in eligible building lots."[21] One is reminded of some of Haussmann's motives for clearing certain sections of Paris.

There is a strong element of historicism and nostalgia in both the garden itself and Whistler's images of it. The paintings recall the work of Watteau and Gavarni as much as that of French modernists. Unlike the railroad bridge at Argenteuil or the Gare St. Lazare, painted by Monet and Manet respectively, Cremorne Gardens was a victim as well as a product of urban renewal. Painted during the last embattled years of the garden's existence, Whistler's Cremorne works were modern history paintings that captured the spirit of pleasure grounds now lost to us and in the process of being taken from Whistler and his contemporaries.

At the same time, however, the works are important aesthetic statements that stretched the definition of permissible abstraction—modern art as it were—a topic that will be discussed at length below. And the ebb and flow of urban crowds at leisure made the gardens a modern subject. Steeped in fashion, public entertainment, and the demimonde, Whistler's Cremorne series argues for the American-born painter as a principal respondent to Baudelaire's challenge for a painter of modern life.

Only an artist could transform such a prosaic quarter into art. A photograph, probably taken from the tower of Old Chelsea Church, offers a glimpse of the Old Battersea Bridge and the trees of Cremorne Gardens that stretched to the river's edge, beyond the crowded, angular homes and businesses of the quarter (Fig. 179). In *The Ten o'Clock Lecture*, Whistler told a rapt audience:

Figure 180.
Nocturne: Blue and Silver—Cremorne Lights, 1872, oil on canvas. Tate Gallery, London.

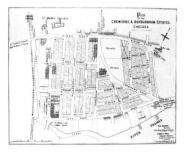

Figure 181.
Plan of the Cremorne and Ashburnam Estates, Chelsea, ca. 1878. Royal Borough of Kensington and Chelsea Libraries and Art Service.

Figure 182.
Plan of Cremorne Gardens, ca. 1870. Royal Borough of Kensington and Chelsea Libraries and Art Service.

Figure 183.
Shield for the Stadium athletic club, 1830s, lithograph. Royal Borough of Kensington and Chelsea Libraries and Art Service.

Figure 184.
Mr. Hampton's Ascent from Cremorne House, Chelsea, Thursday, June 13, 1839, ca. 1839, wood engraving. Royal Borough of Kensington and Chelsea Libraries and Art Service.

> When the evening mist clothes the riverside with poetry, as with a veil, and the poor buildings lose themselves in the dim sky, and the tall chimneys become campanili, and the warehouses are palaces in the night, and the whole city hangs in the heavens, and fairy-land is before us. . . . Nature . . . sings her exquisite song to the artist alone.[22]

The poetic cadence of Whistler's speech parallels the lyric abstraction of paintings like *Nocturne: Blue and Silver—Cremorne Lights* (Fig. 180). It depicts almost the same view as the photograph, but most of the detail is gone, replaced by evocative suggestion. Winking through veils of mist, the lights of Cremorne Gardens drew Whistler into a fairyland. Although Cremorne Gardens was only a tinseled amusement park, Whistler's brush transformed the site into lasting works of art.

The Cremorne series includes seven oil paintings, created from about 1872 to 1877. A number of watercolors and drawings also relate to the group.[23] Prominent among the Cremorne paintings is *Nocturne in Black and Gold: The Falling Rocket* (see Fig. 223), the canvas that provoked John Ruskin's ill-advised insult:

> [The] eccentricities [of the modern schools] are almost always in some degree forced; and their imperfections gratuitously, if not impertinently, indulged. For Mr. Whistler's own sake, no less than for the protection of the purchaser, Sir Coutts Lindsey ought not to have admitted works into the gallery in which the ill-educated conceit of the artist so nearly approached the aspect of willful imposture. I have seen, and heard, much of cockney impudence before now; but never expected to hear a coxcomb ask two hundred guineas for flinging a pot of paint in the public's face.[24]

Whistler's retaliatory libel suit is famous; he later referred to it as a case "between the brush and the pen."[25] His comment underscores the disparity, now familiar to the reader, between printed word and painted image. In the uproar generated by the suit, the concept of abstract painting was the real defendant, and the supposed gap between facture and subject was further widened. Only one farthing in damages was awarded to Whistler, and abstraction lost the case, at least for the time being. Ironically, the Whistler-Ruskin trial coincided with the closing of Cremorne Gardens in 1877, following a similar libel suit in which the proprietor of the grounds was awarded one farthing in damages and then decided not to renew his license. The land was quickly sold off as lots and covered with small houses for mechanics (Figs. 181 and 182). Other constructions—of history and criticism—were to obscure the rich vein of social behavior that Whistler once mined to fuel his Cremorne series with the sooty energy of a theme from modern life.

Situated at the west end of Chelsea between the Thames River and King's Road, Cremorne had been a private estate until it was bought by Charles de Berenger, a nobleman of French and Prussian descent.[26] De Berenger opened a sporting club on the grounds in 1830. He named it the Stadium, and offered activities for "cultivation of various skillful and manly exercises." These included sailing, swimming, fishing, shooting, gymnastics, football, cricket, wrestling, military drill, horsemanship, and skating—in other words, the daring athletic pastimes of the dandy (Fig. 183). Festivals and galas for competitive sports were held, setting the tone for the entertainments that would characterize the gardens in Whistler's day.[27] De Berenger was an experienced pyrotechnist, and in 1836 he sponsored lavish fireworks displayed by Duffel and Derby, famous pyrotechnic

Figure 185.
J. Shury, *Interior of the Banqueting Hall, Cremorne Gardens*, engraving. Reproduced in *Views of Some of the Most Celebrated By-gone Pleasure Gardens of London* (London: H. A. Rogers, 1896).

Figure 186.
Cremorne Gardens: The Crystal Platform. From the *Illustrated London News* (30 May 1857), p. 515.

Figure 187.
Nocturne in Black and Gold: The Gardens, 1872–1877. Metropolitan Museum of Art, gift of Harris C. Fahnestock, 1906.

Figure 188.
Dancing Platform at Cremorne Gardens, daylight view, ca. 1860, wood engraving. Royal Borough of Kensington and Chelsea Libraries and Art Service.

artists of the period. Thus, one of the major themes of Whistler's Cremorne series—fireworks—was an established feature of the park from the beginning. In 1837 de Berenger obtained a license for music and dancing, another activity later depicted in Whistler's paintings. Also in that year the first of many balloon ascents from the park was made by Charles Green in his "Great Nassau Balloon." Balloon ascents were to be another perennial park event (Fig. 184), but one not treated by Whistler, possibly because the majority took place during daylight hours, and the Cremorne paintings are exclusively nocturnal. An American bowling saloon, a "chrystal grotto," a circus, a maze, a theater, marionettes, some gypsy tents, and, significantly for Whistler's interests, a Chinese orchestra, had all been added by 1839. In essence, the spot had by then become the amusement park that Whistler was to frequent more than thirty years later.

De Berenger died in 1845 and the grounds opened to the public under new management as Cremorne Gardens. By 1846 there was a banqueting hall that seated one thousand, and a theater at the south end of the park overlooking the river (Fig. 185).[28] Within the grounds, attractions continued to be added. As the park opened in May 1847, a newspaper article took notice of "another remarkable feature"—the Grand Pagoda Orchestra or Chinese Platform:

> It is ornamented in the most profuse and gorgeous manner, and is surrounded by a vast circular platform, intended to be used as [an] al fresco Salle de Dance, and is capable, it is said, of affording full space for the mazy movements of 4000 dancers at the same time.[29]

Ten years later, a reporter for the *Illustrated London News* admired the Chinese Platform's "inclosing ironwork . . . enriched, by Defries and Son, with devices in emerald and garnet cut-glass drops, and semicircles of lustres and gas jets, which have a most brilliant effect." (Fig. 186)[30] Further particulars of this splendid and glittering edifice can be gained from the auction catalogue compiled when Cremorne Gardens was sold in 1877. The pavilion was about three hundred sixty feet in circumference. It was encrusted with ornamental iron pillars, gas jets, and over forty plate-glass mirrors in black frames. In the upper portion of the pagoda, where the orchestra played, there were seventeen gaslit chandeliers.[31] Details of the platform are readily apparent in works by Walter Greaves, Whistler's pupil (see Fig. 219). Whistler himself depicted the platform filled with dancers in *Nocturne in Black and Gold: The Gardens* (Fig. 187). The painting was originally entitled by Whistler *Nocturne—(Cremorne) Dancing*.[32] But instead of emphasizing the decorative details of the platform, Whistler suggested its presence by bright light which falls from the "inclosing ironwork" and highlights the dresses of the madly whirling dancers. The unarticulated anonymity of the figures conveys the "mazy movements of 4000 dancers" more abstractly than an earlier, more detailed daytime rendering of the crowd from a newspaper illustration (Fig. 188). Lights from the Chinese platform can also be discerned at the left side of Whistler's *Nocturne in Black and Gold: The Falling Rocket*.

By 1857, the grounds had increased from twelve to sixteen acres.[33] In addition to the glittering dancing platform, the garden's "embellishments" by then included "a large picture of Berne, with a model Swiss cottage; a covered circus for horsemanship, two theatres; and a large number of casts from celebrated statues and vases of the classic ages."[34] A poster from the 1850s shows some of the attractions, including a "castellated firework building" which will be discussed later (Fig. 189).

The succession of managers and owners of the gardens after de Berenger's death had strong links with London's restaurant and theater worlds. Not surprisingly, Cremorne became noted for excellent suppers and grew more and

Figure 189.
Cremorne poster, 1850s,
lithograph. Royal Borough
of Kensington and Chelsea
Libraries and Art Service.

Figure 190.
Thames River near
Cremorne Gardens, before
1873, photograph. Royal
Borough of Kensington and
Chelsea Libraries and Art
Service.

Figure 191.
Walter Greaves, *Chelsea
River-Front Scene*, ca. 1860.
Reproduced in Reginal
Blont, *By Chelsea Reach:
Some Riverside Records*
(London, 1921). Reprinted
courtesy of Mills and Boon, Ltd.

Figure 192.
Walter Greaves,
*Hammersmith Bridge on
Boat-Race Day*, 1911, oil on
canvas. Tate Gallery,
London. Reproduced in
Pocock, frontispiece.

more theatrically oriented.[35] The grounds were managed from 1870 until their closing by impresario John Baum, who gave particular emphasis to musical and theatrical attractions. Baum built yet another theater on the grounds, and during the years that Whistler frequented Cremorne Gardens, he could have seen the Ballet Gische, or a production of Offenbach's *Rose of Auvergne*, or the Viennese Ladies Orchestra, or any one of a number of *tableaux vivants*.

Here is a typical round of entertainments presented in the gardens during the 1870s:

2:00 p.m.	Selections by the brass band
4:30	Acrobatic performance by the Boisset family
5:00 f.f.	In the small theatre, the Kostroma people
6:00	Instrumental concert
7:00	Theatre Royale. Hungarian Dancers
7:20	Serio-comic singer, dancer: Miss Fanny Leslie
7:30	Prof. Reinhard: ventroloquist, mime
8:00	Boisset family, part II
8:30	Vocal and instrumental concert
9:00	Operetta: in Marionette Theatre
10:00	Comic Ballet. Theatre Royale
10:30	Grand display of fireworks by Wells
10:45	Boisset Family in Ball Room
11:00	Concert till close [36]

Earlier pleasure gardens, including Vauxhall and Ranelagh, had been frequented by the upper classes, but no London resort was the exclusive preserve of the nobility. By the time Cremorne was established, such gardens were specifically intended for a working-class audience, as the above program may suggest. A visitor observed in 1871, at about the time Whistler began his series on Cremorne, that "everything has been done to render this once elegant place suitable for cockney tastes."[37] Poor Ruskin! To the affront of "cockney impudence" had been added the insult of cockney subject matter.

Managers at Cremorne made extensive use of advertisements, plastering their handbills on walls around the city. They even exploited their featured balloon ascents as opportunities for advertising. During one ascent in 1861, four thousand handbills served the twin purposes of ballast and bombast, being scattered over London to lighten the craft.[38]

It was easy to reach the gardens by water, and a landing dock was installed at the river's edge by about 1850. The dock and the waterside gate, dimly visible in the background of a contemporary photograph, can be more clearly seen in a view by Walter Greaves (Figs. 190 and 191). It was a "pleasant steamboat ride" up the Thames from all piers between London Bridge and Cremorne. Boats ran every five minutes at a fare of twopence and threepence. On land, omnibuses could reach the garden from all over London at a fare of fourpence to sixpence (Fig. 192). Passengers were discharged near the King's Road entrance.[39] Indeed, mass transportation was a key factor in making the park accessible to the many. The gardens lost favor with smart society mainly because of "the number of trippers whom modern methods of locomotion convey to such places in ever-increasing crowds," according to one historian.[40]

Cremorne entrance fees were lower than those at other gardens. The proprietors usually charged one shilling, and only sixpence on Sundays, as opposed to two shillings or more at Vauxhall Gardens, depending upon the entertainments scheduled.[41] A season ticket to Cremorne cost two pounds and two shillings. Sometimes one did have to pay at Cremorne for the entrance to individual

Figure 193.
Percy Cruikshank, *May 11
Sunday at Cremorne,
Fortune Telling, 8 p.m.*,
1850s, lithograph. Royal
Borough of Kensington and
Chelsea Libraries and Art
Service.

Figure 194.
Henry and Walter Greaves,
*The Dancing Platform,
Cremorne Gardens*, 1870s,
gouache. Museum of
London.

Figure 195.
*A General Prospect of Vaux
Hall Gardens, Showing at
One View the Disposition
of the Whole Gardens*,
1754, engraving. From
*Views of Some of the Most
Celebrated By-gone
Pleasure Gardens of
London.*

Figure 196.
*A Supper Party in a Cabinet
at Cremorne*, ca. 1860,
wood engraving. Royal
Borough of Kensington and
Chelsea Libraries and Art
Service.

entertainments, however (Fig. 193). Suppers were priced at a reasonable two shillings sixpence, which allowed the visitor all he could eat, an enticement still familiar in certain of today's chain restaurants, and one which contrasted sharply with the stinginess of repasts offered elsewhere.

The buildings at Cremorne were shiny and new, while Vauxhall Gardens, Cremorne's venerable downriver competitor, looked shabby, having been in operation for almost two centuries. Vauxhall was temporarily closed in 1857, while its rival assumed the title "Royal Gardens Cremorne." A newspaper article that year averred:

> *The place is many times gayer than Vauxhall on its most brilliant nights . . . and Cremorne, with its countless attractions, may be enjoyed at a quarter the expense of its costly prototype. Fine weather brings several thousand persons to the Gardens in one evening; and fireworks at an early hour conclude the entertainments of this very popular resort.*[42]

When Vauxhall was permanently closed two years later, a contemporary writer noted that "it had long lost all chance of rivaling the 'Chelsea Elysium.' "[43]

Half a century earlier, a visitor to London had written an awestruck assessment of Vauxhall Gardens, cast in similar language. In 1805 the American Benjamin Silliman beheld at Vauxhall "a scene . . . splendid beyond description, and almost beyond conception, exceeding all that poets have told of fairy lands and Elysian fields."[44] His enthusiasm reminds us that visitors tend to respond to different pleasure gardens in a similar manner over the years, taking them as fertile grounds for the exercise of fantasy and imagination. Although both packaging and content have changed, Disneyland evokes similarly enraptured first reactions. Cremorne, the Disneyland of its day, was itself the descendant of earlier programmatic gardens, with Vauxhall serving as a major model.

There had once been many pleasure resorts in and around London. For the most part, entertainments offered at Cremorne were not new. As early as the 1760s, the Rosoman Street Grotto had offered Londoners an "enchanted fountain" and a water mill which "when set to work represented fireworks, and formed a beautiful rainbow."[45] A century later one could view at Cremorne "a handsome fountain with female on stork supports" lit by gas jets (Fig. 194), or "Eve's Fountain with its stalactite rock-work, seven figures and vases," or even enter the "Astrologer's cave."[46] The "lavender bowers, Chinese walks [and] trees illuminated with colored lamps" at Cremorne were actually some of its most old-fashioned features. All were to be found in eighteenth-century gardens. The "discrete bowers" and double-tiered supper boxes that could accommodate 1,500 people at Cremorne echoed similar, if more modestly scaled, dining arrangements at Vauxhall (Figs. 195 and 196). Some of the paintings by Hogarth and others, which had once decorated boxes at Vauxhall, were purchased at the sale in 1859 and reinstalled at Cremorne.[47]

By bringing their theatrical experience to Cremorne, proprietors simply carried on tradition. The music of Mozart and Handel had wafted out over the Thames from the riverside grounds of Ranelagh and Vauxhall a century before strains from Offenbach's waltzes rose from the grounds of Cremorne. Jonathan Tyers, proprietor of Vauxhall after 1728, had also run the Drury Lane Theatre. He introduced a number of theatrical spectacles to the older garden.[48] The fireworks that excited visitors to Cremorne had long been a feature of pleasure gardens. Fireworks were set off at Ranelagh after 1767.[49] By the late eighteenth-century they were also popular at Vauxhall and other London pleasure gardens. The love of spectacle led nineteenth-century audiences to thrill to imitation

Figure 197.
Cremorne Gardens: Grand Aquatic Tournaments on the Thames, ca. 1857, lithograph. Royal Borough of Kensington and Chelsea Libraries and Art Service.

Figure 198.
Cremorne poster for *Madame Poitevin As Europa*, mid-nineteenth century, lithograph. Royal Borough of Kensington and Chelsea Libraries and Art Service.

Figure 199.
The Chinese House, the Rotunda, and the Company in Masquerade in Ranelagh Gardens, eighteenth century, engraving. Royal Borough of Kensington and Chelsea Libraries and Art Service.

Figure 200.
Variations in Flesh Colour and Green: The Balcony, 1865, oil on panel. Freer Gallery.

battles. "Waterloo" was repeated at Vauxhall, and a medieval "Grand Aquatic Tournament" was staged at Cremorne thereafter (Fig. 197). Cremorne opened the 1861 season with the exciting spectacle of "the female Blondin" crossing the Thames on a tight-rope. This dangerous stunt repeated earlier offerings at Vauxhall, where, in 1816, Madame Saqui of Paris had descended an inclined rope amidst a "shower of Chinese Fire."[50] Similar events were promised on Cremorne posters. Even the constantly elaborated balloon ascensions at Cremorne (Fig. 198) had precedents in the eighteenth century.

There was much of a traditional nature that Whistler saw when he visited the gardens. Perhaps one reason why the artist felt free to paint Cremorne in abstract terms was that the "exhaustless amusements every day," promised on poster after poster, would have been familiar to audiences of his day and could be conjured up by the merest suggestion.

The weight of tradition is particularly important for our understanding of Whistler's application of Oriental art to his own work. While he, like most painters, was particularly struck by the Japanese art that poured into Europe during the 1860s, his response and his eclectic use of such new stimuli had a wholly Western basis in the chinoiserie of the eighteenth century. His Cremorne series was no exception, and the same stimuli had actually been felt in the gardens themselves. The taste for Oriental decorations and themes at Cremorne reflects the tradition of Oriental follies used in English gardens since the early 1700s. Vauxhall had included Chinese pavilions by 1751, while its rotunda was redecorated as a "superb Eastern tent" of eclectic description in 1789. The "Chinese Walk" there was hung with lanterns, and Cremorne's proprietors were to follow suit. Cremorne's Chinese dance platform was preceded by an Oriental folly at Ranelagh Gardens, used in the eighteenth century as both a bandstand and the setting for masquerades (Fig. 199).

Long before Whistler moved to Chelsea, attendants dressed "in the Eastern manner" had served lemonade at the Ranelagh Gardens rotunda, not far from the house where Whistler eventually lived in Chelsea.[51] Whistler's figures in *The Balcony*, painted in 1860, are also wearing Eastern garb (Fig. 200). They could have heard the music from the Chinese bandstand at Cremorne Gardens on any afternoon. The woman leaning out and looking to her right would have been able to see the lofty trees that shaded Cremorne, which projected out into the river at the west end of the quarter.

Whistler did not even have to take a boat or a bus to reach Cremorne, for it was only a couple of blocks from his house in Cheney Walk. But proximity does not entirely explain Whistler's interest in the gardens. He did not start painting the subject until 1872, nearly a decade after he moved to Chelsea. A more important factor is the predominance of French themes that run as leitmotifs through his art. By the 1870s, Whistler and his contemporaries on the other side of the English Channel were well aware of the power of parks and pleasure gardens as subjects for paintings—they were excellent spots for observing fashionable life (Fig. 201). A French visitor to London remarked, "I have been told that fifty thousand people gather in Hyde Park on the days when the bands are playing—it would be difficult to find a better chance of observing the different elements which compose smart society."[52]

If Whistler's paintings touch upon French as well as British themes, the pleasure garden itself had French as well as British antecedents, for it was an international phenomenon. By 1847 Cremorne Gardens boasted a "very imposing entrance . . . erected at the river side, on the model of the gate at the Jardin de Mabille in Paris." The report continued that Mabille, a "celebrated pleasure-garden, has also been successfully imitated in some other particulars" at Cre-

Figure 201.
Claude Monet, *Hyde Park London*, 1871, oil on canvas. Museum of Art, Rhode Island School of Design, gift of Mrs. Murray S. Danforth.

Figure 202.
Walter Greaves, *The Waterside Entrance to Cremorne Gardens*, 1859, oil on cardboard. Museum of London.

Figure 203.
Nocturne: A Street beside a Park, 1872–1877, ink and wash. Hunterian Art Gallery, University of Glasgow, Birnie Philip Bequest.

Figure 204.
Cremorne poster for the sailing balloon *L'Esperance*, 1865, wood engraving. Royal Borough of Kensington and Chelsea Libraries and Art Service.

Figure 205.
Edgar Degas, *Mlle. Becat aux ambassadeurs*, ca. 1877, lithograph. Courtesy of the Library of Congress.

morne.[53] The gate is visible in a painting by Walter Greaves and is probably the subject of a much more abstract pen drawing by Whistler (Figs. 202 and 203). Consistent with the rest of the series, Whistler's is a nighttime view, with lamps shining out of the darkness as bent figures move, almost surreptitiously, toward the gate. Another French attraction at Cremorne was the "Versailles Promenade" (see Fig. 189). The opening program at Cremorne in 1860 promised a "cirque orientale" doubtless modeled upon circuses popular in Paris at this time.[54] Two years later, Cremorne presented "another startling novelty," Delamarne's sailing balloon *L'Esperance*. A broadside poster announced that the balloon came direct from "the Gardens of the Luxemburg in Paris," where it had been exhibited "before the Senate of France and a vast multitude of people." (Fig. 204). Entertainments like seriocomic singing and fireworks were offered in French as well as English gardens and can be seen in Degas's lithograph *Mlle. Becat aux ambassadeurs*, executed in about 1877 (Fig. 205). This is only one of many such images of outdoor restaurants and café concerts by Degas, Manet, and Renoir.

Although they differ considerably in appearance, Whistler's paintings of the outdoor garden and its entertainments coincide with those of his French contemporaries. Renoir depicted a joyous *Afternoon Dancing at the Moulin de la Galette, Montmartre* in 1877 (Fig. 206). In contrast, Whistler preferred the vague darkness that pervades his sketch of the entrance to Cremorne. Although the gardens opened those gates in the afternoon, Whistler confined himself to nighttime scenes. Greaves later told the Pennells that Whistler "never tried to use colour at night or at Cremorne Gardens, but made notes on brown paper in black and white chalk."[55] Whereas Renoir included clearly distinguishable portraits of some of his friends, Whistler's figures are difficult or impossible to make out. We recall that Whistler's *Ten o'Clock Lecture* made it clear that he did not want his paintings to depend upon local or personal interest. Perhaps the seated figure at the far right in *Cremorne Gardens, No. 2* is Whistler (Fig. 207).[56] But such information adds little to our understanding of the purpose of Whistler's painting as a glimpse of the anonymity of modern life.

The vague obscurity of the subjects in the Cremorne series firmly establishes Whistler as a *flâneur*, the impartial, nonjudgmental observer of contemporary life. By creating impersonal generalizations where figures are barely distinguishable types, identifiable only by their clothing—i.e., the tall silk hat of the gentleman out on the town or the white dress that indicated a woman of means in soot-ridden London—Whistler acts as the observant "stranger" defined by the sociologist Georg Simmel. The stranger enjoys physical proximity yet maintains psychological distance from his fellows.[57] The *flâneur* was a sort of detective shadowing his subject under the cover of shadows. Baudelaire wrote:

> For the perfect flâneur, *for the passionate spectator, it is an immense joy to set up house in the heart of the multitude, amid the ebb and flow of movement, in the midst of the fugitive and the infinite . . . to be at the centre of the world, and yet to remain hidden from the world—such are a few of the slightest pleasures of those independent, passionate, impartial natures which the tongue can but clumsily define. The spectator is a* prince *who everywhere rejoices in his incognito.*[58]

Recognizing the limitations of words—the "clumsy tongue" that Baudelaire decries—Whistler spoke in an abstract language of form and color. He takes us incognito to the gardens, and through his dense, veiled atmosphere the viewer absorbs the mood of the place. Degas and Manet painted pictures of Parisian

Figure 206.
Pierre Auguste Renoir,
*Dancing at the Moulin de la
Galette, Montmartre*, 1877,
oil on canvas. Musées
Nationaux de France,
Musée d'Orsay, Galerie du
Jeu de Paume. (Photograph
courtesy Musées Nationaux
de France.)

Figure 207.
Cremorne Gardens, No. 2,
1872–1877, oil on canvas.
All rights reserved.
Metropolitan Museum of
Art, John Stewart Kennedy
Fund, 1912.

Figure 208.
Phoebus Levin, *The
Dancing Platform at
Cremorne Gardens*, 1864,
oil on canvas. Museum of
London.

Figure 209.
*Nocturne: Cremorne
Gardens, No. 3*,
1872–1877, oil on canvas.
Freer Gallery.

nightlife that focus upon implied relationships glimpsed at close hand, as individuals arrange their assignations. But Whistler expressed the darker side of the pleasure garden with palpable painted darkness itself. He used a bituminous and rather sinister palette of blacks, browns, and yellow-whites, occasionally relieved by harsh spots of color. Enough detail is provided to inform the viewer of his location, but that is all. Nevertheless, there can be no doubt that Whistler, in his own way, joined his French contemporaries in the pleasures of *flâneurie*.

The pleasure garden was by definition a haven for social freedoms not to be enjoyed elsewhere. For a century, such gardens had enjoyed racy reputations as illicit meeting spots. Even Ranelagh Gardens, regarded by many writers as the most decorous of London's resorts during the 1700s, still "had a tolerable reputation as a place of assignation."[59] Perhaps the perception of the pleasure garden as a meeting spot for lovers stems from an eighteenth-century interpretation of the classical Arcadian landscape as a setting for the loves of the shepherds. This theme figured prominently in British collections of landscape paintings, as well as British writings about classical poetry.[60] Well versed in such material, audiences of the nineteenth century might have applied the concept to their public gardens.

Benjamin Silliman found many "genteel people" at Vauxhall in 1805, yet he averred that "no small part of the crowd is composed of courtezans." He went on to warn that while Vauxhall was "superlatively elegant," he was convinced that it was "a most successful school of corruption."[61]

Cremorne, in its turn, rapidly acquired a reputation as the territory of the demimonde, most clearly recorded in Phoebus Levin's painting *The Dancing Platform at Cremorne Gardens*, 1864 (Fig. 208). Clad in traditional garb, and probably fresh from the country, a sturdy Scot looks on while a young woman of impeccable dress but questionable morals accosts a dandified potential escort. The dancing platform glitters in the midground, and supper boxes, promising seclusion, can be seen in the distance. Lest the viewer miss the message, Levin includes dogs and monkeys, obvious sexual symbols, in profusion.

Against such blatant anecdote, Whistler implies the same message abstractly in *Nocturne: Cremorne Gardens, No. 3* (Fig. 209). We have only a glimpse of a couple swiftly departing one of the theaters or restaurants. A man in his top hat and domino, or evening cape, escorts a woman in her fashionable still-white dress. The darkness is about to swallow them, but like Poe's "man of the crowd," Whistler figuratively follows "in pursuit of an unknown, half-glimpsed countenance that has, on an instant, bewitched him."[62] Similarly, his *Nocturne in Black and Gold: The Gardens* (see Fig. 187) offers a tantalizing peek at abandoned dancing on the Chinese platform and the private haven of the supper boxes, but all is understated, anonymous, as clandestine as the types of relationships that were initiated at Cremorne Gardens.

A common event at pleasure gardens, one that greatly facilitated assignations, was the masked ball. Balls at Cremorne were another holdover from the 1700s. During that century Ranelagh was distinguished for masked parties whose main attraction was the freedom and anonymity supposedly conferred upon the wearer by his or her costume. According to one contemporary critic, masks served "not for pretending to hide blushes, but to conceal the inability to blush."[63] Vauxhall, too, held its pageants and masquerades. These continued to be popular into the nineteenth century. At the "Grand Chinese Pageant," on July 13, 1846, seven thousand people crowded the grounds at Vauxhall. Not to be outdone, Cremorne staged similar costumed pageants, as well as costumed theatrical presentations.[64] A French visitor to Cremorne in 1857 reported sitting through a crowded performance of

Figure 210.
Mephistophelian Figure,
1870s, ink. Collection
unknown. (Photograph,
Hunterian Art Gallery,
University of Glasgow.)

Figure 211.
Standing Figure in Japanese
Brocaded Robe, fabricated
chalks on brown paper.
Hunterian Art Gallery,
University of Glasgow,
Birnie Philip Bequest.

Figure 212.
Sheet-music cover, 1850s,
lithograph. Royal Borough
of Kensington and Chelsea
Libraries and Art Service.

Figure 213.
Marriott's Cremorne
Quadrilles, 1850s,
lithograph. Royal Borough
of Kensington and Chelsea
Libraries and Art Service.

> *a farce acted by pierrots, harlequins, policemen and field-marshals.*
> *There were waterfalls, snow-capped mountains and polar bears in*
> *white cotton trousers. The actors oozed sentiment, the actresses*
> *danced, the chorus bellowed. As a conclusion the devil appeared in*
> *pink tights with gilded horns—he went through various transforma-*
> *tions and ended up as an attorney.*[65]

Such entertainments continued in Whistler's day. For example, in 1874 the program of entertainments included the comic ballet *Marguerite la Bouquetière,* with a "Diavolo" as a featured character.[66] The costumes at balls were frequently copies of those used in stage performances. Among Whistler's drawings possibly associated with the Cremorne series are a number of fancy-dress figures from some kind of masked ball or presentation, a satanic costume among them (Fig. 210). The anonymity conferred by masks and costumes was a source of lasting fascination for Whistler. At the end of his career, Whistler created an exquisite pastel that puns upon both the studio model, whose mask preserved her identity, and the costume ball, where masks and costumes protected the reputation of the wearer (Fig. 211).

Deviltry was the rule at Cremorne, whether or not costumes were worn. As was the case at the Jardin de Mabille in Paris, every evening at the London resort ended with wild dancing:

> *In a Chinese bandstand an orchestra struck up a schottische. A*
> *minute later the carefully levelled open space was filled with couples*
> *and the surrounding tables with onlookers . . . while I still gasped*
> *for breath, Lionel seized the hand of a young person of doubtful*
> *morality and flung himself with entire abandon into a Bacchanalian*
> *rendering of the polka. People dance here with their hips and their*
> *shoulders, seeming to have little control over their legs. . . . Frivolous*
> *young things improvise all sorts of indecorous antics.*[67]

Sheet-music covers document society's toleration of a certain degree of wanton public behavior. The lyrics of numerous waltzes and quadrilles were based on amorous activities at the gardens (Figs. 212 and 213). A contemporary visitor remarked, "Nobody here takes the slightest notice of his neighbor's doings," which seems to confirm the innuendo of Whistler's Cremorne series as a veiled look at modern social behavior through the eyes of an unnoticed, anonymous voyeur.[68]

However, there were limits to the amount of toleration accorded to garden visitors. Cremorne's threat to morality caused disputes between the management and other segments of the community during and after the 1850s, a factor that certainly informs Whistler's treatment of the site. In 1857 the Chelsea Vestry petitioned to refuse the renewal of Cremorne's license. The gardens were attacked or ridiculed in cartoons like "Dissipation: A Tale of Cremorne."[69] Over the next fifteen years, opposition grew, galvanized by several tragic accidents connected with ballooning and other stunts staged in the gardens. There were demands for stricter controls (Fig. 214). In 1873 Canon Cromwell, the principal of St. Mark's College, led opposition to a renewal of the garden's license, attacking the "loose women" to be found there. A pamphlet written by a Baptist minister in 1876 satirized the park in no uncertain terms:

> *. . . the public mind—at least the best*
> *Say that your Gardens are a real pest:*
> *Degrading minds—I've heard this twice or thrice*
> *A nursery for every kind of Vice.*

Figure 214.
Cremorne As It Will Be under Future Regulations, ca. 1870, wood engraving. Royal Borough of Kensington and Chelsea Libraries and Art Service.

Figure 215.
Harry Furniss, *The Last of Cremorne Gardens,* 1878, wood engraving. Royal Borough of Kensington and Chelsea Libraries and Art Service.

Figure 216.
The Derby Night at Cremorne—Keeping It Up, wood engraving. From *The Day's Doings* 2, no. 44 (27 May 1871). Royal Borough of Kensington and Chelsea Libraries and Art Service.

Figure 217.
Cremorne No. 1, 1872–1875, oil on canvas. Courtesy of the Fogg Art Museum, Harvard University, bequest of Grenville L. Winthrop.

> *They say that baits are laid, the young to trap*
> *And moral honor you delight to snap.*[70]

The author was sued for libel by John Baum, the gardens' proprietor. As noted above, the trial and Baum's one-farthing damages coincide with the Whistler-Ruskin trial. After his Pyrrhic victory, however, Baum abandoned his efforts to renew the license. The following year, 1877, the contents of the grounds were dismantled and disposed of at auction. The land was sold for development almost immediately (Fig. 215).

With its sexually charged atmosphere, the public pleasure garden was an appropriate trysting place for Whistler and his muse. His written metaphor for art itself was the capricious yet generous mistress. Like the harlot with a heart of gold in many a French novel of the period, Art—"the cruel jade"—denied her favors to many a supplicant, but lavished treasures upon her artist-lover. Whistler wrote:

> *With the man, then, and not with the multitude, are her intimacies; and in the book of her life the names inscribed are few—scant, indeed, the list of those who have helped to write her story of love and beauty.*[71]

Whistler flatly denied Ruskin's pious equation of morality and art, insisting that moral laxity had nothing to do with limited artistic creativity. Whistler's mistresses of the 1850s, 1860s, and 1870s appear regularly as models for his paintings and prints, and he denegrated as "sublimely vain" the belief that a nation "shall live nobly or art perish." "At our own option is our virtue," he went on. "Art in no way we affect."[72]

A newspaper illustration, *The Derby Night at Cremorne—Keeping It Up,* records the level to which the gardens' reputation had fallen by the time Whistler took up the subject (Fig. 216). The illustration appeared in 1871, about a year before Whistler is thought to have started his Cremorne pictures. The two unescorted females that stand out from the murky background of *Cremorne No. 1,* begun in about 1872, may be none other than the brazen hussies who lift their glasses in the newspaper illustration of the preceding year (Fig. 217). One of Whistler's women has dropped her handkerchief, but with typical restraint the artist avoids obvious anecdote in favor of a suspenseful moment fraught with ambiguous possibilities. We do not see the male—whether chivalrous or designing—that may emerge from the gloom, picking up the kerchief before the stooping woman can retrieve it. Afterward, we may presume, that a round of entertainments promised by the lights of the theater at the left of the painting could begin. Eventually the would-be gallant may end up under the table, like the besotted swain in the newspaper illustration. Undertaken during the twilight hours of Cremorne Gardens' forty-year existence, Whistler's series of suggestive nocturnal scenes contributes toward a redefinition of history painting.

Whistler's career can be literally interpreted as a lifelong battle for the acceptance of artistic license and lyrical abstraction. Seen in a warlike context, his determined posture as a dandy is an understandable tactic. Although Whistler lacked independent means, he maintained his public stance, alternately nonchalant and waspish, by dint of labor performed in private. Fellow artists were quick to distinguish between the public fop and the private worker.[73] Whistler's elaborate toilette, his dramatic white forelock, his elegant long coat, his attenuated walking stick and affected monocle, even his succession of mistresses, were all part of a long-established code of dandyism, originated by Beau Brummell in the early nineteenth century and carried on in both England and France (Fig.

Figure 218.
Spy [Sir Leslie Ward] *A Symphony* (caricature of Whistler as a dandy for *Vanity Fair*), 12 January 1878, lithograph. Reproduced A. E. Gallatin, *Portraits of Whistler: A Critical Study and an Iconography* (New York and London, 1918), no. 242.

Figure 219.
Walter Greaves, *The Dancing Platform, Cremorne Gardens*, 1870s, etching. Museum of London.

Figure 220.
Sketches of butterflies for *The Gentle Art of Making Enemies*, ca. 1890, ink. Freer Gallery.

218).[74] As Whistler sought to establish his place in the Anglo-French artistic community during the late 1850s and early 1860s, Baudelaire was still discussing the dandy in terms that had an obvious impact upon the young Whistler. Baudelaire pointed out that sartorial splendors (which Whistler could *just* afford at that time) were "no more than symbols of [the dandy's] aristocratic superiority of mind." The dandy was "in love with *distinction* above all things."[75] In an etching by Greaves, who later imitated Whistler's dandified costume in his own dress, we see Whistler at Cremorne as a natty *flâneur*, striding along with, yet separate from, the crowd (Fig. 219). There can be no doubt that Whistler set himself apart from the common herd:

> *This one unspoken sympathy that pervades humanity, is—Vulgarity! Vulgarity—under whose fascinating influence "the many" have elbowed "the few," and the gentle circle of Art swarms with the intoxicated mob of mediocrity, whose leaders prate and counsel, and call aloud, where the Gods once spoke in a whisper!*[76]

For nearly half a century Whistler maintained his pose as a dandy. He never tired of "the joy of astonishing others, and the proud satisfaction of never oneself being astonished."[77] With pen and brush, he persisted in shocking and irritating the critics and the art establishment, even after having won grudging acceptance within their ranks. His butterfly signature (Fig. 220) was a dandy's choice—at the same time both trivial and filled with meaning, its whiplash tail a visual barb to Whistler's written commentary on the foibles of others in letters like "The Critic-Flâneur," 1888, which was reprinted in *The Gentle Art of Making Enemies*.[78]

Whistler's dandyism was, in short, a type of battle dress, worn with a sure and firm purpose. Baudelaire noted, "Whether these men are nicknamed exquisites, *incroyables*, *beaux*, lions or dandies, they all spring from the same womb; they all partake of the same characteristic quality of opposition and revolt."[79] Whistler's bellicose dandyism was a means to an end, as was the ostensibly careless yet stinging bon mot which kept him constantly before the public eye. Baudelaire called dandyism "the last spark of heroism amid decadence" and observed:

> *Dandyism appears above all in periods of transition, when democracy is not yet all-powerful, and aristocracy is only just beginning to totter and fall. In the disorder of these times, certain men who are socially, politically and financially ill at ease, but are all rich in native energy, may conceive the idea of establishing a new kind of aristocracy, all the more difficult to shatter as it will be based on the most precious, the most enduring faculties, and on the divine gifts which work and money are unable to bestow.*[80]

Two decades after Baudelaire published his remarks upon dandies, Whistler announced to the audience at his *Ten o'Clock Lecture*: "We have then but to wait—until, with the mark of the Gods upon him—there come among us again the chosen [artist]."[81] Whistler saw himself as that divinely appointed agent, and it is significant that both his lyrical painting and dandified posing occurred just as the old aristocracy of literal realism was fading.

Whistler's Cremorne series was an early and important salvo against the *ancien régime* of realism in painting. His *Falling Rocket* was more than a pot of paint flung in the face of an unreceptive public. It was an incendiary cocktail tossed by an aesthetic terrorist. The artist's choice of subject matter was wholly

Figure 221.
Shuntosai, *Fireworks over Bridge*, 1857, woodcut, Japan. From Whistler's studio. Hunterian Art Gallery, University of Glasgow, Birnie Philip Bequest.

Figure 222.
Lepautre, *Fête of 1676: The Fifth Day: Fireworks on the Grand Canal, Versailles,* engraving. Collection Cabinet des Estampes, Bibliothèque Nationale, Paris. Reproduced in Patrick Bracco and Elisabeth Lebovici, *Fireworks: Feux d'artifices. French Fireworks from the Seventeenth to the Nineteenth Century* (exh. cat.) (Washington: International Exhibitions Foundation, 1971), fig. 10. Reprinted courtesy of the International Exhibitions Foundation.

Figure 223.
Nocturne in Black and Gold: The Falling Rocket, ca. 1875, oil on oak panel. Courtesy of the Detroit Institute of Arts, gift of Dexter M. Ferry, Jr.

appropriate, dictated not only by the contemporary meaning of the actual site, but also by the traditional meanings behind displays of fireworks. For centuries, fireworks had dual connections to battle. A Chinese invention, fireworks were used not only in battle but also to represent battle in pageants and spectacles.[82] Among the Japanese prints found in Whistler's studio after his death was Shuntosai's *Fireworks over Bridge*, a woodcut of 1857 (Fig. 221). We do not know when the print came into Whistler's hands. Yet the woodcut is important as a contemporary representation of an old Oriental tradition that had spread to the West, and it also emphasizes Whistler's strong link to Oriental art, seen in his own *oeuvre*.

Fireworks retained their martial overtones when they were brought to the West. *Feu d'artifice*, or artificial fire, was used as a showy political tool in France during the seventeenth and eighteenth centuries. Artists and architects created elaborate stage settings from which both stationary and moving rockets were fired to commemorate events in the life of the nation. It is important to recall that such events were only symbolized; viewers actually experienced some degree of abstract suggestion during a fireworks display. Moreover, stylization carried over into the prints and paintings that tried to record such evanescent events (Fig. 222).

Displays of fireworks changed very little over the centuries, and the spectacles of the 1870s would have been similar to earlier programs. A printed leaflet that accompanied a display at Cremorne in 1836 conveys some idea of the pyrotechnics Whistler might have witnessed later:

> *A representation of a Chinese Pagoda, formed in white and yellow diamond lights, concluding with four semi-suns, in contrasted positions, volly of reports.*
>
> *A double verticle wheel, decorated with all the colours of the rainbow, changing to a twelve-pointed star, formed by diamond lights and concluding with a double sun, of forty-eight radii.*
>
> *A beautiful piece called Le Soleil tournant, commencing with a coloured wheel, changing to a curious figure with concatenated centre, surrounded by alternate green, crimson and purple wheels, concluding with display of brilliant fire.*
>
> *Rockets of large calibre, shedding amber coloured stars [and] gold rains.*[83]

By the time Whistler was in attendance at Cremorne, the principal pyrotechnist was one J. Wells:

> *As the night advances, the Firework Temple receives its votaries, and Mr. J. Wells, in a succession of dazzling devices, vindicates his claim to a foremost place among pyrotechnic artists.*[84]

We may comfortably speculate that it was Mr. Wells who fired the shell immortalized in Whistler's painting *Nocturne in Black and Gold: The Falling Rocket* (Fig. 223). But perhaps it is more profitable to note that Wells's displays "elicited those ejaculative encomiums which have so long been considered the proper compliment to pay to the successful flight of the far-reaching rocket."[85] An encomium was the natural response to the wordless experience of abstract light, smoke, and noise during a fireworks display. But, as the printed program of 1836 implies, a substantive written interpretation was helpful for injecting each display with comprehensive narrative meaning. The beholder could read, for example, of "le Guillache," as "a variety of contrasted fires, representing the engine-turning of a watch, concluding with a brilliant sun; the whole richly decorated with coloured fires." [86]

Presumably the program helped the spectator make the symbolic vault from watch to sun. Here is revealed the imagistic limitation of fireworks—many of the forms seem to have been just lines or circles. And again we find the predictable resort to language to convey meaning to an audience confronted by unfamiliar images. This practice had been followed earlier by engravers of fireworks spectacles who did not distinguish between various parts of the display, as rockets versus cannon balls, but who provided an accompanying text to help the viewer understand what was taking place.[87]

That the pyrotechnist's abstract conceits were unclear is demonstrated by a satirical piece of writing, "Letters from Night Latitudes, No. 15. A Visit to Cremorne," printed in the magazine *Fun* in 1862. The writer complained, "These fireworks all seem to come from splendid palisades and royal evidences, but no one seems to know what these edifications are meant for." [88] The malapropisms are contrived, but the confusion may well have been genuine.

Whistler's paintings of fireworks, appropriately, concentrate much more on capturing the physical experience of darkness broken by almost blinding light and noise. Whistler's is a kinetic verism, keyed to the viewer's visual confrontation with the work of art. A wide line of red and yellow pigments is the strongest passage of color to stand out from the bituminous depths of *Nocturne in Black and Gold: The Falling Rocket*. Whistler placed this band at the bottom of the painting, and thus the viewer's eye begins a journey across the canvas that mimics the path of a real rocket. Intense dots of bright red, orange, and green are placed at the top of the picture, drawing the eye upward into Whistler's murky night sky. Finally the eye moves down along the right side of the canvas, past clusters of pale red and yellow dots whose relative weakness parallels the dying sparks of a spent rocket.

Under the French kings, the symbolism of fireworks was greatly enhanced by elaborate stage settings that helped celebrate royal births and marriages—international political alliances to be more precise. Wartime victories were also occasions for fireworks. The traditional stage set employed in victory celebrations was a bastioned tower or medieval city gate (Fig. 224). Photographs of the fireworks platform at Cremorne Gardens still survive at the National Monuments Record, and the platform can also be seen on posters as well as in a painting by Greaves (Figs. 225 and 226). Obviously the platform at Cremorne is descended from the baroque stage set that had symbolized the capture of a city. The one at Cremorne was made of "four pillars, with ornamental cast iron panels, [a] deal platform, with stout joists under, and zinc front." [89] *Nocturne in Black and Gold: The Falling Rocket* actually contains battlelike imagery, not only in the exploding rockets, but also in the glimpse of the platform from which the rockets were launched. Two of the towering pillars emerge from the smoky darkness, above the ring of lights from the dancing platform at the left side of the painting.

A circular apparatus stood in front of the fireworks tower at Cremorne (Fig. 227). This device would have been used for firing the Grande Girande, or Catherine Wheel, the awe-inspiring explosion that ordinarily ended an elaborate

Figure 224.
Fireworks Scenery Arranged by Merchant Guilds to Celebrate the Taking of Ypres, 1744, engraving after a painting by the Dumesnil brothers. Collection Cabinet des Estampes, Bibliothèque Nationale, Paris. Reproduced in Bracco and Lebovici, fig. 28.

Figure 225.
Cremorne, fireworks platform (the Grotto), ca. 1870, photograph. Royal Commission on Historical Monuments (England), National Monuments Record, London.

Figure 226.
Walter Greaves, *Cremorne: Fireworks Platform* (the Grotto), ca. 1862. Museum of London.

Figure 227.
Cremorne, fireworks
platform (the Grotto), ca.
1870, photograph. Royal
Commission on Historical
Monuments (England),
National Monuments
Record, London.

Figure 228.
*Nocturne: Black and
Gold—the Fire Wheel,*
1872–1877, oil on canvas.
Tate Gallery, London.

program of fireworks.[90] Whistler's compelling work *Nocturne: Black and Gold—the Fire Wheel* captures this cataclysmic image in a violent manner (Fig. 228). Again, abstraction adds to, rather than detracts from, the force of the painting. *The Fire Wheel*, along with *The Falling Rocket*, exemplifies Whistler's aggressive intention to shock the viewing public.

Unlike Ruskin, Baudelaire expected his encounter with a new artwork to begin with a shock. *Volupté* was the shock of pleasure that the critic experienced when first contemplating a painting. His further examination and analysis transformed the initial shock into knowledge: "Je résolus de m'informer du pourquoi, et de transformer ma volupté en connaissance."[91] Such knowledge was

> *far from being the same thing as the cold textbook knowledge which [Baudelaire] had long ago rejected as a critical instrument; it is a knowledge charged and quickened by the pleasure which has logically preceded it, and . . . it is far more likely to take the form of a sonnet than an algebraic equation—a witty and suggestive interpretation than a piece of scientific, or pseudo-scientific, analysis.*[92]

Pseudoscientific analysis and textbook knowledge were ineffective tools for bringing about an understanding of Whistler's art during the Whistler-Ruskin lawsuit. Commentary on paintings introduced as evidence indicates the degree to which conservative members of the London art establishment received the shock. They maligned Whistler's paintings as unfinished, hence unintelligible. Bound by preconceptions, witnesses for Ruskin's defense neither found the shock pleasurable nor managed to transform it into knowledge. While Whistler's mastery of color was conceded, the Royal Academician Frith commented sarcastically that the *Nocturne: Blue and Silver—Old Battersea Bridge* "does not represent any more than you could get from a bit of wallpaper or silk."[93] Frith was unable to accept any decorative art as a suitable inspiration. It would be left to later generations, painters like Vuillard, Braque, and Picasso, to create paintings, prints, and collages in which fabrics and wallpaper played a role evident to all. But Whistler's atmospheric yet frankly decorative canvases stand at the beginning of this artistic development.

Speaking to the members of the jury, Whistler said of *The Falling Rocket*, "If it were called a view of Cremorne, it would certainly bring about nothing but disappointment on the part of the beholders. It is an artistic arrangement."[94] Yet the artist had responded to the site in an appropriate manner, using the subject matter cleverly, as an insidious weapon against literal painting. At the trial's conclusion, Whistler's damages amounted to only one contemptuous farthing. But the damage he inflicted on the established mode of realism was significant. As Whistler's reputation steadily rose during the next two decades, greater leeway was permitted for artists interested in abstraction.

If a single symbolic theme was conveyed by displays of fireworks during the *ancien régime*, it was the victory of Order over Chaos or Light over Darkness. The rulers of France were not above celebrating a victory with great pomp as a means of restoring public confidence in the midst of a war.[95] Whistler's Cremorne series, likewise, must have encouraged the camp of avant-garde painters, lighting a path through the darkness of academic realism that led toward abstraction and the rich possibilities of the decorative surface that eventually revolutionized the art of the twentieth century.

Notes to Artist and Patron

1 For an idea of the scope of the Freer Gallery's American holdings, see Burns A. Stubbs, *Paintings, Pastels, Drawings, Prints, and Copper Plates by and Attributed to American and European Artists, Together with a List of Original Whistleriana in the Freer Gallery of Art* (Washington, 1967).

2 Freer vouchers indicate that a large number of Oriental decorative objects entered the collection shortly after Freer's death, presumably because of previous arrangements. However, these objects were not subject to Freer's usual thorough scrutiny and his customary rejection of part of each shipment.

3 See Thomas W. Brunk, "The House That Freer Built," *Dichotomy* 3, no. 4 (Spring 1981):5–53. See also Betsy Fahlman, "Wilson Eyre in Detroit: The Charles Lang Freer House," *Winterthur Portfolio* 15, no. 3 (Autumn 1980):257–270.

4 Whistler to Freer, 29 July 1899, Freer Archive.

5 "Facts Concerning the Freer Art Collection," *Washington Star* (11 March 1906), p. 10.

6 Freer to W. S. Marchant & Co., London, 19 December 1901, in Freer letter book, vol. 8, p. 497.

7 The year 1886 is the earliest date of ownership that appears in the collector's own records.

8 Freer acquired works by Francis Seymour Haden, Whistler's brother-in-law; Ignace-Henri Delatre, one of Whistler's printers; Otto Bacher, Alphonse Legros, and Henri Fantin-Latour, Whistler's fellow artists; and even Joseph Pennell, the biographer that Freer would come to detest.

9 The other major collection is at the Hunterian Art Gallery, University of Glasgow. That collection is based upon items in the studio left to Rosalind Birnie Philip, Whistler's sister-in-law and executrix. Miss Birnie Philip was also a good friend to Charles Lang Freer.

10 Freer owned states 1, 8, 9, and 11 of the Bracquemond print. All of his Bracquemond prints were given to the Library of Congress in 1920.

11 In 1901 Freer wrote, "I have practically given up buying prints excepting those by Mr. Whistler." Freer to F. Meder, 11 November 1901, Freer Archive. Surviving vouchers show that Freer made only sporadic purchases of non-Whistler prints after 1892. These purchases ceased by 1907.

12 In 1892 Freer wrote, "In reply to your inquiry . . . I collect the work of Whistler, Gravesand, Legros, Buhot and a few other modern painter-etchers." Freer to Mssrs. Deupez and Garenkopf, 1892, Freer Archive.

13 Other nocturnes with monochromatic, printlike surfaces in the collection include Plates 22, 23, 28, 29, 30, 31, 43, and 47.

14 For example, vouchers reveal that the cost of the "Second Venice Set" in 1886 was $300. In 1892 Freer paid about $5,000 for his first Whistler oil painting, *Variations in Flesh Color and Green: The Balcony.* Vouchers, Freer Archive.

15 Freer to W. K. Bixby, 7 November 1900, Freer Archive. Bixby was a business associate, and Freer's correspondence with Bixby contains some of the collector's most candid comments about his activities. Ernest Fenollosa, the art historian upon whom Freer often relied, phrased the thought more elegantly. "He of all our collectors is the most wisely aware of the dangers and weaknesses involved in uncertain aim and omnivorous purchase." See Ernest Fenollosa, "The Collection of Mr. Charles L. Freer," *Pacific Era* 1, no. 2 (November 1907):15.

16 Various letters reveal Freer's culling and upgrading of the collection. He noted that he was weeding out "some of the Dutch school" and was glad not to have any more Seymour Haden prints. Freer to J. H. Jordan, 2 October 1892. His discrimination is evident in another letter: "I beg to say that the watercolor is not sufficiently interesting to add to my collection." Freer to George E. Hopkins, 4 April 1900. Regarding an early Whistler copy on the market he wrote that it was "undoubtedly by the Master, but I do not feel it important enough to add to my collection. A couple of years ago, I had a long talk with Mr. Whistler about this painting and two or three others which he copied during the first year he was in Paris." Freer to Howard Mansfield, 6 July 1904. It would appear that Whistler advised against acquiring such pieces. All letters Freer Archive.

17 James McNeill Whistler, *Mr. Whistler's "Ten o'Clock"* (London, 1886), p. 7.

18 See Freer's diaries, Freer Archive. Freer usually paid a visit to Bing when he was in Paris.

19 Freer to Rosalind Birnie Philip, 24 January 1905, Freer Archive.

20 Fenollosa, 57.

21 Ernest Fenollosa, "The Symbolism of the Lotos," *Lotos* 9, no. 8 (February 1896):579.

22 Freer to Bradley Redfield, 2 October 1893, Freer Archive.

23 For the Goncourt brothers' holdings, see *Collections des Goncourt, Dessins, aquarelles et pastels du XVIIIe (dont la vente aura lieu Hôtel Drouot . . . les . . . 15 . . . 16 . . . 17 Février 1897)* (Paris, 1897), and *Collection des Goncourt, Arts de l'Extrême-Orient (dont la vente aura lieu Hôtel Drouot . . . les 8, 9, 10, 11, 12, 13 Mars 1897)* (Paris, 1897).

24 Walter Benjamin, *Reflections, Essays, Aphorisms, Autobiographical Writings* (New York, 1978, p. 155. Far from venal, Freer's attitude toward his collection was one of stewardship. He sought and respected the desires of the artists represented in the collection. In a typical letter he told Thomas Wilmer Dewing, "You should . . . consider your own wishes must control your own work in which you and I have joint ownership." Freer to Dewing, 7 June 1892, Freer Archive. The patron's concern included generous exhibition and publication permissions when it was deemed benficial to the artists' careers.

25 Freer to Elbridge Kingsley, 7 December 1892, Freer Archive.

26 Freer to Messrs. Proctor, New York (ca. 1892), Freer Archive. Dewing's wife, Maria Oakey Dewing, also contributed to the decorations in Detroit. She was the author of *Beauty in the Household* (1881) and the sister of Alexander Oakey, who wrote extensively on architecture and interior decoration. See Susan Hobbs, "Thomas Wilmer Dewing, The Early Years," *American Art Journal* 13, no. 2 (Spring 1981):5–35, esp. 29 ff.

27 "Facts Concerning the Freer Art Collection," *Washington Star* (11 March 1906), p. 10.

28 For design and construction of the Freer Gallery of Art, see Keith N. Morgan, "The Patronage Matrix: Charles A. Platt, Architect, Charles L. Freer, Client," *Winterthur Portfolio* 17, no. 2/3 (Summer/Autumn 1982):121–134.

29 Freer called Ernest Fenollosa "the greatest of living critics of Japanese art" and consulted him freely, at the same time proving a supportive friend who assisted Fenollosa in arranging lectures and so forth. At one point Freer wrote, "Thank you in advance for your willingness to inspect and criticise the paintings brought over by Matsuki [a dealer]. . . . I not only desire to know concerning their genuineness, but also your opinion of their worthiness." Freer to Fenollosa, 3 October 1904, Freer Archive. Numerous letters between the historian and the collector reveal Fenollosa's influence. See Seiichi Yamaguchi, "Unpublished Letters of Ernest Francisco Fenollosa to Charles Lang Freer," Supplement II, *Saitama University Record* (Foreign Languages and Literatures) 15 (1981). Fenollosa was one of several specialists consulted by Freer over the years. For a fuller discussion, see Helen Nebeker Tomlinson, "Charles Lang Freer, Pioneer Collector of Oriental Art" (Ph.D. diss., Case Western Reserve University, 1979).

30 Fenollosa, "Collection of . . . Freer," 60. See also Ernest Fenollosa, "The Place in History of Mr. Whistler's Art," *Lotos* Special Issue (December 1903):14–17.

31 Fenollosa, "Collection of . . . Freer," 61.

32 Freer to Richard Canfield, 8 April 1904, Freer Archive.

33 Fenollosa, "Collection of . . . Freer," 60. Elsewhere Fenollosa clearly espoused aestheticism over subject matter: "Painting primarily is the creation of a pure idea in terms of beautiful line, dark and light, and color. The representative function of a painting may or may not exist without modifying it as a secondary consideration." Ernest Fenollosa, "The Nature of Fine Art, I," *Lotos* 9, no. 9 (March 1896):669.

34 See "List 1: Oriental Ceramics, Descriptions of Object, purchase date, voucher number, and cost. Marginal notes on disposition," typed manuscript, Freer Archive, p. 19, entry 93.

35 Freer to D. W. Tryon, 21 March 1898, Freer Archive.

36 See "List 1: Oriental Ceramics," items 1682, 1683, Freer Archive.

37 In 1893 Freer ordered a group of Transcendentalist texts. See Martha T. Hamilton to *The Path*, New York, February 1893, Freer Archive. Freer's interest in Okakura's *Ideals of the East, with a Special Reference to the Art of Japan* (1903) was such that he gave copies to several friends as gifts.

38 Freer to Rufus E. Moore, 18 November 1901, Freer Archive.

39 Freer to Mssrs. Long Sang Ti & Co., New York, 1 February 1904, Freer Archive.

40 "List 1: Oriental Ceramics," entry 2456, Freer Archive.

41 Louise Cort, Freer Gallery of Art. I am grateful to Miss Cort for her many suggestions regarding both current and past opinions about Japanese and Chinese ceramics.

42 Freer to L. G. Warrington, 28 October 1904, Freer Archive.

43 Freer to Dewing, ca. 1893, Freer Archive.

44 Fenollosa, "Collection . . . of Freer," 61.

45 *Ibid.*, 65. The modern spelling for Kano Yeitoku is Kano Eitoku.

46 Ernest Fenollosa, "The Nature of Fine Art, II," *Lotos* 9, no. 10 (April 1896):755.

47 *Ibid.*, 761.

48 Whistler, p. 16.

49 Freer to Platt, 12 July 1917, Freer Archive.

50 Freer to Halsey C. Ives, 26 April 1904, Freer Archive.

51 Freer to D. J. R. Ushikubo, 22 July 1904, Freer Archive.

52 Fenollosa, "The Collection of . . . Freer," 62.

53 *Ibid.*

54 *Ibid.*, 63.

55 *Ibid.*

56 Fenollosa, "Nature of Fine Art, II," 762.

57 Fenollosa, "Nature of Fine Art, I," 669.

58 Tomlinson, pp. 10–49.

59 He wrote W. K. Bixby, "I have had just enough of active idleness to begin to fully appreciate its advantages. The intellectual life is, after all, the only one

worth while, except that of an opposite nature, which makes the real one possible—the means to the end." Freer to Bixby, 2 February 1903, Freer letter book, vol. 10, p. 315. Elsewhere Freer told Bixby, "It behooves us in the future to confer together on things intellectual as we used to on things material." Freer to Bixby, 26 March 1901, Freer Archive.

60 See "Report of the Law Committee of the Board of Regents Appointed to Consider Material Papers Relating to the Freer Gift and Bequest," no. 3022 (Washington, D.C.: Smithsonian Institution, 5 June 1929). The collection of paintings includes a full-length portrait of Roosevelt, painted by Gari Melchers in 1908.

61 The inventory lists are invaluable for understanding the formation of the Freer collection over time. They were prepared by Freer and his helpers. However, they must be used with a certain amount of caution, especially those compiled in 1906. During that year Freer assigned accession numbers to objects that his vouchers reveal were purchased much earlier. For example, the *Bognor Nocturne*, Plate 26, was purchased in 1899 but given a 1906 accession number.

62 Freer to Bixby, 16 March 1901, Freer Archive. Freer also counseled against petty emphasis on personalities. Advising Sheridan Ford, whom Whistler certainly had wronged grievously in the publication of *The Gentle Art of Making Enemies*, Freer wrote, "Why drag in Jimmie's backstair methods? Forget for the moment his habits, and remember his art." Freer to Ford, 13 July 1900, Freer Archive.

63 He wrote Mansfield in 1893, "I wonder when Whistler intends to send my impressions of the Venetian plates. . . . He has several of my orders still unfilled. I presume some day however the things will come." Freer to Mansfield, 3 March 1893, Freer Archive.

64 Whistler to Freer, 29 July 1899, Freer Archive.

65 Whistler to Freer, 4 August 1899, Freer Archive.

66 Freer to Marchant, 11 August 1900, Freer Archive.

67 Following the death of his wife Beatrix, Whistler wrote in gratitude for a rare songbird that Freer had sent the dying woman: "Shall I begin by saying to you, my dear Mr. Freer, that your *Little Blue and Gold Girl* is doing her very best to look lovely for you? . . . though steamer after steamer leave me in apparently ungracious silence, it is that only of the pen. I write to you many letters on your canvas—and one of these days, you will, by degrees, read them all, as you sit before your picture. And in them you will find, I hope, dimly conveyed my warm feelings of affectionate appreciation for the friendship that has shown itself to . . . both of us." Whistler to Freer, 24 March 1897, Freer Archive.

68 On a trip to Paris in 1901, Whistler "took me in tow," Freer told another friend. "The result was I left Paris without accomplishing practically any of the things I had hoped to do. Of course I had a delightful time." Freer to Lendall Pitts, 13 August 1901, Freer Archive.

69 Freer to Caffin, 2 May 1901, Freer Archive, regarding a loan of Whistler paintings to an exhibition.

70 The methods he used in assembling a significant and cohesive collection of American paintings were also applied to the collection of Oriental art.

71 Whistler to Murray Marks, early 1870s, quoted in Andrew Mclaren Young et al., *The Paintings of James McNeill Whistler*, 2 vols. (New Haven and London, 1980), I, cat. no. 100, p. 58. See also Whistler's comments to the dealer D. Croal Thompson at the Goupil Gallery on 5 May 1893, quoted *ibid.*, pp. 58–59.

72 Whistler to Freer, dictated to Miss Birnie Philip, 25 October 1901, Freer Archive. Freer wrote immediately to the owner, Mr. Cowan, saying: "I received

a letter from our mutual friend, Mr. Whistler, telling me that you had decided to sell the Thames in Ice . . . and he recommended that I cable you promptly." Freer to Cowan, 11 November 1901, Freer Archive. He later confided to a friend, "Mr. Whistler advised me at once to buy it, sight unseen. I followed his advice, paying ten thousand dollars for the picture, and am delighted with my purchase." Freer to Bixby, 7 February 1902, Freer Archive. For the watercolor of Mrs. Whibley, see Plate 136.

73 Freer thanked Birnie Philip for her help, 24 January 1905, Freer Archive.

74 Freer to Mansfield, 22 September 1892, Freer Archive.

75 Freer dealt with the Kennedy Gallery in New York at the beginning of his collecting career but eventually broke with them. In London he often dealt with William Marchant, sometimes through the Goupil Gallery, other times independently. He also frequented Obach and Company, London, as well as J. J. Cowan in Edinburgh. Freer seldom went to D. C. Thompson in London or Georges Petit in Paris.

76 The collector recalled at one point, "I had been the guest of Lord Battersea at his country place at Cromer, where I had gone for the purpose of examining . . . *The Gold Screen*. . . . I think this picture one of the most perfect things in composition and colouring in the whole range of Mr. Whistler's art, and in talking with him about it, he compared it with *The Thames in Ice*, and told me that they belonged to the same year. Mr. Whistler had just . . . helped me to purchase *The Thames in Ice* from Mr. Cowan, and was anxious for me to also own *The Gold Screen*, but Lord Battersea wisely declined to part with his treasure." Freer to August F. Jaccaci, 4 April 1904, Freer Archive. In December 1902 Freer had contacted Marchant hoping for news: "Will [Lord Battersea's] absence lead to the disposal of his collections? If it should, do keep me informed concerning the probable fate of the *Gold Screen*." Freer to Marchant, 9 December 1902, Freer Archive.

77 Freer to Marchant, 5 July 1904, Freer Archive.

78 Freer to Marchant, 2 January 1903, Freer Archive.

79 Thompson seems to have retained control of the picture's potential sale as late as January 1919. See Young et al., I, no. 24, p. 8.

80 Freer to Birnie Philip, 8 September 1904, Freer Archive.

81 Freer to Canfield, 28 June 1904, Freer Archive.

82 Freer to Canfield, 2 February 1904, Freer Archive.

83 Freer to Bixby, 10 April 1902, Freer Archive.

84 Freer to Bixby, 5 April 1902, Freer Archive.

85 Freer to Marchant, 20 February 1902 and 8 April 1902, Freer Archive.

86 Freer to Randall Davies, 1913, Curatorial File for the *Harmony in Grey and Green*, The Tate Gallery, London.

87 Freer diary, entry for 16 May 1902, Freer Archive.

88 Freer made similar group purchases of Eastern art collections, including jades, Egyptian glass, and Persian manuscripts.

89 See Young et al., I, cat. no. 74, p. 43, for a discussion.

90 "You will recall that one day you . . . asked me if I would like to see [Way's] Whistlers . . . you promptly said you would arrange the matter, and then I told you that only a few days before, Mr. Whistler had advised me to see Mr. Way personally, and had outlined a plan for me to follow, in order that I might surely secure the work. His advice was

followed to the letter." Freer to Marchant, 2 January 1903, Freer Archive.

91 T. R. Way, Jr., to Freer, 1 July 1902, Freer Archive.

92 The Pennells reported, "For some time the *Venus*, one of the Projects, hung or stood about." Elizabeth Robbins Pennell and Joseph Pennell, *The Life of James McNeill Whistler*, 2 vols. (London and Philadelphia, 1908), II, p. 138.

93 Way quoted in Young et al., I, cat. no. 164, p. 94.

94 Whistler quoted in Young et al., I, cat. no. 169, p. 96. The painting was sold to Arthur H. Studd in 1896 and exhibited in New York in 1902, Boston in 1904, and Paris in 1905. Freer knew the painting well and would have seen it at the exhibitions and during a visit to Studd in 1902.

95 Freer to Way, Jr., 18 June 1904, Freer Archive.

96 Freer to Birnie Philip, 13 August 1904, Freer Archive.

97 Freer to Birnie Philip, 8 September 1904, Freer Archive.

98 For provenance of the painting, see Young et al., I, cat. no. 420, p. 187.

99 In 1897 Whistler testified in support of Joseph Pennell in Pennell's successful libel action against Sickert for a *Saturday Review* article which argued that lithographs drawn on paper and transferred to the stone, a practice used by Whistler among others, misled "the purchaser on the vital point of commercial value." Whistler was rightly incensed at his old pupil. See Young et al., I, p. 163. In the letter offering the portrait sketch to Freer, Sickert acknowledged that Whistler thought him a "traitor" because they had disagreed about Whistler's highhanded action in an unfulfilled commission for a portrait of Lady Eden. Sickert to Freer, 22 January 1905, Freer Archive.

100 Freer to Birnie Philip, 24 January 1905, Freer Archive. The portrait in question is Young et al., I, cat. no. 351, now in a private collection.

101 For Canfield's gambling and Wall Street activities, see Allen Johnson, ed. *Dictionary of American Biography* (New York, 1929), III, pp. 472–473.

102 At one point Freer wrote to Canfield, "For your cooperation and kindness . . . I am greatly obliged. As I dictate these lines, I realize how unusual our cooperation is, and I want you to feel that I appreciate your generous treatment." Freer to Canfield, 8 April 1904, Freer Archive.

103 See Young et al., I, cat. no. 72, for the painting's provenance. According to Young, the date that the painting was sold to Canfield is unclear, but it must have been after the telegram was sent on 3 April 1903. Telegram in Freer Archive.

104 Keeping track of just who had Whistler works for sale was difficult. For example, Freer analyzed the situation regarding oils and drawings from the Forbes estate in a letter to Canfield: "Word comes concerning the Forbes pictures of rather a mixed nature. You will remember, I told you that a part of them were under Marchant's control, and the others in the hands of Obach. The two small marines in the Obach end, I have just been advised are mine. . . . The others in Obach's hands, I have had no word concerning; but those in charge of Marchant, the executors have decided not to sell for the present. . . . I guess the truth of the matter is that the executors are very loath to part with the pictures, thinking they will help to advertise the large lot of pictures at the time of their eventual [estate] sale, but, on the other hand, both Marchant and Obach, who have running accounts with the estate, are anxious to turn whatever they can into ready cash." Freer to Canfield, 1 August 1904, Freer Archive.

105 See Young et al., I, cat. no. 185, p. 108.

106 Speer to Canfield, 7 January 1904, Freer Archive.

107 Freer to Canfield, 2 February 1904, Freer Archive.

108 "Your plans in connection with the Spier picture seem to me admirable, and I fully agree with you that it will be wiser for you to see the picture in Europe. After an examination of the same . . . I am confident that we can between ourselves easily determine the question as to who should be its future caretaker. This being the case, I feel that for the present, we had better not mention the matter at all to Mr. Marchant." Freer to Canfield, 11 February 1904, Freer Archive.

109 Freer to Canfield, 20 February 1904, Freer Archive.

110 Freer to Birnie Philip, 28 January 1904, Freer Archive. The photograph must have been poor indeed. Spier noted that in 1898, even though Whistler had granted his permission, the then-owner of the painting had decided not to have it reproduced in a German periodical because the photograph was terrible. See Freer to Birnie Philip, 7 March 1904, Freer Archive.

111 Cable copy of telegram, Kennedy (Freer's secretary) to Freer, 20 March 1904, Freer Archive. Spier's information came from a letter exchanged by Dr. Linde and Josef Oppenheimer, an artist living in London. See also Spier to Canfield, 26 March 1904, Freer Archive.

112 Duret to Freer, 1 April 1904, Freer Archive.

113 He also commented somewhat sourly: "Duret has been more or less a dealer practically all of his life time. He has had to do with the buying and selling of a number of Whistlers during his career . . . he has also been associated with George Petit (and) Durand-Ruel. . . . It is a strange fact that in every large art market, there are more or less 'hangers-on', who, it seems, prey upon things of beauty. I believe that in this instance, Duret has induced the owner to send the picture to Paris on sale, the understanding being that Duret himself is to have all that he can get above a certain figure." Freer to Canfield, 26 March 1904, Freer Archive.

114 Freer paid 62,500 French francs. After shipping costs Freer had laid out $12,350 for the painting; almost three times what the work brought in London in 1897. Freer's draft to Duret is in the Freer Archive.

115 Duret to Freer, 6 September 1904, Freer Archive. For Whistler-Bernheim relationship, see Young et al., I, cat. no. 312, p. 153.

116 Freer was critical of Duret in a letter to Canfield, 1 August 1904. However, he lent six photographs of works in his collection to Duret for an English translation of the book. Freer to Duret, 1914. He spoke of his delight in the work in Freer to Canfield, 28 June 1904. Perhaps that delight eventually softened him toward Duret. All letters, Freer Archive.

117 Freer conveyed Canfield's cable to Birnie Philip, 29 April 1905, Freer Archive.

118 Freer voucher to William Marchant and Company, for £3,000, about $14,617, was dated 8 May 1905, Freer Archive.

119 Freer to Birnie Philip, 5 January 1908. Freer Archive.

120 Freer noted, "Throughout the entire range of Mr. Whistler's art in painting, etching and lithography, one feels the exercise of spiritual influences similar to those of the masters of Chinese and Japanese art." Freer to John Gellatley, 30 March 1904, Freer Archive.

121 Whistler, Ten o'Clock, p. 29. Fusi-yama refers to Mt. Fuji.

122 Freer to Gellatley, 30 March 1904, Freer Archive.

Notes to Artist and Model

1 At the Louvre, Whistler copied Ingres's Roger délivrant Angélique, as well as Greuze's La Cruche cassée and Boucher's Diane au bain. See Andrew Mclaren Young et al., The Paintings of James McNeill Whistler, 2 vols. (New Haven and London, 1980), I, nos. 11, 14, 20. For information on other copies by Whistler, see ibid., I, nos. 5, 12, 13, 15–19. For an excellent discussion of Whistler's work at West Point, which included copies of nineteenth-century French prints by Daumier, Gavarni, and others, see Nancy Pressley, "Whistler in America: An Album of Early Drawings," Metropolitan Museum Journal 5 (1972):125–154. Whistler had access to great European collections once his family moved to St. Petersburg in 1843. The use of prints and books for copying was part of his training in the United States.

2 J. Pennell and E. Pennell, The Life of James McNeill Whistler, 2 vols. (London, 1908), I, p. 145. His schooling in Paris, while regarded by some as desultory, was by no means atypical. Whistler's reputation as a lazy student began with his expulsion from West Point in 1854 and followed him for the rest of his life. George du Maurier fixed the concept in the Whistler literature when he characterized the artist as an idle bohemian in the unexpurgated magazine version of Trilby. See Harper's New Monthly Magazine 77 (January–August 1894):523–531. Whistler forced the writer to expunge the unflattering portrayal in the book version. Most fellow painters, on the other hand, consistently and carefully distinguish between Whistler the dedicated, conscientious artist and Whistler the social gadfly. See, for example, William Merrit Chase, "The Two Whistlers, Recollections of a Summer with the Great Etcher," The Century 80; no. 2 (June 1910), 218–226; and Kenyon Cox, "Whistler and Absolute Painting," Scribner's Magazine 35 (April 1904), 637–639. It was clearly recognized, at least by other artists, that Whistler's public façade had hurt the general perception of his art. Cox wrote, "There can be little doubt that the just recognition of Whistler as a serious artist was long delayed by the very qualities of the man which kept his name constantly before the public." Cox, p. 637. For Whistler's training, see Young et al., I, pp. lvii–lxii. Essentially, his belief that "the study of the masters could have no other end than to evolve something entirely personal" indicates Whistler's acquiescence to a long-established training system for artists: study, copy, synthesize, finally permit the imagination to soar. Sir Joshua Reynolds cautioned would-be painters against "the imaginary power of native genius, and its sufficiency in great works," in "Discourse Six, Delivered to the Students of the Royal Academy on the Distribution of the Prizes, December 10, 1774." See Discourses on Art (1797 ed.; reprinted New York, 1966), pp. 85–101.

3 Charles Baudelaire, The Painter of Modern Life and Other Essays, trans. Jonathan Mayne (London, 1964), p. xi.

4 Carol Duncan, "The Persistence and Re-emergence of the Rococo in French Romantic Painting" (Ph.D. diss., Columbia University, 1969).

5 Gautier quoted by Hélène Adhemar, Watteau: sa vie—son oeuvre (Paris, 1950), p. 188.

6 See Donald Poesner, "Watteau mélancolique: la formation d'un mythe," Bulletin de la Société de l'Histoire de l'Art Français 1973 (1974):345–361. See also Francis Haskell, "The Sad Clown: Some Notes on a Nineteenth-Century Myth," in Ulrich Finke, French Nineteenth Century Painting and Literature (Manchester University Press, 1972), pp. 2–16.

7 For an extensive treatment of Watteau's impact on nineteenth-century French taste, see Hôtel de la Monnaie, Pèlerinage à Watteau (exh. cat.), 4 vols. (Paris, 1977).

8 See Ronald W. Johnson on the importance of Gautier and Baudelaire for Whistler: "Whistler's Musical Modes: Symbolist Symphonies, Numinous

Nocturnes," Arts 55 (April 1981):174–175. For a fascinating discussion of the effect upon later writers of unclear subject matter in Watteau, see Norman Bryson, "Watteau and Reverie: A Test Case in Combined Analysis," The Eighteenth Century: Theory and Interpretation 22, no. 2 (Spring 1981):97–126. I am grateful to Bruce Robertson for this reference.

9 Journal des Arts (25 May 1855), quoted in Pèlerinage, II, pp. 357–358. For other nineteenth-century artists inspired by Watteau, see "Le XIXe Siècle/Peintures," Pèlerinage, II, pp. 353–384. Watteau imitations included not only paintings, drawings, and prints, but also fans and ceramics decorated with Watteauesque compositions. During the nineteenth century, admired models frequently inspired re-creations at a much larger scale, especially in public architectural projects.

10 Pressley, 139–145. For Robert W. Weir's "Outline of Instruction in Drawing," which was taught to Whistler at West Point, see Irene Weir, Robert W. Weir, Artist (New York, 1947), pp. 66–67. Instruction included drawing on tinted paper, a support that is often seen in Whistler's chalk and pastel drawings, as well as "finished drawings from standard works." The items frequently copied by Weir's students are listed on pp. 117–118.

11 Jean de Jullienne gathered engravings after most of Watteau's oeuvre, publishing Figures de differents caractères, de paysages et d'études in two volumes in 1726 and 1728. The engravings were republished as L'Oeuvre d'Antoine Watteau (Paris, 1734). J. de Crozat published Recueil d'estampes (Paris, 1736), and J. F. Gersaint published a catalogue raisonné in 1744. For other publications of the 1740s and 1750s, see Edgcumbe Staley, Watteau and His School (London, 1902), p. 153.

12 Horace Walpole, Anecdotes of Painting in England, 4 vols. (1762; reprinted New York, 1969), II, pp. 295–296.

13 Additional publications appeared on Watteau from 1815 to 1848—that is, on the eve of Whistler's own advent as an artist. See Staley, p. 153.

14 See ibid., pp. 153–154, for a partial list. For the La Caze collection, see Musée National du Louvre, Département des peintures, des dessins et de la chalcographie, Notice des tableaux Lègues au Musée Impérial du Louvre par M. Louis La Caze (Paris, 1870). La Caze, whose twin interests were art and medicine, died on 28 September 1869. The Watteau paintings that he left to the Louvre were Gilles, L'Indifférent, La Finette, Assemblée dans un parc, L'Escamoteur, Le Jugement de Paris, Le Faux Pas, L'Automne, and Jupiter et Antiopé.

15 See "Petite histoire chronologique des monuments à la gloire de Watteau," in Pèlerinage, I, pp. 225–236. Quotation from "La Statue de Watteau," Revue de la mode (19 October 1884), in Pèlerinage, I, p. 232.

16 Mortimer Menpes, Whistler as I Knew Him (London, 1904), p. xxi.

17 Whistler might have seen Gilles while it was still in the La Caze collection housed in the Rue Cherche-Midi. Whistler might also have seen the painting when it was included in a large exhibition of eighteenth-century art held in Paris in 1860: Catalogue de tableaux et dessins de l'école française principalement du XVIIIe siècle, tirés des collections d'amateurs . . . rédigé par M. Ph. Burty, (Paris, 1860?). For the engraving after the painting, which appeared in the Gazette des Beaux-Arts in 1860, see Anne Coffin Hanson, Manet and the Modern Tradition (New Haven and London, 1977), fig. 16.

18 "Suivant l'usage, un tableau à la porte de chaque jeu sollicitait les spectateurs; la parade achevait de les décider à prendre place." For discussion and supporting material see Émile Dacier and Albert Vauflart, Jean de Julliene et les graveurs de Watteau au XVIIIe siècle, I (Paris, 1929), pp. 68–70.

19 *The White Girl* was exhibited in Berners Street, London, in 1862 after being rejected by the Royal Academy.

20 Théodore Duret commented that the *White Girl* "fut encore refusée par le jury, ennemie alors de toute originalité et ancre dans les vieilles traditions." *Histoire de James McN. Whistler* (Paris, 1904), p. 20. Anchored in tradition or not, the jury missed Whistler's historicism completely.

21 Quoted in Young *et al.*, I, no. 38, p. 17. See Johnson, "Whistler's Musical Modes," for Whistler's choices of a red-haired model and the use of white lead paint, as related to the English Pre-Raphaelites.

22 Quoted in Young *et al.*, I, no. 38, pp. 17–20. The realist Courbet objected to the *White Girl*'s spiritual quality, an aspect of the painting that departed from Courbet's canons of realism.

23 Staley, pp. 84, 80.

24 Claude Phillips, *Antoine Watteau* (London, 1895), pp. 69–70. Monochromatic palettes dominated many of Whistler's portraits as well as his *Nocturnes*.

25 Paul Mantz, "Salon de 1863," *Gazette des Beaux-Arts* 15 (1863):60–61. Quoted in Gordon Fleming, *The Young Whistler, 1834–66* (London, 1978).

26 See note 17 for a catalogue citation.

27 While Oudry was primarily noted as an *animalier*, he had other interests more in keeping with those of Watteau and Whistler. For example, he designed tapestries for the Beauvais works.

28 "Les fonds blancs réussissent très-bien à M. Oudry. Il y en a eu un cette année d'un genre toute nouveau, et qui sert à nous instruire, que les objets les plus semblables en apparence, ne laissent pas que de différer par des nuances qui les caractérisent.... Sans doute qu'il faut beaucoup d'art pour tout détacher avec la même couleur. Ces tableaux font rarement de grands effects, mais ils laissent toujours connaître les grands talens des artistes." Mssr. Estève, "Letter . . . sur . . . le grand Salon," 25 August 1753, quoted in Hal N. Opperman, "*Jean-Baptiste Oudry*" (Ph.D. diss., University of Chicago, 1972; New York: Garland, 1977), I, p. 208. Opperman includes a number of critical reactions to the painting, all in this vein.

29 See Poesner, "Watteau Mélancolique," and Haskell, "Sad Clown." During the eighteenth century Pierrot costumes were considered gay and amusing. For example, Oudry, painter of the *White Duck*, was fond of dressing up in a Pierrot costume and playing the guitar for relaxation. He painted two works *à la Watteau*, with Pierrot singing and dancing. See Opperman, *Jean-Baptiste Oudry, 1686–1755*, (exh. cat.) (Fort Worth: Kimball Art Museum, 1983).

30 Goncourts in Adhemar, p. 183. "Pierrot un moment a oublié la salle; en pleine foule, il rêve (combien de choses! la vie dans un eclair)—il rêve, il est comme abîmé . . . Salut peuple, je vais mourir." Michelet, *ibid.*, p. 187.

31 "Des qualités pittoresques supérieures, une imagination amoureuse de rêve et de poésie." Ernest Chesneau, *L'Art et les artistes modernes* (Paris, 1864), quoted in Duret, p. 22. Chesneau's comments first appeared in *Le Constitutionel*, 19 May and 5 June 1863.

32 "C'est le portrait d'une spirite, d'un médium." Quoted in Duret, p. 22. Desnoyers's remarks originally appeared in a brochure, *Salon des Refusés: La Peinture en 1863* (Paris, 1863).

33 Goncourt brothers, *L'Art au XVIIIe siècle* (1860), quoted in Adhemar, p. 185.

34 See Nancy Olson, *Gavarni: The Carnival Lithographs* (exh. cat.) (New Haven, 1979). I am immensely grateful to Miss Olson for her generosity in sharing insights about this material as well as for her sensitive editing of my work.

35 Olson, no. 48. *Cannotage* was the sport of rowing on the river. The *cannotier*'s (sailor's) costume was popular for fancy dress balls. Clandestine assignations could result in duels. See Haskell, "Sad Clown," pp. 2–4. Duels were painted by several artists.

36 Jules-Antoine Castagnary, *Salons (1857–1879)*, 2 vols. (Paris, 1892), I, pp. 179–180. "Un tour de force de votre métier de peintre, consistant à enlever des blancs sur blancs? Permettez-moi de ne pas le croire. Laissez-moi voir dans votre oeuvre quelque chose de plus élève, *le lendemain de l'épousée*, cette minute troublante où la jeune femme s'interroge et s'étonne de ne plus reconnaître en elle sa virginité de la veille . . . [il y a] les rideaux blancs d'une alcove fermée, derrière lesquels *l'autre* sommeille encore sans doute. . . . Vous rappelez-vous *la Cruche cassée* ou la *Jeune fille pleurant son oiseau mort*, sujets folâtres que Greuze a tant aimés. . . . L'interpretation de M. Whistler est plus grave, plus sévère, plus anglaise. Sa *Dame blanche* est mariée, evidemment: la nuite qu'elle a passée est régulière, légitime, approuvée de l'Église et du monde . . . [mais] interrogez la fleur effeuillée qu'elle tient à là main: . . . c'est la continuation de l'allégorie commencée par la cruche casée et le petit oiseau mort."

37 The present location of Whistler's copy is not known. See Young *et al.*, I, no. 14, p. 5.

38 This is the gist of the rhyme that accompanies Watteau's *Les Habits sont Italiens*. Dacier and Vauflart, II, pp. 24 and 25. See also *ibid.*, IV, pp. 97, "Ce que t'offre ici le pinceau Quoique pris de la Comédie, n'est que trop souvent le tableau de ce qui se passe en la vie."

39 *Ibid.*, IV, pp. 1, 82.

40 See J. Armelhault and E. Bocher, *L'Oeuvre de Gavarni: Lithographes originales et essais d'eau-forte et de procédés nouveaux* (Paris, 1873), nos. 1766–1771.

41 Thelma Niklaus, *Harlequin Phoenix* (London, 1956), p. 42.

42 Niklaus also points out that Caruso sang in Leoncavallo's short opera *I Pagliacci*, helping to establish Pierrot-as-dreamer. The clown's connections with love perhaps reached their nadir late in the century in a rowdy play called *Pierrot pornographe*. This play was presented at the Théâtre d'Ombres, a shadow-puppet theater. See Paul Jeanne, *Les Théâtres d'Ombres à Montmartre de 1887 à 1923: Chat Noir, Auat'z'arts, Lune Réussi* (Paris, 1937), p. 44.

43 Niklaus, p. 42.

44 Kate Greenaway, *The Language of Flowers* (1884; reprinted New York, 1978). White lily, p. 27; white lilac, p. 27; pansy, p. 32. Meaning in the etiquette of flowers is not precise. However, a second source, roughly contemporary with the first, recorded similar symbolism: lilacs: first love; white lily: majesty and purity. See "Flora's Wreath," *Ballou's Pictorial and Drawing-Room Companion* 8 (13 January 1855):27, illustrated p. 32.

45 For the wolf, see Young *et al.*, I, no. 38, pp. 17–20. On the bear, see Johnson, 166.

46 Armelhault and Bocher, no. 1706, "Ils . . . ont sur le visage des loups à nez proéminents." For bear costumes, see nos. 257, 407, and 2017. Gavarni's sexually charged images were not confined to wolves and bears. In another print, a young girl refuses to become an older man's mistress:

Man: Réfléchissez, mon chère ange . . . une conchette de noyer, toute neuve! et la commode . . . et quatre belles petites chaises . . . avec les rideaux jaunes et la flèche . . . c'est un avenir, ça!

Girl: Je ne dis pas! Monsieur Coquardeau; mais j'aime mieux Henri sans rien.

47 Francis Wey, *A Frenchman among the Victorians*, trans. Valerie Pirie (1858; New Haven, 1936), p. 174.

48 Guy de Tervarent, *Attributs et symboles dans l'art profane, 1450–1600* (Geneva, 1958), pp. 291–292. See also Angelo de Gubernatis, *Zoological Mythology* (London, 1872), II, p. 112. In one saint's legend, that of Saint Maximin, a bear is transformed into an ass. Perhaps Whistler has done the opposite in *The White Girl*. See *ibid.*, II, p. 119. According to Gubernatis, during the Middle Ages "it was customary to lead a bear round and make him play indecent games." See *ibid.*, II, p. 117. For those who insist the rug is a wolfskin, symbolism can again be marshaled. The wolf is generally a malignant symbol. A wolfskin could refer to the French *loup garou*, a diabolical form to which Whistler might appropriately have added the demonic white wolf of Russian legend, known to him from his childhood stay in Russia. On the other hand, the wolf could simply refer to Jo's position as Whistler's mistress. The she-wolf who had nourished Romulus and Remus was associated with a strumpet, and Jo's extramarital relationship with Whistler was certainly a nurturing one. "The nurse of the Latin twins was a strumpet, because lupoe or lupanoe foeminoe were names given to such women, whence also the name of lupanaria given to the houses to which they resorted." See *ibid.*, II, pp. 144–145. There are a few legends where wolves take a heroic or sympathetic form. For example, a hungry wolf shows compassion by sparing a maiden traveling to fulfil a promise. Whistler's depiction of a skin could be significant, given his relationship with Jo. In several stories a woman uses a wolfskin as a disguise in order to feed a child or a hero without her husband's knowledge. A wolfskin was supposed to have healing or protective powers as well. *Ibid.*, II, pp. 146–147.

49 See J. Lafayette, *The Duchess of York (H.M. Queen Mary)*, 1894, photograph, illustrated in Helmut Gernsheim, *Masterpieces of Victorian Photography* (London, 1951), no. 66.

50 Kenyon Cox, "The Art of Whistler," *Architectural Record* (May 1904):471.

51 Today, the word *decorative* is a loaded term. I take it to mean an emphasis upon aesthetic surface qualities—texture, color, shape—apart from any intended meaning conveyed by the picture's subject matter. In Whistler's case, the one did not obviate the other, although later critics chose to focus upon the aesthetic side of his work. This is further discussed in "Artist and Site."

52 See Ron Johnson, "Whistler's Musical Modes," on the cult of beauty for own sake. For a discussion of a particular example, see my Plate 3.

53 *The Saturday Review* (26 March 1892), p. 357.

54 For Watteau's association with Audran and the earlier impact of the *ornamentiste* Gillot, see Phillips, pp. 13–16.

55 See Helena Hayward, ed., *World Furniture* (Seacaucus, N.J., 1965), sections VI, VII.

56 Goncourt brothers, quoted in Adhemar, p. 183.

57 The drawing served as a study for one of the figures in *Symphony in Blue and Pink*.

58 Phillips, p. 21. In the *Manga*, it is usually male figures that carry large umbrellas.

59 Quote from "La Statue de Watteau," *Revue de la Mode* (19 October 1884), in *Pèlerinage*, I, p. 232. For examples of Watteau-inspired fashion items, see "Le XIXe Siècle/Modes," *Pèlerinage*, II, pp. 396–404.

60 Quoted in Christine Garnier, "La Mode," in "Le XIXe Siècle/Modes," *Pèlerinage*, I, p. 171, no. 460. A Watteau dress similar in cut to Mrs. Leyland's is illustrated.

61 Staley, p. 74. For the portrait of Mrs. Frances Leyland, see Young *et al.*, I, no. 106, pp. 65–66.

62 The painting was engraved in 1732, and it seems to have been in France until 1866, when it entered a Prussian collection. John Sunderland and Ettore Camesasca, *The Complete Paintings of Watteau* (New York, 1968), p. 126–127, cat, no. 212.

63 Denys Sutton, *Antoine Watteau: Les Charmes de la Vie. The Music Party in the Wallace Collection* (London, n.d.), p. 8.

64 The drawing was part of a collection formed by Richard Bull during the eighteenth century, ostensibly for his friend Horace Walpole to use in illustrating *Anecdotes on Painting*. See *Watteau et sa génération*, (exh. cat., Galerie Cailleux) (Paris, 1968), no. 42. The Watteau drawing was sold by Sotheby's in London on 23 May 1881, cat. no. 14. It was bought by Thibaudeau and then entered the collection of J. P. Heseltine. The drawing is currently in the collection of F. Lugt, Institut Néerlandais, Paris. On the Whistler-Heseltine relationship, see Pennell, 1908, I, p. 245.

65 Beatrix's head is in profile, while Watteau's model looks slightly downward. Whistler added a pillow between hand and head while turning the hand itself in another direction.

66 Young *et al.*, I, no. 97, pp. 56–57. For an etching of Fosco, see Edward G. Kennedy, *The Etched Work of Whistler* (New York, 1910), no. 99.

67 See Freer drawing, Plate 235. For discussion, see Deborah Gribbon, "Whistler's Sketch of an Unfinished Symphony," in *Fenway Court* (Boston, 1980), pp. 26–33. See also Young *et al.*, I, no. 87–89, pp. 49–53.

68 The painting's whereabouts during the nineteenth century are unclear. I am able to propose the comparison on visual evidence only at this time. See Posner, "Watteau's Reclining Nude and the Remedy Theme," *Art Bulletin* 54 (December 1972):385–389, for a discussion of Watteau's painting and the drawing that preceded it.

69 The composition's obvious source is Botticelli's *Birth of Venus*.

70 Whistler to Freer, 29 July 1899, Freer Archives.

71 Phillips, p. 14.

72 Sutton, *Nocturne: The Art of James McNeill Whistler* (Philadelphia and New York, 1964).

73 Donald Posner, *Watteau—"A Lady at Her Toilet"* (London, 1973), p. 62.

74 Carol Duncan, "Happy Mothers and Other New Ideas in French Art," *Art Bulletin* 55 (December 1973):570–577. I am most grateful to Susan Zilber for this and other helpful bibliographical suggestions.

75 This example, by Watteau, also circulated as a print engraved by Boucher.

76 For example, Watteau's *Cupid Disarmed by Venus*, now at the Musée Condé. This image circulated as an engraving.

77 Diane Pilgrim, "The Revival of Pastels in Nineteenth-Century America: Society of Painters in Pastel," *American Art Journal* 10, no. 2 (November 1978):43 ff.

78 In catalogues of eighteenth-century works on paper, they are classified as drawings. In Watteau's day, the red, black, and white chalks were natural. By the time Whistler was active, the supply was exhausted and most artists used fabricated chalks, which are also called pastels. For a brief summary of Whistler's pastel technique and its relation to French art, see Betsy Fryberger, *Whistler: Themes and Variations* (exh. cat.) (Stanford, 1978), p. 39. For a detailed discussion, see Robert Getscher, "Whistler and Venice" (Ph.D. diss., University of Michigan, 1970), 101–140.

79 Charles Baudelaire, *The Painter of Modern Life and Other Essays*, trans. Jonathan Mayne (London, 1964), p. xvii.

80 Watteau's tiny format also could have stimulated Whistler to create his many oil paintings on little canvases and boards about the size of a cigar-box top.

81 Mantz is quoted in Staley, p. 81.

82 Quoted by Léonce Bénédite in "Artistes contemporains: Whistler," *Gazette des Beaux-Arts* 34 (1905):232–234, the letter was written in 1867. There is a copy in the Library of Congress, Pennell collection.

83 Pennell, 1908, I, p. 146.

84 Robin Spencer, *The Aesthetic Movement* (London, 1972), p. 31.

85 "Ces croquis si brefs, malgré leur spontanéité, révèlent l'appréciation des lignes qui forment ou soutiennent le mystère de l'équilibre." The sketches are now at the Musée Ingres in Montauban, France. See Raoul Brie, 1972, quoted in *Pèlerinage*, II, p. 363.

86 Albert Moore's biographer aptly remarked in 1893 that "the unsurpassable and unsurpassable sculptures from the Parthenon" were "mere decorations" for a public building. The sculptural linearity of the marbles served as a library of established solutions to the complex problem of rendering three-dimensional volumes that would be seen from a great distance as nearly two-dimensional planes. The shadows of their sculptured surfaces were reduced to black lines. Whistler's problem was to create the illusion of three dimensions on a two-dimensional surface.

87 Once again, a description of Watteau seems tailored for Whistler: "The incomparably suggestive pencil of Watteau expresses a temperament more than normally tender, sensitive, and febrile. . . . What interests Watteau the draughtsman is swiftness, momentariness of movement and attitude, the strong physical sense of life, the definition of what is essential to the type or defined group of individuals, rather than the expression of physical or mental individuality in the narrower sense. He loves to note down in infinite variety of motive, and of bodily, as distinguished from physiognomic expression, woman rather than a particular woman." Phillips, pp. 32–33. The models are Lily Pettigrew and her baby, but it is the red hair that counts in Whistler's rendition.

88 According to mythology, Phryne was the model for Venus, which makes her a logical subject in Whistler's continuing series of Venus figures. Series of similar themes created by other artists at this time range from Cassatt's images of women and children to Degas's monotypes that depict the inmates of Parisian brothels.

89 Whistler to Fantin, from typed manuscript, dated "about August 31, 1867," Freer Archive.

90 Goncourt brothers, quoted in Cormack, p. 6.

Notes to Artist and Architect

1. See Gillian Naylor, *The Arts and Crafts Movement: A Study of Its Sources, Ideals and Influence on Design Theory* (Cambridge, Mass., 1971), pp. 18–20.

2. Andrew Saint, *Richard Norman Shaw* (New Haven and London, 1976), p. 152.

3. The most thoughtful of many reviews to appear following an official press visit on 9 February 1877 was E. W. Godwin's "Notes on Mr. Whistler's Peacock Room," *Architect* (24 February 1877), pp. 118–119. Most of the reviews are frivolous, concerned only with the room as an "event" in fashionable London society. A reporter for the *Examiner* remarked, "Commonplace dining would seem out of place here, where opium should be the most substantial food" (17 February 1877, p. 216).

4. There is no anger evident in the letter to Whistler. See Thomas Jeckyll to Whistler, 11 November 1876, University of Glasgow Library, 1969-AM-M/53.

5. Jeckyll died in Norwich at age fifty-four. See "Our Office Table," *Building News* 41 (16 September 1881):378. The obituary makes no mention of the Peacock Room. See also "Notes on Current Events," *British Architect* 16 (23 September 1881):471–472. This obituary doesn't even mention an association between Jeckyll and Whistler, even though a large puff piece on Whistler appeared on the same page! For a biographical sketch of Jeckyll's career, see Mark Girouard, "Ken Hill, Norfolk," in *The Victorian Country House*, rev. enl. ed. (New Haven and London, 1979), pp. 366–374. I am indebted to Lynn Bell for her help in locating material on Jeckyll.

6. Elizabeth Robins Pennell and Joseph Pennell, *The Life of Whistler*, 2 vols. (London and Philadelphia, 1908), I, p. 207. I wonder whether the source for this probably garbled tale may be a surviving letter from Leyland to Whistler, in which the patron suggested that they leave the gilding on the stairs until they were able to see how it would wear. See Frederick Richards Leyland to Whistler, 17 August 1876, University of Glasgow Library, BP 23/37, L105. The Pennells were aware that there was gilding on the Leyland staircase.

7. On 2 September 1876, the *Academy* took its first notice of the decorations at Prince's Gate (p. 276), noting that the leather had been "modified and enriched by the introduction of a fair primrose tint in the flowers patterned upon the deep ground of gold." Whistler sent the notice to Leyland with a letter that "there will be a little letter of mine in next week that Tommy may have his full share of the praise as is right." Whistler's generous comments about Jeckyll appeared in "Notes and News," *Academy* 10 (9 September 1876).

8. *Builder* 35 (24 February 1877):182.

9. Freer arrived at Obach's, a London dealer, on 15 May 1904, and he purchased the entire Peacock Room the next day, although earlier correspondence indicates an initial reluctance to purchase more than the shutters and the south-wall panel. See Susan Hobbs, *The Whistler Peacock Room* (Washington, 1980), p. 18.

10. Whistler to Leyland, July 1877, University of Glasgow Library, BP II 23/34, Letter 133.

11. Charles Lockwood reviewing Mary Haverstock's *An American Bestiary* (1979) in "Books on America's Artistic Tradition," *Architectural Digest* 37, no. 4 (May 1980):262. The popular and impossible supposition that Leyland was absent from his house in Prince's Gate during the many months that the decoration was going on is based on misinterpretation of the patron's letter of August 1876: "I don't think I shall be in town again for some time—probably not before you start for Venice." Leyland to Whistler, University of Glasgow Library, L105. At that point Whistler was slated to leave for Venice in just a few weeks. However, he stayed through the winter and spring to work on the room. The artist certainly did not have to sneak into Prince's Gate to complete the room. Leyland was anxious to have it finished and did not forbid Whistler to enter the house until July 1877.

12. Found in Whistler's studio after his death, the cartoon eventually went to the Hunterian Art Gallery as part of the Birnie Philip Bequest.

13. Diary of Alan Cole, 4 December 1876, transcript notes made by Rosalind Birnie Philip; University of Glasgow Library, no. LB6. There is another series of notes from the diary in the Library of Congress, Pennell collection. The texts correspond, although not exactly. I do not know the whereabouts of the actual diary.

14. However, the collector generously lent paintings to various exhibitions. See M. Susan Duval's unpublished paper, "A Reconstruction of F. R. Leyland's Collection: An Aspect of Northern British Patronage," Courtauld Institute, 17 May 1982. I am most grateful for the opportunity to read this helpful research.

15. Whistler's visitors included the Princess Louise and the Marquis of Westminister. Whistler told his mother that such visitors were not really good judges of the decorations, but that the publicity was helpful. Whistler to Anna McNeill Whistler, September 1876, University of Glasgow Library, BP II, Res 18d/22–5, LB4.

16. In its press notice, the *Morning Post* called the patron "Naylor Leyland" on 8 December 1876.

17. The importance of the Leyland family's privacy, and Whistler's awareness of the need for it, is demonstrated in an undated letter (probably fall 1876), from the artist to Mrs. Lyulph Stanley: "My sister Mrs. Haden tells me that you would care to see the Peacock Room." Whistler gave her a date, "tomorrow at about 6.00 p.m." He continued, "The family returns on Tuesday which is my apology for this hurried invitation and during the past week they were daily expected, so that no time could be fixed." University of Glasgow Library, J36.

18. See Cole diary, 5 March 1877, "Whistler trying to finish peacocks on shutters."

19. While shillings are usually reported, Theodore Child called them shekels in "A Pre-Raphaelite Mansion," *Harper's New Monthly Magazine* (December 1890), p. 83.

20. The first time I found this passage was in the 1890 Child article. It was repeated in the sales catalogue, *The Mansion Formerly the Residence of the Late F. R. Leyland, Esq.* (London: Osborne and Mercer, 17 June 1892).

21. Whistler's comment is preserved on the back of a letter from Frederick Richards Leyland to the artist, ca. 22 July 1877. See University of Glasgow Library, BP II, 23/29, L125.

22. Arthur Symons, a contemporary of Whistler, quoted in Pennell and Pennell I, p. 256.

23. See Andrew McLaren Young *et al.*, *The Paintings of James McNeill Whistler*, 2 vols. (New Haven and London, 1980), I, nos. 208–210, pp. 120–122.

24. The first documented references to the work are from 1879. See *ibid.*, I, no. 208, pp. 120–121.

25. "I imagine it was meant to complete the 'Peacock Room,' as a panel over the mantelpiece, after differences between painter and patron had brought the work to an untimely end, but I never could get from Whistler (who was delighted to find it in my keeping) what was its genesis—except that when his effects at the 'White House' were sold, he knew that its being knocked down to the highest bidder would annoy Leyland intensely." George Jacomb-Hood, *With Brush and Pencil* (London, 1925), p. 47.

26. Author's memo of 5 October 1981, and a report by John Winter, Freer Technical Lab, 6 May 1982, Freer Curatorial File. I am extremely grateful to Dr. Winter for his lengthy analysis of the paint layers used in the Peacock Room. I presented my conclusions based on his technical analysis at the College Art Association's annual meeting in February 1983 as "Unrequited Patronage: Technical Evidence in the Whistler-Leyland Quarrel, 1877" for the session entitled "The Art Historian and the Laboratory." I am grateful to Gridley McKim Smith and Elizabeth Packard for their helpful suggestions in dealing with the material.

27. Since the bole is nearly the color of gold, it may have made the peacocks seem complete before metallic paint had actually been added, confusing visitors to the dimly lit room during Whistler's press viewing on 9 February 1877. The absence of scattered feathers would not mar the composition as a whole.

28. See University of Glasgow Library, letters BP II 23/13 L106, BP II 23/14 L107, BP II 23/15 L108, BP II 23/16 L109, and BP II 23/19 L114. In L109, Whistler to Leyland, it was agreed that each party would pay 1,000 guineas toward the decorations. Whistler signed this letter "Your promising pupil in business wisdom."

29. See Leyland to Whistler, 30 October 1876, University of Glasgow Library, BP II 23/17 L110.

30. See Whistler to Leyland, BP II 23/16, L109, dated ca. 24–30 October 1876, University of Glasgow Library. Earlier, Whistler must have demanded 2,000 guineas. Thus began the overinterpretation that Leyland refused to pay Whistler's fee. In a letter dated 21 October 1876, Leyland acknowledged a telegram from Whistler but said that he was not prepared to pay the 2,000 pounds mentioned by Whistler, who was trying to get more money for the three sets of shutters which Leyland had not commissioned. The constant vacillation between figures in pounds and guineas during October and November of 1876 in the Whistler-Leyland correspondence during October and November of 1876 suggests to me that tradesmen's pounds versus gentlemen's guineas was *not* the real issue at the time Whistler and Leyland were disputing about the fee. However, as noted above, Whistler *did* make it an issue in the spring of 1877.

31. Whistler to Leyland, Tuesday, 31 October 1876, University of Glasgow Library, BP II 23/18, L111. This letter probably furthered the idea that Leyland refused to pay Whistler's fee.

32. Leyland to Whistler, 1 November 1876, University of Glasgow Library, L114.

33. Whistler to Leyland, Friday, October (1876), BP II 23/20, L112. It was in this letter that Whistler offered to "share" the cost of the decorations, charging Leyland only 1,000 guineas.

34. We can also infer that Whistler finished the docile peacock before the angry one.

35. Reprinted as "Noblesse Oblige" in James McNeill Whistler, *The Gentle Art of Making Enemies* (London, 1890), pp. 174–175.

36. The single really good article in print was written by Peter Ferriday. See "Peacock Room," *Architectural Review* 125 (June 1959):407–414. The London dealer Jeremy Cooper has compiled a helpful manuscript on the room, which he very kindly shared with me. Finally, M. Susan Duval's unpublished manuscript, cited in footnote 14 above, is most helpful for understanding Leyland's role in the commission.

37. Godwin is pointed on the room's eclectic nature. See Godwin, p. 118.

38. Saint, p. 152. I am extremely grateful to Mr. Saint for a long and detailed letter which has helped me enormously in my efforts to keep straight the chronology of renovations at 49 Prince's Gate.

39. See *English Cabinets* (London: Victoria and Albert Museum, 1972), fig. 20.

40. For an explanation of the process, see A. S. Godeau, "Louis-Amédée Mante: Inventor of Color Photography?" *Portfolio* 3, no. 1 (January–February 1981):40–45.

41. This comment was probably made by Whistler after the controversy died down, perhaps during one of his interviews with the Pennells. It was not published until Pennell 1908, I, p. 204.
The thickness of the paint layers in conjunction with the artist's use of metal leaf has prevented analysis by infrared equipment to date. I am indebted to Molly Faries of Indiana University for her generous aid in attempting to check up on this bit of Whistler mythology.

42. See "The Music Room," in *The Royal Pavilion at Brighton* (guidebook) (Brighton: Royal Pavilion, Museums and Art Gallery, n.d.), for additional illustrations. A design for the room is now in the collection of the Cooper-Hewitt Museum in New York.

43. Quoted in Oliver Impey, *Chinoiserie: The Impact of Oriental Styles in Western Art and Decoration* (New York, 1977).

44. Child, p. 82.

45. For their holdings, see sales catalogues. Whistler's collection: Sotheby, Wilkinson and Hodge, *Catalogue of the Decorative Porcelains, Cabinets, Paintings and other works of art of J. A. McN. Whistler, removed from the White House, Fulham, including numerous pieces of Blue and white china . . . (etc) . . . (London, 12–13 February 1880)*. Leyland's collection: Christie Manson and Woods, *The valuable and extensive collection of old Nankin porcelain, old Chinese enamelled porcelain and cloisonné enamels, decorative objects, furniture and tapestry, the property of Frederick Richards Leyland, Esq. Deceased* (London, 26–27 May 1892).

46. I am grateful to Susan Casteras for sharing this image with me.

47. C. G. Williamson, *Murray Marks and His Friends* (London and New York, 1919) pp. 31–50.

48. Saint, p. 152.

49. Williamson, p. 94. There was nothing simple about the elaborately painted and gilded leather in its original state. Emphasis mine.

50. *Ibid.*, p. 95.

51. See the Leyland sales catalogue, cited in footnote 45, above.

52. Several of these photographs, made by Bedford Lamere, are now in the collection of the National Monuments Record, London. See Figures 127 and 174.

53. See *The Peacock Room, painted for Mr. F. R. Leyland by James McNeill Whistler, Removed in its entirety from the late owner's residence and exhibited at Messrs. Obach's Galleries at 168 New Bond Street, London, W.* (sales cat.) (London, June 1904), Freer Archive. The catalogue includes the following notice: "Messrs. Obach & Company are indebted to A. T. Hollingsworth, Esq., for the loan of a considerable portion of the Nankin Porcelain shown in the Peacock Room."

54. Freer to Birnie Philip, 22 July 1918, Freer Archive.

55. Katherine M. Ball, "The Peacock," in *Decorative Motifs of Oriental Art* (London and New York, 1927), pp. 219–224.

56. Elizabeth Aslin, "Red Brick and Sunflowers," in *The Aesthetic Movement: Prelude to Art Nouveau* (New York, 1981), pp. 36–51.

57. For examples in pressed brick, see *ibid.* pp. 53–61.

58. See letter, Whistler to Thomas Jeckyll's brother, University of Glasgow Library, BP II 23/62 J28.

59. Lewis Day, "A Kensington Interior," *Art Journal* (London) (May 1893):138–144. The quote appears on p. 144.

60. *Ibid.*

61. See Girouard, p. 369. The overmantle was made in 1872.

62. Day, p. 144.

63. This piece is now in the collection of the Cecil Higgins Art Gallery, Bedford, England.

64. See Plate 75 for discussion.

65. "Jeckyll writes to know what colours to do the wall, doors and windows in the dining room. . . . I wish you would give him your ideas." Leyland to Whistler, 26 April 1876, University of Glasgow Library, BP II, 123/35 L103.

66. I had the *Princesse* taken down in 1982, but the leather was gone. Similar "cordova" leather with painting and gilding covers a walnut chair by Luigi Frullini. The chair is roughly contemporary with the Peacock Room, as it came from Chateau sur Mer in Newport, Rhode Island. The chair is now in the collection of the Philadelphia Museum of Art, no. 69-198-2.

67. Pennell, 1908, I, p. 204.

68. Whistler to Leyland (n.d., Fall 1876), Box 6B, Pennell collection, Library of Congress.

69. Pennell, 1908, I, p. 204.

70. Whistler wrote this small broadside, printed by Thomas Way in 1877, and distributed it to publicize the decorations at 49 Prince's Gate. The document is ephemeral and hard to find; copies exist at the Rare Book Room of the Library of Congress, and in the University of Glasgow Library, special collections department. I include the entire brief text: "*Harmony in Blue and Gold. The Peacock Room.* The Peacock is taken as a means of carrying out this arrangement. A pattern, invented from the Eye of the Peacock, is seen in the ceiling spreading from the lamps. Between them is a pattern devised from the breast feathers. These two patterns are repeated throughout the room. In the cove, the Eye will be seen running along beneath the small breast or throat feathers. On the lowest shelf the Eye is again seen, and on the shelf above—these patterns are combined: the Eye, the Breast-feathers, and the Throat. Beginning again from the blue floor, on the dado is the breast-work, *Blue on Gold*, while above, on the Blue wall, the pattern is reversed, *Gold on Blue*. Above the breast-work on the dado the Eye is again found, also reversed, that is *Gold On Blue*, as hitherto *Blue on Gold*. The arrangement is completed by the Blue Peacocks on the Gold shutters, and finally the gold Peacocks on the Blue wall."

71. The back of the screen has been restored since this photograph was made. The Japanese painting, by Nampo Jhoshi, was made in 1867 for export to the West, where it was intended to be mounted as a screen.

72. Godwin, p. 118.

73. Curatorial file, *Butterfly Cabinet*, Hunterian Art Gallery, University of Glasgow.

74. George Ashdown Audsley and James Lord Bowes, *The Keramic Art of Japan* (London, 1875), pp. 184–185.

75. E. R. Pennell, "Whistler as a Decorator," in *The Whistler Journal* (Philadelphia, 1921), pp. 299–306.

76. Whistler to Jeckyll's brother, University of Glasgow Library, BP II 23/62 J28.

77. Godwin, p. 118.

78. Lady Archibald Campbell, *Rainbow Music; or the Philosphy of Harmony in Colour-Grouping* (London, 1886), pp. 12–15.

79. P. G. Hamerton in the *Saturday Review* (1 June 1867), reprinted as "Critic's Analysis," in Whistler, *The Gentle Art of Making Enemies*, p. 44.

80. Whistler's response, dated "Chelsea, June, 1867," appeared as "The Critic's Mind Considered," in *The Gentle Art of Making Enemies*, p. 45.

Notes to Artist and Site

1 Editing a group of essays by modern artists, Robert Herbert noted the "coined words and assertive, energetic mood" in Gleize's *Cubism*. One might draw a parallel with the cubists' new ways of inflecting the vocabulary of painted forms. Herbert also pointed out the "clipped and precise language that so beautifully suited the machine esthetic of Purism" in the writings of Ozenfant and Le Corbusier. See Robert L. Herbert, ed., *Modern Artists on Art: Ten Unabridged Essays* (Englewood Cliffs, N.J., 1964), pp. 2, 59. Likewise, Hubert Damisch has written about the organization of Viollet-le-Duc's treatise *Dictionnaire de l'architecture*, observing that the structure of the book itself reflects the structuralist interpretation that the architect Viollet applied to the architecture he was studying, restoring, and often actually recreating. See *L'Architecture raisonnée, extraits du Dictionnaire de l'architecture française*, réunis et présentés par H. Damish (Paris, 1964). Similar occurrences can be found in contemporary art. For example, Peter Eisenman's obscure language is entirely similar to his convoluted drawings. See Rainer F. Crone *et al.*, *Numerals: 1924–1977* (exh. cat.) (New Haven: Yale University Press, 1978). It will soon become clear to my readers that I am deeply indebted to Professor Herbert for the methodology upon which this chapter rests.

2 Charles Baudelaire, "The Painter of Modern Life," in *The Painter of Modern Life and Other Essays*, trans. Jonathan Mayne (London, 1964), p. 36.

3 James McNeill Whistler, *Mr. Whistler's Ten o'Clock Lecture* (London, 1888), p. 16. First delivered in London on 20 February 1885, and later that year delivered at Cambridge and Oxford.

4 In an era of intense specialization, Whistler's talents as a writer hurt him as an artist. It was inconceivable that an individual be gifted in both areas. For example, Swinburne decried "the light and glittering bark of the brilliant amateur in the art of letters." For an early discussion of this problem, see Max Beerbohm, "Whistler's Writing," *Metropolitan Magazine* (September 1904):728–733.

5 Whistler, pp. 17, 18.

6 *Ibid.*, pp. 15, 16.

7 Ernest F. Fenollosa, "The Collection of Mr. Charles L. Freer," *Pacific Era* 1, no. 2 (November 1907):60. See also Fenollosa, "The Place in History of Mr. Whistler's Art," *Lotos* special issue (December 1903):14–17.

8 Jonathan Mayne, introduction to Baudelaire, pp. xiii, xxi–xxviii.

9 See Whistler, "The Red Rag," in Denys Sutton, *James McNeill Whistler: Paintings, Etchings, Pastels and Watercolours* (London, 1966), p. 58; and Algernon Swinburne, *Essays and Studies* (London, 1875).

10 One may point out, moreover, that as a poet Swinburne found such analogies dear to his own heart.

11 Whistler, "Et Tu, Brute!" in *The Gentle Art of Making Enemies* (1892); reprinted New York, 1967), pp. 259–261.

12 Robert Venturi took the idea of "both-and" from literary criticism and applied it to architecture: "Cleanth Brooks refers to Donne's art as 'having it both ways' but, he says, 'most of us in this latter day, cannot. We are disciplined in the tradition of either-or, and lack the mental agility—to say nothing of the maturity of attitude—which would allow us to indulge in the finer distinctions and the more subtle reservations permitted by the tradition of both-and.' The tradition 'either-or' has characterized orthodox modern architecture." Robert Venturi, *Complexity and Contradiction in Architecture, the Museum of Modern Art Papers on Architecture*, vol. I (New York, 1966), pp. 30–31.

13 Whistler, "The Red Rag," in Sutton, p. 58. Italics mine.

14 Fenollosa, "Collection of . . . Freer," 60.

15 Baudelaire, p. ix.

16 *Ibid.*, p. 13. Baudelaire formulated his concept earlier. His essay "On the Heroism of Modern Life" was part of his discussion of the Salon of 1846. See Baudelaire, pp. xviii, xiii.

17 *Ibid.*, pp. xii, 3, 14.

18 Nerina Shute, *London Villages* (London, 1977), pp. 22–23. See also William Gaunt, *Chelsea* (London, 1954), p. 15.

19 David H. Pinckney, *Napoleon III and the Rebuilding of Paris* (Princeton, 1958).

20 Francis Wey, *A Frenchman among the Victorians*, trans. Valerie Pirie (1856: New Haven, 1936), p. 154.

21 *Daily Telegraph* (6 October 1877), p. 102, Cremorne Gardens scrapbook II, Chelsea Public Library.

22 Whistler, *Ten o'Clock Lecture*, p. 15.

23 There are six oils, all nocturnes, specifically identified with Cremorne Gardens. See Andrew McLaren Young *et al.*, *The Paintings of James McNeill Whistler*, 2 vols. (New Haven and London, 1980), I, nos. 163–166, 169–170. Related paintings include a distant view, *Nocturne: Blue and Silver—Cremorne Lights*, in Young *et al.*, no. 115. The view of Battersea Bridge with fireworks in it, *Nocturne: Blue and Gold—Old Battersea Bridge*, includes fireworks, although given the composition which looks north and east, it is hard to imagine Cremorne as the firing site. See Young *et al.*, no. 140. There may have been additional views which are now lost. See Young *et al.*, nos. 167–169. Whistler's watercolors of Amsterdam by night are stylistically related to the Cremorne series.

24 John Ruskin, Letter 79, Fors Clavigera, 2 July 1877, in E. T. Cook and Alexander Wedderburne, *The Works of Ruskin*, vol. XXIX (New York and London, 1907).

25 Joseph Pennell and Elizabeth Pennell, *The Life of James McNeill Whistler* 2 vols (London, 1908), I, p. 229.

26 The site's previous history is as follows. Theophilus, ninth earl of Huntington, built a villa there and called it Chelsea Farm. He died in 1746 and was succeeded by his widow, Lady Selina Shirley, an avid Calvinist and patron of the preacher George Whitfield. In 1778 Chelsea Farm was acquired by Thomas Dawson, Baron Dartrey, who was created Viscount Cremorne in 1785. He had the house improved and enlarged by the architect James Wyatt, and he collected Flemish and Italian paintings. On his death the house passed to his widow Philadelphia Hannah, granddaughter of William Penn. Her cousin and heir Granville Penn put the property up for sale in 1826. In 1829 or early 1830 it was finally sold to Charles Random de Berenger, Baron de Beaufain. He founded the sporting club, and the old house was turned into a hotel.

27 For a description of the Stadium, see Reginald Blunt, *By Chelsea Reach: Some Riverside Records* (London, 1921), pp. 173–175. Skilled as a rifle instructor, draftsman, and pyrotechnist, de Berenger had apparently served as an officer in a foreign regiment before coming to England. He spent about a year in prison for a stock-exchange fraud before embarking on his activities at the Stadium. Information from an unpublished manuscript for an exhibition at Chelsea Public Library. Some of de Berenger's ideas were preserved in his book, *Helps and Hints: How to Protect Life and Property, with Instruction in Rifle and Pistol Shooting, etc.* (London, 1835). The rules for membership at the Stadium appear on pp. 265 ff.

28 Thea Holme, *Chelsea* (New York: Taplinger, 1971), p. 184. See also unpublished manuscript, Chelsea Public Library exhibition.

29 "Entertainments during Whitsun Week" (May 1847), newspaper clipping, scrapbook, SR 130, p. 15, Chelsea Public Library.

30 *Illustrated London News* (30 May 1857), p. 516.

31 The pagoda-shaped orchestra was fitted with an eight-light gasalier as well as sixteen two-light bracket gasaliers. It had a zinc roof. There were a dressing room and seven cabinets in the center section. The orchestra was completely surrounded by gas jets; blank walls were covered with plate-glass mirrors in black frames. The platform was made of thirty-two sections with stout timber joists and had an ornamental iron panel enclosure with sixteen pairs of iron pillars decorated with arches and gas jets, protected by glass globes. See Furber, Price and Furber, *Cremorne Gardens Auction Sale, 8 April 1878 and on Following Days*, lots 1376–1392, in scrapbook, *Papers upon the History of Cremorne Gardens, Chelsea, 1840–1878*, Chelsea Public Library.

32 Young *et al.*, I, no. 166, p. 96.

33 At some point, the proprietor Simpson purchased the grounds to Ashburnum House, which was west of the Cremorne Estate. Information from unpublished manuscript, Chelsea Public Library exhibition. A Cremorne guidebook of 1852 mentions twelve acres, while the *Illustrated London News* article of 1857 commented that the grounds included sixteen acres.

34 *Illustrated London News* (30 May 1857), p. 516. The statuary that was auctioned off represents a library of Victorian popular taste. Included were Burn's *Cottage Fireside*, *The Duke of Wellington*, and *Napoleon* (all three life-sized); *Lacoön*, a pair of lions, *Three Graces*, *Dying Gladiator*, two cupids, *Venus*, *Paul and Virginia*, *Innocence*, *Three Rustic Figures*, *Mercury*, *Apollo*, *Tragedy and Comedy*, *Hercules*, a Warwick vase, and *Diana*. See Furber, Price and Furber, auction catalogue, Chelsea Public Library. Many of these pieces were situated down the long walkway near the fireworks pavilion.

35 In 1845 the grounds were managed by Littlejohn, previously of Rosherville Gardens in Gravesend, in partnership with Tom Matthews, the clown from Drury Lane Theatre. In 1846 the grounds were rented at £585 a year by James Ellis. He went bankrupt in 1850. From 1850 until he retired in 1861, Thomas Bartlett Simpson, who had also been lessee of the Drury Lane Theatre, was proprietor at Cremorne. He purchased the grounds, and his widow sold them after the gardens closed in 1877. From 1861 Edward Tyrell Smith managed the grounds. After nine years John Baum took over. See Blunt, p. 192. See also unpublished manuscript, Chelsea Public Library exhibition.

36 *Papers upon the History of Cremorne Gardens*, scrapbook, p. 33. See also Blunt, p. 192.

37 Isabella Burt, *Historical Notices of Chelsea, Kensington, Fulham, and Hammersmith* (Kensington, 1871), p. 42.

38 Reginald Blunt, "A Balloon Ascent from Cremorne," in *The Crown and Anchor: A Chelsea Quarto* (London, 1925), p. 87. The event took place in 1861.

39 From a guidebook of ca. 1851–1852, in *Papers upon the History of Cremorne Gardens*, scrapbook, pp. 115–120.

40 Ralph Nevill, *The Gay Victorians* (London, 1930), p. 24.

41 Guidebook of ca. 1851–1852, from scrapbook, Chelsea Public Library.

42 *Illustrated London News* (30 May 1857), p. 516.

43 See James G. Southworth, *Vauxhall Gardens: A Chapter in the Social History of England* (New York, 1941), p. 181, for this contemporary quotation.

44 Benjamin Silliman, *A Journal of Travels in England, Holland and Scotland . . . in the Years 1805 and 1806*, 2 vols. (Boston, 1812), I, p. 211.

45 Miles Hadfield, *History of British Gardening* (London and New York, 1969), p. 222.

46 See Furber, Price and Furber, Cremorne, auction sales catalogue, 1877, lots 1337, 1412, 1417, scrapbook, Chelsea Public Library.

47 Edward Tyrell Smith bought them for the Banqueting Hall at Cremorne according to Southworth, p. 181.

48 Hadfield, p. 223. Tyers had another garden, a programmatic one, at Denbies near Dorking. It was a labyrinth of walks symbolizing human life and its inevitable end.

49 Warwick Wroth, *The London Pleasure Gardens of the Eighteenth Century* (London, 1896), p. 204.

50 *Ibid.*, p. 314. "Amid the blaze of meteors seen on high, Etherial Saqui seems to tread the sky," p. 313. Such thrilling feats continued to intrigue audiences and artists alike. For example, Degas's painting, *Miss La La at the Cirque Fernando*, 1879, now at the National Gallery in London, shows a performer hanging by her teeth from a rope.

51 Southworth, p. 58. The gardens were at the east end of Chelsea, on the Thames.

52 Wey, p. 165.

53 "Entertainments during Whitsun Week," May 1847, clipping from an unidentified London newspaper, scrapbook, Chelsea Public Library. Earlier, British pleasure gardens had an impact in France, where both Ranelagh and Vauxhall were imitated.

54 Scrapbook III, Chelsea Public Library.

55 Unfortunately no such drawings survive to confirm the Pennells' report. However, Whistler used this "memory" technique for nocturnes and other works as well. Quote from E. R. Pennell, *The Whistler Journal* (Philadelphia, 1921), p. 117.

56 See Young *et al.*, I, no. 164, p. 94.

57 Georg Simmel, *On Individuality and Social Forms*, ed. Donald N. Levine (Chicago and London, 1971), pp. 143–149.

58 Baudelaire, p. 9.

59 Wroth, p. 208.

60 Changing interpretations of Claude's *oeuvre* were discussed at a symposium on the artist held in 1982 at the National Gallery of Art, Washington, D.C.

61 Silliman, I, p. 215.

62 See Baudelaire, p. 7. Baudelaire borrowed the concept from Poe, and he also used it for his poem "To a Passerby." The building could be either the old hotel or Ashburnam Hall.

63 Blunt, *By Chelsea Reach*, pp. 99, 117–118.

64 An advertisement for a "second grand bal masque" is included in *Papers upon the History of Cremorne Gardens*, scrapbook, p. 11.

65 Wey, p. 174.

66 See scrapbook III, Chelsea Public Library. Among the costumes auctioned at the Cremorne sale were twenty-four Harlequin outfits (Furber, Price and Furber, auction catalogue, lot 1056).

67 Wey, p. 176.

68 *Ibid.*

69 *Punch* (24 July 1858), in scrapbook II, p. 43, Chelsea Public Library. See also "The Battle of Cremorne," *Punch* (24 October 1857).

70 The poet went on to give graphic examples. See "The Trial of John Fox, or Fox John, or The Horrors of Cr-m-rne" (October 1876), SR 141, L/1180, Chelsea Public Library. Fox John represented the proprietor of the Gardens, John Baum.

71 Whistler, *Ten o'Clock Lecture*, pp. 27–28.

72 *Ibid.*, p. 26.

73 See, for example, William Merritt Chase, "The Two Whistlers: Recollections of a Summer with the Great Etcher," *Century Magazine* 80 (1910):218–226.

74 For a study, see Ellen Moers, *The Dandy: Brummell to Beerbohm* (New York, 1960).

75 Baudelaire, p. 27.

76 Whistler, *Ten o'Clock Lecture*, p. 22.

77 Baudelaire, p. 28.

78 Ready with his pen if not with his pistol, Whistler wrote an aggressive letter warning this particular critic that "the foolish critic only—*looks*—and brings disaster, upon his paper—the safe and well-conducted one 'informs himself.' " See Whistler, *The Gentle Art of Making Enemies*, pp. 197–198.

79 Baudelaire, p. 28.

80 *Ibid.*

81 Whistler, *Ten o'Clock Lecture*, p. 29.

82 Patrick Bracco and Elisabeth Lebovici, *Fireworks: Feux d'artifices. French Fireworks from the Seventeenth to the Nineteenth Century* (exh. cat.) (Washington: International Exhibitions Foundation, 1976), p. 6.

83 Twenty different items were included in the event. See "Programme of a Grand Display of Fire Works: Executed by J. G. d'Ernst at Cremorne House, Chelsea, 14 July 1836," scrapbook III, Chelsea Public Library.

84 *Daily Telegraph* (28 July 1875), in scrapbook II, p. 97, Chelsea Public Library.

85 *Daily Telegraph* (1877), scrapbook II, p. 101. Item on Wells not further dated.

86 "Programme of a Grand Display of Fire Works."

87 Bracco and Lebovici, p. 12.

88 Mary Anne Hodgkinson, "Letters from Night Latitudes, No. 15. A Visit to Cremorne," *Fun* (14 June 1862), scrapbook, p. 121, Chelsea Public Library.

89 "Deal" indicates inexpensive wood. Information from Furber, Price and Furber, Cremorne auction catalogue, lot 51.

90 Bracco and Lebovici, p. 10.

91 Baudelaire, p. x.

92 *Ibid.*

93 Frith quoted in Pennell and Pennell, I, p. 240.

94 Whistler quoted *ibid.*, p. 235.

95 Bracco and Lebovici, pp. 6, 10.

Chronology

At the Piano, 1858, oil on canvas, 66 × 90 cm. Taft Museum, Cincinnati, Ohio, Louise Taft Semple Bequest.

Symphony in White, No. 2: The Little White Girl, 1864, oil on canvas, 76 × 51 cm. Tate Gallery, London.

Nocturne in Blue and Silver: Cremorne Lights, 1872, oil on canvas, 49.5 × 74 cm. Tate Gallery, London.

Arrangement in Grey and Black, No. 2: Portrait of Thomas Carlyle, 1872–1873, oil on canvas, 171 × 143.5 cm. Glasgow Art Gallery & Museum.

Nocturne in Blue and Gold: Old Battersea Bridge, 1872–1875, oil on canvas, 66.6 × 50.2 cm. Tate Gallery, London.

1834–1843

James Abbott Whistler was born to George Washington Whistler and Anna Matilda Whistler on July 11, 1834. The year before, Major Whistler had resigned his commission in the United States Army and moved the family to Lowell, Massachusetts, where he was a civil engineer. Whistler's mother descended from the McNeills of the Isle of Skye, Scotland. After entering West Point, Whistler adopted his mother's family name, calling himself James McNeill Whistler.

1843–1851

The family lived in Russia for several years when Major Whistler was a consulting engineer for the railroad from St. Petersburg to Moscow. In Russia, the young Whistler received his first instruction in art. Whistler spent most of 1848 in London with his sister, who was married to Seymour Haden, a prominent surgeon and an accomplished amateur etcher. After the major died in 1849, Whistler's mother took her son to London and then back to America, enrolling him in a school at Pomfret, Connecticut. His drawing ability was noticed, and the Freer Gallery owns two watercolor paintings from this period (see Plates 74 and 77).

1851–1855

Mrs. Whistler hoped her son would follow his father's example, becoming a soldier after attending West Point, but Whistler was discharged for deficiency in chemistry in 1854. He was at the head of the class in drawing. Several ink sketches from this period are in the Freer collection (see Plates 141–144). Late in 1854 Whistler received an appointment to the Coast and Geodetic Survey to work on drawing and etching plates for map making, but he resigned after four months. One of his copper plates with unauthorized sketches of heads and figures is in the Freer collection (see Plate section, Fig. 168.1).

1855–1859

With the financial assistance of his family, Whistler went to Paris to study art. Much of his time was spent in the Latin Quarter (see Plates 147, 194, 197). In June 1856 he entered Gleyre's studio. In 1858 he made a sketching tour of the Rhineland (Plates 168–171). Subsequently, he began to experiment with printing, and he published his first set of etchings (see Plate section, Fig. 148.1). In 1859 *At the Piano* was exhibited in François Bonvin's Paris studio, marking the end of what Whistler called his "student days."

1859–1863

In 1859, Whistler exhibited two etchings, his first works to be shown in England. Many of his Thames etchings were made that year.

Whistler's prints were an important part of the etching revival that swept Britain and France during the 1860s and 1870s.

In 1860 *At the Piano* again received praise, this time at the Royal Academy in London. By 1860 Whistler was seriously interested in executing paintings of the Thames River. *The Thames in Ice* was painted late that year (see Plate 20). Although Whistler established his home in London, he made frequent trips to Paris. But *The Music Room*, an interior scene taken from modern life, is one of the last of Whistler's works to be painted in the manner of French realists (see Plate 3). Whistler's later arrangements, nocturnes, and symphonies moved away from Courbet's realism, emphasizing abstraction and evoking analogies with music. Whistler "pitched" his paintings in one or two related color tones, and color harmonies became the focus of his work. Whistler's central idea was that art should appeal to the eye without depending upon the expression of ideas or emotions, although the latter are not absent from his paintings (see "Artist and Site"). To Whistler's disappointment the *Symphony in White, No. 1: The White Girl* was rejected for an exhibition at the Royal Academy in 1862. It was one of Whistler's earliest paintings to defy established convention. After a subsequent showing of the *White Girl*, Whistler wrote his first letter to the press, denying any literary associations for the painting. Whistler continued to correspond with the public via the newspapers throughout his career. As his work in oil became more avant-garde, Whistler gradually estranged himself from the British public. Unlike his paintings, Whistler's etchings continued to be well received.

In 1862 Whistler moved to Chelsea. Illustrated magazines engaged him to make drawings for them. The *White Girl* joined Manet's *Déjeuner sur l'herbe* in causing a sensation at the Salon de Réfuses in Paris in 1863. Meanwhile, Whistler's etchings drew honors in England, France, and Holland.

1863–1879

Whistler began to use Oriental costumes, screens, fans, and pottery as props in figure paintings. *The Golden Screen, The Balcony*, and *La Princesse du Pays de la Porcelaine*, all in the Freer collection, were painted during this period (see Plates 4–6). Eventually, Whistler was to assimilate the principles of Oriental art into his own work.

In 1866 Whistler traveled to South America, where he painted his first night scenes. Returning to Chelsea, Whistler conceived his nocturnes, twilight or late evening scenes along the Thames. A number of these are now in the Freer collection (see Plates 22, 23, 25–31). By the 1870s Whistler was also concentrating on large portraits. These include images of his mother and of the Scottish philosopher and historian

Arrangement in Grey and Black, No. 1: Portrait of the Painter's Mother, 1872, oil on canvas, 145 × 164 cm. Louvre, Paris.

Harmony in Grey and Green: Miss Cicely Alexander, 1873, oil on canvas, 218.4 × 99 cm. Tate Gallery, London.

Symphony in Flesh Colour and Pink: Mrs. F. R. Leyland, 1873, oil on canvas, 189.5 × 96 cm. Copyright The Frick Collection, New York.

Cremorne Gardens, No. 2, 1875, oil on canvas. 68.6 × 134.9 cm. Metropolitan Museum of Art, John Stewart Kennedy Fund.

Harmony in Flesh Colour and Pink: Portrait of Lady Meux, 1881, oil on canvas, 190.5 × 90.5 cm. Copyright The Frick Collection, New York.

Thomas Carlyle. The two portraits were the first works by Whistler to enter public museum collections (see Plates 222 and 223).

Another two portraits depict Whistler's mistress Maud Franklin and his patron Frederick Richards Leyland. Both arrangements, painted in black and white, are now in the Freer Gallery (Plates 15 and 19). Whistler continued to work on a series of decorative schemes for Leyland. His "Six Projects," begun in 1868, combined Oriental and classical motives with colors inspired by French rococo art (see Plates 7–12).

By the early 1870s, recognition of Whistler's etchings was widespread. His paintings, however, were not so readily accepted. In 1872 Whistler sent *Arrangement in Grey and Black, No. 1: Portrait of the Painter's Mother* to the Royal Academy for exhibition. After an initial refusal, the committee finally decided to display the work, but their reluctance caused permanent offense. The artist never again showed a painting at the Royal Academy and was scornful of the British art establishment thereafter.

Commissions to paint the members of the Leyland family led to Whistler's visits to Speke Hall, near Liverpool, during the early 1870s. Although he finished standing portraits only of Mr. and Mrs. Leyland (see Plate 15), a number of watercolors, pastels, and prints also resulted (see Plates 224–237). In 1876 Whistler began work on Leyland's house in Prince's Gate, London. He created the dado of the front hall staircase before going on to decorate the famous Peacock Room (see Plate 72, and "Artist and Architect"). The controversial interior stimulated great publicity, but the commission ended with a quarrel and a permanent break between the artist and his first important patron.

Whistler's minute attention to detail gradually gave way to the use of fewer lines and strokes in etchings that achieve suggestive images akin to the nocturnes painted in oil earlier in the decade. Whistler was introduced to lithography in 1878. The Ruskin libel suit, caused by harsh criticism of Whistler's abstract painting, came to trial that year, but Whistler won only a farthing in damages. His finances were already strained to the breaking point as he had just built his White House to a design by Philip Godwin. In May 1879, Whistler was declared bankrupt and lost the house. Many of his paintings were dispersed at auction. The Fine Art Society commissioned Whistler to make twelve etchings in Venice for them. Whistler spent the rest of 1879 and most of 1880 in Venice, making numerous etchings and pastels, as well as a few watercolors and oils (see Plates 91, 244–261).

1880–1887

Following his return to London, Whistler exhibited the twelve Venetian etchings at the Fine Arts Society. In 1881 he displayed his Venice pastels to great acclaim. In 1883 he held an important showing of fifty-one etchings, accompanied by a catalogue that made witty sport of earlier critics. At the Dowdeswell Gallery in May 1884, Whistler held his first large showing of watercolors. They reflect his mastery over the medium. Most were executed in washes without preliminary drawing (see Plates 98, 104, 109, 125–127, 129–131). In 1885 Whistler delivered his *Ten o'Clock Lecture*, setting forth his basic aesthetic credo. The following year, he published the *Set of Twenty-six Etchings*, which made up Charles Lang Freer's first purchase of work by Whistler (see Plate section, Fig. 110.1). Also in that year, Whistler was elected president of the Society of British Artists, which he set about to reform in an autocratic manner.

1888–1897

On August 11, 1888, Whistler married Beatrix Birnie Philip Godwin, widow of the architect of the White House. Encouraged by Beatrix, he took up lithography again, making many prints from about 1890 until 1896. Whistler continued to receive honors for his works. In 1889 a large and successful exhibition of oils, watercolors, and pastels was held at Wunderlich's in New York. Whistler and Freer met in London the following year. Publication of *The Gentle Art of Making Enemies*, a carefully edited volume of Whistler's correspondence occurred in 1890 with a reprint in 1892. Illustrations from the book are now in the Freer collection (see Plates 283–293).

Early in 1892, a retrospective exhibition of Whistler's works in London was a complete success. Growing respect for the artist was directly reflected in a flood of commissions, and his earlier works commanded escalating prices. Printmaking absorbed much of his energies, but Whistler did embark on a number of portraits in 1893–1894. Few of these were finished. Mrs. Whistler was stricken with cancer and declined steadily from 1894 until her death in 1896. The grieving artist was too distracted to appreciate honors or to complete commissions. Miss Rosalind Birnie Philip, Mrs. Whistler's sister, who lived with the Whistlers beginning in 1895, was made Whistler's ward and the executrix of his estate. Miss Birnie Philip became a close friend of Freer, aiding his efforts as a collector.

1897–1901

After the winter of 1897–1898, Whistler's poor health forced him to stop work from time to time. Nearing the end of his career, he executed a number of small but powerful nudes now in the Freer collection (see Plates 62 and 63). In 1900, he traveled to Tangier, hoping to recuperate. Whistler stopped at Gibralter, where he made a number of sketches.

1901–1903

After returning to London, the restless, ailing artist moved from place to place. He started a portrait of Charles Lang Freer in 1902 but left it unfinished (see Plate 66). On July 17, 1903, Whistler intended to go driving with Freer in London, but the artist died shortly before his patron reached the house. After Whistler's death, Freer continued to collect representative examples of the artist's work, eventually amassing one of the two largest Whistler collections in the world.

Plates

Plate 1.
Portrait of Whistler with a Hat

1857–1858
oil on canvas
46.3 × 38.1 cm.
Inscription: "Whistler," artist's hand.

As is frequently the case when a young artist creates a self-portrait, Whistler identified himself with a past master. Theodore Duret reported that Whistler was particularly struck by Rembrandt's *Portrait of a Man in a Beret* in the Louvre.[1] Whistler adopted Rembrandt's general format as well as his rich, dark palette. The artist Kenyon Cox detected the impact of Courbet's realism in Whistler's use of "rather violent light and shade, with black shadows, the yellowish tone of the flesh, and the attempt at powerful modeling."[2] The self-portrait exhibits a fastidious fashion consciousness: the artist is wearing a flat-brimmed brushed silk hat—the "Quartier Latin type," as one friend described it.[3] By the time Freer acquired this self-portrait in 1906, it had been frequently exhibited in America and reproduced as both a woodcut and an engraving.

Plate 2.
Portrait of Major Whistler

ca. 1857–1859
oil on panel
30.3 × 25.1 cm.

The authenticity of this portrait of Major George Washington Whistler has been questioned. Whistler is known to have copied a painting for Dick Palmer in 1857, and the Freer's portrait was bought from Miss Emma W. Palmer, stepniece of the artist's mother. However, it is odd that the portrait would have left Whistler's immediate family, had the artist actually painted it.[1] Whistler attempted to copy a lithographed image of his father in 1859, but the Freer's portrait does not resemble the most logical lithographic source available to Whistler.[2]

The Freer's oil portrait of Major Whistler most closely resembles another portrait, made by Chester Harding and now in the collection at Glasgow University. From about 1840 until 1842, Major Whistler and Harding were neighbors in Massachusetts. Harding painted Major Whistler during this time. He also allowed his student W. S. Elwell to copy his portrait of the major. The Freer's portrait is not by Elwell. But Harding himself frequently made replicas of his own paintings, and it is possible that this portrait was executed by Harding rather than by the son of the sitter.[3]

Plate 3.
Harmony in Green and Rose:
The Music Room

1860–1861
oil on canvas
96.3 × 71.7 cm.

Harmony in Green and Rose depicts the music room at 62 Sloane Street, the London home of the Seymour Haden family. Whistler's niece, Annie Harriet Haden, sits reading a book. Miss Isabella Boott, a family connection, stands at the right, clad in a black riding habit.[1] Whistler's half-sister, Deborah Delano Whistler Haden, is reflected in the mirror. It is impossible to tell whether Deborah is rising to greet Miss Boott or to see her out. For that matter, Deborah's bent posture may indicate that she is playing the piano. Annie ignores them both, and ambiguity sets the tone for this enigmatic picture.[2]

Even before his imagination was caught by Japanese woodblock prints,[3] Whistler constructed his painting in a manipulative manner that emphasized artistic decisions. In concert with contemporary developments in France, Whistler stressed the painted surface as a two-dimensional colored plane. The space itself, while rendered in terms of pictorial realism, is physically impossible. Whistler placed Miss Boott so as to obscure the corner of the niche where Annie sits. The edge of a picture frame on axis with Miss Boott is logically the corner at which the niche should angle back from the wall on the right. The dado changes levels on either side of the standing figure to suggest spatial recession, but the two framed pictures above the woman and child seem to hang side by side on a continuous wall, denying that same recession. The lamp above Annie's head floats before the wall. There is no place for it to stand, but we know from an etching that it was indeed a standing lamp with a wide base (Fig. 3.1). Another etching depicts what is probably the same corner of the music room, showing part of the shelf with its mirror and vase as well as the large window to the left (Fig. 3.2). The area above the lighted lamp is dark and hard to read, but the etching indicates how much Whistler flattened and foreshortened the space in the painting. He echoed the triad of women with a triad of picture frames. Even though the frames are the most distant objects in the scene, they are cut off at the top, bringing the picture plane sharply forward. Three areas of strident floral fabric repeat the other triads, while emphasizing the vertical format and the precariously tilted foreground. Similar spatial innovations were later employed by Degas.[4]

The Music Room carries forward Whistler's early interest in popular illustrations by artists such as Gavarni, from whose work the figure of Annie may be derived (Fig. 3.3). The painting also is concerned with fashion. Miss Boott wears an instantly recognizable costume—that of the "Amazon," or horsewoman (Figs. 3.4 and 3.5). The Amazon costume was strictly defined in fashionable circles and was sometimes associated with dandyism.[5] Miss Boott wears a tricorner hat rather than the more dramatic top hat, but either was fashionable in 1860.[6] Her riding whip was the iconic emblem of the Amazon, seen in fashion illustration and painting alike. The costume was credited to the English, but was adopted by the French as well. While it was not uncommon for women in either country to ride, Parisian courtesans were especially proud of their abilities as horsewomen, and the word *Amazon* became a euphemism for ladies of questionable virtue.[7] Whistler referred to the painting as "le tableau avec l'amazone."[8]

If Isabella Boott in a riding costume implied freedom, Deborah Haden's presence evoked a conventional marriage. Her union to the prominent surgeon Seymour Haden was an advantageous one, arranged by the artist's mother. Whistler studiously avoided such bourgeois social sanction until he finally married in the late 1880s. It is, therefore, perhaps significant that Deborah appears only as a reflection. Whistler scraped the pigment defining Deborah's dress to a low-toned gray. In contrast to the vigorous black shape of the Amazon, Whistler's half sister appears almost ghostly. Dressed in white, Annie sits between the two women, looking at neither. The viewer receives little information about either her thoughts or her prospects. Whistler avoids a clearly stated message, but it is not too much to speculate that he has painted an ambiguous allegory of choice, couched in what Baudelaire called "the beauty of circumstance and the sketch of manners."[9]

Figure 3.2.
The Music Room, etching, K33, Freer Gallery.

Figure 3.3.
Gavarni, *Laure*, 1833, lithograph. From Paul-André Lemoisne, *Gavarni, peintre et lithographe, 1804–1847* (Paris: H. Floury, 1924), p. 55.

Figure 3.4.
Gavarni, *Amazone*, 1830, watercolor drawing. From Lemoisne, opp. p. 34.

Figure 3.5.
Adrien Tournachon (Nadar), *Mlle. Jenny in Costume of an Amazone*, photograph. From Nigel Gosling, *Nadar* (London: Secker and Warburg, 1976), p. 289. Reprinted courtesy of Archives Photographiques de la Caisse Nationale des Monuments Historiques et Sites.

Figure 3.1.
Reading by Lamplight, etching, K32, Freer Gallery.

Plate 4.
Caprice in Purple and Gold:
The Golden Screen

1864
oil on panel
50.2 × 68.7 cm.
Inscription: (r) "Whistler. 1864," artist's hand; (v) "No. 2:
The Golden Screen (oil painting)," artist's hand (label).

Whistler's mistress Jo Hiffernan sits looking at
Hiroshige woodblock prints in one of the
quintessential paintings from the artist's early
phase of *japonisme*. The prints and other Oriental props, both Chinese and Japanese, may
have been objects Whistler had gathered for
his own collection. The genre is familiar in
Western art—a woman's beauty has been contrasted by exotic, expensive, and fashionable
art objects arranged in luxuriant profusion.
Whistler himself considered the work "ravis-
sant," but the painting was maligned in a caricature when it was exhibited at the Royal
Academy in 1865 (Fig. 4.1). Despite the painting's eclectic nature and Western approach, its
assymetrical composition and brightly patterned surface are aspects of Oriental art that
Whistler later integrated more subtly into his

work. Late in life, Whistler sketched *The
Golden Screen*, along with *The Music Room*,
another painting now in the Freer collection,
on a compiled list of his works (Fig. 4.2). Freer
actively pursued *The Golden Screen* for several
years before finally acquiring it. During the
1890s he owned woodblock prints similar to
those depicted here, and the patron also hoped
to discover a Japanese screen like the one seen
in the painting.

Figure 4.1.
Cartoon, *Fun Magazine*,
August 5, 1865, p. 118.
Courtesy of the Library of
Congress.

Figure 4.2.
List of paintings with
sketches of *Caprice in
Purple and Gold: The
Golden Screen; Harmony in
Green and Rose: The Music
Room; Purple and Rose:
The Lange Leizen of the Six
Marks,* and three other
pictures, pencil. Hunterian
Art Gallery, University of
Glasgow.

Plate 5.
La Princesse du Pays de la Porcelaine

1863–1864
oil on canvas
199.9 × 116.1 cm.
Inscription: "Whistler 1864–," artist's hand.

Whistler's painting of Christine Spartali, a noted beauty of the 1860s, is another in his series of clearly Western compositions that depict languid young women amid Oriental props. Later writers saw parallels between this work and Japanese images, such as woodblock prints by Utamaro, but the painting is just as firmly based upon eighteenth-century French chinoiserie.[1] The *Princesse* is one of several early works for which preparatory sketches are known to have been used. One surviving sketch shows the artist blocking in the general composition and colors, but leaving out details of rug, screen, and costume that were added to the final work (Fig. 5.1). The spray of flowers at the left of the oil sketch were later eliminated. Whistler's decision isolated Miss Spartali's profile and increased the impact of her exotic visage. However, her father refused to purchase the work as a portrait of his daughter. Whistler was not willing to reduce the size of his signature for another potential purchaser, and the Pennells believed that this incident caused him to develop his butterfly cypher. However, the butterfly did not actually appear until several years later.[2]

Figure 5.1
Sketch for *Rose and Silver: La Princesse du Pays de la Porcelaine*, oil on paperboard. Worcester Art Museum, Bequest of Mary G. Ellis as part of the Theodore T. and Mary G. Ellis collection.

Plate 6.
Variations in Flesh Colour and Green: The Balcony

1864 ff.
oil on panel
61.4 × 48.8 cm.
Inscription: butterfly.[1]

The Balcony was one of the early figure paintings that occupied Whistler over a long period of time. Begun in 1864, it seems to have undergone alterations as late as 1870, and there are several preliminary works, including a watercolor sketch that corresponds almost exactly with the Freer oil (Fig. 6.1).[2] As so often happened with Whistler, his plans to enlarge the composition into a life-size work were never brought to completion, although an oil sketch squared for transfer does survive.[3]

The Balcony was criticized for its obvious Oriental content. The *Art Journal* called it "singular and eccentric" in 1870 while in 1873 a French critic complained, "Le désir d'atteindre à la franchise des estampes japonaises est flagrant."[4] However, typical of Whistler's early japonesque works, *The Balcony* relates as closely to Western fashion of the period as to any actual example of Oriental art.[5] If *The Balcony* was "a Japanese fancy realized on the banks of the gray Thames," it was divorced neither from its actual setting nor from earlier Western art.[6] The painting depicts the view from the artist's own balcony in Chelsea, and the background includes unadorned smokestacks and factories on the south side of the Thames. A short distance from Whistler's house, the Chinese Bandstand at Cremorne Gardens linked nineteenth-century orientalism with that of the eighteenth. Whistler's model, standing and looking to the right, could have heard the music, which started in the early afternoon.[7]

The unsettling blend of then-fashionable *japonisme* with a view of an industrialized river lined with factories suggests that Whistler may have intended to paint a scene from modern life. Several balcony scenes were undertaken by Whistler's contemporaries. Constantin Guys, the ultimate "painter of modern life," had sketched one. Manet's famous balcony picture, another modern view, was painted in 1868 (Fig. 6.2). However, by using "a group in Oriental costume on a balcony, a tea equipage of old China," as his mother put it,[8] Whistler achieved a bizarre exoticism, furthered by the lavish blossoms that decorate the bottom edge of the work and the strident, flat passage of brilliant blue flooring.[9] It is, perhaps, this combination of the exotic with the prosaic that gives the work its strange power.

The Balcony was the first major oil by Whistler to enter the Freer collection.

Figure 6.1.
Study for "The Balcony," watercolor. Hunterian Art Gallery, University of Glasgow, Birnie Philip Bequest.

Figure 6.2.
Édouard Manet, *The Balcony,* 1868, oil. Musées Nationaux de France.

Plates 7–12.
"The Six Projects"

ca. 1868
oil on millboard, mounted on wood panel
Inscription: (*Venus*) two butterflies (added ca. 1902).

7. Venus
61.8 × 45.6 cm.

8. Symphony in Blue and Pink
46.7 × 61.9 cm.

9. Symphony in White and Red
46.8 × 61.9 cm.

10. Variations in Blue and Green
46.9 × 61.8 cm.

11. The White Symphony: Three Girls
46.4 × 61.6 cm.

12. Symphony in Green and Violet
61.9 × 45.8 cm.

"The Six Projects" are a group of oil sketches that set out Whistler's ideas for a never-completed scheme of architectural decoration. The purpose of the sketches was to establish color harmonies that would have dominated the final paintings. The sketches remain as a lexicon of the stylistic influences with which Whistler allied himself, and they witness his powerful skills at synthesis. Moreover, the projects reveal the artist's working sequence, in which color harmonies had priority over the depiction of volumetric human figures.[1] Finally, the projects show how early Whistler immersed himself in issues of decoration, issues that suffuse the creative act as practiced by Whistler for the rest of his career.

These early paintings were like pressed blossoms that Whistler took out for contemplation and inspiration over the years. "The Six Projects" are surrounded by a large group of related works, for they contain favorite compositions and themes to which the artist returned over and over. Of all the projects, *The White Symphony: Three Girls* occupied Whistler for the longest period. This oil sketch is the first in a long series of drawings and paintings that were produced in the course of more than a decade.[2] The English poet Algernon Swinburne recognized the slow workings of Whistler's creative process when he described *The White Symphony* in 1868:

> *The great picture which Mr. Whistler has now in hand is not yet finished enough for any critical detail to be possible; it shows already promise of a more majestic and excellent beauty of form than his earlier studies . . . [in] a sketch for the great picture, the soft brilliant floor-work and wall-work of a garden balcony . . . set forth the flowers and figures of flowerlike women.*[3]

7

Figure 7-12.1.
Study for Three Decorative Panels Representing "The Landing of Columbus," "Queen Isabel la Catolica of Spain," and "Queen Elizabeth of England," oil on wood panel. Print Department, Boston Public Library; Albert H. Wiggin collection. (Photo, Stein-Mason Studio.)

Figure 7-12.2.
Annabel Lee, pastel. Freer Gallery.

Figure 7-12.3.
Greek Girl, black and white chalk. Freer Gallery.

Whistler never completed the commission, although a fragment of the larger work survives in a private collection.[4] While the promise of majestic form went unfulfilled, the fresh brilliance of the "flowerlike" color studies was never surpassed in Whistler's *oeuvre*.

Venus reappeared in 1892–1893 as a muse presiding over the landing of Columbus when Whistler undertook an oil sketch for a mural at the Boston Public Library (Fig. 7-12.1). But the mural, like the "Six Projects," was never completed. Whistler may have reworked the *Venus* panel itself in 1902.[5] The composition of *Symphony in Blue and Pink* was seen again as a design for a fan.[6] Other pieces from the projects were brought to a high state of finish. The standing figure at the left of *Variations in Blue and Green* became *Annabel Lee*, one of the artist's most compelling figure drawings and one which recalls the art of Albert Moore (Fig. 7-12.2).[7]

Whistler joined Moore and other artists during the 1860s, studying classical art, particularly the Elgin marbles which had been reinstalled at the British Museum in 1865. Several other drawings give evidence of Whistler's interest in large, isolated sculptural images. One of these was even entitled *The Greek Girl* (Fig. 7-12.3).

The Elgin marbles were not Whistler's only classical source, however. Given the artist's talent for creating what Swinburne called the "delicacy and melody of ineffable color," it is not surprising that he was attracted to small Mediterranean decorative sculptures which date from the third and second centuries B.C. Powdery bits of color clung to the ridges and furrows of these diminutive terra-cotta figurines. Candy pink and robin's egg blue are among the most frequently encountered colors, and the same shades are prominent in several of the "Six Projects." Mediterranean statuettes had been added to the collection of the British Museum by 1856, and there was a vogue for collecting Tanagra figures from Boetia during the early 1870s.[8] Eventually, Whistler owned a photograph album of Tanagra figures from the Ionides collection.[9] Comparison of one album photograph with a pencil drawing and a pastel by Whistler shows that he studied both the linear and textural quality of the figurines (Figs. 7-12.4–7-12.6). A chalk drawing related to the "Six Projects" reveals the artist's effort to create strong linear drapery like that of the figurines (Figs. 7-12.7 and 7-12.8). Many of the Mediterranean statuettes are images of goddesses like Venus. Groups of women such as we see in the "Six Projects" were also common (Fig. 7-12.9).

Feminine imagery also dominates the Japanese woodblock prints left in Whistler's studio (Figs. 7-12.10 and 7-12.11). Scholars have been reluctant to draw firm conclusions about the impact of any particular image upon Whistler. While he owned Japanese woodblock prints

8

9

Figure 7-12.4. Tanagra figure, from Whistler's photo album. Hunterian Art Gallery, University of Glasgow, Birnie Philip Bequest.

Figure 7-12.5. *Drawing after Tanagra*, bound in Whistler's photo album. Hunterian Art Gallery, University of Glasgow, Birnie Philip Bequest.

Figure 7-12.6. *Pastel after Tanagra*, bound in Whistler's photo album. Hunterian Art Gallery, University of Glasgow, Birnie Philip Bequest.

Figure 7-12.7. Tanagra figure, from Whistler's photo album. Hunterian Art Gallery, University of Glasgow, Birnie Philip Bequest.

during the 1860s and 1870s, these were sold at the time of his bankruptcy. Even though it is not entirely certain when he acquired the prints left in the studio, it does seem likely that images of this type did inform the "Six Projects." Freer compared "the shore scene girls and sea," perhaps *Variations in Blue and Green*, with woodcuts by Kiyonaga.[10] Whistler could have absorbed obvious elements: architectural settings that act as a graph to chart the pictorial space; the juxtaposition of land and water; the use of flowering branches; and the generally asymmetrical composition of such prints. He also observed flattened figures grouped in rhythmic combinations of various heights. Linear treatment of drapery is again a component, as it was with the Tanagra figurines. None of the Japanese woodblock prints from the studio was imitated exactly, and examples of linear drapery and friezelike arrangements of figures are conjoined with similar examples from Greek art. Whistler's tendency to corroborate his artistic decisions with models from diverse works of art is thereby clarified.

Eighteenth-century architectural decorations in the Chinese taste are another type of imagery that the artist conflated in the "Six Projects." Although ostensibly japonesque, Whistler's drawing for the umbrella-carrying figure in *Symphony in Blue and Pink* suggests a rococo French model for his orientalism (Fig. 7-12.12).[11] Evocative color can also be traced to rococo France. Of course, the very concept of such a decorative plan for an interior recalls the rococo revival, and Whistler did complete at least one scheme, conflating the arts of France and Japan in the Peacock Room.

The *Venus* panel may be an important clue to an interpretation of the "Six Projects," for it demonstrates the artist's early interest in the subject of the goddess long worshiped as the embodiment of Love and Beauty. Whistler was to paint her many times in the course of his extensive career. The intended order of the "Projects" is not known. Such abstract paintings are open to multiple interpretations.[12] However, the panels seem to imply a journey in search of Venus, and may represent a modern version of the voyage to Cythera, an important subject in eighteenth-century French art.[13]

Loosely painted in a refined and subdued palette, the *Symphony in Green and Violet* is the most difficult of the "Six Projects" to fit into a sequential progression. This panel is the least complete and one cannot be certain whether it depicts an interior or an exterior scene. The colors set it somewhat apart from the rest. This panel was the favorite of Fenollosa and other scholars of Oriental art, who compared it to the work of Sesshu and juxtaposed it with Oriental flower painting (Fig. 7-12.13).[14]

10

11

Figure 7-12.8.
Standing Draped Figure, black and white chalk, Freer Gallery.

Figure 7-12.9.
Tanagra statuette, photograph from Whistler's studio. University of Glasgow, special collections.

The poet Swinburne provided the voluptuous verbal equivalent to Whistler's elegant brush work, following a common impulse to describe abstract painting with musical metaphor: "The main strings touched are certain varying chords of blue and white, not without interludes of the bright and tender tones of floral purple or red." Alive to the colorful vibrance of the paintings, Swinburne also noted their feminine charm, filled with the "exquisite fluttered grace of action." He was particularly taken with the imagery of the sea "lightly kindling under a low clear wind." Whistler's lavish brush stimulated Swinburne's written extravagance: "Between the dark wet stair-steps and piles of the pier the sweet bright sea shows foamless here and blue." Of *Variations in Blue and Green*, Swinburne wrote:

We have again a gathering of women in a balcony; from the unseen flower-land below, tall almond-trees shoot up their topmost crowns of tender blossom; beyond the warm and solemn sea spreads wide and soft without wrinkle of wind. The dim floorwork in front, delicate as a summer cloud in color, is antiphonal to the wealth of water beyond: and between these the fair clusters of almond-blossom make divine division. Again the symphony or (if you will) the antiphony is sustained by the fervid or the fainter colors of the women's raiment as they lean out one against another, looking far oversea in that quiet depth of pleasure without words when spirit and sense are filled full of beautiful things, till it seems that at a mere breath the charmed vessels of pleasure would break or overflow, the brimming chalices of the senses would spill this wine of their delight.[15]

Swinburne's recourse to musical imagery reminds us that even before he began to paint nocturnes, Whistler was deeply involved with intoxicating schemes of visual melody.

12

Figure 7-12.10.
Kiyonaga, *Women in an Interior*, ca. 1790, woodblock print. British Museum.

Figure 7-12.11.
Kiyonaga, *Gentlemen and Ladies at a Window Overlooking a Snowy Landscape* ca. 1790, woodblock print. Hunterian Art Gallery, University of Glasgow, Birnie Philip Bequest.

Figure 7-12.12.
François Boucher after Jean-Antoine Watteau, *Nikou, Femme Bonze*, engraving.

Figure 7-12.13.
Wisteria Blossoms, Japan, Edo period, style of Honami Koetsu, color and gold on paper, Freer Gallery.

Plate 13.
Venus Rising from the Sea

ca. 1869–1870
oil on canvas
60.3 × 49.8 cm.

Venus literally rises from the sea on a recycled
canvas. A vertical dark area to the right of the
figure indicates the remains of an abandoned
seascape underneath the present composition.
More easily visible pentimenti reveal multiple
changes to the figure itself, which is related to
the *Venus* of the "Six Projects." In this work,
Whistler reused both theme and support.

Plate 14.
Self-Portrait

1870–1875
oil on canvas
70.0 × 55.3 cm.

Freer purchased this portrait at the same time
he acquired the Peacock Room. A reporter
who saw the painting exhibited at the Metropolitan Museum of Art in 1910 thought it was
"the most vital and characteristic self portrait
by the artist."[1] The painting was reproduced
as a frontispiece to the 1910 catalogue. On the
basis of this or some other reproduction,
Joseph Pennell doubted the work's authenticity.[2] However, Pennell can hardly be praised
for his connoisseurship of Whistler's painting,
and it should also be pointed out that Pennell
and Freer were bitter enemies because of
Freer's championship of Rosalind Birnie
Philip. Together the patron and Whistler's executrix made many joint efforts to stop publication of the Pennells' biography of Whistler.

Plate 15.
Arrangement in Black: Portrait of F. R. Leyland

1870–1873
oil on canvas
192.8 × 91.9 cm.
Inscription: butterfly.

In his Paris studio, Charles Gleyre taught aspiring young artists that "ivory black is the basis for tonal painting."[1] Whistler put that lesson to use in a full-length portrait of Frederick Richards Leyland, his first important patron. The image occupied Whistler for several years, and related works both precede and follow it.[2] Reduced to black, white, and gray, the dramatic, if difficult, palette also demonstrates Whistler's interest in the work of Velásquez. In 1857 Whistler saw fourteen works by or attributed to the Spanish master at an exhibition in Manchester. Half a century later, Whistler left several large photographs of standing portraits by Velásquez in his studio (Fig. 15.1). For his full-length figures, Whistler ordinarily favored a tall, narrow format, with the sitter set well within the frame. Such a format had been used in court portraiture of preceding centuries, as comparison to *Philip IV* by Velásquez demonstrates. Neither Whistler nor Leyland would have missed the parallel between a seventeenth-century monarch and a nineteenth-century magnate.

Figure 15.1.
Diego Rodriguez de Silva y Velásquez, *Portrait of Philip IV*, photograph from Whistler's studio, University of Glasgow Library, special collections.

Plates 16 and 17.
The Blue Girl, fragments

1872–1874
oil on canvas, attached to wood panel.

16. Yellow and Blue

76.5 × 22.0 cm.

17. Purple and Blue

76.8 × 22.0 cm.

These two panels are all that is left of Whistler's full-length oil portrait of Elinor Leyland, entitled *The Blue Girl*. Having acquired a pastel drawing for the oil in 1905 (see Plate 228), Freer may have decided to acquire the fragments as well.

Plate 18.
Portrait Sketch of a Lady

mid-1870s
oil on canvas
67.5 × 50.1 cm.

This incomplete portrait may have been one of
the canvases that was rejected by auctioneers
during Whistler's bankruptcy in 1879. Presumably it fell into the hands of the Way family at
that time.[1] Although unfinished, the portrait
records Whistler's rather tradition-minded use
of a dark background upon which he built
layers of related dark tones as the basis for
portraiture. The paint was so thinly applied
that it ran and dripped at the bottom of the
canvas, which suggests a date of the mid-
1870s.[2] The sitter in a possibly related drawing
was unfortunately not identified when it was
published by Way in 1912. Along with the portrait, Freer acquired the frame later found to
belong to another painting, *Caprice in Purple
and Gold: The Golden Screen*. This helps substantiate a mid-1870s date. In the scramble
that followed Whistler's bankruptcy and sales,
more than one painting was put into a frame
originally intended for another work.[3]

Plate 19.
Arrangement in White and Black

ca. 1876
oil on canvas
191.4 × 90.9 cm.
Inscription: butterfly.[1]

For Charles Lang Freer, Whistler's *Arrangement in White and Black* was one of the most evocative works in the collection. Freer associated the portrait with the subdued elegance of Sung period Chinese painting. Freer's associations, as well as his eager pursuit of the *Arrangement*, are discussed at length in the first essay in this book.[2]

Maud Franklin, the last of Whistler's "White Girls," appears in a fashionable costume of the mid-1870s. The composition is firmly wedded to contemporary fashion plates, but a photograph of Maud shows that Whistler did not have to exaggerate her regal presence (Fig. 19.1).[3] Whistler's sense of fashion was recognized by writers of the period. Henry James's novel *Democracy* contains a passage that evokes precious Whistlerian imagery translated into the world of fashion:

> *Schneidekoupon, who was proud of his easy use of the latest artistic jargon, looked with respect at Mrs. Lee's silver-grey satin and its Venetian lace, the arrangement of which had been conscientiously stolen from a picture in the Louvre, and he murmured audibly, "Nocturne in silver-grey!"*[4]

After the painting was sold to a German collector in 1897 it acquired an erroneous title, *L'Américaine.* Apparently there was confusion between Whistler's expatriate status and the national origin of his subject, Maud Franklin.[5] Miss Franklin, Whistler's mistress for a decade, was actually British.

The frame, decorated with an incised basketweave pattern, is original to the painting but has been restored.

Figure 19.1.
Photograph of Maud
Franklin, mid-1870s.
Courtesy of the Library of
Congress, Pennell
collection.

Plate 20.
The Thames in Ice

1860
oil on canvas
74.6 × 55.3 cm.
Inscription: "Whistler," artist's hand.

Opinion on the success of Whistler's technique varies over time. In 1908 Whistler's handling of the rigging in *The Thames in Ice* was admired but his color found wanting. The opposite conclusion was put forth in 1980.[1] What has not changed is the recognition of *The Thames in Ice* as a powerful image of the river.

Part of that power comes from the wealth of data Whistler recorded. A popular subject for British artists and writers, the teeming river thrilled Victorian sensibilities with a *frisson* based on the heady combination of vitality and danger, the picturesque alongside the mundane.[2] The large ship in the foreground is a flat-bottomed collier brig, used to transport heavy cargoes up the tidal river to London. When the tide went out it remained upright and motionless. Unloading—or in Whistler's case, painting—could proceed uninterrupted. Ships of this size could not pass beyond London Bridge, and they never appear in Whistler's images of Chelsea, located upriver. The brig's heavy masts supported windlasses for transferring cargo to smaller boats, called lighters. One is seen at the right of the painting, and similar boats fill many of Whistler's nocturnes.

Whistler recorded an unusual weather event: the river had been frozen for fourteen weeks by January 19, 1861.[3] However, his artistry was not confined to mere reportage. Formal choices enhance the impact of the chilly subject. A figure on the snowy bank is identified with the brig, he is painted with the same black pigment. Whistler carefully placed the brig's anchor line to lead the eye back to the solitary figure. As the man is anonymous so is the boat—Whistler has not added a name on the prow. A four-masted seagoing vessel also lies at anchor. Its spindly masts echo the factory stacks, making a visual connection between shipping and manufacturing. The sails of the boldly painted collier brig are lowered. Several sailors can be discerned in the rigging—Whistler's brittle handling evokes the chill of icy ropes and canvas sails frozen stiff.

Whistler subtly contrasted the factories—hallmarks of the industrial revolution with its attendant progress and problems—with the old-fashioned sailing craft, which were already being replaced by steam-driven boats. Here the two largest boats lie motionless, either clearly tethered to the snowy bank or seemingly entrapped in the ice. The man on shore stares out toward the distant factories; he is separated from them by the oily brown water with its cold, yellowish sheen. Whistler's personal feelings on this state of affairs are as neutral as his palette. He simply presents us with a frozen moment from modern life in London on a wintry day in 1860.

Plate 21.
Blue and Silver: Trouville

1865
oil on canvas
59.3 × 72.8 cm.

Blue and Silver is probably one of several works painted on the beach at Trouville in the company of Courbet during October–November 1865.[1] Light, bright passages of blue and white are fairly thickly applied, and the resulting surface is a sensuous one. But Whistler also had practical reasons for wielding a generous brush—the thick paint obscures the figures of a man and woman at the bottom of the composition, immediately to the left of the rocks in the corner. The heads of the couple are still faintly visible as pentimenti.

Plate 22.
Nocturne: Blue and Gold–Valparaiso

1866
oil on canvas
75.4 × 50.3 cm.

Whistler's succession of abstract nocturnes
from the 1870s developed directly from this
painting, which he executed during a brief visit
to Chile in 1866. It would seem that his physical separation from the artistic communities
of London and Paris played a role in his ability
to break stylistically with the realism of Courbet. Whereas his earlier works depicted Oriental objects in an anecdotal manner, Whistler
incorporated Oriental compositional devices
into the actual structure of his view of the harbor at Valparaiso. Whistler visited Chile during its battle for liberation from Spain; accord-
ingly, he portrayed the city's harbor filled with
ships and the night sky lit by rockets. His own
liberation was an artistic one. He arranged
forms asymmetrically and created a composition in which the foreground was tilted sharply
up. This general arrangement can also be seen
in *Valparaiso Harbor*, another oil, which may
have preceded the Freer's painting (Fig. 22.1).
But darkness increases the sense of abstraction.
Coupled with blurred forms, compositional
asymmetry encourages the viewer to see
Whistler's canvas as a flat arrangement of patterns on a picture plane, an aesthetic familiar
to the artist from his own collection of Japanese prints. Whistler was to use this abstract
vertical format many times in subsequent
years.

Figure 22.1.
Valparaiso Harbor, 1866,
oil on canvas. National
Museum of American Art,
Smithsonian Institution,
gift of John Gellatly.

Plate 23.
Symphony in Grey: Early Morning, Thames

1871
oil on canvas
45.7 × 67.5 cm.
Inscription: butterfly, "71."

Symphony in Grey offers an abstract view of Battersea, located on the Thames River across from Whistler's Chelsea home. The lyrical monochromatic palette presages Whistler's comment that "colours are not more since the heavy hangings of night were first drawn aside, and the loveliness of light revealed."[1] Here Whistler paints light rather than color. Although night has faded, the colors of nature, already reduced by the wintry fog, are further muted by the semidarkness. Whistler's grays had great charm for Freer and the scholars of Oriental art associated with him. Ernest Fenollosa believed that Whistler's grays "pulsate with imprisoned colors." He noted, "The old Chinese school . . . conceived of color as a flower growing out of a soil of grays. But in European art I have seen this thought exemplified only in the work of Whistler."[2] Other orientalizing elements include the division of the canvas into horizontal bands and a geometric butterfly signature enclosed in a rec-

tangular cartouche not unlike the seals on Japanese prints. A white puff of smoke at the right is carefully balanced by the signature cartouche in a touch of Japanese asymmetry. Whistler was interested in the work of art as a self-contained object. He emphasized the picture plane by allowing the finely woven canvas to show through thinly applied paint. The viewer is never unaware that *Symphony in Grey* is a painted piece of fabric. Additional formal devices help to balance and emphasize the flat surface of the painting. The prominent verticality of the factory smokestack is repeated by the mast of a small boat, effectively negating the spatial distance and pulling the factory back toward the picture plane. The artist's brush work is gestural—almost calligraphic. Long horizontal strokes suggest the flow of the icy river. Whistler's symphony is a quiet one, evoking the hush of a foggy winter morning.

Plate 24.
Variations in Pink and Grey: Chelsea

1871–1872
oil on canvas
62.7 × 40.5 cm.
Inscription: butterfly; "Variations in pink and grey—
  Chelsea," artist's hand, on the back of the frame.

Variations in Pink and Grey belongs to the second stage of Whistler's orientalism, when he began to adopt the pictorial constructions of Japanese art instead of using actual Oriental objects as props.[1] The asymmetrical angularity of the composition, along with its series of flat, sharply tilted spatial registers, reveals Whistler as an avid student of Japanese woodblock prints. However, the scene is not without its sense of place. Whistler may have painted *Pink and Grey* from the second story of Lindsey Houses, which are located by the river.[2] Such a high vantage point was frequently taken by French modernists.[3] A photograph of the river, roughly contemporary with the painting, depicts almost the same spot on the north bank (Fig. 24.1). Whistler has observed the sharp geometries of rigging, the misty quality of light on the river, and even heavily loaded boats riding low in the water. The board fence may indicate that the construction of the Chelsea Embankment had begun. The artist simply made his data abstract, avoiding reportage in favor of artistic synthesis. Even the frame for this painting was designed by the artist and signed with a butterfly.

Figure 24.1.
View of the Thames River,
photograph, ca. 1870.
Royal Borough of
Kensington and Chelsea
Libraries and Art Service.

Plate 25.
Nocturne: Blue and Silver—
Battersea Reach

1870–1875
oil on canvas
49.9 × 76.5 cm.

This nocturne was revarnished more than once
during Whistler's lifetime, and it is possible
that the artist repainted the work in 1892.[1]
Moreover, the painting was treated several
times after it had entered the Freer collection.[2]
However, despite rather a hard life in and out
of conservation laboratories, the painting still
conveys the eloquent beauty that Whistler discovered along the riverfront. His visions of the
1870s had a strong effect upon later percep-
tions of nocturnal beauty. In 1901 Jean Lorraine, a critic of the Belle Epoque in France,
described the Seine in Whistlerian terms: "The
most beautiful sight of all is the dark, reflecting
span of the river, the Seine suddenly constricted between the Palaces of the Rue des Na-
tions and the greenhouses of the Rue de Paris,
bearing reflections and flames in its waters.
. . . Oh! The magic of the night, night with its
everchanging forms! Then the Porte Binet and
its grotesque towers change into translucent
enamel and assume a certain grandeur."[3]
Whistler had recognized such beauty in the
humble warehouses and smokestacks of the
Thames three decades earlier.

Plate 26.
Nocturne: Blue and Silver—
Bognor

1871–1876
oil on canvas
50.3 × 86.2 cm.
Inscription: butterfly.

Nocturne: Blue and Silver—Bognor was one
of Whistler's favorite nocturnes.[1] It was probably the *Bognor* that intrigued a reporter in
1876. He described a picture of "moonlight on
the sea . . . with fishing-boats pushing out
from the shore. A perfect stillness controls the
scene, save where the tide, rippling in upon the
sand, catches with its movement the white
shine of the moon. One little wing-like cloud
hovers above a sea of intensest blue, which
seems to reflect and to contain the fairer tones
of the star-lit blue sky."[2] Anyone who has
stood upon a beach at nightfall, watching one
form melt into another, can recognize that
Whistler's painting has a veristic quality quite
different from his contrived interiors of the
1860s, such as *The Music Room*, which is executed in the manner of French realists. Yet
Whistler was never content with reportage. A
poetic feeling invests this painting with serene
calm. In 1872, about the time the *Bognor* was
painted, Whistler's friend Degas wrote to
Tissot, "Remember me to . . . Whistler who
has really found a personal note in that well-
balanced expression, mysterious mingling of
land and water."[3]

Plate 27.
Nocturne in Black and Gold: Entrance to Southampton Water

ca. 1875–1876
oil on canvas
47.6 × 63.1 cm.

The *Nocturne in Black and Gold* was described in 1882 as follows: "It is a mystery, the charm and fidelity of which we acknowledge, composed of the darkest grey and dusky olive tints, among which a beacon lamp rises on a pole above a space of apparently irresolvable gloom, but which may be a cottage or a light vessel. Subtly graded gleaming bars and long lines of golden dots in the distance attest the existence of Southampton Water and the town lights."[1] Some of Whistler's very early drawings were made from the decks of river steamers. His tendency to consistently reuse certain vantage points leads to the conclusion that he painted this view from a boat. Its prow points toward the distant harbor. The "pole" is presumably a mast. The 1882 account may be taken as evidence that the work was always rather dark and impenetrable. H. E. Thompson's comment in 1921 that the canvas was "virtually ruined" is certainly an exaggeration.[2] However, the nocturne is one of several works in the Freer collection that have suffered from gradual darkening over the years.

Plate 28.
Nocturne: Cremorne Gardens, No. 3

1872–1877
oil on canvas
44.9 × 63.1 cm.

This view of Cremorne Gardens, a popular London resort on the west edge of Chelsea, is one of a series of Whistler's nocturnal scenes from modern life, discussed at length in the essay "Artist and Site."[1] The specific spot depicted may be either the old hotel on the grounds, or else Ashburnum Hall.[2] The somber canvas was one of the last works of art to enter Freer's huge collection. He died a month after buying the *Nocturne*.

Plate 29.
Nocturne: Trafalgar Square,
Chelsea—Snow

ca. 1875–1877
oil on canvas
47.2 × 62.5 cm.

In this nocturne, Whistler concerned himself with the effects of winter weather in a small urban square. Snow scenes were frequently painted by Impressionist artists, and both Whistler's theme and its treatment remind us of his lasting ties to the Parisian art community. Like many of his French contemporaries, Whistler chose to avoid well-known parts of his city. He did not paint the Trafalgar Square beloved of tourists, adorned with Nelson's Column and the National Gallery of Art. Instead he focused upon a modest square of the same name on London's west side, far

removed from crowds of visitors.[1] Similarly, Impressionist painters often elected to paint out-of-the-way sections of Paris and its suburbs.

Trafalgar Square, Chelsea, was located between Kings Road West and New Brompton Road. A map from a London guide book printed in 1867 includes outlines of buildings.[2] Whistler probably painted a view of the square's northwest corner, looking toward New Brompton Road in the distance. The blocky architecture of the square is rendered in a slightly warm gray-brown. Overlapping the

roof lines, cool grays and blues mingle, softening the geometry of the long buildings that face the park. Like fog, a haze of gray pigment seems to seep in from the edges of the canvas. The bare limbs of trees are shrouded in the mists of what may be early evening, yet no human is present. Street lamps have been lit and they form an inviting band of yellow, orange, and red spots across the canvas, suggesting the shelter to be found indoors away from the chilly, gathering gloom.[3]

Plate 30.
Nocturne: Grey and Silver— Chelsea Embankment, Winter

1879
oil on canvas
62.6 × 47.5 cm.

During the winter of 1879 there was so much ice floating on the Thames that "between the bridges the river appear[ed] as if it had been frozen over."[1] Such natural weather conditions stimulated Whistler's imagination. His resulting wintery nocturnes combine verism with poetry.[2] By the end of Whistler's career, it was the poetic side of his work that was most readily apparent. The critic Jacques-Émile Blanche noted in 1905 that Whistler was generally perceived as "une sorte de Mallarmé de la peinture." Such artist-writer equations abound in the Whistler literature. Blanche also emphasized that the fashionable success of Whistler's art in Paris at the turn of the century coincided with similar developments in other spheres: "En effet, le succès parisien de Whistler éclata à une époque d'alanguissement général. En peinture, dominaient les teintes grises; en musique, une mièvrerie maladive, dans les lettres, un goût malsain de bizarrerie et de mystère factices, joint à une manie . . . de l'exceptionnel et de l'occulte."[3]

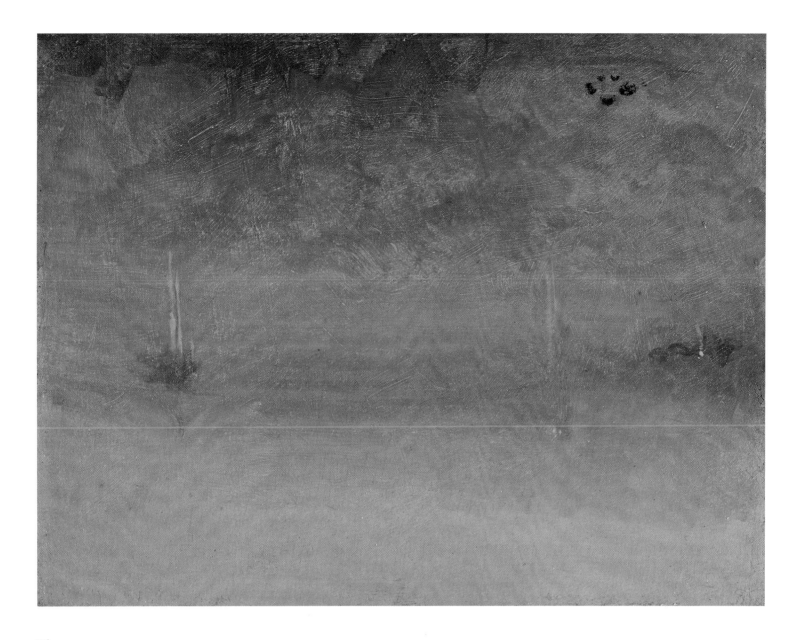

Plate 31.
Nocturne: Silver and Opal— Chelsea

early 1880s
oil on panel
20.3 × 25.7 cm.
Inscription: butterfly.

The Chelsea Bridge, built in 1858, serves less as a subject than as a formal element in this nocturnal view of the Thames River.[1] Whistler has positioned the structure as a divider separating water from sky, a familiar formula in his work. The artist differentiated the two registers further by varying the brush work in each one. However, even though *Silver and Opal* seems abstract, there is an element of verism here. In 1892 a newspaper critic pointed out how "the suspension bridge seems to grow on you and then to fade away just as in the foggy twilight, when the lamps are being lit, it really does."[2] In contrast, Whistler's early works of the 1860s, while executed in the mode of Courbet's realism, involve highly manipulated surfaces and pictorial spaces.

Plate 32.
Chelsea Shops

early 1880s
oil on panel
13.5 × 23.4 cm.
Inscription: butterfly.

This view of an unidentified Chelsea street
could be the earliest of Whistler's studies of
shop fronts. It is certainly among the most detailed.[1] However, a roughly contemporary
photograph of Chelsea shows that Whistler
simplified what he saw from the very beginning of the series (Fig. 32.1). Grid patterns
were a common feature of the streetscape as
Whistler knew it. But he regularized his subject
further by eliminating the jostle of disparate
roof lines. Small rectangles of the brightest
yellow, along with a few touches of red and
blue, hold the center of the composition, and
its tectonic structure seems appropriate for an
architectural subject. It has been pointed out
that Whistler's division of the picture plane
into regular units anticipates geometric abstraction of the twentieth century.[2]

Figure 32.1.
Chelsea, Corner of Danvers
Street and Cheyne Walk,
photograph. Royal
Borough of Kensington and
Chelsea Libraries and Art
Service.

Plate 33.
Red and Blue: Lindsey Houses

ca. 1882–1884
oil on panel
13.4 × 23.5 cm.
Inscription: butterfly.

The Lindsey Houses were completed by 1674 and had been divided into seven separate dwellings by 1774. They are still one of Chelsea's most famous landmarks.[1] Whistler lived here from February 1867 until he moved to the White House in 1879.[2] Sometime after leaving, he decided to paint a picture of the residences, but he shows the back rather than making a more conventional choice to depict the riverfront façade (Fig. 33.1). The open field at the left of the painting was the Moravian Burial Ground.[3]

Figure 33.1.
Lindsey Houses, River Façade, photograph, ca. 1870. Royal Borough of Kensington and Chelsea Libraries and Art Service.

Plate 34.
Harmony in Brown and Gold:
Old Chelsea Church

ca. 1884
oil on panel
8.9 × 14.8 cm.
Inscription: butterfly.

The Chelsea section of London was dominated
by the square tower of Old Chelsea Church,
"the waterman's landmark of weathered Car-
oline brick that was always the pivot of village
life." [1] The light-colored block of J. Johnson's,
coal merchant, can be made out to the left of
the tower. Further to the left, there is a white
building that may be the Adam and Eve Tav-
ern, the subject of an earlier Whistler etching,
or another tumble-down structure at the
river's edge. [2] A panoramic photograph, made
about 1870, demonstrates the artist's accuracy
(Fig. 34.1). It is somewhat unusual for Whistler
to adopt an old-fashioned topographical viewpoint, and it may be that he was evoking a
memory. The building of the Chelsea Embankment began in 1871. Although Old Chelsea
Church survived, the Adam and Eve was destroyed along with many of the crooked little
shops and houses visible in the photograph. [3]
Whistler used very thin oil, and the woodgrain
of the underlying panel shows through in this
ghostly image of Chelsea as it once was.

Figure 34.1.
Panoramic View of
Chelsea, photograph, ca.
1870. Royal Borough of
Kensington and Chelsea
Libraries and Art Service.

Plate 35.
An Orange Note: Sweet Shop

1884
oil on panel
12.2 × 21.5 cm.
Inscription: butterfly; "An Orange Note—Sweet Shop. No.
    38   Catalogue, **Notes, Harmonies, Nocturnes** 1884.";
    signature, butterfly, artist's hand (on back of panel); "W.
    Flower Old Swan House. Chelsea" (on back of panel).

An Orange Note: Sweet Shop received much
favorable comment in newspaper reviews of
the Dowdeswell exhibition held in 1884.[1] Although the site for the scene may have been St.
Ives, Cornwall,[2] a contemporary photograph
of a typical Chelsea side street shows the type
of heavy, low architecture that Whistler would
have found in either town (Fig. 35.1). He dispensed with most architectural detail, however. His street became a shallow stage set for
the group of figures in the doorway. The lus-
cious allure of goods displayed in the window
is intensified by the absence of color elsewhere
in the painting, save for the reds in the clothing
of the children. Whistler painted a variation on
this theme at about the same time.[3]

Figure 35.1.
Back Street in Chelsea,
photograph. Royal
Borough of Kensington and
Chelsea Libraries and Art
Service.

Plate 36.
Black and Emerald: Coal Mine

1883–1884
oil on panel
8.8 × 14.0 cm.
Inscription: butterfly.

Changes wrought by the industrial revolution provided some stirring imagery for mid-century British painters. The coal mines of Britain fueled the country's industrialization, and, not surprisingly, coal miners were sometimes an artist's chosen subject.[1] While Whistler's early paintings and etchings of the 1860s include laborers along the Thames River, he painted no miners, and the artist's neutral or non-polemical air moves away from the ambitious allegories of the British.

French painters also admired the worker-hero and sometimes depicted the coal industry.[2] Whistler's composition for *Black and Emerald* conjures up Claude Monet's *Unloading Coal*, painted in 1872 (Fig. 36.1). However, Whistler differed from Monet in choosing to paint the other end of the supply chain. His quiet country setting is devoid of human activity. Monet subordinated his subject to design considerations, possibly related to Japanese prints.[3] Whistler also used asymmetry, balancing the structure of the mine against a large blank foreground space which is opposite on the diagonal.

The work was exhibited during the 1880s.

Its lack of finish would have been immediately apparent to any viewer. As Linda Nochlin has pointed out, sketchy paintings "constituted a serious challenge to traditional values both by being a statement of contemporary reality and by embodying a forceful, innovating viewpoint towards it."[4] This issue occupied young French painters of the 1860s, at the outset of Whistler's career. Twenty years later, *Black and Emerald* carried on the celebration of the oil sketch as a complete (as opposed to finished) work.[5] Noted for his wit, Whistler may have engaged in a pun to invest this tiny painting with a significance out of proportion to its modest size. The subject, a coal mine, relates *Black and Emerald* to earlier allegories about honest labor. A hard-working artist, committed to the concept of the artist-as-hero, Whistler left the miners out of the composition but did record his own presence through expressive brush work.[6] Exhibited in Paris in 1887 as *La Mine abandonnée*, the painting may also constitute Whistler's comment upon academic tradition, that is "finished" painting as a played out ideological vein for artists.

Figure 36.1.
Claude Monet, *Les Déchargeurs de Charbon à Argenteuil*, oil. Private collection. (Photograph: Giraudon/Art Resource, Inc.)

Plate 37.
Note in Green: Wortley

ca. 1884
oil on panel
13.5 × 23.4 cm.
Inscription: butterfly.

Whistler was a visitor to Wortley Hall in the early 1880s.[1] Wortley is a remote country village located in Yorkshire, six miles southwest of Barnsley.[2] In Whistler's freely painted composition, the modest geometries of the village buildings are isolated from the viewer by an expanse of thinly applied green pigment striated with calligraphic brush work. The actual location of the scene is far less important than the viewer's sense of the artist at work.

Plate 38.
Note in Blue and Opal:
The Sun Cloud

1884
oil on panel
12.4 × 21.7 cm.
Inscription: "No. 52 Catalogue Notes Harmonies
    Nocturnes 1884. The Sun Cloud, Note in blue and opal.
    J. McN. Whistler," artist's hand, on original backing.

Whistler is credited with such remarks as
"There are too many trees in the country," and
he avowed that "seldom does nature succeed in
producing a picture."[1] Yet frequent visits in
the countryside or at the seashore provided
him with points of departure for tight compositions whose precise balance always reveals
conscious artistry. Probably painted in St. Ives
during Whistler's winter sojourn in 1884, *The
Sun Cloud* is more abstract than what Whistler
actually would have witnessed, but the bright,
cool colors embody a lasting freshness that
made such free sketches appealing to modern
artists of Whistler's era.

Plate 39.
Green and Silver:
The Devonshire Cottages

1884
oil on canvas
32.0 × 62.8 cm.
Inscription: butterfly.

Green and Silver is large compared to other landscapes painted by Whistler during the 1880s. The artist personally considered the painting to be a special one, and it was owned for many years by his brother.[1] In composition, however, it is remarkably similar to *Liverdun*, a much earlier etching (Fig. 39.1). When *Green and Silver* came up for sale in 1895, Whistler revealed his anglophobia, specifying that it "must be sold to Scotsman American German Frenchman whoever you please—but *not* to an Englishman."[2] Whistler would have been pleased to know that the painting eventually fell into the hands of his patron and friend Freer.

Figure 39.1.
Liverdun, etching, K16,
second state. Freer Gallery.

Plate 40.
The White House

ca. 1884–1885
oil on panel
13.6 × 23.6 cm.

Pencil lines show that Whistler began this composition by placing his white house at the far
right edge of the panel. His decision to shift the
strip of architecture to the left increased the
illusion of spatial depth. Had the right edge of
the white building touched the frame, it would
have flattened the pictorial space by bringing
the building forward and giving it a formal
relationship to the picture frame. Whistler's architectural configuration resembles the buildings seen at closer remove in *Green and Silver:
The Devonshire Cottages*, which was painted
at about the same time as this small panel.
Fresh colors evoke a sense of the brisk sea air
that whips up white clouds above the house.

Plate 41.
Low Tide

ca. 1883–1884
oil on panel
13.8 × 23.5 cm.
Inscription: butterfly.

Low Tide may belong to the series executed in and around St. Ives, but it is an unusual composition for Whistler and the colors are richer than in the other St. Ives panels. Perhaps the painting was exhibited at Dowdeswell's in 1884, but it cannot be identified by title. The jumble of boats next to fishermen's huts recalls works by Monet painted at Étretat in western France at about the same time.

Plate 42.
Blue and Grey: Unloading

ca. 1883–1884
oil on panel
8.9 × 14.8 cm.
Inscription: butterfly.

This diminutive work focuses upon a large subject—the constant transfer of goods along British waterways. *Unloading* continues a theme seen much earlier in Whistler's etched scenes of the Thames River.[1] However, the image is altogether different in treatment, with far less detail provided. A few starkly silhouetted lines convey a mast used as a winch with block and tackle. Round, commalike strokes are sufficient to represent heavy barrels. The panel is a good example of the proximity of Whistler's oil and watercolor techniques during the 1880s.

Plate 43.
Grey and Silver: Mist—
Life Boat

1884
oil on panel
12.3 × 21.6 cm.
Inscription: butterfly.[1]

The rigorous lives of hardy English fishermen and their families inspired many painters of Whistler's generation. One is reminded of Winslow Homer's series begun at Tynemouth on the North Sea in 1881. Freer owned one such painting (Fig. 43.1).[2] However, in contrast to the monumentality of Homer's figures, which convey the strength of honest laborers pitted against the sea, Whistler presented a more subtle message in this image from St. Ives. His palette is restricted to elegant gray-greens, and the figures are tiny. Rust-red defines the jacket of one woman on shore. A brighter peach-pink stroke draws the viewer's eye to the lifeboat. By means of an aesthetic solution, Whistler solved the problem of how to connect the women on shore with the men in the boat upon which their survival depended. But he also painted his butterfly signature rust-red, formally balancing the touches of bright color on an otherwise almost monochromatic surface. Whistler insisted that "the picture should have its own merit, and not depend upon dramatic, or legendary, or local interest."[3]

Figure 43.1.
Winslow Homer, *Early Eve ning*, 1881–1907, oil on canvas. Freer Gallery.

Plate 44.
The Angry Sea

1884
oil on panel
12.4 × 21.7 cm.
Inscription: butterfly (possibly added later).

According to Whistler, he painted this small
but eloquent panel at St. Ives, Cornwall, during a visit that lasted from January to March
1884.[1] The use of an emotive title is unusual
for the artist, but Whistler was the veteran of
many a channel steamer crossing and has managed to convey something of the rigors of
travel in rough waters. The skies are a forebod-
ing gray. A steamer is pinned on the horizon
line, churning through heavy seas. Judiciously
placed whitecaps form a decorative parallel to
the shape of the steamer, but they outnumber
the ship and exceed it in size. The flat open
beach, contrasted with the rolling ocean,
evokes the promise of relief to be found on dry
land, yet the amount of unpopulated empty
space between the viewer and the struggling
ship serves as a reminder of the ocean's might.

Plate 45.
The Sea and Sand

1884
oil on panel
13.4 × 23.4 cm.
Inscription: butterfly.

There is little textural difference between sea
and sand in this thinly painted panel. Whistler
grounded it with a warm mauve-gray before
brushing on a thin glaze of gray-blue for sea
and a slightly thicker glaze of gray-brown for
sand. The two elements are divided by breaking waves, rendered in bluish-white. The panel
is abstract and elegant in its emptiness. The
figures on the beach counterbalance the heav-
iest surf, at the upper left. The white ribbons of
paint that represent waves are wet and runny,
incorporating tiny air bubbles, as surf is comprised of churning water mixed with air.

Plate 46.
Violet and Silver:
The Great Sea

ca. 1884
oil on panel
13.8 × 23.5 cm.
Inscription: butterfly.

Heavy surf and boiling clouds are captured as
much by Whistler's gestural use of the brush as
by the silvery whites, mauve-grays and deep
blue-greens that make up the painting's
vibrant palette.[1] Whistler kept a newspaper
cutting that described this panel as "rough and
vigorous."[2] *The Great Sea* is elegant rather
than rough, yet the brisk colors are as invig-
orating as bracing sea air.

Plate 47.
Grey and Brown:
The Sad Sea Shore

1885
oil on panel
12.5 × 21.7 cm.

Probably painted during the fall of 1885, *Grey and Brown* carries the sense of approaching winter. The panel is unusual in Whistler's *oeuvre* for it shows no visible horizon.[1] After several efforts evident in pentimenti above and to the left of the seated woman, Whistler arrived at the final placement of people on the beach. Strollers at the far right follow the artist's common practice of using figures as vertical transitional points between horizontal registers of sea and sand. Backs turned, they emphasize a sense of departure, and the eye is drawn to them by a brick-red umbrella, the only bit of strong color in the painting. Whistler decided to engulf the central trio in brush work whose sweep evokes a chill autumn wind off the channel. The somber palette is as sad as the title, and Whistler reinforces the mood with a pair of abandoned chairs to the left of the panel.

Plate 48.
The Summer Sea

1880s
oil on panel
12.9 × 21.6 cm.
Inscription: butterfly.

This panel is not accepted as a Whistler painting, although it was acquired from J. J. Cowan through Marchant, the London dealer, along with *The Angry Sea*.[1] The painting was not included on a list of works about which Cowan asked Whistler for information in 1902, but it was exhibited as a Whistler in Edinburgh in 1904. There is no indication that Freer questioned the painting's authenticity. Nonetheless the composition is loose, almost flaccid, in comparison to *The Angry Sea* or any one of the other seascape panels in the collection. The boats fail to perform Whistler's characteristic taut transition from sea to sky, and the figures are fussy and weakly drawn. A photograph of this work in the Pennell collection has Menpes's name, and "Dieppe" on the verso. Whistler's pupils Mortimer Menpes and Walter Sickert accompanied the master during his 1884 visit to St. Ives, and Whistler stayed with Sickert in Dieppe in September 1885, after he traveled to Holland with Menpes.[2] Perhaps the painting was executed by one of Whistler's students.

Plate 49.
Red and Pink:
La Petite Mephisto

early 1880s
oil on panel
25.4 × 20.3 cm.
Inscription: butterfly.

La Petite Mephisto is closely related to
Whistler's watercolor *Milly Finch*, with its
pentimento of a seated nude. This image of a
woman on a couch contains the ghost of another behind and to the right. The sketchy handling of forms as well as the hot colors translate comfortably from watercolor to oil, and it
would be difficult to say which was painted
first.[1] The painting probably makes reference
to Ellen Farren, one of the prime stars of the
Gaiety Theatre in London. Whistler frequented the Gaiety during the 1870s. "Our
Nellie," as Miss Farren's public called her, appeared in *Little Dr. Faust* in October 1877.[2]
She was noted for her ability to electrify the
audience. As one newspaper critic put it, "Elle
a la diable au corps." [3] Whistler's image, while
general, evokes devilish high spirits. Rendered
in bright reds and pinks, the subject peeks
coyly out from behind her enormous fan.

Baudelaire had written earlier on courtesans
and actresses: "Against a background of
hellish light . . . red, orange, sulphur-yellow,
pink (to express an idea of ecstasy amid frivolity), and sometimes purple (the favourite
colour of canonesses, like dying embers seen
through a blue curtain)—against magical
backgrounds such as these, which remind one
of variegated Bengal Lights, there arises the
Protean image of wanton beauty." He went on,
"These reflections concerning the courtesan
are applicable within certain limits to the
actress also; for she too is a creature of show,
an object of public pleasure." [4] Whistler's allu-
sion to a burlesque stage star links *La Petite
Mephisto* to café concert scenes by Degas
(Fig. 49.1).

Figure 49.1.
Edgar Degas, *Cabaret*,
1875–1877, pastel over
monotype. Corcoran
Gallery of Art, William A.
Clark collection.

Plate 50.
Note en Rouge: L'Eventail

ca. 1884
oil on panel
8.8 × 14.7 cm.
Inscription: butterfly.

Although the composition of *L'Eventail* is generally similar to *The Little White Sofa* (Fig. 50.1), Whistler used the vibrant colors of *La Petite Mephisto*. Whistler again orchestrated gesture and color. The placement of the model's finger in her mouth is suggestive, while the open fan may be read as an open invitation, according to "fan language" of the late nineteenth century.[1]

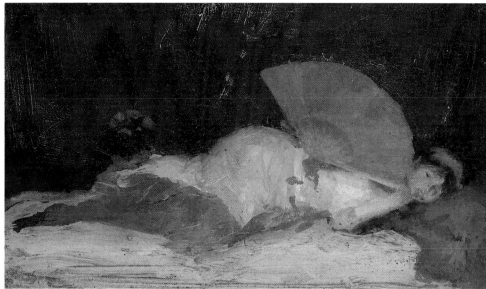

Figure 50.1.
The Little White Sofa, oil on panel. Courtesy of the Fogg Art Museum, Harvard University, Bequest of Grenville L. Winthrop, 1943.

Plate 51.
Arrangement in Grey: Portrait of Master Stephen Manuel

ca. 1885
oil on canvas
50.8 × 38.1 cm.
Inscription: butterfly.

The ineffable delicacy of Whistler's grays and blacks are nowhere better exemplified than in this sensitive portrait of Stephen Manuel, Whistler's young relative by marriage.[1] Fluid execution and thinly applied paint were characteristic of Whistler's portraits during the 1880s. The elegant palette would appeal later to Freer and to historians of Oriental art, who "conceived of color as a flower growing out of a soil of grays."

Plate 52.
The Butcher's Shop

late 1880s
oil on panel
12.5 × 21.8 cm.
Inscription: butterfly; "Butcher Shop—Dieppe" (on verso of
frame).[1]

Like Rembrandt and Daumier before him, Whistler found the butcher shop a suitable subject for art.[2] Although diminutive, the panel is compelling. The rust-reds, pinks, and oranges of hanging meat are repeated in the awning above them. The reds are not particularly bright, but surrounded by neutral grays and ochres they gain intensity. Whistler rivets the viewer's eye on the subject with a graphic circular splotch of red underneath one of the two beef carcasses. To the right of the red splotch, a large pink planter repeats the color of the meat. However, Whistler leaves the passage of red under the beef obscure. It is up to the viewer to determine whether it represents another planter or a dripping puddle of blood.

Plate 53.
The Grey House

1889
oil on panel
23.6 × 13.8 cm.

Whistler probably painted this panel during his visit to Amsterdam in September 1889. The painting conflates ideas that appear in two etchings from the same trip. The composition, set in a vertical format, recalls *The Embroidered Curtain* (Fig. 53.1), but the panel depicts the site Whistler used for *Jews' Quarter, Amsterdam* (Fig. 53.2). Although the painting was left incomplete, Whistler put in a few strokes of peach and red. Through contrast, this modest amount of color is sufficient to bring out the vibrancy of the silvery-grays.

Figure 53.1.
Embroidered Curtain,
etching, K410, fourth state.
Freer Gallery.

Figure 53.2.
Jews' Quarter, Amsterdam,
etching, K415. Courtesy of
the Library of Congress.

Plate 54.
Gold and Orange:
The Neighbors

ca. 1894–1895
oil on panel
21.6 × 12.8 cm.
Inscription: butterfly.

There is a thin, almost ghostly quality about
some of Whistler's late views of back streets
and alleyways. His familiar formula uses a grid
pattern to lock figures into an overall decorative design. Titles combining various color
combinations have been used over the years to
describe *The Neighbors*. Together the changing titles record the elusive quality of
Whistler's subtle palette.[1]

Plate 55.
The Little Nurse

1895
oil on panel
12.6 × 21.7 cm.
Inscription: butterfly; Goupil label (back of frame).[1]

According to Whistler, he painted this scene in
Lyme Regis during his visit there from September to November 1895.[2] The careful placement of figures in relation to the dark rectangle
of an open door and the motif of one child
carried by another recall earlier shop-front
scenes painted in Chelsea. Whistler consistently transferred his general formal vocabulary from one site to the next.

Plate 56.
Vert et Or: Le Raconteur

1896–1900
oil on canvas
51.4 × 31.3 cm.

Whistler's attraction to "typical" street urchins
with some sort of exotic or foreign characteristic recalls an established tradition in European art—that of painting national or regional
types. Whistler abhorred narrative art, but
here the subject of the painting is the telling of
a story, not the story itself. In the expressive
face and gesture of the sitter, Whistler captured
everyone's delight in a tale well told.

Plate 57.
The Little Faustina

1896–1900
oil on canvas
50.9 × 30.4 cm.

Whistler was always in search of interesting models. With her level gaze and self-possessed calm, this engaging urchin is capable of captivating the viewer as well as the artist. Freer believed the sitter to be the sister of the young storyteller in *Vert et Or: Le Raconteur*. He saw these and related paintings of Italian children in Whistler's studio.[1] In his diary Freer wrote of Faustina, "The marvellous little girl, full face, eyes looking into futurity—Her two little hands folded and resting in her lap." [2] The title may be a somewhat melodramatic reference to the child's future potential as a temptress.[3]

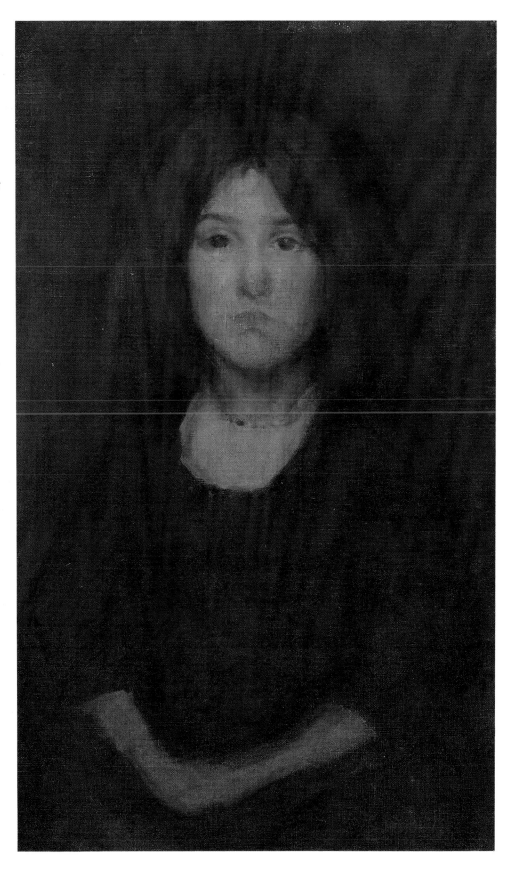

Plate 58.
Green and Gold:
The Little Green Cap

1896–1901
oil on canvas
51.0 × 30.9 cm.
Inscription: butterfly.

For a discussion, see Plate 59.

Plate 59.
The Little Red Glove

1896–1902
oil on canvas
51.3 × 31.5 cm.

Plates 58 and 59 are two in a series of about ten portraits Whistler began in 1896. They all depict Lillie Pamington, a girl whose red hair caught Whistler's eye as he passed through one of London's somewhat squalid thoroughfares near his Fitzroy Street studio.[1] In a sense, the portraits can be viewed as variations on a theme. Each has a dominant color scheme, but the composition does not change markedly from one painting to the next. It is possible that Whistler based his composition on a large study photograph of a Dürer image.[2] Like Dürer's young boy, Whistler's Lillie has an oval face with finely drawn features. Her wide,

folded sleeves and soft cap atop long, flowing hair, as well as the choice of a head and shoulders floating against an empty background, all recall the photograph (Fig. 59.1). Freer was eager to have these paintings, which he saw in Whistler's studio. He recorded *Green and Gold* in his diary as "Little girl with perfectly painted face . . . Superb," but he did not manage to acquire it until 1907.[3] However, Freer got Whistler to agree in advance to his purchase of *The Little Red Glove*, which Freer bought in June 1903.

Figure 59.1.
Albrecht Dürer, *Portrait of a Young Boy*, photograph from Whistler's studio. University of Glasgow Library, special collections.

Plate 60.
Rose and Gold: The Little Lady Sophie of Soho

1898–1899
oil on canvas
64.5 × 53.5 cm. (oval).
Inscription: butterfly.

The painting is modeled on Sophie Burkitt, the daughter of the artist's landlady at 8 Fitzroy Street.[1] Freer found that Whistler's picture appealed "as perhaps of his very best" yet found it "so illusive" that it would "baffle the cleverest photographer."[2] When the painting was exhibited at the Metropolitan Museum in 1910, a reviewer called it "one of the most perfect of Mr. Whistler's productions, with its dignity of repose, its wonderfully vital expression, now smiling, now earnest, the very essence of soul and movement, which alone was Mr. Whistler's power to convey to the canvas."[3] But the very language in which the painting is discussed points toward its historical underpinnings. One need not search far for Whistler's muse. *The Little Lady Sophie of Soho* represents his attempt to capture the enigmatic half smile of Leonardo's *Mona Lisa*.[4]

61

Plate 61.
Harmony in Blue and Gold: The Little Blue Girl

1894–1903
oil on canvas
74.7 × 50.5 cm.
Inscription: butterfly (on frame).

Freer's request for a picture "hinting at Spring" eventually resulted in this young standing nude. The somewhat overworked surface is a palimpsest that records multiple changes to the image, some of which were made following the death of Mrs. Whistler. At that time the anguished artist told Freer, "I write you many letters on your canvas." But one wonders whether Whistler was ever actually satisfied with the work. Although his patron paid for the picture in 1894, it was still in the studio at the time of the artist's death in 1903.

Plate 62.
Purple and Gold: Phryne the Superb!—Builder of Temples

1898 ff.
oil on panel
23.6 × 13.7 cm.
Inscription: butterfly.

Painted at the end of Whistler's long career, this small panel is something of a reprise, combining several of the leitmotifs that run throughout Whistler's *oeuvre*—Venus, the courtesan, and the mistress as model.[1] Phryne was a wealthy courtesan who offered to pay for the rebuilding of Thebes after it was destroyed by Alexander during the fourth century B.C. Moreover, she was the mistress of Praxiteles, the Greek sculptor.[2] As his mistress, she may have served as the model for Praxiteles' statue of Venus. *Purple and Gold* was begun early in 1898 as part of a planned series of large decorative compositions that also would have included an Eve, a Dannae, an Odalisque, and a Bathsheba.[3] However, like the "Six Projects" of the 1860s, Whistler's late plans for large decorative figural paintings never were fully realized. Freer saw this panel in Whistler's studio in 1900 and arranged to purchase it upon completion. Whistler exhibited the panel, and then worked on it again in 1901. Although Freer paid for *Phryne* in 1902, the painting was still in Whistler's studio at the time of the artist's death. The scrubbed and overworked surface of the panel is a testament to the intensity with which Whistler continued to explore these well-worn motifs.

Plate 63.
Rose and Brown: La Cigale

1899
oil on panel
27.7 × 12.6 cm.

Rose and Brown: La Cigale typifies Whistler's ability to create a complex work of art stimulated by current events yet based upon ideas that had interested him for years. On March 17, 1898, a group of London theater personalities took part in a five-hour benefit for Ellen Farren, once the greatest attraction of the Gaiety Theatre.[1] Shortly thereafter, Whistler painted this youthful nude, one of many that he created at the end of his own career.[2]

Miss Farren first caught Whistler's interest two decades earlier in *Little Doctor Faust*.[3] The Gaiety next presented a French play called *La Cigale*. Rewritten as a burlesque vehicle for Miss Farren, the play opened in December 1877 as *The Grasshopper*, and Whistler attended it more than once.[4] *The Grasshopper* poked fun at "Impressionist" painting, however loosely understood, and the sets included a comic portrait of Whistler by Pellegrini.[5]

The grasshopper in the play was an acrobat. Whistler's diminutive nude image evokes ancient statuettes of athletes. But during the 1890s, Nellie Farren was crippled with rheumatism and could no longer sing and dance on the stage. Another character in *The Grasshopper* was Pygmalion Flippit, "the artist of the future." In mythology, the sculptor Pygmalion fell in love with an ivory statue which was brought to life by the goddess Aphrodite. Whistler's slender, ivory-colored young girl seems a gentle hommage from one aging star to another.

Plate 64.
Grey and Gold:
High Tide at Pourville

1899
oil on panel
13.9 × 23.4 cm.
Inscription: butterfly.

Although Whistler's last years were marked by illness, he was not entirely unproductive. Late in July 1899, he rented a house at Pourville-sur-Mer, a resort near Dieppe. He was there on and off for convalesence until October, but he found time to paint at least eight small marines.[1] This panel can be compared with Whistler's view of Trouville, another French resort, executed thirty-four years earlier (Fig. 64.1). *Harmony in Blue and Silver: Trouville* is a much larger work, but it presents essentially the same composition. What has changed is the scale, now tiny, and the brush work. While the surface of the earlier painting is a series of thinly applied paint films, *High Tide* is made up of ribbons of buttery soft green, gray, and blue pigments, a palette typical of the Pourville works.

Figure 64.1.
Harmony in Blue and
Silver: Trouville, oil on
canvas, Isabella Stewart
Gardner Museum, Boston.

Plate 65.
Blue and Silver:
Boat Entering Pourville

1899
oil on panel
14.1 × 23.4 cm.
Inscription: butterfly.

An extremely loose and unusually smudgy handling of pigment characterizes this view of the beach at Pourville. A steamer approaches the port while a crowd looks on. Although he has chosen to depict a scene of anticipated arrival, Whistler suggests a sense of loneliness. His palette is subdued, save for a single bright red spot that centers the composition. A lone figure stands off at the left side. Whistler's grief after his wife died in 1896 was to haunt him for the rest of his life. Yet, in formal terms, the placement of images also makes perfect sense. A diagonal, formed by the crowd on the beach, slopes toward the left, reinforced by a single thin brush stroke of dark gray. The boat, the isolated figure, and the butterfly signature form the points of a long wedge that emphasizes the thrust of the arriving boat's intended path.

Plate 66.
Portrait of Charles Lang Freer

1902–1903
oil on panel
51.8 × 31.7 cm.

Although they met in 1890, Freer was closest
to Whistler near the end of the artist's life.
Whistler began this portrait in May 1902.[1] The
sitter was then forty-six years old. In June, artist and patron traveled to Holland with the
intention of viewing works by Rembrandt.
Rembrandt's rich tonalities might have governed the appearance of the portrait had it
been completed. But Whistler was stricken
with illness and spent six weeks in The Hague
with Freer at his side, so dangerously ill that
the *London Morning Post* printed a premature
obituary.[2] Whistler's health was impaired for
the remainder of his career, and the unfinished
portrait was still in the studio when Whistler
died in July 1903. Despite all this, Freer seems
to be one of the few patrons who actually enjoyed sitting to Whistler.[3] He wrote, "Whistler
is great just now! I am spending much of my
time with him and in doing my portrait he is
making me look like a pope, but then that is all
right as there will of course be *little* of Freer in
it. It will surely be all Whistler!!"[4]

Plate 67.
Frame for Caprice in Purple and Gold: The Golden Screen

ca. 1864
gold leaf on wood and gesso
76.2 × 93.4 × 4.5 cm.

Whistler intended that gold and deep red would surround *Purple and Gold*, but at some point this frame became separated from its painting. Decorated with bamboo motifs and whorls, as well as circular motifs based upon the paulownia leaf, the frame bears cast ornament as well as carving, and is related to another frame designed by Whistler for *Purple and Rose: The Lange Leizen of the Six Marks*.

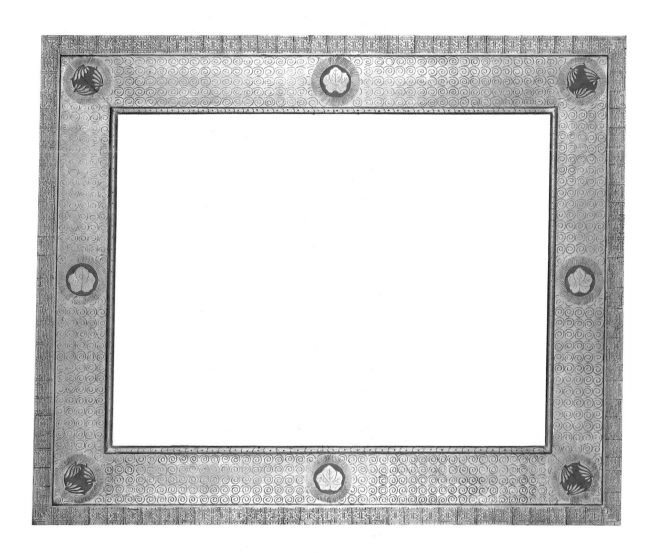

Plate 68.
Frame for **La Princesse du Pays de la Porcelaine**

ca. 1864
gold leaf on wood and gesso
235.6 × 148.6 × 4.5 cm.

A combination of carved and cast motifs similar to those on the frame for *Caprice in Purple and Gold: The Golden Screen* suggests that Whistler had a standard vocabulary of decorative patterns which he liked to apply to frames for his orientalizing pictures of the early 1860s. The patterns are drawn from the *Grammar of Ornament* or another pattern book of the day.

Plate 69.
Frame for **Variations in Pink and Grey: Chelsea**

ca. 1871–1872
gold leaf and oils on wood
82.5 × 60.3 × 2.8 cm.

Whistler might have found the pattern of incised lines that decorates this frame on blue and white porcelain. As Ira Horowitz has pointed out, Whistler was probably not familiar with the Eastern significance of the patterns he borrowed.[1] The frame also includes reeding that eventually became the most recognizable element of the "Whistler frame." The butterfly was thickly painted on. The frame is similar to another that surrounds the artist's self-portrait of 1871–1873, now at the Detroit Institute of Arts.

Plate 70.
Frame for **Arrangement in White and Black**

ca. 1876
gold leaf and oils on wood
218.5 × 118.1 × 5.1 cm.

This frame again combines the indented, colored parallel lines and elegant reeding of Whistler's frames designed in the 1870s.

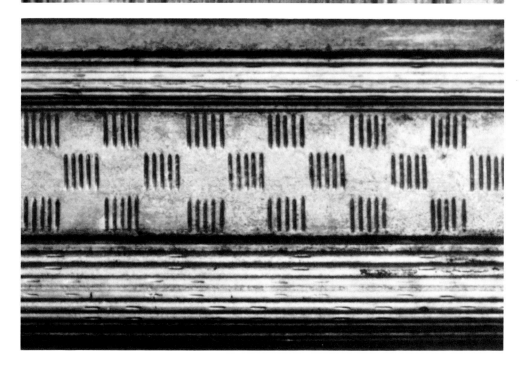

Plate 71.
Frame for
Harmony in Blue and Gold: The Little Blue Girl

1894–1903
gold leaf, oil on wood
105.4 × 81.3 × 7.6 cm.

The last frame to be decorated by Whistler carries on patterns in the painting itself. The blue squares alternate with gold in a checker motif that echoes the pattern on the rug underneath the model's feet. In this case, the blue and gold of the frame repeats the blue and gold harmonies of the painting, and Whistler signed only the frame of his carefully integrated pair.

Plate 72.
Staircase dado panels for entrance hall, 49 Prince's Gate

1876
oil and metal leaf on wood
51.1 × 36.8 cm. (typical size).[1]

Seventeen staircase panels represent fragments of the first decorative scheme that Whistler undertook for Leyland at 49 Prince's Gate, London. The panels were completed during the fall of 1876 (Fig. 72.1). Immediately afterward, Whistler began his much better known Peacock Room, also at Prince's Gate. In June 1904, following several months of negotiations, Freer finally completed purchase of the Peacock Room, Whistler's most important program of interior decoration. In July Freer added the staircase dado panels to his collection.[2]

The panels provide insight into Whistler's attitudes toward interior decoration and demonstrate that he drew what he needed from the vocabulary of contemporary decorative art in Britain. However, rather than subscribing to any set ideas, Whistler combined present theories with past practices. His eye was always turned toward the total effect, for his was an individual aesthetic statement, not a generally applicable theory. As he would shortly do in the Peacock Room, Whistler mixed Eastern and Western elements into an eclectic whole. Its central message was sensuous luxury.

Whistler's work on the staircase was the key by which he gained access to the dining room. However the project served not only as entry but also as experiment. The process of gilding, glazing, and painting the dado was to be repeated in the dining room woodwork. Whistler used a Dutch metal process similar to the one employed in the 1890s by Freer for the decoration of his Detroit mansion. Briefly, the process involved five-inch square sheets of Dutch metal foil, an alloy of copper and brass, laid over prepared sizing and covered with semiopaque glazes.[3] Materials for this process were not particularly expensive, considering the splendid effect achieved. A bundle of Dutch metal sheets cost $4.25 in 1900, and three books were sufficient to cover a large dining-room ceiling.[4]

Whistler had previous experience in decorating his own staircase in Chelsea. At No. 2 Lindsey Row he painted flower petals on the dado and a conventional scene with ships on the panels of the hall.[5] Whistler's design was that of a tradition-minded muralist painting realistic distances glimpsed through architectural elements that act as "windows." One drawing combines both the stair decorations and the hall panels with their Battersea-like bridge, boats, and assorted figures (Fig. 72.2). Other extant drawings depict just the boats (Fig. 72.3).[6]

A sketch for the Leyland stair hall describes the essential elements with which the artist

would have to contend: the stair, its balustrade, the Venetian gilt wood carving used as a newel post, the separate panels that form the dado, and a doorway under the stair (Fig. 72.4). The doorway was eventually hidden by a large screen (Fig. 72.1). But Whistler clearly viewed the stair hall as an orchestration of straight and curving lines. His sketch analyzes the design problem in terms of current British design theory. Owen Jones's tenth proposition from *The Grammar of Ornament* reads "Harmony of form consists in the proper balancing, and contrast of, the straight, the inclined, and the curved."[7]

The balustrade itself was gilt bronze, brought to 49 Prince's Gate from the recently demolished Northumberland House at Charing Cross. It was described in 1890 as a "balustrade . . . of admirable design . . . presumed to have been made at the end of the 18th century, at prosaic Birmingham, in the days when taste had not yet utterly abandoned that industrious Town."[8] The staircase is characterized by flowing curves and much open space, punctuated by flat flower heads. As would be the case in the Peacock Room, Whistler faced already installed architectural elements. The artist did not expect style to link his dado decorations to the staircase. Instead, he complimented its sense of openness, using spriggy flower forms that echo the linear quality of the balustrade. He chose japonesque morning glories, stylized according to current series of decorative art. Fine lines tie the flowers to the suggestion of a trellis. The flower heads picked up on the flower forms in the balustrade as well as those in the mosaic floor. Whistler's

Figure 72.2.
Decorations for Lindsey Row, after 1863, pen. Hunterian Art Gallery, University of Glasgow, Birnie Philip Bequest.

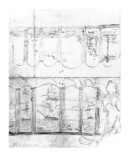

Figure 72.3.
Decorations for Lindsey Row, after 1863, black crayon on brown paper. Hunterian Art Gallery, University of Glasgow, Birnie Philip Bequest.

Figure 72.4.
Sketch of a Stairway at Leyland's House, pencil. Trustees of the British Museum.

Figure 72.1.
"The Stair Case" from *No. 49 Prince's Gate S.W., for Sale by Auction by Mssrs. Osborne & Mercer* (London, 1893).

treatment of illusory space is much more sophisticated than it was when he painted conventional ships seen through architectural elements at Lindsey Row. Heavy moldings again act as "windows" through which we see the morning glories on their trellis. But the flowers float upon the surface. Infinite, dark, unarticulated space is suggested behind the trellis. The abstract evocation of space beyond the wall brought into tension the actual space glimpsed through the balustrade. As one mounted, heavy moldings repeated the rhythmic element of the stair treads, while glints reflecting off the bronze balustrade were echoed by similar glints from the metallic foil on the dado panels. Whistler avoided stylistic imitation of the already present elements of the stair hall in order to bring the whole into spatial harmony, for the balustrade and the dado were in taut and perfect balance.

The dado's overall dark-green color links it to the decorative arts of Jacobean England, as revived by practitioners of the Arts and Crafts Movement. Dark green was a popular choice from the 1860s to the 1880s. At 49 Prince's Gate it was a logical compliment to other Jacobean touches, like the pendant lights based on ceiling drops which were designed by Thomas Jeckyll for the Peacock Room and also used in other parts of the house. In combination with the willow-colored wall paneling above the stair-hall dado, the dark green formed a "greenery-yallery" scheme beloved of British aesthetes and denounced by their critics.[9]

Whistler's use of mottled glazes beneath the flowers in the dado resulted in streaks and striations on each panel. These recalled imitation marble wallpapers of the late seventeenth and early eighteenth centuries (Fig. 72.5). An advertisement from about 1703, taken from a London newspaper, mentioned "Imitations of Marbles and other coloured Wainscots which are to be put in Pannels and Mouldings made for the purpose, fit for the hangings of Parlours, Dining Rooms and Staircases."[10] Again Whistler's choice could be viewed as theoretically orthodox. In Jones's *Grammar*, imitative materials were acceptable whenever the actual material might also have been employed.[11] In France, marble papers were important first as book endpapers, but eventually were used as wallpaper, too.[12] Decorations atop the early marble papers were not unknown in France where "some of Le Breton's loveliest marbles were made on 'royal paper', the size used for octavo books. To these he added stencil decorations of flowers and ornaments in distemper lacquer colours."[13] Whistler also added flowers above his dark, striated glazes on alternating panels of the staircase dado. He was very much intrigued by antique papers, which he avidly sought out for use in his etchings and lithographs. It is not

dangerous to speculate that Whistler would have been acquainted with antique marble papers as well.[14]

Whistler's historicism coupled with current decorative-art theory is further indicated by the inclusion of the trellis pattern that supports the dado's morning glories. A grid pattern evident on all the panels was to some extent dictated by the use of Dutch metal leaf which came in square sheets. However, in numerous panels Whistler chose to emphasize the grid, painting trellislike lines over the metal leaf and glazes before adding the flowers. In some cases he used short cross strokes to bind intersecting lines together as string might bind withes into a real trellis. The morning glories intertwine through and around the grid. This kind of composition can be seen in wallpapers and tiles by some of the era's foremost Arts and Crafts designers, including William Morris, Lewis Day, and William De Morgan. Morris's earliest wallpaper, appropriately named *The Trellis*, had been in production since 1862 (Fig. 72.6). A more abstract design by Lewis Day shows that the concept translated neatly into the "Japanese taste" (Fig. 72.7). Here the vines themselves provide the grid. Whistler was indeed *au courant* when he painted Leyland's staircase. Day's wall paper was designed two years after Whistler had completed his project. A hand-painted De Morgan wall tile from the same period indicates a similar reliance on trellis grids (Fig. 72.8). Whistler went further than De Morgan, avoiding any machinelike quality whatsoever by ensuring that no two of his panels matched. Yet the underlying grid, coupled with the stylization of the flowers themselves, would have met with the approval of more than one theorist supposedly at odds with Whistlerian "art for art's sake."

Japonesque elements in the staircase dado are perhaps the most obvious part of its make-up. Many comparisons with woodblock prints, painted books, and screens from the Edo period could be cited, showing the kind of available inspiration upon which Whistler could model his morning glories (Figs. 72.9 and 72.10). In the late nineteenth century, the panels were likened to aventurine lacquer.[15] However this connection reflects the general disinterest in historical accuracy on the part of early admirers of Japanese art. The aventurine process involves sprinkling gold bits onto layers of wet, opaque lacquer and covering them with transparent amber lacquer. Whistler's Dutch metal leaf process is the opposite, with metallic layers at the bottom, clouded with semiopaque glazes, and finally decorated with painted images. A much more likely inspiration for this technique would be the Japanese screens of the Momoyama and Edo periods (Fig. 72.11). These often had backgrounds of tissue-thin gold or silver leaf laid in slightly overlapping squares. They re-

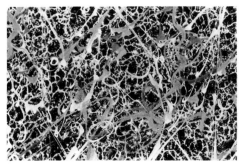

Figure 72.5.
Marble paper, from Sugden and Edmondson, *A History of British Wallpaper 1509–1914* (London, ca. 1914), pl. 50. Reprinted courtesy of B. T. Batsford.

Figure 72.6.
William Morris and Philip Webb, *The Trellis*, designed 1862, wallpaper, from Sugden and Edmondson, pl. 109. Reprinted courtesy of B. T. Batsford.

Figure 72.7.
Lewis Day, *Trellis Dado*, 1877, wallpaper, from Elizabeth Aslin, *The Aesthetic Movement: Prelude to Art Nouveau* (New York, 1981), fig. 10. Reprinted courtesy of Bookthrift of Simon and Schuster, Inc.

flect the light in a cloudy, murky manner suggestive of infinite distances. Opaque flowers and other decorations are painted on top of the metal leaf.

Once completed, the eclectic stair hall at 49 Prince's Gate became a showcase which featured works from Leyland's important collection of Italian primitive and English Pre-Raphaelite paintings. With its impressive and richly decorated stair, the hall served an important role in determining the visitor's initial impression of the house.[16] Whistler's dado was intended to enhance his patron's art collection. Yet Whistler also managed to insert his own art into this showcase, for he made no hierarchical divisions between painting and decoration. The japonesque morning glories on the dado were equally appropriate in his pastel drawing of a draped figure (Fig. 72.12). At Prince's Gate, heavy moldings served to isolate the individual panels like independent, precious little screens. Experienced sequentially, the panels demonstrate Whistler's masterful grasp of the subtleties of Japanese screens decorated with gold leaf:

> *In the darkness of the innermost rooms . . . the gold leaf of a sliding door or screen will pick up a distant glimmer . . . then suddenly send forth an ethereal glow, a faint golden light cast into the enveloping darkness, like the glow upon the horizon at sunset . . . you may find that the gold dust of the background, which until that moment had only a dull, sleepy luster, will, as you move past, suddenly gleam forth as if it had burst into flame.*[17]

Figure 72.9.
Ando Hiroshige. *Flowers in Four Seasons*, fan print. Courtesy of Museum of Fine Arts, Boston, Spaulding collection.

Figure 72.12.
Morning Glories, ca. 1870–1875, pastel on brown paper. Freer Gallery.

Figure 72.10.
Hokuga (follower of Hokusai), *Blue Morning Glories with a Frog*, album leaf. Freer Gallery.

Figure 72.11.
Peonies and Willows, screen, Japan, Momoyama period, late sixteenth century, Hasaegawa school, color and gold on paper. Freer Gallery.

Figure 72.8.
William De Morgan, ceramic tile, 1870s. Private collection.

Plate 73.
Portrait of Whistler

1845
pencil, watercolor
11.8 × 7.8 cm.
Inscription: (v) "Portrait of Whistler in 1845," Freer's hand.

There is no particularly compelling evidence that Whistler did more than sit for this portrait. It resembles images made of him by others during his childhood (Fig. 73.1). The watercolor does not correspond in style or feeling to works known to date some years after 1845.[1] While the attribution has been published three times, in no case was any substantive discussion included.[2] Freer's inscription on the verso leaves doubt as to whether he believed the artist actually created the piece. One possible explanation for the drawing's facility is that Whistler was helped by an adult hand. A more likely explanation, however, is the eagerness with which an accomplished object is attributed to a young artist as evidence of future genius.

Figure 73.1.
The Whistler Brothers, ca. 1845, pastel. Freer Gallery.

Plate 74.
A Fire at Pomfret

ca. 1850
(r) watercolor on brown paper; (v) pen
12.8 × 19.6 cm.
Inscription: (v) "Sketch at Pomfret by James W."

In this early drawing of young men putting out a fire, Whistler concerned himself with volumes and shadows to a degree that entirely disappeared in his mature work. The fragment of a building plan, not necessarily drawn by Whistler, appears on the verso.

Plate 75.
Woman with a Dog and Bird

ca. 1850–1851
ink and watercolor on brown paper
8.8 × 6.9 cm.

Whistler probably made this drawing during
his days at Pomfret, Connecticut. Similar in
style to another drawing now at the Metropolitan Museum of Art,[1] Whistler's standing
woman with a hunting dog and hooded bird is
another example of the Gothick imagery that
entranced him at an early age. Whistler added
touches of pink and blue watercolor to the
woman's plumed hat. His attempt at stylized
elegance foreshadows that characteristic of his
mature full-length portraits.

Plate 76.
Two Lovers and an
Old Woman
Leaf from the **Album of
Archie Gracie**

ca. 1852
ink and watercolor on lace paper
6.3 × 9.9 cm.

While he was at West Point, Whistler employed the somewhat eclectic working manner
of an illustrator. He combined fine lines and
crosshatching with sweetly sentimental expres-
sions, revealing that popular prints and book
illustrations were a major stimulus at this
point in his career. The face of the old woman
in this watercolor is virtually identical to the
chaperone that appears in another flirtation
scene now in the collection of the Metropolitan Museum of Art. Whistler applied watercolor after completing his drawn image. Related drawings without watercolor are
reproduced as Plates 141–144.

Plate 77.
The Cobbler

1854–1855
watercolor
10.4 × 14.9 cm.

Whistler sketched numerous illustrations of novels by Dickens, Dumas, and Hugo in the margins of his notebooks at West Point. This watercolor probably dates from that time or shortly thereafter.[1] *The Cobbler* approximates a passage from *The Pickwick Papers*. Sam Weller, a lovable cockney souse, was one of Charles Dickens's most popular characters. Sam met a cobbler in "The Fleet," the London debtors' prison:

> *His face was a queer, good-tempered, crooked featured piece of workmanship, ornamented with a couple of eyes that must have worn a very joyous expression at one time, for they sparkled yet. . . . He was a little man, and, being half-doubled up as he lay in bed, looked about as long as he ought to have been without his legs. He had a great red pipe in his mouth, and was smoking, and staring at the rush light, in a state of enviable placidity.*[2]

In general *The Cobbler* recalls eighteenth-century illustrations, but contemporary sources can also be found. Dickens's novels were profusely illustrated by Robert Seymour, Hablot K. Browne, R. W. Buss, and others.[3] As is typical of Whistler's early work, the image conveys a strong sense of the anecdote illustrated:

> *"Do you always smoke arter you goes to bed, old cock?" enquired Mr. Weller of his landlord, when they both retired for the night. "Yes, I does, young Bantam," replied the cobbler. "Vill you allow me to en-quire vy you make up your bed under that 'ere deal table?" said Sam. "Cause I was alvays used to a four-poster afore I came here, and I find the legs of the table answer just as well," replied the cobbler. "You're a character, sir," said Sam."*[4]

Plate 78.
A Street at Saverne

1858
watercolor, pencil
29.8 × 23.3 cm.
Inscription: "S.H.," "1858," Haden's hand; "——, Place St.
Thomas 3."

Whistler's visit to Saverne, a village in Alsace
Lorraine, occurred in August 1858. That fall
he returned to Paris, where he printed *Twelve
Etchings from Nature*, also known as *The
French Set*. An image related to this watercolor
was included as number 6 in the set. Etching
and watercolor share the same title, although
certain changes were made. The etching is
much smaller than the watercolor, and the image is reversed. The watercolor shows blue
skies and has a free and sketchy linear quality.
But successive states of the related etching become darker, with the lines coming closer and
closer together in straight verticals and hori-
zontals that tend to simplify the masses and
heighten the scene's dramatic impact in a manner reminiscent of Charles Meryon (Figs. 78.1
and 78.2). Whether or not *Street at Saverne*
was drawn from memory, as reported by the
Pennells, it probably was used by Whistler in
the development of his etching.[1]

Figure 78.1.
Street at Saverne, etching,
K19, second state. Freer
Gallery.

Figure 78.2.
Street at Saverne, etching,
K19, fourth state. Freer
Gallery.

Plate 79.
Boutique de Boucher—Saverne

1858
watercolor, pencil on blue paper
21.7 × 14.4 cm.
Inscription: "Boutique de Boucher Saverne.—," artist's
hand.

Having met an Alsatian named Dabo at
Gleyre's studio in Paris, Whistler was invited
to visit eastern France during the summer of
1858. He began at Saverne, or Zaberne, a village located to the northeast of Nancy. *Boutique de Boucher* is one of the picturesque village views made during his stay. Whistler drew
the entire composition in pencil before adding
blocks of wash to focus the viewer upon the
butcher and his wares. These are contemplated
by a little boy while a young girl sits off to one
side. Whistler balanced his group of figures
and shop details with large empty spaces that
occupy the upper part of the sheet. For most of
the ancient building, Whistler let his tinted paper support suggest the soft texture of a plastered façade struck by bright sunlight. Whistler
bracketed the composition with the jutting angular wall of the building on the left as well as
the vertical block of shadowed space on the far
right.

This early view of a little village store presages oils and watercolors of shop fronts made
during the 1880s.

Plate 80.
The Kitchen

1858
watercolor, pencil
19.3 × 14.2 cm.

The Kitchen was preceded by a pencil drawing,
A Kitchen at Lutzelbourg (Fig. 80.1). Both the
drawing and the watercolor contain ideas
which the artist utilized for an etching also
entitled *The Kitchen* (Fig. 80.2). The pencil
drawing exhibits a strong sense of spatial recession. Whistler built the drawing up from
back to front. The woman was added after the
window frame was drawn; the jug and box
came after the fireplace and shelf. Although
Whistler smudged in shadows with his finger,
the drawing is full of light. The related watercolor is much richer in contrasts. It was drawn
in pencil before dark washes were added.
Again, the drawing is built from back to front,
with the figure of the woman added atop the
window frame and so on. Whistler's emphasis
on orthagonals and spatial recession has a relentless, pedantic quality. By increasing the size
of the woman in relation to the window, and
by adding the heavy dark mass that frames her
figure, Whistler greatly dramatized the image.
He retained the compositional geometries of
objects first seen in the pencil drawing, but the
objects themselves have changed. The angle of
the fireplace wall became a broom handle; the
double doorway with its hatrack was replaced
by a massive cupboard. The space itself has
been narrowed considerably. Whistler's etching retained the dark figure against the light-
filled opening of a cavelike space.

Figure 80.1.
A Kitchen at Lutzelbourg,
1858, pencil. Freer Gallery.

Figure 80.2.
The Kitchen, etching, K24,
second state. Freer Gallery.

Plate 81.
The Kitchen

1858
watercolor, pencil
30.4 × 19.7 cm.
Inscription: (v) "Drawing for The Kitchen W.19," Freer's
    hand.

Despite Freer's inscription, neither this watercolor nor the pencil drawing that preceded it,
entitled *Cuisine à Lutzelbourg* (Fig. 81.1), is
directly related to an etching. Similar subject
matter treated in a similar sequence—from
pencil drawing to watercolor to etching—may
have confused Freer (see the previous entry).
As was consistent with his technique at this
time, Whistler added the figure of a woman
after he drew details of the room, including the
large box which the woman partially obscures.
Other details, like the straw hat hanging by the
door, are taken from Whistler's standard formal vocabulary.

This watercolor translated the pencil drawing into bold areas of light and dark. A rather
weak pencil sketch was substantially enhanced
by wash blocks that create and maintain the
space. Whistler gave the composition a strong
tectonic structure by extending the shelf completely across the far end of the room parallel
to the picture plane. The woman's relation to
stove and oven as well as other details from the
drawing were changed in the watercolor. The
scene in Figure 81.1 may be a view of the opposite end of the kitchen discussed in the previous entry. Alternatively, the space could have
been invented in Whistler's studio after he returned from his trip armed with pencil
sketches.

Figure 81.1.
Cuisine à Lutzelbourg,
1858, pencil. Freer Gallery.

Plates 82–89.
Illustrations for A Catalogue of Blue and White Nankin Porcelain

1876–1877
82. 21.8 × 16.2 cm.
83. 22.3 × 17.9 cm.
84. 20.5 × 14.1 cm.
85. 22.5 × 17.5 cm.
86. 22.6 × 17.1 cm.
87. 22.5 × 17.2 cm.
88. 20.3 × 13.4 cm.
89. 20.3 × 13.8 cm.
watercolor
Inscription: butterfly (all).

Charles Lang Freer did not care to own blue and white porcelain, yet he did gradually acquire eight watercolor illustrations made by Whistler for a catalogue of Sir Henry Thompson's collection of blue and white porcelain that was published in 1878. The sumptuous final versions of Whistler's illustrations, in combination with preliminary studies, provide important evidence of the artist's developing watercolor technique. At the same time, they remind us that many aspects of Whistler's *oeuvre* must be seen as facets reflecting the shared interests of a tightly interwoven, frequently quarrelsome artistic community.

Whistler eventually fought with both of his collaborators on this lavish publication project—they were the collector Thompson and the dealer Murray Marks.[1] Whistler had been among the earliest collectors of blue and white porcelain, and one of his primary suppliers was Marks, who lauded Whistler's collection as one of the most important in England.[2] The watercolor illustrations for Thompson's collection can be dated to the period between October 1876 and January 1877. Presumably, the Freer objects should belong near the end of the period since they are all final renderings.[3] The watercolors coincide with Whistler's decoration of the Peacock Room, another scheme involving a collection of blue and white porcelain assembled with the help of the dealer Marks. That scheme also ended in personal discord for Whistler.

Whistler's appreciation of blue and white porcelain was aesthetic rather than historical. The artist went so far as to create designs for

his own blue and white china, adapting motifs from his paintings and frames (Fig. 82–89.1). While it is not known whether any dishes were actually produced, Whistler's designs are contemporary with those of more practical artists like Félix Bracquemond, whose table services based upon comic sketches from Hokusai's *Manga* were put into production in France.[4]

Blue and white pieces decorated both Whistler's home and his atelier (Fig. 82–89.2). The artist was fond of using such porcelain for his eccentric breakfast and dinner parties.[5] Perhaps in imitation of Whistler, Marks staged an elaborate dinner on blue and white to celebrate the publication of the Thompson catalogue and the accompanying exhibition of his collection. Whistler's watercolor illustrations were also exhibited. Foods were carefully selected for the color harmonies they would produce against blue and white dishes. The period's recherché appreciation of the china for its color alone can be seen in remarks made by guests, such as "observe the effect of the exquisite pink [smoked salmon] on that lovely blue."[6]

On the printed invitation to the private viewing of the Thompson collection, Whistler is portrayed wearing his metal-rimmed glasses and scrutinizing a piece of blue and white pottery (Fig. 82–89.3). The illustration suggests that Whistler adopted an analytical approach to studying blue and white for the catalogue. Earlier, Whistler had exploited the aesthetic appeal of blue and white pieces from his own collection in several oil paintings. *Purple and Rose: The Lange Leizen of the Six Marks*, 1864, depicts Whistler's model-mistress Jo Hiffernan in a completely fanciful vignette as a "Chinoise en train de peindre un pot" (Fig. 82–89.4).[7] As a collector, Whistler was perfectly aware that blue and white decoration involved an underglaze technique, yet Jo is shown "painting" upon a shiny pot whose high gloss identifies it as an already completed studio prop. In the Thompson catalogue project, Whistler went beyond the anecdotal employment of pots as props, for his purpose in creating the illustrations was to convey information about particular objects. Watercolor was an appropriate medium, for blue and white porcelain was actually decorated using a

Figure 82–89.3.
Invitation to Thompson exhibition, 1878, from C. G. Williamson, *Murray Marks and His Friends: A Tribute of Regard* (London and New York, 1919), repr. opp. p. 40.

Figure 82–89.4.
Purple and Rose: The Lange Leizen of the Six Marks, 1864, oil on canvas. Philadelphia Museum of Art, John G. Johnson collection.

Figure 82–89.5.
Drawing of porcelains submitted by Whistler to Sir Henry Thompson as suggestion for illustrations in his catalogue, from Williamson, repr. opp. p. 44.

Figure 82–89.6.
Sir Henry Thompson, Plate VII, from *A Catalogue of Blue and White Nankin Porcelain* (London, 1878).

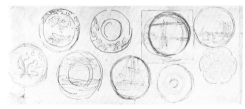

Figure 82–89.1.
Designs for blue and white plates, photograph. Courtesy of the Library of Congress, Pennell collection.

Figure 82–89.2.
Whistler's dining room, Lindsey Row, photograph. Courtesy of the Library of Congress, Pennell collection.

watercolor technique, with lines and washes of cobalt oxide painted directly onto unfired, absorbent white clay.[8] Nonetheless, as the following entries will show, Whistler retained a good deal of artistic license in illustrating individual pieces.

Whistler first prepared a page of sketches, supposedly from memory (Fig. 82–89.5). But soon the artist was carefully examining individual pieces in order to capture their essential qualities. He made preliminary sketches which are more like still-life painting than informational illustrations. A letter from Whistler to Marks confirms that he was working directly from the porcelain. He wrote, "Come down tomorrow morning at about 11 or 12 and take your drawings—they are charming. Bring a lot more pots and take away the old ones."[9]

Margaret MacDonald has discussed Whistler's illustrations of several porcelains, following his artistic process from the initial study to the final catalogue illustration.[10] In general, the final illustrations, including those in the Freer collection, are flatter in treatment than the preliminary studies. They have a more hard-edged quality, coupled with the suppression of shadows and the illusion of depth. However, by making comparisons with actual porcelains, MacDonald shows that Whistler did summarize decorative motifs rather than record every detail.

Whistler's final illustrations stand in sharp contradistinction to the six plates rendered by the collector Thompson (Fig. 82–89.6). Thompson's work is muddy compared to Whistler's. It has a lifeless quality that is unequal to Whistler's crisp summations, which suggest that the artist was already well advanced in the handling of watercolors by the late 1870s. Their quality was confirmed by their rapid sale. As Whistler told the dealer Marks in his letter requesting more pottery, "Your drawings I think you will find much more valuable than you expected."[11]

Plate 82.
Thompson, plate XII, no. 172

Whistler's preliminary sketch in gray wash bisects the form of the vase, probably as an aid to the capture of its symmetrical curving form (Fig. 82.1). The line is eliminated in the final version, but the two drawings are so close in size that Whistler might have traced the form from one sheet to the next. The vase is described in the Thompson catalogue as one of two, even eleven inches high, decorated with persons of rank and marked on the base with a leaf. The decorations depict a mandarin, but were erroneously described in the catalogue as "a lady rising to receive a petition: behind her an attendant," which indicates the state of scholarship at the time the Thompson catalogue was compiled. It is possible that the leaf mark was the artemisia leaf, used in the K'ang-hsi period, 1662–1722.

Figure 82.1

Plate 83.
Thompson, plate XVII, nos. 134, 202

The Freer watercolor combines two preliminary sketches, both of them quite painterly and rich with shadowy suggestion. As MacDonald has pointed out, the final version retained much of this artistic spontaneity, making it somewhat difficult to discern the subjects that decorate the porcelains (Figs. 83.1 and 83.2). Whistler used a composition similar to this one in a large painting, *The Blue Girl*. Although the painting is destroyed, a fragment survives as *Purple and Blue*, now in the Freer collection.

The dish was one of two in Thompson's collection. Thirteen inches in diameter, it was decorated with "sharply drawn flowers and leaves painted in white enamel, which form a raised pattern on a ground of bright powder blue." It would have been more common for the decoration to be reserved in white rather than enameled on top of blue, so the description may be incorrect. In any case, neither Whistler's sketches nor the final version are sharply drawn.

There were three covered quadrilateral vases in the Thompson collection decorated with "similar" court scenes "slightly different in detail." One of the vases is now at the Fitzwilliam Museum, Cambridge. Whistler chose to include the panel with a "person of rank seated within a room, on each side two attendants carrying tall fans, before her a female figure dancing on a carpet; at an open window another female figure holding something in a cover; in the foreground four female musicians." In other words, Whistler selected the same type of scene he favored in his own paintings like *The Balcony* (see Plate 6). The vases were marked with beribboned leaves, indicating that they date from the K'ang-hsi period.

Figure 83.1

Figure 83.2

Plate 84.
Thompson, plate XIII, no. 130

Two preliminary sketches preceded the final version of this Rouleu vase clumsily described in the Thompson catalogue as a "cylindrical vase, with thick neck." The elegant vase stood eighteen inches tall and was probably an eighteenth-century piece. Prunus branches decorate the vase—these were popularly called "hawthorne blossoms" during the 1870s. One of Whistler's sketches is awkward in outline, executed on blue paper in gray and blue wash heightened with white (Fig. 84.1). The other has a midline that helps establish the balanced symmetry of the form (Fig. 84.2). In the final version Whistler eliminated most of the shadowy "still life" background and tilted the vase slightly forward, emphasizing its undercut foot and strong silhouette. It was drawn with light-colored ink before the dark background was filled in using a rich wash that left the prunus blossoms in reserve as they would have been on the original porcelain.

Figure 84.1

Figure 84.2

Plate 85.
Thompson, plate XIV, no. 195

Whistler's quick preliminary sketch captured the general proportions and areas of decoration on one of three covered quadrilateral vases in the Thompson collection (Fig. 85.1). The final version has much more detail, rendered in washes of varying density. It shows female figures, described in the catalogue as "Lange Lysen"—the "Long Elizas" familiar in Whistler paintings such as *Lange Leizen of the Six Marks*. The women on the vase are flanking a potted shrub, another motif in Whistler's own paintings (see *The White Symphony: Three Girls*, Plate 11). Described as being marked with the cipher for jade, the vase was probably made in the eighteenth century.

Figure 85.1

Plate 86.
Thompson, plate I, no. 3

The vase in this drawing was one of a pair in Thompson's collection. It was decorated in underglaze cobalt blue and was probably another eighteenth-century piece. Whistler's preliminary design is sketchy, but it clearly differentiates between the two types of decoration on the vase: flowers and leaves in reserve on a light ground, and dark linear cartouches and bands (Fig. 86.1). In the final version the artist again tipped the vase forward, giving the drawing a stronger outline and a somewhat greater illusion of volume.

Figure 86.1

Plate 87.
Thompson, plate XIV, no. 242

By now Whistler's method is familiar. He proceeded from sketchy first versions (Fig. 87.1) to more fully realized renderings. In his final images he consistently increased the tilt of each piece and added lightly washed shadows.

Here Whistler clearly depicts the vase panel with "two mandarins or persons of rank giving instructions to a warrior." Harder to make out are "a rocky landscape with two figures carrying baskets." Least comprehensible are the "lotus flowers and symbols" that decorate the neck.

Figure 87.1

Plate 88.
Thompson, plate III, no. 292

Both the early sketch (Fig. 88.1) and the final version of this oviform covered jar evidence Whistler's concern with the uneven blue underglaze that characterized the piece. The Thompson catalogue described the jar's "transparent wavy blue (brilliant colour)." Areas of dark and light are not consistent from first to final sketch and we may presume that Whistler exercised artistic license. His intimate knowledge of porcelain with its infinitely variegated color was to prove important when he used Leyland's large collection of porcelains as a glittering blue and white "glaze" over the blue-green walls of the Peacock Room. The prunus, or "hawthorne" pattern was so popular during the 1870s that it was also chosen as the decorative motif for the Thompson catalogue cover, and a jar like this one appeared on Murray Marks's trade card.

Figure 88.1

Plate 89.
Thompson, plate III, no. 8

Two sketches precede the Freer version of a globular bottle, one of a pair from the Thompson collection.

Whistler made both a linear sketch and a volumetric drawing with lightly washed shadows before completing his final version (Figs. 89.1 and 89.2). The Freer drawing is rendered in the same technique as other watercolors in the collection—thinly outlined and then filled in with washes of varying density. About seven and a half inches high, the bottle was decorated with "vases, implements and leaves" on a translucent pale blue ground. Such motifs can be identified as part of the "hundred antiques" design which included books, bronzes, paintings, vases, and so forth.

Figure 89.1

Figure 89.2

Plate 90.
Dragonflies and Butterflies

1870s[1]
watercolor on brown paper
26.7 × 17.3–17.4 cm.

Whistler tried drawing several insects on this
sheet. The large dragonfly at the upper left has
a flat linear quality, similar to Whistler's earliest geometric butterflies, which adorn paintings and drawings of the 1870s. Over the
years, Whistler's signature butterflies vary
greatly in appearance but are always highly
stylized.[2] In contrast, Whistler painted the butterfly at the bottom center of this sheet in a
fairly naturalistic manner. The wings are rendered in dewey brushfuls of moist turquoise
and black, suggesting the evanescent beauty
that attracted Whistler to such fragile creatures
as the fitting symbol for his own artistic
presence.

Plate 91.
Venice Harbor

1879–1880
watercolor
12.2 × 27.8 cm.
Inscription: butterfly.

In scale and composition, *Venice Harbor* resembles the broad and distant Venetian views
in related prints and pastels. Except for a
smear of ocher, red, and black in the large boat
at the right, the colors have a dry and scrubbed
appearance, with a great deal of paper left
showing. Touches of semiopaque gouache help
give substance to the buildings strung across
the center of the sheet. While Whistler received
a good deal of attention for his etchings and
pastels of Venice, little notice was generated by
scenes of the city executed in watercolor.[1]
J.M.W. Turner was noted for his watercolors
of Venice, and the critic John Ruskin had
championed Turner while attacking Whistler.
Since Whistler came to the Italian city immediately after the financially disastrous Ruskin
libel suit, it is possible that he decided not to
create his vision of Venice using Turner's
medium.

Plate 92.
Design for the Coloring of a Room

1870s–1880s
watercolor
25.2 × 17.8 cm.
Inscription: (r) "Ceiling—; Cornice; Wall—Venetian Red—
White—Yellow ochre; Skirting board—Venetian Red—
White—Raw Sienna; Waxed floor," artist's hand,
butterfly; (v) "Design for the coloring of a room. A
Symphony in red, white and yellow!" Frederick Keppel's
hand.

Whistler created this interior decorative
scheme in horizontal bands of color akin to his
abstract landscape paintings. Whistler prepared his walls as he would a canvas, in layers
of color that broke through one another to
give life and interest to a seemingly blank wall.
On the back of another color scheme Whistler
explained his method (Fig. 92.1). While none
of Whistler's simple interiors survives, they are
known through little sketches like this one,
and an occasional glimpse of a Whistlerian interior can be seen in the backgrounds of some
of his portraits.

Figure 92.1.
Instructions for coloring a
room, Letter Book 9/4.
Special collections,
University of Glasgow
Library, special collections.

Plate 93.
(r) Study for the Tall Flower and (v) Design for a Wall Decoration

1880s
watercolor
25.3 × 17.6 cm.
Inscription: (r) butterfly.

This study entered the Freer collection with its
current title, although I have not located a finished work called *The Tall Flower*. In general,
the nude standing with her head cocked resembles a number of Whistler's late oils.[1] Although Whistler seems to have partially obliterated it, his scheme for wall decoration on the
verso firmly establishes his interest in rococo
revival interiors. The design just above the
dado is similar to feather patterns used in the
Peacock Room, and the single blossoms recall
a design for a stairway.[2] Together, these elements suggest a date of the late 1870s or early
1880s for the decorative scheme.

Plate 94.
Standing Nude (destroyed)

1880s
watercolor
17.6 × 25.5 cm.
Inscription: "Paris" artist's hand; "Newman" (stamped on
matboard backing).

Although Whistler obliterated this standing
figure in a pink cap, its ghostly remains recall
such compositions as *La Cigale* and *The Little
Blue and Gold Girl*. It is also similar in pose to
the preceding entry. On the verso is a drawing,
Plate 272.

Plate 95.
Miss Alexander

1870s
etching, with watercolor
22.5 × 14.9 cm.

Whistler painted over this etching of one of the
Alexander sisters. He used black washes which
vary in thickness to give the figure greater volume. The scratchy etched lines are absorbed to
some extent in the atmospheric shadows he
added to the sheet. At times Whistler used watercolor upon a proof to indicate intended
changes to the plate. However, in this case it
would seem that he wanted to create an independent work of art.

Plate 96.
Grey and Silver: The Mersey

1880s
watercolor
15.0 × 17.1 cm.
Inscription: butterfly.

The significance of Freer's earliest acquired painting by Whistler is closely related to the patron's previous activity as a print collector (see "Artist and Patron").

Plate 97.
London Bridge

1880s
watercolor
17.5 × 27.5 cm.

Whistler's decision to paint London Bridge in a glowing gray and gold palette recalls the expressive images of bridges on the Thames by J.M.W. Turner (Fig. 97.1). Turner's impact upon Whistler remains an issue still ripe for exploration. Whistler had copied Turner's work by 1855,[1] and he probably viewed the exhibition of Turner's paintings at the National Gallery in London in 1857. However, standard biographies tell us that Whistler "reviled" Turner. Whistler complained that "neither Turner nor Ruskin had the brains to carry on tradition."[2] Turner's art was championed by the art critic John Ruskin, who later became Whistler's adversary in the famous libel suit. This connection may well have something to do with the negative verbiage on Turner that Whistler left behind. However, some of Turner's titles, like *Shade and Darkness* or *Light and Color* seem to presage Whistler's aesthetic concerns, and watercolors like *London Bridge* offer visual evidence that Whistler did not revile Turner completely.

Figure 97.1.
J. M. W. Turner, *The Thames above Waterloo Bridge*, ca. 1830–1835, oil on canvas. Tate Gallery.

Plate 98.
Opal Beach

early 1880s
watercolor
17.7 × 25.3 cm.

In 1884, *Opal Beach* was included in *Nocturnes—Harmonies—Chevalet Pieces*, Whistler's first major exhibition of watercolors. The facility with which the artist painted *Opal Beach* suggests that he had been working with watercolor for some time. Perhaps his early experiments in color lithography of 1879–1880 were an impetus for watercolor painting.[1] But Whistler's monochromatic watercolor illustrations for the Thompson catalogue demonstrate considerable skill by 1878. Earlier pencil drawings related to etchings had been covered with wash blocks as part of Whistler's working process, and even some surviving objects from his youth are water-

colors. By the mid-1870s Whistler was thinning out his oils to achieve translucent layers of color that parallel the effects of watercolor painting. Although Whistler applied his thinned-oil technique to both portraits and landscapes, it seems particularly suited to river and beach scenes—subjects concerned with water. All this argues for a certain amount of cross-fertilization of Whistler's technique as he shifted his interest from one medium to the next. Some of his watercolor beach scenes from the 1880s have a similar visual impact to small seascapes executed in oil during the same period.

Plate 100.
The Mouth of the River

early 1880s
watercolor
17.7 × 25.2 cm.

Various types of river traffic are contrasted in this small watercolor. The subject—ships traveling up the river—is reinforced through compositional means. Whistler narrowed the river mouth into a thin wedge moving to the left. Clouds of steam from several boats trail off in a complementary diagonal. The composition is centered and stabilized by a bright red sail, furled into a thin vertical line.

Plate 99.
Note in Blue and Opal: Jersey

1881
watercolor
13.8 × 25.5 cm.
Inscription: (r) butterfly; (v, on card) "Note in Blue and
   Opal—Jersey. Whistler [butterfly] 13 Tite Street—
   Chelsea," artist's hand.

Note in Blue and Opal: Jersey was probably
painted early in 1881. Whistler's mother died
in Hastings on 31 January 1881. Shortly thereafter, Whistler painted seascapes in Jersey and
Guernsey, before leasing a flat and studio at 13
Tite Street in Chelsea on 22 March 1881.[1]
Whistler used brilliant blues to capture the
bracing effect of winter sunshine and brisk
sea air.

100

Plate 101.
The Bathers

early 1880s
watercolor
25.3 × 17.7 cm.

If the scale of this watercolor is small, its ostensible subject is tiny. Whistler painted an expanse of empty sand as a prelude to minuscule dots which, despite their size, easily can be read as figures in the shallow water. Two bathing machines, wagons in which swimmers of the Victorian era entered the ocean, stand near the figures. Two boats with sails furled act as parentheses around the bathers.

Plate 102.
The Anchorage

early 1880s
watercolor
25.3 × 17.8 cm.
Inscription: butterfly.

Conscious design dominates *The Anchorage*, revealing the impact of Japanese art. We look downward from an unspecified vantage point, while the spatial recession has been flattened and sharply tilted forward. Whistler divided the paper into horizontal registers: beach, sea, and sky. Further registers were created within each element—the linear fence echoes stripes of gray and green water. These formal divisions never become boring, however. The fence is set at a slight angle, repeated by dry little jackstraws of rust and gray-brown that represent masts. Anchored ships form a dark mass asymmetrically placed on the sheet but held in perfect balance by equally dark rocks at the left and a figure silhouetted on the beach. Whistler's butterfly was colored and placed to maintain the surface tension.

Plate 103.
Southend: The Pleasure Yacht

early 1880s
watercolor
25.4 × 17.9 cm.

Again, size and handling relates this watercolor to the foregoing works. Wind fills the
mauve-grey sails of the pleasure yacht. In contrast, an anchored "lighter" with furled sails is
placed in the midground. Lighters were among
the workhorses of river traffic, used to move
goods from place to place. *Southend: The
Pleasure Yacht* reminds us that Whistler, like
his contemporaries in France, was interested in
depicting the leisure activities of the urban
bourgeoisie. Middle-class leisure was earned—
pleasure was one of the rewards of work.

Plate 104.
Grey and Silver: Pier, Southend

early 1880s
watercolor
16.0 × 24.7 cm.

Grey and Silver: Pier, Southend argues for the holistic nature of Whistler's art. The reticent tonalities here achieved in watercolor approach those of Whistler's earlier etchings, such as *Long Lagoon* (Fig. 104.1). The very familiarity of the composition, with its elegant network of dark lines thrown out over a stretch of neutral sky and water, serves as evidence that Whistler applied a consistent vision to different subjects from different sites rendered in different media.

Figure 104.1.
Long Lagoon, etching, K203, first state. Freer Gallery.

Plate 105.
Southend Pier

1880s
watercolor
18.2 × 25.7 cm.
Inscription: butterfly.

The effect of this watercolor is brisk, almost jarring. Most of the forms, including the boats, the pier, and the figures in black, have a transparent quality. But the artist added a few people in bright, thick gouache at the bottom center of the composition. These include one couple wearing sharply contrasted black, white, and pink, and another where the woman's flounced gown is pink and chartreuse. Electric-blue garments worn by members of the group with a child make a third strident passage of color. Whistler broke the horizontal bands of sand, sea, and sky with figures and masts, and he flattened the pictorial space with two touches of brick red—one in the face of the man at dead center on the beach and the other in the sail of the tiny boat out in front of the long pier.

Plate 106.
Southend: Sunset

1880s
watercolor
25.5 × 17.9 cm.

During the early 1880s Whistler executed several watercolor views of Southend on paper this size. However, *Southend: Sunset* is much more abstract and is executed in a rococo-inspired pink and blue palette first seen in architectural decorations of the late 1860s, such as the "Six Projects." Whistler tends to divide landscapes into horizontal bands of color, three or four in number. His treatment of nature does not differ significantly from his designs for walls. Similar color schemes in striated registers can also be found in Whistler's designs for rugs (Fig. 106.1).

Figure 106.1.
Design for a rug, pastel on brown paper. Courtesy of the Fogg Art Museum, Harvard University, Grenville L. Winthrop Bequest.

Plate 107.
The Thames Near Erith

early 1880s
watercolor
16.2 × 22.2 cm.
Inscription: butterfly.

Whistler included enough information in this scene to let viewers identify the industrialized river, but he reduced what he saw to a subtle orchestration of gray and black, brightened with touches of rust at the center of the composition. In 1885, not long after this work was painted, Whistler delivered his *Ten o'Clock Lecture*. Whistler stated: "Nature contains the elements, in colour and form, of all pictures, as the keyboard contains the notes of all music. But the artist is born to pick, and choose, and group with science, these elements, that the result may be beautiful." Whistler's rust-colored butterfly marks the artist's presence. It is very carefully placed, counterbalancing all the visual information that "nature" provided.

Plate 108.
Erith: Evening

ca. 1883
watercolor
14.5 × 24.1 cm.

Whistler here employs a wet technique that allows his curious mauves, ochres, and blue-greens to blend and melt into one another. He has kept the addition of dryly brushed ship's rigging to a minimum in this scene, which contrasts sailing and steam-driven vessels.

Plate 109.
A Little Red Note: Dordrecht

1883–1884
watercolor
12.6 × 21.5 cm.

Whistler's travels to Holland during the summer of 1883 and in January and February of 1884 included visits to Dordrecht, and he may have painted this watercolor then.[1] His sketchbook from the trip contains a similar watercolor note (Figure 109.1). Whistler was elected to the Society of British Artists in November 1884.[2] Among the works he exhibited at the society's Winter Exhibition held in their Suffolk Street galleries was *A Little Red Note: Dordrecht*. The luminous little watercolor was praised in the newspapers as "masterful," "delightful," and "charming." Earlier that year, Whistler had printed "Proposition No. 2," which begins, "A Picture is finished when all trace of the means used to bring about the end has disappeared." One journalist, who must have taken "Proposition No. 2" to heart, found *A Little Red Note* "perfectly magical in the amount and nature of the effects, contrasted with the means employed."[3]

Figure 109.1.
Sketchbook E, p. 41, watercolor, Hunterian Art Gallery, University of Glasgow, Birnie Philip Bequest.

Plate 110.
St. Ives, Cornwall

1883
watercolor
17.6 × 12.6 cm.
Inscription: (r) butterfly; (v) "Thos. Way."

A guidebook of the period described St. Ives as "a quaint old town" occupied with "the coasting trade and pilchard fishery." Whistler displays little interest in detailing the tourist attractions of the place, however.[1] Instead, he depicts the beach, populated with occasional strollers. The long curve of the shoreline is emphasized by a large blank foreground, while its strong geometric shape is anchored by tightly massed buildings. Although greatly simplified, the composition recalls a view of the Riva in Venice, executed only a few years earlier (Fig. 110.1).[2]

Figure 110.1.
The Riva, No. 2, etching, K206, first state. Freer Gallery.

Plate 111.
St. Ives: Sunset

1883
watercolor
12.3 × 17.2 cm.

Whistler left any sense of place behind in this liquid sunset view. Passages of gold, gray, and blue melt into one another, a few semitransparent comma-shaped strokes manage to evoke small boats hurrying back to port. A single gull, black against the sunset, pulls the eye forward, reminding the viewer that *St. Ives: Sunset* is an artistic vision of the day's end, painted on a flat sheet of paper.

Plate 112.
The Ocean Wave

ca. 1883
watercolor
12.7 × 17.6 cm.
Inscription: butterfly.

The size, palette, and liquid handling of this abstract marine relates it to watercolors executed in and around St. Ives. The title recalls Whistler's realistic early oil, *Blue and Silver: Blue Wave, Biarritz*, painted in Courbet's company (Fig. 112.1). Courbet was using photographs by Gustav Le Gray as tools, and Whistler could have known them. But twenty years later, he had no need of such aids. Whistler still organized a marine composition in a few horizontal bands of color. But by the 1880s, he suggested a wave breaking upon the shore using only an ellipse of whitened space at the center of the composition, and paper saturated with wet color represents the ocean he once tried to capture within the canons of photographic realism.

Figure 112.1.
Blue and Silver: Blue Wave,
Biarritz, 1862, oil on
canvas. Hill-Stead Museum,
Farmington, Connecticut.

Plate 113.
The Sea Shore

1883–1885
watercolor
21.5 × 12.8 cm.
Inscription: butterfly.

The Sea Shore demonstrates Whistler's operating opinion that nature alone was incapable of painting a picture. The generalized scene compares to any particular beach as an idealized Greek statue related to the average citizen of Athens. Whistler divided the paper into three registers. He made a visual transition from sky to sea with a trio of sails that break the far horizon line. Three figures on shore break the division between sea and sand. Two figures hold parasols painted the same red and gray as the boats' sails.

114

115

Figure 114–117.1.
Nocturne: Dance-House,
etching, K408, first state.
Freer Gallery.

Figure 114–117.2.
Little Drawbridge,
Amsterdam, etching, K412,
first state. Freer Gallery.

Plates 114–117.
"Amsterdam Nocturnes"
114. Nocturne: Black and Red—Back Canal, Holland

22.0 × 28.4 cm.

115. Nocturne: Grey and Gold—Canal, Holland

29.3 × 23.1 cm.

116. Nocturne: Grand Canal, Amsterdam

22.7 × 28.4 cm.

117. Nocturne: Amsterdam in Winter

20.3 × 27.3 cm.

1883–1884
watercolor
Inscription: butterfly (all).

The "Amsterdam Nocturnes" immediately bring to mind Whistler's series on Cremorne Gardens, executed in oil during the previous decade.[1] These four watercolors bear strong compositional affinities to the earlier group. Once again, large blocks of murky color create abstract patterns broken by scattered sources of light and occasionally punctuated by dimly perceived figures. Margaret MacDonald has called these "the most extreme of his water-colors," pointing out that the artist "almost entirely rejects the qualities of the paper itself, and deluges it with wash over wash of dark colours to obtain effects nearly impossible to realise."[2] The views of Amsterdam and Cre-morne could be related by subject matter as well. The most active scene, *Amsterdam in Winter*, recalls public pleasures at Cremorne, for it depicts an urban crowd at leisure. This time the crowd is skating rather than dancing, but Whistler generates a sense of abandon through both the agitated, ominous atmo-sphere and the indecorous postures of the skat-ers. *Black and Red: Back Canal, Holland*, in-cludes two figures, one clad in black, the other in white, probably a couple on the order of the one furtively leaving the London pleasure garden in *Nocturne: Cremorne No. 3*. Figures walking along the quays in *Grand Canal* and *Grey and Gold* are shrouded in the anonymity afforded by the fog and the night. An etching titled *Nocturne: Dance-House* is clearly re-lated to the Amsterdam watercolors and helps to substantiate this analogy with the Cremorne series (Fig. 114-117.1).[3] Although Whistler chose typical tourist views for some of his daylight etchings of the Dutch city (Fig. 114-117.2), night seems to have found him once again the discreet observer of slightly un-savory scenes from modern life.

116

117

Plate 118.
Reach in Upper Thames

1880s
watercolor
17.8 × 25.4 cm.

The contrast between city and country fascinated artists of Whistler's generation. Many
city dwellers spent their leisure time upriver
from the bustling urban waterfronts of Paris or
London. Whistler's glimpse of a peaceful
Thames backwater was probably made close
to the city, but its idyllic emptiness is a gentle
invitation to brief respite from crowded and
dirty city streets.

Plate 119.
The Rows, Chester

mid-1880s
watercolor, pencil
8.6 × 14.1 cm.
Inscription: butterfly.

Established by the time of the Roman occupation, Chester is located in Cheshire on a sand-
stone height above the river Dee. A number of
ancient structures dotted the town, and its medieval city walls are still intact. However,
Whistler chose to record a more modern phenomenon. The Rows were a sort of arcade
formed by the projection of second-stories out
along the main streets of the town.[1] The rows
housed various stores, and Whistler offers a
glimpse of women shopping, one of the most
remarked-upon activities to characterize the
nineteenth century.

Plate 120.
Chelsea Shops

mid-1880s
watercolor
12.5 × 21.0 cm.
Inscription: (r) butterfly; (v) "stair landing," artist's hand,
   "No. 33."

In both color and composition, *Chelsea Shops*
resembles an oil painting, *Street Scene in Old
Chelsea*, executed by Whistler ca. 1880–1885.[1]
The oil scene can be pinpointed since it includes Maunder's Fish Shop, but in the watercolor the artist has obscured enough detail to
make it difficult to ascertain the exact location. The watercolor may depict shopfronts
farther up or down along the same street. A
topographical drawing of Cheyne Walk west
of Old Chelsea Church shows that Whistler's
art works were based upon remarkably accurate observations of the busy neighborhood
(Fig. 120.1).

Figure 120.1.
View of Cheyne Walk,
pencil, W.W.B. Borough of
Kensington and Chelsea
Libraries and Art Service.

Plate 121.
Chelsea Children

mid-1880s
watercolor
12.7 × 21.6 cm.
Inscription: butterfly.

Most of the children in the painting peer
through the windows of what may be a curi-
osity or art shop of some kind, although one
little girl stands apart from the rest, gazing into
a fishmonger's shop under a sign reading
"Stewed Eels." The artist's butterfly signature
is next to the art-shop entrance. Whistler
wanted to have an art dealership himself, as is
seen in a surviving drawing (Fig. 121.1). In
1897 Whistler finally leased rooms at No. 2
Hinde Street, Manchester Square, to house the
Company of the Butterfly, formed to sell his
work without the intervention of dealers.[1] Although it seems that Freer bought *Chelsea
Children* from Whistler's enterprise, the artist
was no businessman, and he did much better
painting shops than running them.[2] Whistler
has allowed spots and lines of primary red,
yellow, and blue to soak into the paper, im-
parting a shimmering brightness to this
glimpse of his Chelsea neighborhood.

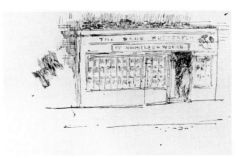

Figure 121.1.
The Blue Butterfly, ink.
Hunterian Art Gallery,
University of Glasgow,
Birnie Philip Bequest.

Plate 122.
Flower Market: Dieppe

1885
watercolor
12.8 × 21.0 cm.
Inscription: (v) "3¾ reeded Whistler" "8 × 4⅝."[1]

A letter written by Walter Sickert confirms
that *Flower Market: Dieppe* was one of several
watercolors given to him by Whistler and that
it was painted in 1885.[2] The master was visiting his pupil in Dieppe that September.
Whistler also painted a number of oils, including *Grey and Brown: The Sad Sea Shore* (Plate
47). In contrast to the gloomy beach scene,
Whistler's view of the flower market is exuber-
ant, full of bright light in which the colorful
blossoms, the awnings, and some of the
women's costumes vibrate in joyous visual harmony, dominated by complementary blues and
oranges. Earlier in 1885, Whistler had delivered his *Ten o'Clock Lecture* for the first time.
Among the many epigrammatic passages was
his observation that the artist "delights in the
dainty—the sharp, bright gaiety of beauty." [3]

Plate 123.
Green and Silver: Beaulieu, Touraine

ca. 1888
watercolor on canvas board
12.9 × 21.6 cm.
Inscription: (r) butterfly; (v) "Beau Lieu Touraine," artist's
    hand, and "E. Mary et Fils, 26 Rue Chaptal, Paris"
    (stamp).

During the summer of 1888 Whistler spent
time in the Touraine region of the Loire Valley,
making a number of etchings which depict
both genre scenes and tourist attractions. Just
south of Tours, Beaulieu-les-Loches is on the
right bank of the Indre River, only about a mile
from Loches, where many of the etchings were
made. (Fig. 123.1).[1] Whistler painted what appears to be a country house in the vicinity. The
child in the foreground is echoed by a tiny
figure behind him, making a formal transition
from the vast green meadow to the house in
the distance. The composition began with dark
clouds which were scraped away before
Whistler painted the pinkish-gray sky. The use
of a canvas support for a watercolor is unusual
in Whistler's work.

Figure 123.1.
From Agnes Sorel's Walk,
etching, K385. Freer
Gallery.

Plate 124.
Breakfast in the Garden

1880s
watercolor[1]
12.7 × 21.9 cm.
Inscription: (v) "Studios"?

While the model for this fluidly rendered watercolor was Maud Franklin, her setting is debatable. Thomas Way, who sold the drawing
to Freer, believed that Maud was sitting in
Ranelagh Gardens, and the work has been
published under that title.[2] Ranelagh Gardens
flourished as a public pleasure ground in
Chelsea from 1742 to 1803. Its popularity
waned during the early nineteenth century,
and it was replanned and planted with shady
walks and undulating lawns between 1859 and
1866. It would have been a restful and se-
cluded spot by the time this watercolor was
painted.[3] However, it seems troublesome to
have dragged furniture to a public garden.[4]
Freer believed that the painting depicts the private garden at the Vale, where Maud and
Whistler were living by 1885.[5] In any case the
watercolor was made in Chelsea, and whether
the spot was public or private, Whistler's gray-
green image is evocative of "old London gardens . . . like pale wraiths of the past."[6]

Plate 125.
Bravura in Brown

early 1880s
watercolor
22.0 × 17.8 cm.
Inscription: butterfly.

Art and music are pointedly conflated in this interior scene. Whistler placed a young woman at the piano, her hands on the keyboard, her music spread in front of her. Above the figure, a small painting has been hung. An empty chair sits next to the musician—it is the artist's. As we must imagine Whistler's presence, we must conjure up the tune played by his mistress. For the musician, bravura connotes brilliant technique or style. Whistler has kept pace with bravura brush work.

Plate 126.
Note in Opal: Breakfast

early 1880s
watercolor
25.2 × 17.6 cm.
Inscription: butterfly.

Maud Franklin posed for a number of elegant little interior views during the early 1880s. *Note in Opal* captures an inviting bourgeois scene: a breakfast table at which the artist's mistress sits reading. The empty chair at the left can again be presumed to be Whistler's, and his artistic presence is particularly strong on that side of the sheet, where he has dampened the paper to exploit the fluid evanescence of his medium. Thus, as the room is awash in light, the paper has literally been flooded with opalescent color. The dissolution of forms in light was a major impressionist theme, and these works correspond in period and feeling to the brightly lit interiors of Berthe Morisot (Fig. 126.1).

Figure 126.1.
Berthe Morisot, *In the Dining Room*, 1886, oil on canvas, National Gallery of Art, Washington, Chester Dale collection, 1962.

Plate 127.
Pink Note: The Novelette

early 1880s
watercolor
25.3 × 15.5 cm.
Inscription: butterfly.

Whistler has constructed a taut and flat pictorial space whose bright colors and patterns
predict the work of the Nabis in France at the
end of the century. Once again the artist's mistress is placed in an intimate setting. Wearing a
pink jacket, she sits on the edge of a rumpled
bed, engrossed in her novel. Entwined with the
bedsheets is a swath of pink fabric that looks
suspiciously like a domino or evening cape.
Whistler painted a portrait of the art critic
Théodore Duret holding such a cape at about
the same time that he executed this watercolor.[1] Duret holds the cape over his arm with
the proprietary air of a man waiting for his
mistress. In the watercolor, another touch of
pink appears in the painting that rests on the
mantlepiece. Surrounded by fans, the prominently displayed painting serves to remind the
viewer that this is an artistic household. The
color pink is used to suggest a link between the
woman reading and the absent artist. Common plots in French novels of the period involved the relationships between young painters and their mistresses.

Plate 128.
Resting in Bed

early 1880s
watercolor
17.0 × 24.0 cm.

Resting in Bed is seductively painted, and Whistler created a sexually charged image of artist and mistress by using much the same vocabulary that informs *Pink Note: The Novelette*. At the far end of the room, a male presence is declared by a black silk top hat. The hat is entangled in the black and pink folds of an evening cape, and we may safely presume a romantic attachment between the woman in bed and the invisible male symbolized by the hat. Again, fans and a picture on the mantle are related by color and suggest artistic occupants, implying that Whistler's watercolor is based upon his relationship with his mistress Maud Franklin. Several related images testify to Whistler's fondness for the general composition (Fig. 128.1). However, variations in the details alter the meaning of each work. By changing the setting to an outdoor hammock, Whistler captured an atmosphere of pleasant idleness (Fig. 128.2). Another watercolor is given a gently domestic turn with the substitution of a coffee pot, napkin, and plate for the domino and silk hat (Fig. 128.3).[1] In 1896 Whistler used a reversed and elaborated variant of the composition to depict his dying wife Beatrix, lying by her balcony at the Savoy Hotel in London (Fig. 128.4).

Figure 128.1.
Girl Reading in Bed, ink.
Courtesy of the Art
Institute of Chicago,
Charles Deering collection.

Figure 128.2.
*Maud Reading in a
Hammock*, watercolor.
Courtesy of the Fogg Art
Museum, Harvard
University, Grenville L.
Winthrop Bequest.

Figure 128.3.
The Convalescent,
watercolor, fig. 10 from *The
Studio Whistler Portfolio*
(London, 1905), Freer
Archive.

Figure 128.4.
By the Balcony, 1896,
lithograph, K124. Freer
Gallery.

Plate 129.
Moreby Hall

early 1880s
watercolor
19.5 × 28.3 cm.
Inscription: butterfly.

Moreby Hall is located just south of York in
the East Riding of Yorkshire. The house was
built from 1818 to 1831 in the "Tudor-Eliza-
bethan" style and is "grander inside than outside." The scale of the interior is quite large for
the size of the house.[1] Moreby Hall is noted for
several features, including a central hall lit
from above and a long gallery that ran the
entire length of the building. Whistler may
have chosen one of these two parts of the
house for his interior view. The watercolor
captures the comfortable yet imposing atmosphere of Victorian country houses with their
eclectic mixtures of old-master paintings, fine
porcelains, overstuffed furniture, and interesting weekend guests, one of whom must have
been Whistler.

Plate 130.
Pink Note: Shelling Peas

early 1880s
watercolor
23.4 × 14.6 cm.
Inscription: butterfly.

Whistler's exploration of standard compositions over the decades was not confined to
landscapes and studio nudes. *Pink Note: Shelling Peas* harks back to his earliest genre scenes,
such as the seated figure with a work bowl,
framed by a doorway, called *La Vieille aux
Loques*, 1858 (Fig. 130.1). The volumetric
treatment of the woman in *Pink Note*, unusual
for Whistler in the 1880s, recalls his sculptural
figure drawings of the late 1860s. The bright
color scheme, on the other hand, reflects a general move away from dark Dutch-inspired tonalities toward the lighter palette associated
with Impressionism. Images of peasants had
been executed by Millet and others since the
1850s. Ubiquitous in popular literature, the
peasant remained a favorite, if increasingly romanticized, subject for the rest of the century
(Fig. 130.2).[1] Elaborate peasant pictures
hardly dominate Whistler's *oeuvre*, but he continued to sketch such figures as late as the
1890s (Fig. 130.3), thereby acknowledging one
of the standard themes of his era.

Figure 130.2.
G. H. Boughton, *Dutch
Peasant*, from *Sketching
Rambles in Holland* (1885),
p. 335. From Whistler's
library. University of
Glasgow Library, special
collections.

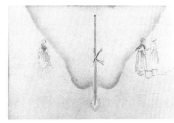

Figure 130.3.
Peasants, pencil, Whistler
Sketchbook, Brittany, 1893,
pp. 30–31. Hunterian Art
Gallery, University of
Glasgow, Birnie Philip
Bequest.

Figure 130.1.
La Vieille aux Loques,
etching, K21, second state.
Freer Gallery.

Plate 131.
Note in Pink and Purple: The Studio

early 1880s
watercolor
30.4 × 22.8 cm.
Inscription: (r) butterfly; (v) "31."

This sketch offers an intimate glimpse of one
of Whistler's studios. The studio interior was a
subject frequently chosen by French, English,
and American artists in Whistler's day. Familiar furnishings include the gaudy rococo revival couch, the square table, now serving as a
stool, and the folding table.[1] Stacks of canvases and swaths of drapery make up the background. Whistler is reputed to have said
"Mauve? Mauve is just pink trying to be purple." Nonetheless, he has skillfully orchestrated pink and purple notes into a rich mauve
chord.

Plate 132.
Milly Finch

early 1880s
watercolor
29.8 × 22.5 cm.
Inscription: butterfly.

During the early 1880s, Whistler created a
number of oils and watercolors using the
model Milly Finch. The group as a whole
forms another block of evidence placing
Whistler firmly within the context of French
modernism. This watercolor, with Miss Finch
reclining and holding a large fan, seems close
to a host of women with fans on couches
painted by Manet during the previous two decades (Fig. 132.1).[1] Whistler's image is a composite, for a partially finished nude sits at the
other end of the couch. The portrait lacks specific overtones of either Spanish or Japanese
exoticism, yet hot colors and a languid pose,
with Miss Finch's little finger raised to her lips
and her bright red fan held aloft, are as suggestive as some of Degas's pastels of café-con-
certs, where singers on stage arrange assignations by signaling with their fans.[2]

Figure 132.1.
Édouard Manet, *Le Repos,*
1870, oil. Rhode Island
School of Design. Bequest
of Mrs. Edith Stuivesant
Vanderbilt Gerry.

Plate 133.
Harmony in Violet and Amber

1881–1884
watercolor
25.2 × 16.3 cm.
Inscription: butterfly.

For discussion, see Plate 134.

Plate 134.
A Note in Green

1881–1884
watercolor
25.2 × 17.5 cm.
Inscription: butterfly.

Whistler's reinterpretation of established poses recalls the self-referential *oeuvre* of his French contemporary Edgar Degas. Both *A Note in Green* and the *Harmony in Violet and Amber* are part of a complex of works that revolve around what is essentially the same pose. The pose could be reversed, turned slightly, or altered here and there, but the most important variations are found in the artist's use of different color combinations.

The pose struck by Miss Finch in *Harmony in Violet and Amber* appeared in Whistler's *oeuvre* about a decade earlier. Whistler was then painting Florence, the daughter of his first significant patron, F. R. Leyland.[1] Miss Finch's pose for *A Note in Green* can also be seen earlier, in an unfinished sketch for the portrait of Leyland himself.[2] Whistler found the pose effective for both sexes, and he seems to have added it permanently to his formal vocabulary. Among the finished oil portraits that precede the two watercolors of Miss Finch are *Arrangement in Black: Portrait of F. R. Leyland*, 1870–1873, and *Arrangement in White and Black*, ca. 1876, a portrait of Whistler's mistress Maud Franklin.[3] In each of these, Whistler explored the use of a monochrome palette.

Whistler reworked the *Portrait of Miss Florence Leyland* in about 1881 (Fig. 134.1), at about the same time he created the two watercolors of Miss Finch.[4] Degas may have stimu-

Figure 134.1.
Portrait of Miss Florence Leyland, 1871–1876, oil on canvas. Portland Museum of Art, Maine.

Figure 134.2.
Edgar Degas, *The Little Dancer of Fourteen Years*, 1880–1881, bronze, fabric. All rights reserved. Metropolitan Museum of Art, Bequest of Mrs. H. O. Havemeyer, 1929.

Figure 134.3.
Whistler's studio, 1881, photograph (detail). Courtesy of the Library of Congress, Pennell collection.

Figure 134.4.
Edgar Degas, *Schoolgirl*, 1881, bronze. Courtesy of the Detroit Institute of Arts, gift of Dr. and Mrs. George Kamperman.

Figure 134.5.
Harmony in Coral and Blue: Miss Finch, oil on canvas. Hunterian Art Gallery, University of Glasgow, Birnie Philip Bequest.

Figure 134.6.
Harmony in Fawn and Purple: Portrait of Miss Milly Finch, oil on canvas. Hunterian Art Gallery, University of Glasgow, Birnie Philip Bequest.

Figure 134.7.
Harmony in Blue and Violet: Miss Finch, oil on canvas. Hunterian Art Gallery, University of Glasgow, Birnie Philip Bequest.

Figure 134.8.
Arrangement in Pink, Red, and Purple, 1885, oil on panel. Cincinnati Art Museum, John J. Emery Endowment.

lated Whistler to all this activity. When the French artist exhibited *The Little Dancer of Fourteen Years* at the Impressionist exhibition in 1881, "Paris could scarcely maintain its equilibrium" and Degas "became the hero of the hour. His name was on all lips, his statue discussed by all the art world" (Fig. 134.2).[5] Huysmans commented that "at the first blow" Degas had upset traditional sculpture, "just as he had long ago shaken the conventions of painting."[6] This would not be the first instance in which Whistler was galvanized by a revolutionary event in the art community.[7]

A photograph of Whistler's London studio, taken in 1881, shows a few studio props, including a statuette of a standing woman in a contemporary costume (Fig. 134.3). Not a commercially produced object, the statuette appears to be "the work of a student modeller," possibly Whistler himself.[8] Like the *Little Dancer*, Whistler's figure is a modern one, and it could easily have been inspired by Degas's triumph. Whistler might also have been aware of another Degas statue of 1881 called *Schoolgirl* (Fig. 134.4). Whistler's statuette is as angular as Maud in *Arrangement in White and Black*. It is obviously related to the two water-

colors of Milly Finch as well as the reworked portrait of Florence Leyland.

Unlike Degas, however, Whistler did not really take up sculpture as a sustained interest. Yet the statuette in his studio did serve him as a tool. Whistler's working sequence cannot be exactly determined, and it is unnecessary to assign an object the role of "study" on the basis of its medium. However, the statuette can be detected in his later paintings. Perhaps it served as a sort of pivot around which the variously related watercolors and oils rotate.

Whistler's statuette conflates the poses of the early Leyland portraits along with that of Maud Franklin. The statuette holds one arm akimbo, the other is extended along the body. In the watercolors now at the Freer Gallery, the poses are again separate: in one Miss Finch has her hand on her hip, in the other her hand is extended, and equipped with a large hat, like the one held by the statuette. Yet each work has a completely different visual impact, largely because of the differing color schemes.

During the mid-1880s, Whistler executed three full-scale oil portraits of Miss Finch. *Harmony in Coral and Blue* (Fig. 134.5) is similar to both the statuette and the watercolor

Harmony in Violet and Amber. *Harmony in Fawn and Purple* (Fig. 134.6) approaches the watercolor *Note in Green*, although the hat has become a fan. For *Harmony in Blue and Violet* (Fig. 134.7) Whistler kept the fan, but moved it. Miss Finch's right arm now holds the flounces of her long dress. In all these works, great variations in color occur, but only slight changes in the pose.

The pose reappears yet again in *Arrangement in Pink, Red, and Purple*, which was probably painted during the autumn of 1885 (Fig. 134.8).[9] The portrait is thought to depict Olga Alberta Caracciolo, but the pose is essentially the one held by the Mlles. Leyland, Franklin, and Finch, as well as by the statuette. J.-E. Blanchet, a fellow artist, purchased the Caracciolo painting in 1885, noting that "I bought [it] from the painter . . . because the pose he used was the same as that in my portrait."[10]

The statuette's whereabouts are unknown, and several of the related paintings have disappeared. But enough survive to record Whistler's fascination with an elegant pose, and his ability to rework a few notes into endless complex harmonies.[11]

Plate 135.
Blue and Silver:
The Chopping Channel

1890s
watercolor
14.1 × 24.2 cm.
Inscription: (r) butterfly; (v) "Blue & Silver The Chopping
    Channel," butterfly, artist's hand.

Abstract and free, Whistler's *Chopping Channel* must have been painted from a boat out on the water. His rough brush work serves as a visual metaphor for the channel itself, which was noted for stormy weather. While the piece may seem "modern" in its abstraction, it can be related to plein-air sketches made by French Academicians like Valenciennes in the late eighteenth century. Such sketches were remarkably abstract and were the first step toward the so-called "subjectless" landscape.[1]

Plate 136.
Rose and Silver:
Portrait of Mrs. Whibley

early 1890s
watercolor
28.2 × 18.8 cm.
Inscription: butterfly.

Whistler's sister-in-law, Ethel Birnie Philip, served him as both secretary and model until she married Charles Whibley in 1895. Just before her marriage, Whistler was at work upon several oil portraits of her, and this watercolor may have been executed at the same time.[1] One oil depicts her in a splendid pink silk gown. Another shows her reading in an armchair. The heavily painted watercolor conflates the pink color scheme with the general concept of a seated figure, but here Mrs. Whibley is lively and pert. Turned in her chair to show off her chic costume, she conjures up the era's custom of visits by fashionable women to artists' studios. Whistler arranged for Freer to acquire this watercolor along with *The Thames in Ice* in 1901.[2] Like the artist, the patron was entranced by the subject of feminine beauty. *Rose and Silver* eventually kept company with several hundred images of women made by various American artists and collected by Freer.[3]

Plate 137.
Blue and Gold:
The Rose Azalea

ca. 1890–1895
watercolor on brown paper
27.8 × 18.1 cm.
Inscription: (r) butterfly; (v) "Blue and Gold—The Rose
   Azalea," butterfly, artists hand.

This graceful figure stands as a lexicon of issues Whistler had begun to explore three decades earlier. The curving posture, draperies,
and bowl of flowers recall the women in the
"Six Projects." The screen behind the figure
reminds us of Whistler's occasional forays as a
designer of decorative art. Finally, his use of
watercolor shows that he was able to manipulate one medium to obtain effects characteristic of another. Thickly applied opaque pigments echo the fragile, chalky surfaces of
Tanagra figurines also seen in pastel drawings
Whistler made at about the same time as *The
Rose Azalea*.[1]

Plate 138.
Venus and Cupid

1890s
watercolor
26.7 × 18.2 cm.
Inscription: butterfly.

Venus and Cupid is one of Whistler's last treatments of this mythological theme. The pink and blue color scheme was seen in his work of the 1860s and 1870s, which included several images of Venus (see Plates 7, 13). This watercolor is also related to numerous prints and drawings in the Freer collection.[1] Here, Whistler chose an absorbent Japanese paper, which gives a softness to the lines that delineate the figures. He has arranged drapery behind the child to suggest large wings.

Plate 139.
Design for a Decorated Fan

1895
watercolor, pencil
17.6 × 11.2 cm.
Inscription: (r) butterfly; (v) "Sketch for Fan. Given to me
by Mr. Whistler, August 1899. C.L.F.," Freer's hand.

Art and music are again associated in this tiny
watercolor design of a girl dancing. Whistler
was one of several artists who contributed to
an elaborate wooden fan (Fig. 139.1).[1] Legible
signatures include those of painters Millais,
Lord Leighton, Alma Tadema, Burne-Jones,
and the concert pianist Paderewski. The fan
was decorated on both sides. A number of the
signatures bear dates, suggesting that the fan
was passed from hand to hand for decoration
during the first half of 1895 (Fig. 139.2). While
portrait busts dominate the decorations,
Whistler's design incorporates an entire figure
in a composition adapted to the rounded end
of the fan rib (Fig. 139.3). The artist made a
pun upon the object decorated, for his little
dancer holds a fan as well as embellishes one.
The only other full figure visible in the photographs is Alma Tadema's woman seated
upon a cushion (see Fig. 139.1). The two
women are symmetrically placed facing one
another. Whistler's butterfly signature recalls
the long-tailed insects that decorate *The Gentle Art of Making Enemies*, published in 1890,
while his puckish little nude relates to many
drawings, paintings, and prints of dancing figures he created during the last decade of his
career. The fan must have been a very special
present for its lucky recipient. Whistler made a
gift of his design to Freer in August 1899.

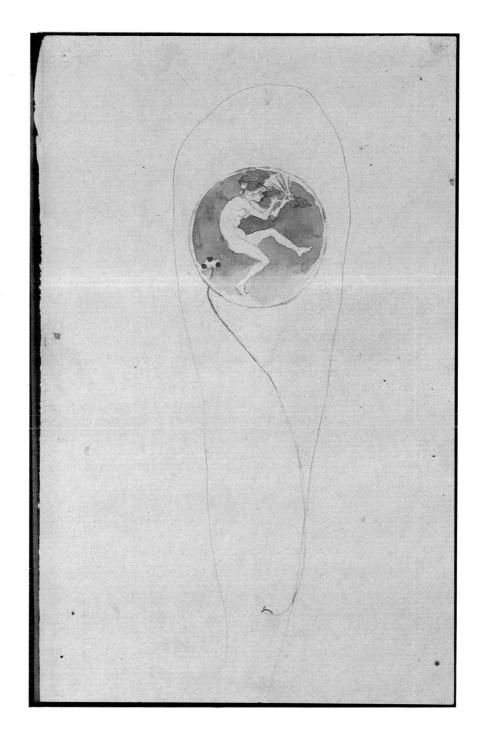

Figure 139.1
Decorated wooden fan,
1895, photograph.
University of Glasgow
Library, special collections.

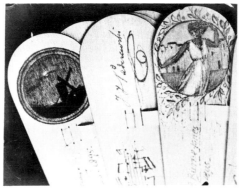

Figure 139.2
Fan detail, verso, with
Paderewski signature.

Figure 139.3.
Fan detail.

Plate 140.
St. Augustine and
Other Figures

ca. 1849–1851
pencil, ink
17.0 × 13.4 cm.
Inscription: "J.W.," "St. Augustine," artist's hand.

This drawing was probably made during
Whistler's sojourn at Pomfret, Connecticut,
between August 1849 and July 1851. It is similar to another drawing of monks now in a
private collection.[1] St. Augustine shows
Whistler's youthful penchant for romanticized
subjects. Whistler first drew the monk with a
child in pencil, then went over the head in ink.
The other figures in ink presumably followed.[2]

Plates 141–144.
Leaves from the Album of
Archie Gracie
141. The Game of Chess

5.2 × 8.6 cm.

142. À la Yankee

3.1 × 5.0 cm.

143. An Outside

3.0 × 5.0 cm.

144. The Corkscrew

22.7 × 18.5 cm.

ca. 1852
(141–143) ink on lace paper; (144) ink on paper[1]
Inscription: "J. Whistler"; (161) "J.W.," artist's hand.

Whistler's style at this point reflected his
awareness of popular prints and book illustrations. His figures are created using crosshatching and fine lines, a method practiced by illustrators of the period. *À la Yankee* and *An
Outside* are each one of two sketches on a
single album page.

141

143

142

144

208

Plate 145.
A Group of Figures at West Point

1852–1854
ink, pencil
22.7 × 18.4 cm.

This sketch is another leaf from the *Album of Archie Gracie*. Nancy Pressley attributed the drawing to Whistler but pointed out that its style is more advanced than the little ink sketches, indicating that it was executed at a later date.[1]

Plate 146.
Portrait of John Ross Key

1854
crayon, white chalk on brown paper
51.5 × 31.0 cm.
Inscription: (v) "Portrait of John Ross Key, grandson of Francis Scott Key, drawn by James McNeill Whistler, in the Coast Survey Office, Washington, in 1854."

Key was a draftsman at the U.S. Coast Guard Survey during Whistler's brief tenure, which lasted from November 1854 until February 1855. Half a century later, Key's article in *The Century Magazine* presented Whistler as a somewhat indifferent member of the survey staff. However, Key recalled that Whistler was frequently inspired to sketch or draw. "One day he took up one of my crayons and began to draw me as I sat at my student's sketch-board. He was not pleased with his effort, and finally threw the half-completed sketch upon the floor; but when I asked him to finish the drawing, he picked it up, and rubbed and erased it several times, something I had never seen him do before. . . . Much displeased with his effort, Whistler again threw the sketch upon the floor, and I picked it up and put it away."[1] The ambitious drawing shows almost no evidence of rubbing or erasure, but it is in poor condition. Key was born on July 16, 1837, and would have been seventeen years old at the time the piece was executed. However, Whistler drew an overscaled head and upper body, making the figure seem childish.

Plate 147.
An Artist in His Studio

ca. 1856
ink, pencil
23.4 cm. diameter.
Inscription: "J. Whistler Au 5me No. 7 Rue Galeres,
 Quartier Latin," "Fuseli".

Whistler arrived in Paris in November 1855,
and lived at various addresses during his student days. While the exact dates of his residence in Rue Galère are not presently known,[1]
the drawing presumably was executed shortly
after his arrival. Before coming to France
Whistler had already developed a drawing
style that combined the rich shadows and detailed crosshatching of Dutch prints with the
caricatural style of French illustrators that include Gavarni, Monnier, and Bertall.[2] He was
still using that style, but the awkward proportions of the figure suggest that he had just begun his studies at the École Imperiale et Spé-
ciale de Dessin and at Gleyre's studio. As a
format, Whistler chose a somewhat self-con-
sciously artistic tondo. A counterpart to the
drawing is entitled *A Scene from Bohemian
Life* (Fig. 147.1). Both drawings evidence the
type of literary preconceptions of "la vie de
bohème" that Whistler brought with him to
the Latin Quarter. A book labeled "Fuseli" lies
on the floor, giving us a clue to his early taste
for romantic art.

*Figure 147.1
A Scene from Bohemian
Life*, ca. 1856, ink.
Courtesy of the Art
Institute of Chicago.

Plate 148.
Standing Figure

ca. 1855–1858
pencil
11.9 × 7.5 cm.

Whistler's pencil drawing of a rather wizened
figure, possibly an old woman, is rather
Gothick in flavor, suggesting that it dates from
his youth. Etchings like *La Mère Gerard* (Fig.
148.1) and *La Mère Gerard, Stooping* demonstrate that Whistler would soon create much
more sophisticated standing figures that recall
these early attempts.

*Figure 148.1
La Mère Gerard*, etching,
fourth state. Freer Gallery.

Plate 149.
Standing Figure, Profile

ca. 1855–1858
pencil, 12.7 × 6.7 cm.
Inscription: "S.H.," Haden's hand.

See Plate 148.

Plate 150.
Profile Sketch of a Child

ca. 1855–1860
pencil
12.6 × 10.2 cm.

Some of Whistler's earliest works depict children, including both relatives and other tots he met on his travels. While this sitter is unidentified, the drawing comes closest to an early etching, *Seymour, Seated* (Fig. 150.1). The two children have similar profiles. The costumes, with stark white Eton collars, large black bow ties, and jackets, are also analogous, although Seymour's hair seems to be somewhat longer than the unidentified child's.

Figure 150.1
Seymour, Seated, etching,
K29, first state. Freer
Gallery.

Plate 151.
Young Man Smoking a Pipe; Bending Figure

ca. 1855–1859
pencil on buff paper
8.4 × 6.9 cm.

Although the paper support differs from most of the drawings executed on Whistler's travels to western France and Germany, it is possible that this drawing dates from about that time. The leaning figure at the lower right could be bending over the side of a boat, and there are several other scenes with pipe smokers that are associated with Whistler's trip. In any case, the drawing is an early one, executed rapidly and with confidence, direct from life.

Plate 152.
(r) Head of a Man in a Tall Hat and (v) Standing Figure

ca. 1855–1859
(r) pencil on buff paper; (v) red chalk
7.9 × 6.5 cm.

Whistler's quick impression of a gentleman of the Victorian era has been rendered with just a few sharp lines which delineate his features, bracketed by the parenthetical curves of the high collar and hat brim. A very slight sketch of a standing figure was executed on the verso in red chalk. The same type of paper support was used for *Young Man Smoking a Pipe* (Plate 151).

152v

Plate 153.
Heads of Two Men

ca. 1855–1859
pencil
14.1 × 11.9 cm.

These two men appear to be sitting at a table. The one on the right resembles a bald man included in *Seated Seamstress with Male Companion* (Plate 197), a drawing identified with Paris. Perhaps these are artist friends of Whistler. However, in general, the piece recalls genre scenes executed during the course of Whistler's travels in the summer of 1858, and it could have been made then.

Plate 154.
(r) Les Côtes à Dieppe and
(v) Cliff at Dieppe

1857
pencil
10.5 × 18.7 cm.
Inscription: "Les Côtes a Dieppe 1857," artist's hand;
    "La Mer a Dieppe 1857," artist's hand.

Dieppe is located on the west coast of France at the mouth of the Arques River. Once a significant port, Dieppe had become a resort town popular with English tourists by the mid-nineteenth century. It offered visitors a lengthy promenade, warm baths, sea bathing, golf links, and a casino.

Whistler depicted the promenade with its large clock that proclaimed the value of middle-class leisure time. He also included the lofty chalk cliffs and the sea beyond. The tightly drawn figures with highly contrasted pencil strokes are similarly distributed in this and Plate 155, suggesting the studio nature of the compositions. On the verso a looser, partially completed drawing of the chalk cliff edged by a column notes the features of the landscape. It was probably done at the site and then incorporated into the more finished drawing on the opposite side of the sheet.

Whistler visited Dieppe many times as he traveled back and forth between Paris and London. According to a guidebook of 1854, packets between Dieppe and Brighton ran four days a week and the trip took only eight hours.[1]

Whistler's early narrative views captured specific attractions. Numerous oil sketches of Dieppe from the 1880s and 1890s are more abstract and are interchangeable with Whistler's views of other French and British coastal towns.[2]

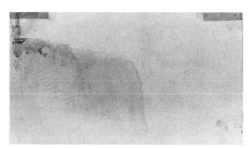

154V

155V

Plate 155.
(r) The Esplanade at Dieppe
and (v) Studies of a Young Boy

(r) 1857, (v) 1858–1860
pencil
10.1 × 17.1 cm.

See the description of Plate 154. Two sensitive studies of a young boy on the verso demonstrate Whistler's facility in drawing young children. Unrelated to the Dieppe scene, the studies were probably made slightly later. The subject may be one of the Haden children.

Plate 156.
A Bridge

ca. 1858
pencil
20.8 × 32.3 cm.

A Bridge follows the canons of eighteenth-century picturesque landscape imagery.[1] The drawing has an academic quality which sets it apart from other sketches executed during Whistler's Rhineland tour, and the actual site has thus far eluded identification. The scene recalls a heavy stone bridge at Mayence, and similar bridges at Bingen and Coblentz were painted by Turner earlier in the century (Fig. 156.1). Whistler could also have created a composite or imagined scene. Whistler drew with a soft lead, and then sharpened details with a harder pencil, while smudging in shadows with his finger. What is most interesting about the drawing is Whistler's consistency of vision. Although he soon abandoned such academic designs, he remained interested in river banks glimpsed through the arches of a bridge. Later etchings, like *London Bridge* (Fig. 156.2), as well as drawings and watercolors are based on such a composition.[2]

Figure 156.1
J. M. W. Turner, *Bingen from the Lorch*, 1817, watercolor. Trustees of the British Museum.

Figure 156.2.
London Bridge, etching, K153, first state. Freer Gallery.

Plate 157.
Whistler Sketching

1858
pencil
20.7 × 15.4 cm.
Inscription: "S.H.," "1858," Haden's hand.

The artist is seated near a shed, making a drawing while three rustics look on. Whistler later described how "we walked 22 miles once in one day, and then I was unable to move out of the way of a mob of hooting Prussian children such as the Prophet Elijah would certainly have set all the wolves in his power upon . . . how for a *glass of milk* had to make the portrait of one of my tormentors."[1] While the appearance of the figure at the far left is somewhat loutish, Whistler and Delannoy did not always encounter unpleasant circumstances. Perhaps he is sketching the young girl standing in front of him here. The three rustics reappear in a rare etching related to the title plate for *The French Set*.[2]

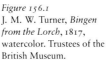

Plate 158.
Seated Man Examining Foot

1858
pencil
17.8 × 14.8 cm.
Inscribed: "Frouare," artist's hand.

Whistler's inscription on this sheet is probably
a phonetic spelling for Frouard, a town located
about five miles northwest of Nancy on the
Marne-Rhine Canal. The straw hat and back-
pack identify the subject as either Whistler or
Delannoy examining a travel-worn foot.
Whistler's letter to Deborah Haden recalled
that at one point on the journey a portrait
sketch was traded for "a piece of black bread
and an egg." Whistler continued, "The white
of [the egg] went to heal my bruised feet."[1]

Plate 159.
A Street Scene

1858
pencil
24.8 × 15.0 cm.

Although the exact location of this scene cannot be pinpointed, Whistler spent enough time
on the drawing to record numerous picturesque details of the half-timbered architecture
that is typical of the Rhine region. The building at the far right has been plastered and decorated with a mural in an oval cartouche and a
bracket supporting a statuette—presumably of
a saint. Whistler also recorded the pots of
plants and flowers in windows that seem to
delight city visitors to the medieval villages of
Germany and France. The figures are sketchy,
but obviously represent local peasants.
Whistler provided anecdotal interest with a
woman in the street conversing with another
framed in the tiny open window above.

Plate 160.
Figures by a Fountain

ca. 1858
pencil
12.2 × 6.7 cm.

The central focus of this pencil sketch is a fountain, perhaps one of the old stone and metal public fountains from the Rhine region. Such fountains were often located in town squares. The two figures at the right are remarkably stiff, and the drawing has an unresolved quality.

Plate 161.
Three Standing Figures

1858
pencil
15.1 × 10.0 cm.

The very sketchy nature of these figures, along with their casual pose, suggests that they were drawn from life. Moreover, Whistler has not gone over the soft lines with harder, more detailed strokes, so he seems not to have reworked this drawing in his studio. The elaborate headpiece worn by the woman at the left must be made of lace. Such headpieces distinguished different provincial regions of France, and we may speculate that Whistler encountered his subjects during his summer travels in 1858.

Plate 162.
À La Ferme de Maladrie

1858
pencil
16.7 × 21.7 cm.
Inscription: "A la ferme de Maladrie," artist's hand; "S.H.,"
  Haden's hand.

This inscribed sketch may indicate that
Maladrie's farm was one of the spots where
Whistler and Delannoy found inexpensive, if
uncomfortable, accommodations during their
Rhineland tour.

Plate 163.
Chambre à la Ferme de Maladrie

1858
pencil
16.9 × 21.7 cm.
Inscription: "Chambre a la ferme de Maladrie," artist's
  hand.

The drawing appears to have been sketched
from life, probably during Whistler's Rhineland tour. The figure at the window is difficult
to read—Wedmore couldn't even tell whether
it was a man or a woman in the later etching.[1]
However it is unlikely that a miser would have
posed to a stranger while counting his hoard.
The figure in the window could as well be
Whistler's traveling companion Delannoy.
Once back in Paris, the drawing became the
basis for a dramatic etching entitled *The Miser*
(Fig. 163.1). The drawn image was reversed
and the composition simplified. Whistler increased the contrast between the dark figure
and the light wall, removed the drapery from
the table and bench, and cropped the space to
the right of the hunched figure. Both the bench
and table were lengthened. By all these means
the artist emphasized spatial recession, and
heightened the dramatic impact of the etching.
Whistler's romanticized reworking of the farm
scene as well as its new title may reflect to
some extent Whistler's struggle to keep traveling once his funds had run out in Cologne. The
artist reported that in some cases he met with
stingy hospitality.[2]

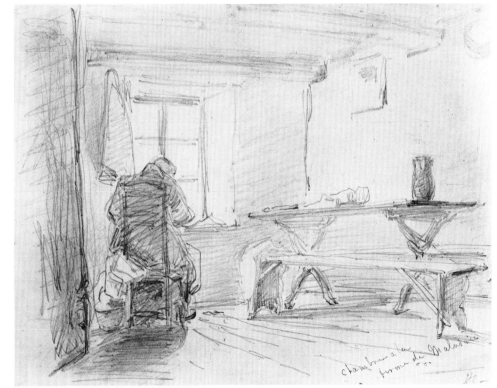

Figure 163.1
The Miser, etching, K69,
first state. Freer Gallery.

Plate 164.
(r) Four Men on a Boat and
(v) Sailor

1858
pencil
10.7 × 14.9 cm.
Inscriptions: "S.H.," "1858," Haden's hand.

Whistler's drawing of figures on a river steamer conjures up the opening sentences of Gustave Flaubert's novel, *The Sentimental Education*:

> The sailors brushed questions aside; passengers caromed into each other; the stack of luggage between the two paddle-boxes rose ever higher; and the uproar was dominated by the hiss of steam escaping through the iron plates, and wrapping everything in a white cloud, while the forward bell jangled incessantly. At last the boat pulled out and the banks . . . slid past like two broad ribbons unfurling. A long-haired young man of eighteen stood motionless . . . a sketchbook beneath his arm. He gazed through the fog.[1]

It is thought that the figure to the far left of this boldly drawn composition may be Whistler himself. Forty years after he undertook the Rhine journey, Whistler was still alert to "all incidents and accidents of travel":

> Attention is drawn to the smallest and most trivial mark on the evenness of the route. The stopping of the train . . . the ringing of a bell, the pulling in of the gangway. All these announcements of freshness, the calling of attention to the thing about to happen—or the thing achieved—the departure or the arrival—these are the moments . . . when the mere joy of being together suffices.[2]

The sailor smoking a cigarette, at the bottom right, was probably the model for the drawing on the back of this sheet.

164v

Plate 165.
Two Figures

1858
pencil
13.4 × 10.2 cm.
Inscription: (v) illegible Axenfeld address.

As he traveled, armed with a pencil and a sketchpad, Whistler was often intrigued by the brief encounters between strangers that he observed along the way. This rapidly drawn image recalls a passage in Flaubert's *The Sentimental Education*. Aboard a river steamer, the artist-hero "noticed a gentleman exchanging flirtatious remarks with a peasant girl" in the midst of an anonymous crowd of passengers and sailors.[1]

Plate 166.
Chez George Sauer

1858
pencil
14.6 × 9.5 cm.
Inscription: "Ou mangez vous?" "Chez George Sauer Au
   Lion Rouge," artist's hand.

Whistler's inscriptions on this quickly drawn
portrait let us assume that the sitter is George
Sauer, owner of the Red Lion. Sauer has a proprietary hand on the small change next to his
glass. This is probably the type of sketch with
which the artist answered the question, "Où
mangez-vous?" for he drew to help pay his
expenses during the trip. In his letter to Deborah Haden Whistler mentioned "how the
first night I made a portrait in pencil . . . for a
plate of soup."[1]

Plate 167.
Le Rhin

1858
pencil
15.4 × 17.0 cm.
Inscriptions: "Le Rhin," artist's hand; "S.H.," "1858,"
   Haden's hand.

Whistler's descriptive powers are exhibited in
this drawing of passengers on a Rhine steamer.
The wealth of detail seems to prefigure another
passage from Flaubert's novel, *The Sentimental Education*:

> *Apart from a few bourgeois traveling first
> class, the passengers were laborers, or shop-
> keepers. . . . In those days it was the custom
> to dress shabbily for a journey, so nearly all
> of them wore old skullcaps or faded hats,
> cheap black suits rubbed threadbare against
> desks, or frock-coats with their buttons
> splitting open from heavy use at the store.
> . . . Some chatted together, standing or
> squatting on their luggage, others slept in
> corners.*[1]

Whistler's precise notations extend to the relaxed pair of feet protruding into the picture
space at the bottom right, and a tantalizing
book strapped to a knapsack: *La Poire aux
Vanitée*, perhaps a sardonic reference to the
recently deposed Louis-Philippe. However, by
about the time Flaubert's novel was published
in 1869, Whistler was already moving beyond
descriptive literalism in his painting and reaching toward abstraction that he believed was
the territory of the painter and the musician, if
not the writer.

Plates 168–171.
"Rhine River Scenes"
168. Worms, Oppenheim

20.7 × 16.4 cm.

169. Près de Mayence

15.5 × 17.0 cm.

170. Untitled (Pfalz)

5.1 × 16.9 cm.

171. Untitled

7.1 × 17.1 cm.

1858
pencil
Inscription: 168, "Worms," "Oppenheim," artist's hand;
169, "Pres de Mayence," artist's hand.

Five views occupy one sheet in Plate 168. As a serial progression, the sketches record Whistler's travels north along the river to Cologne. Named sites include Worms, where Whistler drew part of the city's medieval fortifications near the river, and Oppenheim, a river town north of Worms. Whistler's panoramic view of Oppenheim suggests that he and Delannoy occasionally debarked to view the Rhine valley from its majestic bluffs.

Plate 169 depicts an area of the river near Mayence or Mainz, a town just south of Wiesbaden and Frankfurt. Whistler contrasted wind-driven and steam-powered boats in this view.

Plate 170 was untitled by Whistler, perhaps because it depicts one of the most famous spots on the Rhine: on a rocky little island south of Caub, in the middle of the river, rises the Pfalz, a curious old building with "a pentagonal tower covered with an unsightly roof, numerous turrets and jutting corners, loopholes in every section and one entrance only."[1] The building, which is small, can barely be made out in the drawing. To the left a large baroque building hugs the bluffs.[2]

The panorama at the bottom of Plate 171 recalls the sweep of the river in several places, including both Bingen and Boppard, and one can only speculate on the actual site. Numerous little towns were nestled along the banks of the Rhine, each enclave punctuated by its church spire. Like the preceding drawing, Plate 171 could have been made from either the prow or stern of a steamer. Sailboats in the upper portion of the drawing are part of the river traffic Whistler would have seen. As in Plate 170 the bluffs are reduced to a single elegant line.

Thumbnail sketches are the recognized tool of the academically trained artist. But Whistler's brief notations are more important for establishing the early crystallization of a consistent vision. Whistler's beloved format was characterized by wide stretches of water divided from the sky by a thin strip of land, broken by figures, boat masts, towers or trees that counter the long horizontal line. An "ele-

vation" of the landscape, as seen in the *Coast Survey Plate* of 1855 (Fig. 168–171.1), was a familiar topographical device. It eventually reappeared in many of Whistler's paintings, drawings, and prints of rivers or oceans at sites ranging from London to Venice and from southern England to western France (Figs. 168–171.2 and 168–171.3).

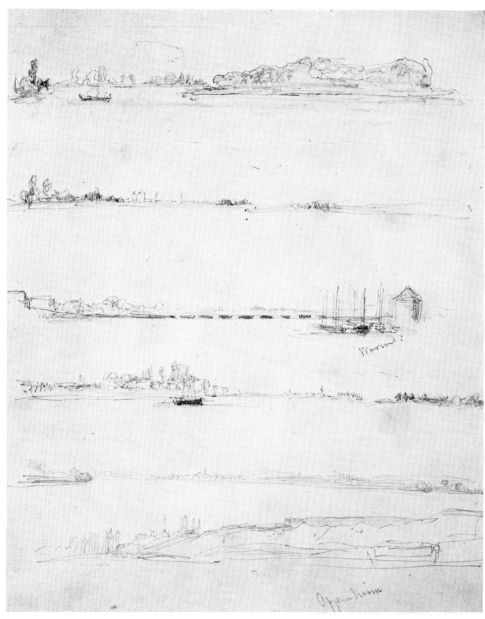

168

Figure 168–171.1.
Coast Survey Plate, 1855,
etching, K1. Freer Gallery.

Figure 168–171.2.
Old Westminster Bridge,
etching, K39, first state.
Freer Gallery.

Figure 168–171.3.
Little Venice, etching,
K183. Freer Gallery.

169

170

171

Plate 172.
Man Asleep on a Pile of Luggage

1858
pencil
9.2 × 9.1 cm.

A weary traveler collapsed upon a pile of heavy luggage represents some of the rigors of travel experienced by Whistler and Delannoy as they spent their wanderlust. This drawing might have been executed before the two artists reached Cologne, for at that point they left their knapsack with their landlord as security until money could be sent from Paris to pay the hotel bill.[1] There is an unrecognizable scribble on the verso of the sheet.

Plate 173.
(r) Group of Travelers and (v) Man Seated on Bench

1858
pencil on cream paper
16.0 × 10.4 cm.
Inscription: "S.H.," Haden's hand.

173v

This lively character study of travelers must be part of Whistler's Rhine experience. Impersonal contact between tightly packed strangers traveling by public conveyance was a subject of much interest to both artists and writers of the period, and Whistler has been careful to suggest a general isolation of each figure. Heads are tilted at different angles, eyes are averted, backs are turned.

Whistler's light underdrawing suggests the general placement of figures on a boat deck. In heavier lines Whistler redrew the features and costumes of several travelers, and he added shading as well. The gentle curve of the boat's side dictates the somewhat circular composition that has the effect of a magazine vignette.

An incomplete drawing of a man on the verso seems to involve a bench and a table. It is probably another glimpse from Whistler's travels.

Plate 174.
Barbier à Mayence

1858
pencil
15.2 × 9.9 cm.
Inscription: "Barbier a Mayence," artist's hand.

Whistler's early interest in nocturnal genre scenes is evidenced here. However, the candle-lit space recalls nighttime interiors by numerous earlier artists, rather than suggesting anything of the unconventional nocturnes Whistler would begin to execute a few years hence. Whistler used a similar approach to light in *The Music Room*, an etching which is roughly contemporary with this drawing (Fig. 174.1). In both the drawing and the print, brightly lit passages form flat, abstract shapes while the rest of each figure emerges as a group of scribbled or crosshatched lines.

Figure 174.1
The Music Room, etching,
K33, first state. Freer
Gallery.

Plate 175.
(r) Brasserie à Mayence and
(v) River Steamer, detail

1858
pencil
9.9 × 15.2 cm.
Inscription: "Brasserie à Mayence," artist's hand.

This sketch captures some of the atmosphere of a candle-lit *Stube*, where artists and others could smoke their pipes, drink beer, and converse. Despite the casual nature of the sketch, Whistler's penchant for symmetry and balanced surface pattern is evident. The semicircular shadow at the back of the drawing leads the eye from the bright light on the table to a large shadow thrown on the wall by the pipe smoker wearing a cap. On the verso is an incomplete detail drawing of a river steamer's deck. Similar forms are seen in Plate 164.

175v

Plate 176.
Entre sur la Grande Promenade à Baden

1858
pencil
15.0 × 19.5 cm.
Inscribed: "Entre sur la grande Promenade a Baden," artist's hand; "S.H.," "1858," Haden's hand.

Located in the Black Forest between Strasbourg and Karlsruhe on the Rhine River, Baden Baden was a fashionable resort, famed for hot baths and genteel vices including promenades and gambling casinos.[1] By 1873 the city was attracting fifty thousand visitors a year.[2] Burdened with backpacks and clad in outlandish attire, Whistler and his companion Delannoy have blundered into polite society during the afternoon promenade of the city's fashionable residents and guests. It is difficult to distinguish one artist from the other. Whistler may be the more distant figure, wearing a cadet cap and a monocle. Delannoy could be in the foreground, since he was described as wearing brown hollands and a straw hat.[3] It is also possible that Whistler used his own face as the model for both. Other drawings from the trip show Whistler in a straw hat, and he sometimes wore iron-rimmed glasses. What *is* certain is Whistler's delight in shocking the spa's bourgeois visitors. Not only the title but also the exaggerated attitudes struck by several figures place this drawing squarely in the tradition of seriocomic reportage as practiced by Hogarth, Rowlandson, Daumier, and Gavarni. Whistler captured the disapproving stares of top-hatted gallantes, not to mention the fluttered consternation of ladies and children dismayed by the artists' appearance. *Entre sur la Grande Promenade* foreshadows the relish with which Whistler would "épater le bourgeoisie" for the next fifty years.

Plate 177.
Baden Baden

1858
pencil
13.4 × 19.6 cm.
Inscription: "Baden Baden," artist's hand.

In this scene, a couple of visitors take refreshment at one of Baden Baden's outdoor cafés while a small knot of men chat nearby. The drawing demonstrates Whistler's early interest in contemporary leisure activities, a dominant theme in the work of French modernists of his generation.

Plate 178.
Promenade à Baden

1858
pencil
15.3 × 19.5 cm.
Inscription: "Promenade à Baden.," artist's hand; "S.H.,"
    "1858," Haden's hand.

Whistler used two pages from his notebook for
this drawing. He later removed the sheets from
the notebook and joined them at the center of
the composition. Sharply incised lines surround the image, suggesting that he would
have brought the viewer closer to the composition and eliminated some of the detail had he
taken the conception further. The scene shows
a group of figures approaching a columned
portico. The general composition recalls earlier views of Dieppe. Architectural features in
this drawing suggest that the spot is one of the
baths or gambling casinos of Baden Baden. In
the distance, buildings nestled against the hills
of the Black Forest can be seen. A French geography book of 1878 attributed the city's appeal
not to any commercial attraction, but to the
beauty of the setting and "les agréments de la
vie."[1]

Plate 179.
Group Conversing

1858
pencil
14.8 × 9.9 cm.

Although Whistler provides few clues to the
location of this drawing, it corresponds almost
exactly in size with Plate 175. The general
treatment of the subject is consistent with
other drawings of 1858, and perhaps Whistler
here depicts a group from Mayence, Baden
Baden, or one of the other towns he visited on
his Rhineland trip.

Plate 180.
Couple Seated at a Table

1858
pencil
16.8 × 11.8 cm.

The anecdote implied by this scene is ambiguous. We cannot be certain whether the woman is reading a small book or holding a hand of cards. Her relationship to the smoker is not clear. However, the drawing does reveal the artist's interest in illustration during the late 1850s. A very slight underdrawing is still visible beneath the two figures, particularly in the faint outline of a head to the left of the bonneted woman and another head to the right of the hatted man. Whistler later elaborated his quick sketch, recording such details as the woman's enormous challis shawl, the plaid pattern of her skirt, and the curve of the man's pipe. Whistler created textural interest by varying the thickness of line, and he added a good deal of shading. He also vignetted the two figures in an oval composition with blank space at the corners. Whistler continued to use this popular device, borrowed from magazine illustration, in later works—for example, some of the Venetian drawings and etchings executed in 1879–1880.

Plate 181.
(r) Group of Figures around a Brazier and
(v) Figures in a Chariot

1858
pencil
16.5 × 10.0 cm.

In an unidentified street scene drawn from life, Whistler applied his pencil in broad, rapid strokes to capture a glimpse of modern life. A crowd presses around a brazier while a bonneted woman at the left stirs something that is heating. Typically, Whistler suppresses enough detail to make the scene ambiguous, but we may speculate that the woman is a chestnut seller. Whistler created several images of street vendors in various media. His etching of *La Mère Gerard* depicts an old woman who sold flowers outside the Bal Bullier in Paris (Fig. 148.1). However, unlike the woman at the brazier, the flower seller is isolated, removed from any contextual reference point. Comparison of the two objects illustrates Whistler's budding tendency to simplify his studio work. On the verso of this sheet a sketchily drawn chariot with two figures may express Whistler's wish that he and Delannoy could ride magically back to Paris once their money had run out.

181v

Plate 182.
(r) Gambling Salon at Baden Baden and (v) Girl Knitting, Street Scene, Cloaked Figure

1858
(r) pencil, charcoal; (v) pencil
22.2 × 26.8 cm.
Inscription: "S.H."; (on mount) "1858," Haden's hand.

Using a free drawing technique that recalls Gavarni's handling of crowd scenes, Whistler here depicts one of Baden Baden's primary tourist attractions. The allure of the city's gambling tables had been described in Thackeray's *Vanity Fair*, and Whistler adopted an illustrational mode. Always interested in formal properties, however, Whistler reinforced his subject matter by centering the roulette wheel and calling attention to it with a large black form, probably a hanging lamp. A circular light space is ringed by heads—wheellike forms dominate even though we are aware that the table is rectangular. It is possible that Whistler later added the rich charcoal to the underlying pencil. On the verso are several pencil drawings. The girl knitting could be "Gretchen," the subject of an etching (Fig. 182.1). That interior scene included Gretchen's knitting needles and a ball of yarn on the little table next to her. The quaint medieval house on this sheet looks like Rhineland architecture. Whistler turned the sheet to sketch a hooded figure similar to the chestnut seller (Plate 181).

182v

Figure 182.1
Gretchen at Heidelberg,
etching, K20. Freer Gallery.

Plate 183.
La Jeunesse à Coblentz

1858
pencil on cream paper
22.9 × 24.2 cm.
Inscriptions: "La Jeunesse a Coblentz," artist's hand;
   "S.H.," "1858," Haden's hand.

Freer believed that the figure at the center of this freely drawn composition might have been Whistler. In several sketches from the Alsatian trip, Whistler depicted himself as an artist at work, surrounded by admiring onlookers, many of them children. This raises the possibility that some of the drawings were executed or reworked in the studio. The foreshortened pictorial space has a crowded theatricality in this scene of a river wharf, with details that include small boats and, in the far distance, the towering bluffs of the Rhine River. The title Whistler inscribed on the drawing records the jubilant good spirits in which his journey was undertaken. The artist was still recounting tales of his adventures years after the trip.[1]

Plate 184.
Deux Artistes Célèbres de Paris

1858
pencil
20.0 × 24.5 cm.
Inscription: "Deux Artistes celebres de Paris! decendus a la
cave Profonde, font des portraits a trrrrois frrrancs!!!"
artist's hand;[1] "S.H.," Haden's hand.

Whistler and Delannoy paid for some of their
travel expenses by making portraits along the
road. Lack of funds was a difficulty, but
Whistler later told his sister Deborah Haden
that they had encountered some "sunnier mo-
ments." He described how they "came upon a
fair—how I there made a portrait of 'butchers,
bakers, candlestickmakers!' for five groschen
apiece—that is a little more than fourpence!!!"[2] In this drawing, Whistler depicts
the amusing side of his predicament. A
huckster rings a bell while bawling out the bar-
gain rate at which the two young artists were
willing to make their sketches.

Plate 185.
Blanchissage à Cologne

1858
pencil
15.1 × 9.8 cm.
Inscription: "Blanchissage a Cologne," artist's hand; "S.H."
("1858" on mount), Haden's hand.

Whistler's record of his laundering activities in
Cologne indicates that his funds were running
short. He had already had some experience in
this line. His fellow artist Thomas Armstrong
reported that clean linen was important to
Whistler, and "during his humble beginnings
in Paris he washed his own clothes, but he was
always dressed impeccably."[1]

Plate 186.
Attendant Que le Linge Sèche!
Cologne

1858
pencil
15.1 × 19.6 cm.
Inscribed: "Attendant que le seche! Cologne," artist's hand;
  "S.H." ("1858" on mount), Haden's hand.

This drawing, with its strong sense of perspective, gives us a view of Whistler's room at Herr Schmitz's hotel in Cologne. The drawing was conceived as a pendant to the preceding drawing.

Plate 187.
Reclining Figure with Table
and Glasses

1858
pencil
12.3 × 17.2 cm.

The figure in this drawing takes a pose similar to that taken in Plate 186. However, the draftsmanship is bolder and less detailed while the setting is ambiguous. Whistler's letter to Deborah Haden recalled primitive lodgings during the Alsatian trip. At one spot a woman "took our *only two groschen* for a bed which she made with an armful of straws, and for the pillow a chair overturned, which was violently withdrawn the next morning at dawn, so that the consequent bump of the head on the ground might awaken us."[1] This scene may represent a similarly uncomfortable resting place.

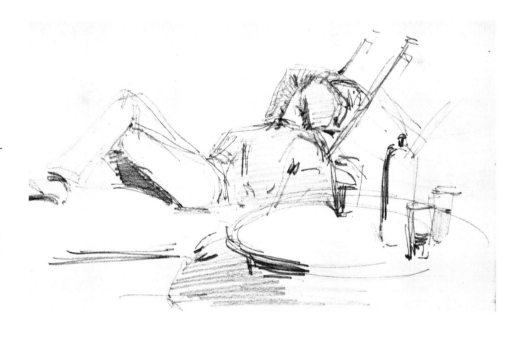

Plate 188.
Marchand de Potirons
à Cologne

1858
pencil
14.8 × 9.4 cm.
Inscribed: "Marchand de Potirons a Cologne," artist's hand.

For discussion see Plate 189.

Figure 189.1
La Marchande de Moutarde, etching, K22, second state. Freer Gallery.

Plate 189.
La Marchande de Moutarde

1858
pencil
15.2 × 9.8 cm.

These two drawings include observations that Whistler combined in an etching, *La Marchande de Moutarde* (Fig. 189.1). Whistler drew with a soft, blunt pencil before using a sharper pencil to refine certain passages, including architectural details and objects in the foreground of each scene. Although the compositions are similar, it is not certain that each drawing represents the same house. The etching contains the angled plane of the countertop in Plate 189 but is more obviously related to Plate 188, whose figures and chimney breast with pots appear in reverse. The narrow doorway from the first drawing was chosen for the etching. During his long career, Whistler repeatedly used the compositional device of a figure or figures silhouetted in a doorway. In Whistler's day, "potiron" meant not only pumpkin, but also drinking glass.[1] The cylindrical forms in both drawings are identifiable as glasses, and there seems to be a pitcher to the right in Plate 189. As hot and thirsty travelers, Whistler and Delannoy would have been much more interested in a refreshing drink than in a pot of mustard. The forms on the countertop in the etching do not look like drinking glasses. Perhaps the designation "moutarde" was applied to the drawing after publication of the etching.[2]

Plate 190.
Woman Seated at Window

1858
pencil
12.5 × 9.7 cm.
Inscription: "Adieu mes enfants: il est l'heure . . . au poste," artist's hand.

Perhaps the genesis of this drawing was Whistler's daily trip to the post office in Cologne to see whether funds had been forwarded to ease his financial straits. Whistler and Delannoy stayed in Cologne for ten days, hoping to receive aid. "Every day they would go to the post office for letters, every day the officials would say 'Nichts! Nichts!' until they got to be known in the town."[1] Herr Schmitz, the landlord at Whistler's hotel, seems to have been relatively sympathetic to the plight of the two young artists. This drawing could portray another friendly person at the hotel.

Plate 191.
Enfant de Choeur de Cologne

1858
pencil
12.9 × 8.4 cm.
Inscription: "Enfant de Choeur de Cologne," artist's hand.

Even though Whistler's brief visit to Cologne was plagued by financial worry, he seems to have found some time to visit the sites. Whistler could have seen this choirboy at the immense Cologne cathedral. The drawing recalls earlier ecclesiastical figures such as Plate 140, but here Whistler's draftsmanship is much more accomplished. He shows interest in the light-dark contrasts between the boy's crisp white surplice and his dark gown. Whistler later explored such contrasts in a number of major full-length oil portraits.

Plate 192.
Succès d'Erneste à Cologne

1858
pencil
9.8 × 15.1 cm.
Inscription: "Succes d'Erneste a Cologne," artist's hand.

Whistler's inscription designates his traveling companion Ernest Delannoy as the subject of this pencil sketch. However, the drawing points up the problem of successfully differentiating between the two artists in sketches from the Rhine trip. Not only did they look somewhat alike, they also were interchangeable for artistic purposes. Whistler used this drawing as the basis for his title etching to the *French Set*. With minimal reworking, Whistler transformed Delannoy into himself (Fig. 192.1). The drawing sheds some light on Whistler's early etching methods. He went over the drawing with a sharpish tool, transferring it to a grounded plate while leaving a ghostly impression on the verso of the sheet (Fig. 192.2).[1] Whistler then reworked the artist's head directly on the plate. It is much darker than Delannoy's head in the drawing, and the hat is flatter. The position of the artist's hands was edited, and Whistler extended several figures, adding feet to the artist and some of the children surrounding him.

Figure 192.1
Title to the *French Set*,
etching, K25. Freer Gallery.

Figure 192.2.
Verso of Plate 192, ghost image.

Plate 193.
Group of Four Men

1858
pencil
9.0 × 11.2 cm.

The younger man in the center of this composition seems to be holding forth while an older companion, in the cap and neckerchief of a laborer, gives him undivided attention. The figure with a cap is similar to men that appear in Whistler's Rhine river-boat drawings. Braggadocio and beer were significant components of student life. The Pennells reported that once Whistler returned to Paris with tales of his adventures, his artist friends saluted him at the Café Molière with loud songs:

> *Car il n'est pas mort, larifla! fla! fla!*
> *Non, c'est qu'il dort.*
> *Pour le réveiller, trinquons nos verres!*
> *Pour le réveiller, trinquons encore!*[1]

Plate 194.
Whistler with Friends

1859
pencil
16.4 × 10.8 cm.
Inscription: "S.H.," Haden's hand.

Whistler shows himself in the midst of a lively discussion. On the basis of a crayon sketch now in the Louvre, *Fantin au lit, 1859*, we can date the Freer drawing and presume that the man in the top hat is Whistler's close friend and fellow artist Henri Fantin-Latour (Fig. 194.1). The woman has not been identified. Illustrational in style, the drawing recalls the artistic milieu in which Whistler and his friends, particularly Fantin, passionately discussed their ideas about modern art.

Figure 194.1
Fantin au Lit, 1859, crayon.
Musées Nationaux de
France, Cabinet des
Dessins.

Plate 195.
Sir Seymour Haden Playing the Cello

1858–1859
ink
18.5 × 10.5 cm.
Inscription: "J.W."; "S.H.," Haden's hand.

Whistler's bold drawing of Seymour Haden, his brother-in-law, demonstrates the artist's progress in handling the human figure with assurance. Haden's pose recalls an earlier, much more comical sketch of a Baltimore friend, Ross Winans, playing a violin.[1] But the figure of Haden has gone beyond dependence upon caricature and exaggeration. It is realized with broad outlines and rich, dark shadows. The dignified image of the cellist had an impact upon Whistler's later etching of Ross Winans. In the etching, Winans was again shown with musical instruments, but this time in a comfortable, naturalistic posture (Fig. 195.1).

Figure 195.1
Ross Winans, etching, K88, first state. Freer Gallery.

Plate 196.
(r) Nelly (Helen Ionides) and (v) Peasant Woman

ca. 1858
pencil
16.8 × 10.0 cm.
Inscription: (r) "Nelly," artist's hand, "S.H.," Haden's hand; (v) "Nelly," Freer's hand.

In 1855, shortly after he arrived in Paris, Whistler met Luke and Aleco Ionides, sons of a Greek shipping magnate, Alexander Ionides. He would have met their sister, Helen, sometime thereafter. The Ionides family were patrons of Whistler at the outset of his career, and Whistler's friendship with "Nelly," as he called her, was long-lasting. On April 17, 1877, Miss Ionides married Whistler's brother, Dr. William Whistler. She outlived both of the Whistler brothers, dying about 1920.[1]

Whistler has drawn Nelly at an early age, slumped down in an indecorous position, with her sleeves rolled up. Clouds of smoke rise from her cigarette. Possibly the drawing was made in the studio, away from parental supervision. However, Whistler has stylized his sitter to some extent, and we are reminded of the degree to which his early drawings relate to magazine illustration. This view of Nelly as a "modern woman" may owe something to the artist's imagination.

An unfinished drawing of a peasant woman appears on the verso. Her masklike face and stylized quality is typical of Whistler's illustrational mode up to about 1858.

Plate 197.
Seated Seamstress with Male Companion

ca. 1855–1859
pencil
12.7 × 9.0 cm.

In this romantic scene Whistler has drawn a young seamstress at her work, watched by a man casually smoking a pipe while seated on the floor. The man would seem to be older, since he is balding. We may speculate that he is a painter, sculptor, or writer. Called "grisettes," seamstresses were popular mistresses for aspiring artists in the Latin Quarter.

196v

233

Plate 198.
(r) Seated Woman, Smoking and (v) Head

ca. 1858–1859
pencil
15.5 × 9.9 cm.

The model in this facile drawing wears a stylish dress with frogging and slashed sleeves. Her cigarette, as well as her hairstyle and her evident youth, recall Whistler's drawing of Nelly Ionides, although she may also be Fumette or some other model. Whistler's early interest in fashion and the relaxed conventions of studio life are evident. Whistler's simple but beautifully rendered head of a child on the verso may depict one of the Haden children.

198v

Plate 199.
(r) Girl Reclining on a Couch, Reading and (v) Female Head, unfinished sketch

1858–1860
pencil
10.2 × 16.6 cm.

Whistler's rapid sketch from an unidentified live model establishes his early interest in compositions that involve young girls wearing voluminous dresses stretched out on a divan. From about 1865 to 1867, he developed this theme elaborately in his *Symphony in White, No. 3*.[1] The brief sketch on the verso was probably taken from the same model.

199v

Plate 200.
(r) **Fumette** and
(v) **Dancing Clowns**

ca. 1855–1859
(r) red chalk, pencil; (v) pencil
21.6 × 15.0 cm.
Inscription: (r) "S.H.," Haden's hand; (v) "Fumette red
 chalk drawing," Freer's hand.

Fumette, or Eloise, was a little modiste with
whom Whistler had an affair during his student days in Paris. Luke Ionides later recalled
that Whistler was a favorite "among the
grisettes we used to meet at the gardens where
dancing went on. I remember one especially—
they called her the *tigresse*. She seemed madly
in love with Jimmie and would not allow any
other woman to talk to him when she was
present. She sat to him several times with her
curly hair down her back. She had a good
voice, and I often thought she had suggested
Trilby to Du Maurier."[1] Another image of
Fumette, closely related to this drawing, was
included in Whistler's first published set of
etchings (Fig. 200.1).[2] At one point during
their tempestuous relationship, Fumette's jeal-
ousy led her to tear up a number of Whistler's
Gavarnilike sketches.[3] One survivor, however,
was the group of dancing clowns on the verso
of this sheet. The clowns are a direct copy of
Gavarni's lithograph, *(Air: Larifla! . . .) Nos
femm' sont cou-cou!*.[4]

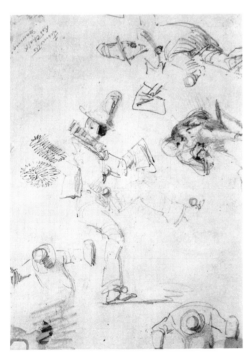

200v

Figure 200.1
Fumette, etching, K13, third
state. Freer Gallery.

Plate 201.
Annie Haden

1858–1859
pencil on gray-blue paper
17.3 × 11.2 cm.
Inscription: "W."

Whistler's drawing of Annie Haden is probably a preparatory drawing related to *At the
Piano*, an oil begun late in 1858 and exhibited
the next year.[1] The Freer drawing could have
been one of several in which the artist explored
the leaning figure from different angles. For
the final work, he chose a profile which formally complements the piano player. X rays of
the painting indicate that the figure of the little
girl may not have been part of the artist's conception at first. *At The Piano* was an important picture, the first one Whistler exhibited in
England, and probably the first to be associated with Velásquez.[2] Freer greatly admired
the "Piano Picture," but was never able to acquire it.[3] He had to content himself with this
drawing.

Plate 202.
Nelly

ca. 1860–1862
pencil on gray-blue paper
21.4 × 14.3 cm.
Inscription: (r) "Nelly," artist's hand; (v) "Nelly," Freer's
    hand.

This picture of Nelly Ionides smoking is
noticeably more lifelike than Whistler's earlier
image of her, as is evident from a photograph
(Fig. 202.1). Although Whistler stylized his sitter less, he related her general pose to the other
drawing. Fascinated with beautiful women
languidly posed in armchairs, Whistler continued to create such images throughout his
career. In 1863 Whistler etched *Weary*; (see
"Artist and Model," Fig. 87), a portrait of his
mistress Jo Hiffernan, which is similar in appearance to his treatment of Nelly, particularly
in the sketchy handling of the voluminous
skirt. Whistler often posed different sitters in
standard positions, making them look somewhat alike.

Figure 202.1
Helen Ionides Whistler,
photograph. University of
Glasgow Library, special
collections.

Plate 203.
Self-Portrait

ca. 1860s
black and white chalk on gray-brown paper
18.9 × 12.5–12.9 cm.

This drawing bears a slight resemblance to
Whistler's early oil portrait of himself wearing
a large dark hat (Plate 1). However, the drawing avoids a self-conscious identification with
the art of past masters. Instead, Whistler offers
a glimpse of his youthful confidence, evident
not only in his frank gaze, but also in his deft
handling of black and white chalks.

Plate 204.
Portrait of the Artist

ca. 1860s
black and white chalk on brown paper
27.8 × 17.7–18.1 cm.

In 1893 Whistler wrote to Thomas Way about
self-portraits. "I remember that at one time I
always made a drawing before going to
bed!!—of myself I mean—though I finally destroyed most of them."[1] This engaging image,
which once belonged to Thomas Way, may be
one of the survivors. Whistler has chosen to
depict "the artist at work," a common enough
theme in self-portraiture. He holds a drawing
instrument in his hand and seems to be sketching on a piece of paper in front of him. He may
have been looking in a mirror as he drew. The
remains of an abandoned nude sketch on the
verso give further evidence of the spontaneous
nature of Whistler's self-portrait. He drew
himself rapidly on a previously used sheet that
must have been handy at the time.

Plate 205.
Greek Girl

ca. 1865
black and white chalk on brown paper
26.2 × 18.5 cm.

Both the title and the treatment of this figure study recall Whistler's fascination with the linear and sculptural qualities of classical art during the mid-1860s when he was associated with Albert Moore. Whistler met the British artist, noted as an Ingriste, in 1865. That year, Moore exhibited *The Marble Seat* at the Royal Academy (Fig. 205.1). Whistler's pensive figure suggests that he may have made this drawing after seeing Moore's work.

Plate 206.
(r) **Female Figure, Seated** and
(v) **Drawing for a Screen**

ca. 1865–1870
black and white chalk on mottled gray-brown paper
27.5 × 18.0 cm.
Inscription: butterfly.

Whistler's perky model seated at an angle in an extremely light chair recalls similar figures on attenuated neo-Grecian furniture by Albert Moore. The drawing for a screen on the verso is a good example of Whistler's two-dimensional approach to furniture and interiors. The screen is all surface: two-dimensional planes surrounded by dark lines. Whistler was to maintain this two-dimensional approach in his decorations for the Peacock Room in 1876–1877.

Figure 205.1
Albert Moore, *The Marble Seat*, 1865, oil on canvas. From Spencer, 1972, p. 31. Reprinted courtesy of Studio Vista Publishers of Cassell & Collier Macmillan Publishers.

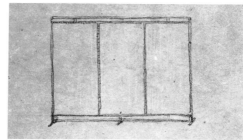

206v

Plate 207.
Woman with Parasol

ca. 1868
black and white chalk on gray-brown paper
18.2–18.3 × 12.9–13.0 cm.
Inscription: butterfly.

This figure's drapery is classical, while her parasol recalls eighteenth-century French chinoiserie.[1] Yet her awkward pose seems derived from caricatures of Japanese laborers laden with heavy burdens, and they wear straw hats on the same scale as this figure's parasol (Fig. 207.1). Japanese umbrellas, on the other hand, are usually rather large (Fig. 207.2). The umbrella lost its ability to designate status in the West during the nineteenth century, but the parasol, a shelter from the sun, remained an important accoutrement in women's fashion: "It exaggerated sexual distinctions by keeping women fair and unfreckled while serving as a prop for coquetry."[2] Unlike the umbrella, the parasol remained a potent element for exploitation in Western paintings with an Oriental bias. This drawing relates to the second figure from the right in Whistler's *Symphony in Blue and Pink*, (Plate 8).

Figure 207.1
Peasants with Burdens,
from *Hokusai Gashiki*,
1819. Freer Gallery.

Figure 207.2.
Woman with Umbrella,
from *Hokusai Gashiki*,
1819. Freer Gallery.

Plate 208.
Draped Female Figure

ca. 1868–1870
black and white chalk on brown paper
25.5 × 19.3 cm.
Inscription: butterfly.

One of the most active figures related to Whistler's "Six Projects," this draped model also appears in a study of four women by a railing (Fig. 208.1). Although Whistler used the pose in *Variations in Blue and Green*, he chose to turn her further around so that her back is to the viewer. Thus, she appears as the woman at the left in the oil sketch (see Plate 10). Whistler's interest in studying figures from different angles reminds one of academic studio practice. Classical draperies recall Whistler's interest in the Elgin Marbles, which he would have surveyed from many angles. This figure, with her filmy swirling gown, has the swift motion of Iris, the messenger of the gods.

Figure 208.1.
Studies of Four Female Figures, fabricated chalks on brown paper. Hunterian Art Gallery, University of Glasgow, Birnie Philip Bequest.

Plate 209.
(r) Draped Figure Standing and (v) Drapery Study

ca. 1868
(r) black and white chalk on mottled brown paper;
(v) black chalk
28.5 × 17.8 cm.

Whistler probably drew several images of a draped figure leaning on a rail during a single modeling session. On the verso of this sheet is an incomplete sketch studying the folds of airy fabric over the model's right shoulder and around under her left arm. Whistler used that study for the recto of this sheet, as well as for the recto of Plate 210. He began the latter starting with the model's left shoulder and arm. However, an infrared photograph makes it clear that soon he decided to move the composition slightly to the right before completing the drawing (Fig. 209.1). Plate 209 is virtually identical to Plate 210, but Whistler has turned the model's head farther over her shoulder, allowing us to see more of her face. The nude figure on Plate 210 verso strikes a pose familiar in previously illustrated drawings from the collection.

Plate 210.
(r) Standing Draped Figure and (v) Standing Nude

ca. 1868
black and white chalk on brown paper
28.5 × 17.7–17.9 cm.
Inscription: (r) butterfly; (v) "34."

For a discussion, see Plate 209.

209v

210v

Figure 209.1.
Infrared photograph of
Plate 210, recto.

Plate 211.
Standing Nude

ca. 1865–1870
black and white chalk on brown paper
27.9 × 19.4 cm.
Inscription: butterfly.

Whistler's study of a standing nude in a hip-sprung pose, partially supported by resting on her arms, reminds us that he tended to stylize his figure drawings in keeping with the canons of classical art.

Plate 212.
Draped Figure at a Railing

ca. 1868–1870
black, white, and gray chalks on brown paper
27.8–27.9 × 17.95–18.1 cm.
Inscription: butterfly.

Drawing from a live model, Whistler here explored the drape of filmy gauze on a figure set against a rail. The composition was one of his favorites and reappears in subsequent drawings, paintings, and prints. While the draperies and hip-sprung stance recall ancient classicism, the gesture of the hand held to the face is reminiscent of Japanese woodblock prints of courtesans laughing behind their kimono sleeves.

Plate 213.
(r) Study for Morning Glories and (v) Standing Nude

ca. 1870
(r) fabricated chalks on brown paper; (v) black and white
   chalk
30.6 × 19.1 cm.
Inscription: (r) butterfly.

Whistler's central concern in this drawing is
the interplay of semitransparent veils swathed
about the figure in contrapuntal harmonies of
light and dark. The model takes the same pose
as seen in Plate 212 and is drawn in the blues
and greens that dominate the final composition. The artist also sketched suggestions for
background boats and flowers. The nude figure on the verso strikes a similar pose. When
Freer bought this drawing, Thomas Way called
it *The Balcony*, but it bears only a tangential
relationship to the finished oil by that name.[1]

213v

Plate 214.
(r) Morning Glories and (v) Nude Study

ca. 1865–1870
(r) fabricated chalks on gray-tan paper; (v) black chalk
26.2 × 16.2–16.3 cm.
Inscription: (v) "7."

Background details developed more fully here
than in earlier drawings are executed in repeating colors that serve to pin the figure in her flat
pictorial space. Whistler surrounded his richly
draped model with brilliant periwinkle blue
and white flowers. Slashes of the same color
enliven her draperies. Scattered blossoms that
decorate the mat at her feet are made the same
pale green as leaves on the morning glories at
her sides. The vertical figure, echoed by upright railings and masts, is countered by a series of horizontal registers that begin with the
matting, ascend through the railing upon
which the model leans, and die away in softer
bands of sea, mountain, and sky. There is a
nude study on the verso of the sheet.

214v

Plate 215.
Annabel Lee

ca. 1870
fabricated chalks on brown paper
32.5 × 17.8 cm.
Inscription: butterfly.

When Freer purchased this drawing of a stat-
uesque figure, he noted that the seller thought
the subject was Niobe. The drawing has carried the title *Annabel Lee* since 1905.[1] Both
subjects are associated with the sense of death.
Niobe was the daughter of Tantalus; she was
turned to stone while bewailing the loss of her
children. Annabel Lee, who probably sym-
bolizes Edgar Allan Poe's young wife, also is
lost:

> *For the moon never beams, without bringing*
> *   me dreams*
> *   Of the beautiful Annabel Lee;*
> *And the stars never rise, but I feel the bright*
> *   eyes*
> *   Of the beautiful Annabel Lee:*
> *And so, all the night tide, I lie down by the*
> *   side*
> *Of my darling—my darling—my life and my*
> *   bride,*
> *   In her sepulchre there by the sea—*
> *   In her tomb by the sounding sea.*[2]

The figure itself has marked affinities with the
neoclassical works of Albert Moore. Like
Degas's ballet dancers, Whistler's draped models continue to reappear, slightly varied and
invested with new meaning. This figure has
been generated from the woman at the left in
Variation in Blue and Green (see Plate 10) and
follows a similar color scheme. A shimmering
inverted rainbow of blue and green gauze
hangs behind the figure, separating the viewer
from the space she occupies. Whistler's butterfly and a single violet iris balance the composition. With her head cast down and her
back turned to us, the figure is as inaccessible
and melancholy as she is beautiful. Whether
the subject is Niobe or Annabel Lee is probably less important than our recognition of the
painter's poetry: "The amazing invention that
shall have put form and colour into such perfect harmony, that exquisiteness is the result."[3]

Plate 216.
Venus

1869
black and white chalk on brown paper
119.4 × 61.4 cm.
Inscription: ". . . Thursday morning . . . ," obliterated;
"69" in cartouche.

Pounced cartoons rarely survive in Whistler's *oeuvre*.[1] Whistler's *Venus* cartoon was meant to transfer the figure to a final work now lost to us.[2] It is also related to an oil now called *Tanagra*, which was executed about 1869 (Fig. 216.1).[3] The oil is sketchy, and it is smaller than the pounced cartoon. The pose of each figure is similar, and the arrangements of fans and pottery, as well as the lines of the drapery, correspond quite closely.[4]

It is possible that the cartoon also played a role in Whistler's unrealized scheme for a mosaic decoration at the South Kensington Museum. Although this commission was never executed, pastel sketches similar in pose to the *Venus* cartoon remain. Background accessories, however, are different (Fig. 216.2).[5]

Whistler's letter to Henry Cole, director of the South Kensington Museum, discussed the use of photography to transfer a cartoon to another surface: "Tomorrow evening I believe that the traced cartoon will be ready for photographing and enlarging upon the big canvas."[6] Whistler also mentioned the use of studio assistants. There is a photograph of the *Venus* cartoon in Glasgow, upon which the artist drew with pencil, making the torso lean more to the left.[7]

Whistler's treatment of the figure here is conventional. It recalls an antique Aphrodite by Praxiteles that existed in multiple Roman copies, but Whistler had many possible models much closer in time. Victorian neoclassical nudes were popular as statuary during Whistler's student days. Hiram Powers's *The Greek Slave*, for example, received loud acclaim at the Great Exhibition in London in 1851 and was copied thereafter in parian statuettes (Fig. 216.3). During the 1860s Whistler was painting with Albert Moore, whose heavily fleshed classicizing nudes included both *A Wardrobe*, 1867, and *Venus*, 1869.[8] Whistler would have known them both. Moreover, he had recently expressed his admiration for Ingres, whose *La Source*, 1867, could easily be the source for Whistler's image of the goddess of love (Fig. 216.4).[9]

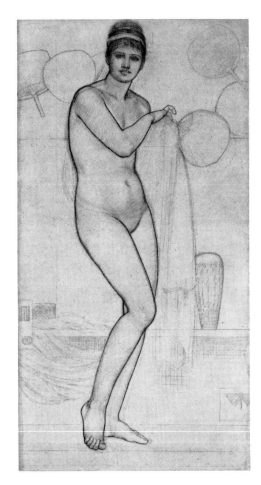

Figure 216.1.
Tanagra, ca. 1869, oil on canvas. Randolph-Macon Woman's College Art Gallery.

Figure 216.2.
The Gold Girl, fabricated chalks on brown paper. Repr. Pennell, 1908, I, p. 150.

Figure 216.3.
Hiram Powers, *The Greek Slave*, marble. National Museum of American Art, Smithsonian Institution, gift of Mrs. Benjamin H. Warder. This version was carved after 1869.

Figure 216.4.
Jean Auguste Dominique Ingres, *La Source*, 1856, oil on canvas. Musées Nationaux de France, Louvre.

Plate 217.
(r) **Nude Study** and
(v) **Standing Nude,** abandoned sketch

ca. 1868–1875
black and white chalk on brown paper
27.5 × 27.5 cm.

In 1867 Frederick Richards Leyland commissioned a large oil painting of three girls, which would have been a more highly finished version of *The White Symphony: Three Girls*, ca. 1868. This somewhat labored drawing of a crouching nude was probably created after *The White Symphony*. In September 1875, the artist reported having hired a model to pose for such studies.[1] More than one image based on the same pose survives, but the worked and reworked quality of this particular drawing marks it as a tool in Whistler's endeavors to create figures with convincing volume. Although it is heavily outlined, like Whistler's cartoon called *Venus*, it has not actually been pounced.[2] An infrared photograph reveals that Whistler drew the figure over an earlier nude study (Fig. 217.1). The bottom half of yet another study can be seen on the verso, but the sheet was trimmed after that drawing had been executed. Closest to the sculptural reality achieved here is an oil fragment, *Girl with Cherry Blossom*, which is thought to be all that is left of Whistler's ambitious composition first envisioned in *The White Symphony*.[3]

217v

Figure 217.1.
Infrared photograph of *Nude Study*.

Plate 219.
Japanese Figure, Seated

ca. 1870–1875
black and white chalk on brown paper
28.2 × 18.0 cm.
Inscription: butterfly.

While this drawing has been exhibited twice with a title that relates it to Japan, it might more appropriately have been called *Luncheon in the Studio*. Perhaps the model was resting between posing sessions for Whistler's "Six Projects" or another japonesque painting.

Figure 218.1.
Study for a Female Attendant in "Dante's Dream at the Time of the Death of Beatrice," ca. 1868, pencil, squared for transfer. Photograph courtesy Sotheby's Belgravia.

Plate 218.
The Purple Iris

ca. 1870
fabricated chalks on brown paper
28.4 × 12.4–12.5 cm.

An unusually stylized quality marks this figure drawing by Whistler. Its color scheme, drapery, and background with iris and a trellis suggest that he made the drawing in the late 1860s or early 1870s, when he was working with the classically draped figures of the "Six Projects." But the odd attenuation of the figure seems closer to the work of Dante Gabriel Rossetti, Whistler's Chelsea neighbor (Fig. 218.1).[1]

Plate 220.
(r) Nocturne: Battersea Bridge and (v) Standing Female Nude

ca. 1872
fabricated chalks on brown paper
18.2–18.5 × 27.9–28.7 cm.
Inscription: butterfly.

One of the most richly colored pastels in the collection, *Nocturne: Battersea Bridge* was probably made at about the same time Whistler painted *Blue and Silver: Screen with Old Battersea Bridge* (Fig. 220.1). A prosaic topographical view by Walter Greaves suggests the degree to which Whistler used simplification and removed spatial reference points to emphasize the height of the bridge (Fig. 220.2).[1] The screen itself has a vertical format, and the artist carried his stylization even further than in the pastel. He eliminated the railing as well as people on the bridge, while increasing the height of the bridge supports.[2] An earlier drawing shows the Albert Bridge under construction (Fig. 220.3). The new bridge was built east of Old Battersea Bridge from May 1871 to August 1873.[3] Whistler incorporated this information about the site into his composition for the screen (Fig. 220.4). However, true to his dictum that a work of art should not depend upon local interest for its impact, Whistler avoided verism in favor of broken lines and shapes that would be hard to interpret without further information.

Figure 220.2.
Walter Greaves, *Old Battersea Bridge*, watercolor. Museum of London.

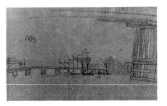

Figure 220.3.
The New Albert Bridge Seen from under the Old Battersea Bridge, black chalk. Hunterian Art Gallery, University of Glasgow, Birnie Philip Bequest.

Figure 220.4.
Battersea Bridge, ca. 1875, charcoal with touches of white chalk and gray watercolor. Albright-Knox Art Gallery, gift of George F. Goodyear, 1958.

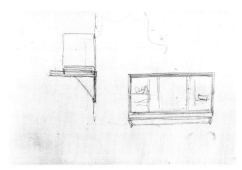

Figure 220.1.
Blue and Silver: Screen with Old Battersea Bridge, 1872, oil on panel. Hunterian Art Gallery, University of Glasgow, Birnie Philip Bequest.

220V

Plate 221.
Two Sketches for Furniture

1870s
pencil[1]
12.7 × 21.9 cm.
Inscription: "Studies"?

Case pieces filled with arrangements of Oriental porcelain, similar to the drawing on the left of this sheet, stood in several rooms occupied by Whistler.[2] It is difficult to determine whether or not the drawing on the right depicts another view of the same cabinet or a different piece altogether. The cabinet on the right appears to have both a stretcher and an extended shelf supported on brackets. These features were sometimes found in art furniture of the period. It is notable that Whistler's consistent approach to furniture seems to have been two-dimensional. He showed no concern whatsoever for the mass of either piece, but concentrated upon gridlike linear patterns made by shelves, supports, and stretchers (Fig. 221.1).

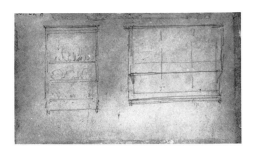

Figure 221.1.
Cabinet design, pencil, from Sketchbook A, p. 3. Hunterian Art Gallery, University of Glasgow, Birnie Philip Bequest.

Plates 222–223.
Portrait Sketches of
Thomas Carlyle

1872
222. 14.5 × 13.1 cm.
223. 28.0 × 18.2 cm.
222: pencil, ink; 223: (r) black and white chalk on brown
    paper

In choosing to paint one of Chelsea's most distinguished residents, Whistler approached the concerns of history painting, using portraiture in modern dress.[1] The Scottish philosopher and historian Thomas Carlyle began sitting to Whistler in 1872, and continued to pose until the summer of 1873. The sittings took place in Whistler's studio at 2 Lindsey Row, Chelsea. The gray walls and black dado of the studio can be seen in the ink sketch, although they are not readily apparent in the chalk drawing.

In general, the final oil portrait, entitled *Arrangement in Grey and Black, No. 2: Portrait of Thomas Carlyle*, was based upon Whistler's earlier portrait of his mother.[2] However, Whistler experimented with compositional variations in the chalk drawing. He set the chair at an angle to the wall and also hinted at a corner to the left of the figure. Carlyle does not have a lap robe in the chalk drawing. These variations seem not to have pleased the artist, for in the final oil he reused the planar composition of the *Mother*, draping a robe

over Carlyle's lap to create a shape similar to Mrs. Whistler's dress. As a result, Carlyle assumes an almost Egyptian monumentality.

A sketch whose regularity indicates that it was made after the portrait is now in the Fogg (Fig. 222-223.1). The Freer Gallery ink sketch was owned by Thomas Way before Freer acquired it. Way believed that Whistler also drew this sketch from memory after the portrait was finished, and Way published another similar drawing (Fig. 222-223.2). However, both sketches once associated with Way are much more scratchy and free. Whistler could conceivably have made them to help determine the distribution of light and dark passages prior to his completion of the oil.[3]

From 1834 until his death in 1881, Carlyle's home was a pilgrimage spot for many intellectuals, although Carlyle was known as a somewhat overbearing conversationalist. Following her visit in 1846, Margaret Fuller complained, "To interrupt him is a physical impossibility. If you get a chance to remonstrate for a moment,

he raises his voice and bears you down."[4] Whistler may have suffered a similar verbal barrage during the sittings. He later reported that Carlyle "told people afterward that he had been there [in the studio], talking . . . and that I had just gone on with my work and had paid no attention to him whatever."[5] Whistler produced a work in which the Sage of Chelsea is wrapped in the iconic silence of a sphinx.

Figure 222–223.1.
Ink sketch after the *Carlyle*.
Courtesy of the Fogg Art
Museum, Harvard
University, Grenville L.
Winthrop Bequest.

Figure 222–223.2.
Ink sketch, probably before
the *Carlyle*. From Way,
1912, opp. p. 44.

Plate 224.
Sketch of F. R. Leyland and Daughter

ca. 1869–1874
ink
8.1 × 10.2 cm.

The heavy light and dark contrasts in this brief sketch parallel Whistler's chiaroscuro drawings and etchings of the Hadens executed in the 1860s. The tiny drawing is a relic from the days when Whistler enjoyed intimate access to the Leyland family circle.

Plate 225.
The Leyland Girls

ca. 1872–1874
black and white chalk on brown paper
28.7 × 17.9 cm.
Inscription: butterfly.

F. R. Leyland and his wife Frances had three daughters: Fanny, born 1857; Florence, born 1859; and Elinor, born 1861.[1] Leyland was Whistler's patron by the late 1860s, but the artist began to frequent the Leyland home, Speke Hall, in Autumn 1869. And he was most actively involved with various portraits of the Leylands from about 1871–1874.[2] When Freer purchased this drawing, the sitters were identified as Florence and Fanny. However, the identification is debatable. Whistler etched Fanny Leyland at the age of about fifteen—that is, around 1872 (Fig. 225.1). The child with long hair in the Freer drawing wears a similar dress, indeed takes a similar, if somewhat more relaxed, pose. But Whistler's habit of using stock compositions is known. Moreover, the girl in the drawing seems to be playing at cat's cradle, a childish game for Fanny as a prim and proper teenager. Perhaps Florence and Elinor are depicted in the Freer drawing. Making allowance for family resemblance, the long-haired girl looks as much like Florence as Fanny (Fig. 225.2). In Whistler's etching of Florence, she holds a hoop, another childish toy. The short hair and puckish face of the younger girl in the drawing most closely resemble other images of Elinor (Fig. 225.3).

Figure 225.1.
Fanny Leyland, etching, K108, second state. Freer Gallery.

Figure 225.2.
Florence Leyland, etching, K110. Freer Gallery.

Figure 225.3.
Elinor Leyland, etching, K109, third state. Freer Gallery.

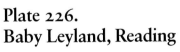

Plate 226.
Baby Leyland, Reading

ca. 1872–1874
fabricated chalks on brown paper
29.0 × 18.7 cm.
Inscription: "Thos. Way, 1905," Way's hand.

Whistler's drawing of Elinor, the youngest Leyland child, argues strongly for his ability to capture the charm of youthful sitters. Touches of salmon, carmine, burnt sienna, and pale pink suggest Whistler's awareness of eighteenth-century drawings executed in "trois crayons"—black, white, and red chalk. Another image made about the same time shows Elinor and her book from another angle (Fig. 226.1). The subject of a young girl reading was popular in both the eighteenth and nineteenth centuries.

Plate 227.
Portrait of Baby Leyland

ca. 1872–1874
black and white chalk on brown paper
28.0 × 18.0 cm.

Although Whistler failed to complete full-length oil portraits of the Leyland girls, he did leave vignetted drawings like this study of Elinor, or "Baby." A related pen sketch is in the British Museum,[1] and another chalk drawing using this format probably depicts Elinor's sister Florence (Fig. 227.1). The oil portrait of Baby Leyland, entitled *The Blue Girl*, was destroyed, but Freer acquired two fragments as well as a pastel sketch of the full-length composition (see Plate 228).

Figure 226.1.
Elinor Leyland Reading, black chalk on brown paper. Hunterian Art Gallery, University of Glasgow, Birnie Philip Bequest.

Figure 227.1.
A Little Girl Seated (Florence Leyland), black and white crayon on brown paper. Hunterian Art Gallery, University of Glasgow, Birnie Philip Bequest.

Plate 228.
(r) The Blue Girl and
(v) Study for a Portière

1872–1874
(r) fabricated chalks on brown paper; (v) black crayon
25.2 × 14.5 cm.

The Blue Girl embodies Whistler's conception for a full-length portrait of Elinor Leyland. The abandoned portrait had been destroyed by about 1880, although two oil fragments survive.[1] Elinor's insouciant stance is derived from *Pablillos de Valladolid*, painted by Velásquez. The image was popular with artists of Whistler's generation. Others copied this work, and Whistler kept a photograph of it in his studio (Fig. 228.1).[2] He used the pose more than once.[3] The brilliant blues in the pastel, possibly inspired by Gainsborough's *Blue Boy*, suggest the impact the final painting might have had. According to the Pennells, Whistler "wished to paint blue on blue as he had painted white on white."[4] However, the two oil fragments are somewhat dark and murky, a reminder of the difficulty Whistler sometimes met when translating his fresh color schemes into completed oil paintings (see Plates 16 and 17). The fragments depict blue and white china, which is faintly outlined in the pastel. Such props may help to explain the black crayon drawing on the verso of this sheet. It could be a piece of Oriental fabric, similar to the hanging that appears in *Arrangement in Grey and Black: Portrait of the Painter's Mother*. At one point, Whistler may have intended to use a fabric backdrop for Elinor's portrait. Sketchy chevrons and flower forms are visible in the pastel.

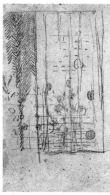

228v

Figure 228.1.
Diego Rodriguez de Silva y Velásquez, *Pablillos de Valladolid*, ca. 1635, photograph, from Whistler's studio. University of Glasgow Library, special collections.

Plates 229–234.
Studies for **Symphony in Flesh Colour and Pink**
229. The Blue Dress

28.1 × 18.5 cm.

230. Study

28.3 × 18.0 cm.

231. Study

27.0 × 17.8 cm.

232. Study

28.4 × 18.2 cm.

233. Study

26.6 × 17.5 cm.

234. Study

28.8 × 18.0 cm.

1871 ff.
fabricated chalks on brown paper
Inscription: butterfly (r) all; (v) no. 252, "Thos. Way, 1905."

This group of drawings relates to the magnificent dress seen in *Symphony in Flesh Colour and Pink: Portrait of Mrs. Francis Leyland.* Whistler designed the dress to harmonize with the sitter's red hair.[1]

The Blue Dress (Plate 229), one of the first Whistler drawings to be acquired by Freer, contains the embryo of the artist's conception. Whistler drew a filmy blue overdress, with a pale pink gown underneath. The model's hair is red, and a deep peach tone appears on the open fan. Although Whistler eventually abandoned the fan, his bare suggestion of peach in the drawing is the prelude to the *Symphony in Flesh Colour and Pink*. Thin vertical and horizontal lines of black chalk hint at the complicated orchestration of carpet, flooring, and dado in the finished oil. At the bottom right of *The Blue Dress*, a single rosette is outlined in black chalk. Eventually, Mrs. Leyland's gown was strewn with such flowers; their relative positions were frequently altered before the artist was satisfied. Whistler also made studies for the type of rosettes and hand-made carpet that appear in the oil portrait (Fig. 229–234.1).

In the remaining five drawings Whistler opted for a dress without blue. Whistler's conscious alliance with eighteenth-century France is evident in his choice of medium. Plates 232 and 234 are drawn with minimal strokes of black, white, and red, again recalling the favored "trois crayons" of Watteau and other eighteenth-century draftsmen.

The figure of Mrs. Leyland seems to revolve in space in this series of drawings. Looking at his subject from different angles, Whistler explored dress details in the margins of several sheets. From the front, his design for the gown resembles classical draperies. A notable feature of the gown is its stately train—the "pli Watteau" that signals interest in both contemporary fashion and the revival of eighteenth-century French art. Variations on the Watteau

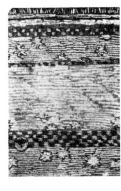 

Figure 229–234.1.
Studies for rosettes and carpet. From Pennell, 1921, opp. p. 302.

230

231

232

dress were in vogue from the 1860s through the 1890s. The stylistic admixture of Greek, Oriental, and French art is frequently found in Whistler's *oeuvre*.

Shortly after Whistler's death the sociologist Georg Simmel wrote about the importance of fashion, observing that it blends conflicting desires. Fashion involves imitation, thereby satisfying "the demand for social adaptation; it leads the individual upon the road which all travel." But change and contrast are also part of fashion, and the "constant change of contents" give current fashion "an individual stamp as opposed to that of yesterday and of to-morrow."[2]

Whistler viewed fashion as an arena for the blending of imitation and innovation. In *The Red Rag* he observed, "The imitator is a poor kind of creature. It is for the artist to do something beyond this: in portrait painting to put on canvas something more than the face the model wears for that one day; to paint the man . . . as well as his features; in arrangement of colours to treat a flower as his key, not as his model. This is now understood indifferently well—at least by dressmakers. In every costume you see attention is paid to the key-note of colour which runs through the composition."[3]

The last pastel drawing in this group is closest in pose to the final oil painting. Intrigued by the elegant "pli Watteau," Whistler finally elected to portray Mrs. Leyland from the back, capturing not the face she wore for a day, but the regal carriage that set her apart as a member of the social elite. By changing the contents of the fashionable French gown, adding both

233

Greek and Japanese elements, Whistler exhibited fashion's union and segregation as later discussed by Simmel.

Both Mrs. Leyland and Maud Franklin posed for the portrait, and perhaps for these drawings as well. The beauty Whistler discerned in Mrs. Leyland is conveyed less by her features than by the roseate glow of his dressmaker's color scheme. The last pastel study

234

also has a sprinkling of white dots to the left of the figure. These became a spray of apple or cherry blossoms in *Symphony in Flesh Colour and Pink*. As Whistler's contemporary, Baron Haussmann, wrote, "J'ai le culte du Beau, du Bien, des grandes choses. . . . J'ai l'amour du printemps en fleurs: femmes et roses."[4]

Plate 235.
Young Girl Standing

ca. 1870–1875
black and white chalk on brown paper
21.2 × 13.5 cm.
Inscription: butterfly.

The pose of this figure, along with its early
butterfly, suggests that it could be a working
drawing related to one of Whistler's uncom-
pleted portraits of the Leyland girls. The pose
is similar to that finally chosen for the portrait
of Mrs. Leyland, but this model looks youthful
and is more likely to be one of her daughters.
The dress resembles the one worn by Fanny
Leyland in an etched portrait (K108) made
about the same time as this drawing.

Plate 236.
Standing Figure with Fan

ca. 1870–1875
black, white, and gray chalks on dark brown paper
20.6 × 13.0 cm.
Inscription: butterfly.

Making studies of the same figure from different angles was a consistent part of
Whistler's method in portraiture. This drawing
of a young girl is part of such a series. Although no finished portrait resulted, the series
is contemporary with Whistler's drawings for
the portrait of Mrs. Leyland. Fanny Leyland
was thirteen years old in 1870, and the figure
depicted here seems to be about the same age.
Related drawings are now at the University of
Michigan Museum of Art and the Carnegie
Institute. The series recalls contemporary fashion prints. Faces were shown in profile, but
bodies were turned at oblique angles to display
the trains of the dresses, like the walking costumes from 1870 shown in Figure 236.1. However, puffed sleeves and an unadorned train
typify the "artistic" clothes of the Aesthetic
Movement. Fanny Leyland's parents, of
course, were involved in the avant-garde art
world of the 1870s.

Figure 236.1.
Walking Costumes, 1870.

Plate 237.
The Lady with the Fan

ca. 1870–1875
black and white chalk on dark brown paper
20.7 × 13.3 cm.
Inscription: butterfly.

Whistler probably created this drawing at the
same time he was busy with the "Six Projects"
as well as portraits of the Leyland family. Indeed, the drawing seems to conflate the two
commissions. The dress resembles the one
worn by Fanny Leyland, and she held a similar
fan.[1] But the composition, with a gracefully
bending figure standing at a railing, recalls
Greco-japonesque women in the "Six Projects." Whistler's treatment of this figure can be
compared to one of the Japanese woodblock
prints found in his studio after his death (Fig.
237.1). He has concerned himself with the sin-
uous curve of a voluminously clad figure, with
a partially concealed face. Her long gown cas-
cades to her feet, giving the artist occasion to
draw a series of linear patterns. The comparison demonstrates Whistler's ability to find
inspiration in Eastern art but to apply it to a
completely Western subject.

Figure 237.1.
Follower of Utamaro, *The
Courtesan Karakoto and an
Attendant*, ca. 1800,
woodblock print.
Hunterian Art Gallery,
University of Glasgow,
Birnie Philip Bequest.

Plate 238.
(r) Resting and (v) Sketch of
Standing Figure

ca. 1870–1875
(r) fabricated chalks on brown paper; (v) black chalk
14.7–16.0 × 7.3–7.7 cm.
Inscription: (r) butterfly; (v) "43" written twice.

Although tiny in scale, *Resting* demonstrates
the range of Whistler's powers as a colorist.
The model, in shades of pink, is held in a tiny
grid of vertical and horizontal elements suggesting a golden balcony. Another bright
streak of golden yellow—her hairband—helps
anchor the figure against a shifting background of cloudy pink and blue. The sheet is
composed with impressive graphic precision.
Whistler maintained balanced tension by making the fan purple and the butterfly orange.
The sculptor William Wetmore Storey said of
these drawings, "Whistler, they are as charming and complete as a Tanagra statue!" (Fig.
238.1).[1] When Freer had himself photographed by Alvin Langdon Coburn, this pastel
was arranged behind him along with two
pieces of Eastern sculpture, and it is clear that
for Freer, *Resting* demonstrated Whistler's
masterful blending of Oriental decorative surface with the classical figure tradition of the
West. The black chalk drawing on the verso
appears to relate to *Morning Glories* (Plate
214).

238v

Figure 238.1.
Tanagra figurine from
Whistler's photograph
album. Hunterian Art
Gallery, University of
Glasgow, Birnie Philip
Bequest.

Plate 239.
Seated Figure

1870s
fabricated chalks on brown paper
26.7 × 17.4 cm.[1]

Vigorous and angular in execution, Whistler's study is drawn with black, white, and shades of coral, pink, orange, and brown that recall eighteenth-century French drawings. A related drawing was published by Way in 1912.[2] Equally energetic draftsmanship can be seen in a lithograph of a standing figure wearing a similar dress and hat (Fig. 239.1). A lithograph, drawn on the stone in 1879, may also be related to the *Seated Figure*.[3]

Plate 240.
Study in Grey and Pink

ca. 1872–1874
fabricated chalks on brown paper
21.5 × 13.9 cm.

Whistler's pastel study relates to two full-length oil portraits from the early 1870s. After receiving a commission to paint the daughters of W. C. Alexander in 1872, Whistler took great pains to design a dress worn by the subject of *Harmony in Grey and Green: Miss Cicely Alexander*.[1] This is one instance where Whistler did indeed "drag in Velásquez," for his general basis of inspiration is obviously *Las Meninas*. A large detail photograph of the Spaniard's painting was found in Whistler's studio (Fig. 240.1). Cicely's dress is short, but Whistler reused the concept of a decorative ruff at the neck, and a large ornament at the waist for the longer dress in the Freer pastel. Each model wears a similar rosette in her hair, while a scattering of flowers appears at the right edge of the oil and is reversed in the pastel. The pastel and another like it (Fig. 240.2) form a bridge to the second portrait, painted from 1872 to 1874. Entitled *Harmony in Grey and Peach Colour*, the oil presumably depicts Maud Franklin (Fig. 240.3).[2] The two pastels correspond closely in composition and detail to the oil painting, although more than one model could be involved. The drawings probably served as studies for *Harmony in Grey and Peach Colour*. But their relation to the portrait of Miss Alexander reminds us how one work by Whistler tended to generate another.

Figure 240.1.
Diego Rodriguez de Silva y Velásquez, *Las Meninas*, detail, photograph from Whistler's studio. University of Glasgow Library, special collections.

Figure 239.1.
Study, lithograph, K1. Freer Gallery.

Figure 240.2.
Lady with a Fan, pastel with watercolor, photograph from Pennell collection, Library of Congress, also marked "C. L. Rothenstein." The drawing was once in the Way collection and is now at the Manchester City Art Gallery.

Figure 240.3.
Harmony in Grey and Peach Colour. Courtesy of the Fogg Art Museum, Harvard University, Grenville L. Winthrop Bequest.

Plate 242.
Standing Figure in Fur Jacket

1870–1875
black, white, and gray chalks on brown paper
28.6 × 17.8 cm.
Inscription: butterfly.

Black and white subject matter dictated the black, white, and gray color scheme for this drawing of an unidentified woman in a short fur jacket and straight skirt. Relatively close-fitting skirts gradually replaced voluminous ones during the 1870s. The drawing was exhibited after the artist's death as *The Sable Jacket* according to a label on the back of its original frame, but the fur could also be ermine, which has white tails tipped in black. In any case, it shows Whistler's continuing interest in fashion, and in making studies that recall his series of black and white full-length oil portraits. In the background, faint lines indicate the underpinnings of a streetscape. Had the artist taken this composition further, it might have been an unusual addition to the series.

Plate 241.
Standing Woman in
Flounced Dress

ca. 1870–1875
black and white chalk on brown paper
32.8 × 18.2 cm.
Inscription: butterfly.

Both Whistler's geometric butterfly signature and his use of black and white chalk on brown paper suggest a date of the early 1870s for this drawing. It is possible that the model is Maud Franklin, Whistler's mistress. She began posing for him then. However, the artist's real interest here was the turn of the figure and the details of the costume. Once again Whistler created an image closely related to fashion plates of the era.

Plate 243.
Maud, Reading

ca. 1878
black and white chalk on brown paper
31.3 × 19.5 cm.
Inscription: butterfly; "Whistler," "2 Lindsay Houses—
    Chelsea—London," butterfly, artist's hand (on wood
    backing).

Women reading in armchairs supplied
Whistler with one of his favorite motifs. This
drawing probably depicts Maud Franklin, absorbed in a book. Another drawing, made at
the same time, shows her from the front (Fig.
243.1). In each drawing, Whistler used thick
white chalk to mark highlights such as the
cuffs of the dress and the pages of the book.
Bright little spots of white disappeared when
the artist executed a related lithotint in 1878. It
recorded almost the same pose as *Maud, Reading*, but the figure is reversed, and tiny highlights gave way to larger areas that include not
only the cuff, but the whole hand and the book
as one continuous passage (Fig. 243.2).[1]

Figure 243.1.
Maud, Seated, black and
white chalk. Hunterian Art
Gallery, University of
Glasgow, Birnie Philip
Bequest.

Figure 243.2.
Study: Seated Figure, 1878,
lithotint, K2. Freer Gallery.

Plate 244.
Venice Bay

1879
fabricated chalks with pencil and watercolor on tan paper
12.7 × 22.7 cm.
Inscription: butterfly.

Clumsy in composition, curious in execution, this drawing causes one to raise the curatorial eyebrow. Underneath the pastel are the beginnings of a watercolor drawing with tiny boats, started at the right side of the paper and then abandoned. The initial attempt in watercolor may explain Whistler's use of an unusually smooth paper, not typical of his pastel drawings. Another abandoned pencil drawing can be discerned, as opposed to identified, at the right side of the page. The pastel itself is dryly applied and does not work well with the sallow tone of the paper. Robert Getscher has argued that *Venice Bay* is one of Whistler's earliest Venetian experiments in pastel.[1] The drawing's provenance is good, but one is hard-pressed to find any reason why Whistler would have signed it so boldly.

Plate 245.
The Grand Canal, Venice

1879
fabricated chalks on tan paper
17.4 × 27.0 cm.
Inscription: butterfly.

There is an awkward and unsettling quality about this pastel, which is not known to have been published or exhibited until after Whistler's death. The *Studio* reproduced it in full color in 1903, perhaps at the behest of the London dealer Obach, who sold the drawing to Freer shortly thereafter.[1] Freer thought highly enough of the work to lend it to the Whistler memorial exhibition in Paris in 1905. Although the drawing is prominently signed, the strip of architecture is too detailed, clumsier than we expect of Whistler at his best. The fussy blocks of buildings recall those in a gouache drawing, *Venetian Atmosphere*, that has been erroneously attributed to Whistler (Fig. 245.1).[2] Moreover, the colors have been awkwardly applied to the rough, mottled gray-tan paper. Unpleasantly scrubbed and smudged in texture, the colors fail to reach the exquisite balance characteristic of Whistler's finest pastels. However, both the gondola in the foreground and the butterfly signature seem to be genuine. It is possible that an unfinished drawing by Whistler received additions to make it more salable. Or perhaps Whistler was just having an extremely bad day.

Figure 245.1.
Attributed to Whistler, *Venetian Atmosphere*, gouache. Courtesy of the Art Institute of Chicago, gift of Walter S. Brewster.

Plate 246.
(r) Venice: Sunrise on the Rialto, and (v) Venetian Scene

1879–1880
fabricated chalks on gray paper
10.4–10.6 × 27.0–27.4 cm.

Acid yellows, hot pinks, and peaches evoke a Venetian morning in *Sunrise on the Rialto*. The etching *Upright Venice* depicts the same bit of skyline in reverse (Fig. 246.1).[1] Underneath the drawing is an earlier one, showing a close-up view of figures in front of a building (Fig. 246.2). This drawing is a variant of the same subject on the verso of the sheet. The figures recall some of the women and children in Whistler's elaborate pastel, *The Steps* (Plate 250). Otto Bacher described Whistler's working methods: "Some motives were finished at one sitting, but more often he made only the crayon outline, charming in its effect, leaving the unfinished sketch for days at its most fascinating point, to be filled in later with the pastels. Many times these outlines needed very little color to complete them. At other times, he would take an old pastel which had been cast aside, and, by adding some new strokes, bring it into a beautiful creation."[2] But now and then, as this sheet demonstrates, Whistler covered an old pastel with a completely new drawing.

Figure 246.1.
Upright Venice, etching, K205. Freer Gallery.

Figure 246.2.
Venice: Sunrise on the Rialto, infrared photograph.

246v

Plate 247.
Venice: Sunset on Harbour

1879–1880
fabricated chalks on gray paper
15.8–16.0 × 25.3–25.5 cm.

Sunset on Harbour is one of a few Venice pastels not on a brown paper support. Here Whistler chose a gray paper, actually made up of blue fibers on a light tan base. The chalks are somewhat harsh in color and application, and it has been suggested that the work stands early in Whistler's corpus of Venetian drawings.[1] Whistler may not have cared much for this pastel. It was not included in the 1881 exhibition in London, and the artist did not bother to sign it.

Plate 248.
Venice

1879–1889
fabricated chalks on brown paper[1]
32.0–32.1 × 20.2–20.3 cm.

Whistler gave this sheet a quarter turn to the right before drawing a broad view of the city over traces of a figure leaning near a large rectangular opening with a heavy ceiling (Fig. 248.1). The early drawing may relate to the artist's effort to rework his etching *The Beggars*.[2] The later composition is similar to another pastel, entitled *San Giorgio* (Fig. 248.2). However, it has been argued that *Venice* is an unfinished drawing,[3] and Whistler did not include it in the 1881 exhibition. Had he taken *Venice* further, Whistler might have created a drawing like *Winter Evening* (Plate 258). At present no color has been applied to the architecture, but, as in *Winter Evening*, Whistler would have added very little. The sea has traces of pale blue-gray, and the sky is enlivened by a brilliant passage of acid yellow touched with orange, set against mixed veils of blue and turquoise. Whistler used just enough color to reveal the importance of the brown paper, which let him easily secure "a ready-made tone."[4]

Figure 248.1.
Venice, infrared photograph.

Figure 248.2.
Church of San Giorgio, Venice. Corcoran Gallery of Art, James Parmelee Bequest.

Plate 249.
Nocturne: San Giorgio

1879–1880
fabricated chalks on brown paper[1]
20.2 × 29.8–30.0 cm.
Inscription: butterfly.[2]

Drawn in black chalk, *Nocturne: San Giorgio* is misted over with pale gray-blues, recalling Whistler's earliest nighttime scenes executed along the Thames River. *San Giorgio* remained unsold at the end of the 1881 exhibition, but Whistler later chose it as part of a group of Venetian pastels for Mrs. H. O. Havemeyer, one of Freer's most important fellow collectors. Mrs. Havemeyer was also a personal friend, and in 1917 she gave the drawings to Freer for his intended museum.[3] Rarely did objects enter the collection in this manner, and once again, the quality of the objects reflects the intervention of the artist. The pastel's subtle beauty appealed to Freer in the same way that he enjoyed the nuances of glazed Oriental pottery.

Plate 250.
The Steps

1879–1880
fabricated chalks on brown paper
19.4 × 30.0–30.3 cm.
Inscription: butterfly.[1]

The Steps offers a glimpse of a quiet corner of
Venice. Women and children are ranged about
in comfortable attitudes, removed from
crowds of visitors bustling to and from the
standard tourist sites. An infrared photograph
indicates changes to the drawing, including the
elimination of two gondolas at the right (Fig.
250.1).[2] Suppression of detail at the edges of
the sheet helps to create a calm frieze of figures
in which all the excitement is carried by small
passages of vibrant color. Whistler applied his
pastel sticks solidly here, although even in such
rich works he avoided stumping and blending.
The women are occupied with various daily
tasks, but one could hardly call this a genre
scene. Rather, Whistler has taken relatively
humble elements and transformed them into a
thing of great beauty. He wrote to his mother,
"The people with their gay gowns and hand-
kerchiefs—and the many tinted buildings for
them to lounge against or pose before, seem to
exist especially for one's pictures—and to have
no other reason for being!"[3]

Figure 250.1.
The Steps, infrared
photograph.

Plate 251.
San Giovanni Apostolo et Evangelistae

1879–1880
fabricated chalks on brown paper
30.0 × 22.1–22.2 cm.
Inscription: butterfly.

Drawing must have been uppermost in the artist's mind as he created this view of a richly ornamented Venetian portal and the courtyard beyond. Like his earliest colored images, *San Giovanni* was completely realized in black before bits of color were added. Whistler captured a similar surface quality with his etching needle in *The Doorway* (Fig. 251.1). An infrared photograph shows that the artist made alterations as he went along (Fig. 251.2). The most striking of these is his elimination of something about to enter the courtyard, and the transformation of two children into a black and orange cat at the base of the column on the left.[1] Unblocking the entrance increases the grandeur of the imposing portal, and the brilliant coloring of the cat distracts the viewer from still-visible pentimenti.[2]

Figure 251.1.
The Doorway, etching, K188, third state. Freer Gallery.

Figure 251.2.
San Giovanni Apostolo et Evangelistae, infrared photograph.

Plate 252.
The Staircase: Note in Red

1879–1880
fabricated chalks on brown paper
28.7–28.9 × 20.2–20.4 cm.
Inscription: butterfly.

One of the brightest of all of Whistler's Venice drawings, *The Staircase* was not particularly well received when it was exhibited in 1881.[1] The heavily applied pastel masks another drawing underneath the present one. The earlier composition was also architectural (Fig. 252.1). Whistler turned the sheet upside down for the current work. Traces of an earlier arch are still visible to the naked eye but they easily escape notice, countered by multiple arches in the opposite direction, as well as the rich red color. The first drawing was signed with a butterfly different in style from the rust and brown one that marks the current drawing (Fig. 252.1). The ghost of the earlier butterfly can still be seen to the left of the seated lion at the top of the staircase.

Figure 252.1.
The Staircase, infrared photograph.

Plate 254.
Quiet Canal

1879–1880
black chalk on tan paper
22.7 × 13.8 cm.

Whistler was skilled at manipulating different tools to achieve similar effects. This view of a Venetian canal shares the somber mood of nocturnes that precede and follow it. Whistler's night views of Cremorne Gardens were executed in oil during the early 1870s. His Amsterdam nocturnes were painted in watercolor during the 1880s. Whistler here achieves the same dark and expressive mood using only black chalk. The composition is consistent with other Venetian pastels that show a narrow passage with a bit of architecture glimpsed at the far end. However, *Quiet Canal* is one of only two monochromatic Venice drawing in the collection. Perhaps Whistler intended to create an etching related to this view.[1] He did not do so, but the brooding atmosphere recalls the heavily inked surface of another Venetian etching, *Nocturne: Palaces* (Fig. 254.1).

Figure 254.1.
Nocturne: Palaces, etching, K202, seventh state. Freer Gallery.

Plate 253.
The Marble Palace

1879–1880
fabricated chalks on brown paper
30.0 × 15.7–15.8 cm.
Inscription: butterfly.

Whistler's travels to Venice immediately followed the Whistler-Ruskin libel suit, and Whistler was to remain contemptuous of Ruskin for the rest of his life. However, it is interesting that in *The Marble Palace*, Whistler chose to depict the crumbling corner of an old building with Gothic arched windows. Passages of shimmering cream pigment suggest marble clinging to the façade, but the artist also showed warm red brick, indicating the structure's state of decay, as the focal point of the composition. It was this very sense of decaying grandeur that fascinated Europeans who visited Venice during the nineteenth century. While Whistler's drawing makes no moralizing statement, it is clear that he observed and appreciated some of the same qualities that prompted Ruskin to write *The Stones of Venice*.

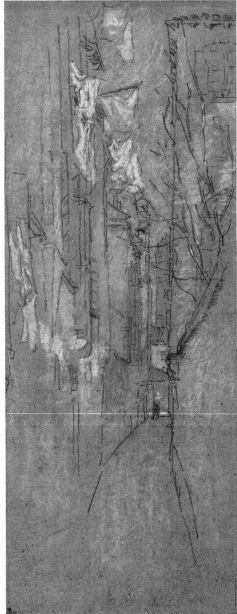

Plate 256.
A Street in Venice

1879–1880
fabricated chalks on brown paper
30.0 × 12.6 cm.

A Street in Venice is dominated by the pinks and blues favored by Whistler for some of his major figural compositions during the late 1860s and early 1870s.[1] Prosaic white linens are transformed into festive banners hanging from windows. Much of Whistler's Venetian corpus displays beauty of color or strength of composition, but he often chose to depict obscure parts of the city, ignoring popular taste. As one outraged critic complained of an etching, "It is not the Venice of a maiden's fancies."[2] The drawing resembles two compositions included in the 1881 exhibition at the Fine Art Society, although it cannot be positively identified as either one.[3] Traces of another drawing survive under *A Street in Venice*, suggesting that the sheet originally bore the image of a building seen horizontally (Fig. 256.1).

Figure 256.1.
A Street in Venice, infrared photograph.

Plate 255.
Bead-Stringers

1879–1880
fabricated chalks on brown paper
27.5–27.6 × 11.6 cm.
Inscription: butterfly.

Whistler has drawn a visual metaphor evocative of the infinite small delights to be found along the city's tortuous byways. One such delight was the colorful peasant life, which fascinated more than one visiting artist during the period. A young girl in a silvery-gray dress sits at the near end of a constricted passage, stringing beads. A light gray façade broken by a dark doorway stands at the far end.[1] Bits of clean linen flutter on the lines like pennants, and a checkered patch of turquoise and deep jade green pulls the eye through the alley toward brightly clothed figures in the distance. These touches of color sparkle like the little glass beads Venetian women strung for sale to tourists.[2]

Plate 257.
The Beggars—Winter

ca. 1880
fabricated chalks on brown paper
30.0–30.1 × 20.2 cm.
Inscription: butterfly, "N 14   10¾ × 6¾."

The purpose of this drawing may have been to serve as an intermediate study for an etching entitled *The Beggars*, which exists in numerous states. Whistler would have completed the first state of the print before making this drawing, for in the first state, an old man and a little girl occupy the archway. The posture of the two foreground figures drawn in chalk is similar to reversed figures in the second state of the etching (Fig. 257.1). Although the little girl is a constant in the various states of the print, the young woman had become old and wizened by the fourth state (Fig. 257.2).

Figure 257.1.
The Beggars, etching, K194, second state. Freer Gallery.

Figure 257.2.
The Beggars, etching, K194, fourth state. Freer Gallery.

Plate 258.
Winter Evening

1880
fabricated chalks on brown paper[1]
30.0 × 20.2 cm.
Inscription: butterfly.[2]

Otto Bacher, a fellow American artist, described Whistler at work in Venice: "In beginning a pastel he drew his subject crisply and carefully in outline with black crayon upon [a sheet] of tinted paper which fitted the general color of the motive. A few touches with sky-tinted pastels, corresponding to nature, produced a remarkable effect, with touches of reds, grays, and yellows for the buildings here and there. The reflections of the sky and houses upon the water finished the work."[3] In *Winter Evening* the color occurs mostly in the sky and water. Bare brown paper, occasionally brightened by a bit of pastel, evokes the aged buildings. Robert Getscher has suggested that Whistler perfected the balance between black line drawing and shimmering clouds of color, as seen in *Winter Evening*, near the end of his Venetian sojourn.[4] Whistler was there until November 1880.

Plate 259.
Sunset in Red and Brown

1879–1880
fabricated chalks on brown paper
30.0 × 20.2–20.3 cm.
Inscription: butterfly.[1]

Sunset in Red and Brown is another Whistler pastel with a completely different drawing underneath it. The earlier work is partially visible to the naked eye but can be even better perceived in an infrared photograph (Fig. 259.1). Whistler used the same sheet of paper for several different purposes.[2] The first drawing on the sheet includes an arched doorway and figure at the center; these elements reappeared in an etching, *The Balcony* (Fig. 259.2). Elements from the second drawing, showing a canal with boats and buildings, can be seen in several other etchings.[3] *Sunset* was shown in its present state at Whistler's 1881 exhibition.[4] The artist willingly displayed sheets upon which unrelated, reusable images were obviously layered. This would seem to complicate assigning the role of "study" to one of these pastels, although it does testify to the experimental nature of Whistler's Venetian works.[5]

Plate 260.
Campo S. Marta: Winter Evening

1880[1]
fabricated chalks on brown paper
22.7–22.8 × 27.7 cm.
Inscription: butterfly.[2]

As in several other pastels with wintery subjects, Whistler confined himself to few and cold colors for this view of Campo Santa Marta. An underlying drawing suggests that Whistler might have started much nearer the water's edge (Fig. 260.1). To the left side of the sheet the trunk of a large tree is now masked by a cloud of cream, peach, and blue chalks. Some of its branches were reworked into small trees in the far distance of the later drawing. To the left of the early tree appears a boat. Its masts also became small tree trunks. The line that bisects the sheet may once have indicated the corner of a building.

Figure 259.1.
Sunset in Red and Brown,
infrared photograph.

Figure 259.2.
The Balcony, etching,
K207, between first and
second state, drawn upon
with ink. Freer Gallery.

Figure 260.1.
*Campo S. Marta: Winter
Evening,* infrared
photograph.

Plate 261.
The Isles of Venice

1880
fabricated chalks on brown paper
9.2–9.4 × 28.4 cm.
Inscription: butterfly.

The Isles of Venice is drawn on part of a previously used sheet, which was cut down and given a quarter turn to the right. The horizon line of the present composition follows the left edge of what was once a building, and the pentimento of a standing figure can be made out at the bottom right of the earlier work (Fig. 261.1). Again, the richness of the chalks was dictated in part by reuse of the support. But the brilliant color also conveys the artist's delight in contemplating the old Venetian city: "Perhaps tomorrow may be fine—And then Venice will be simply glorious, as now and then I have seen it—After the wet, the colors upon the walls and their reflections in the canals are more gorgeous than ever—and with sun shining upon the polished marble mingled with rich toned bricks and plaster, this amazing city of palaces becomes really a fairy land—created one would think especially for the painter."[1]

Figure 261.1.
The Isles of Venice, infrared photograph.

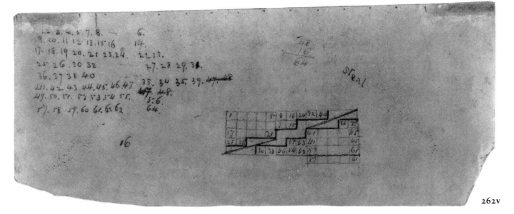

Plate 262.
(r) Seven Sketches of Heads and (v) Chart

ca. 1880
(r) ink on buff paper; (v) black crayon
13.8 × 35.1 cm.
Inscription: "WHISTLER, Venice 80."

More than one artist exercised his talents in the creation of this drawing. The inscriptions upon it are in several hands, none of them Whistler's, suggesting that the drawing might have been made in one of the Venice studios frequented by Whistler and other expatriate artists during the winter of 1879–1880. Only the head at the upper right seems to be drawn by Whistler. The schema on the verso has not been explained, but the word "steal" conjures up the possibility that it relates to some sort of a game, perhaps played by Whistler and his fellow artists.

262v

Plate 263.
Maud Standing

ca. 1881
black chalk on brown paper
27.4 × 17.8 cm.
Inscription: (v) "Thos. Way."

Maud Franklin was Whistler's model and mistress from the early 1870s until his marriage in 1888. She probably stood in this dress as Whistler worked on *Harmony in Pink and Grey: Portrait of Lady Meux*, now in the Frick Collection (Fig. 263.1). The work was painted from 1881 to 1882.[1] The buxom Lady Meux holds a hat in the finished oil, and the bodice of her dress has been altered. However, Maud was known to pose for the portraits of other women, allowing the artist additional study without bothering his socially prominent sitters. The drawing was made on a reused sheet, for there is an underdrawing which resembles fish scales at the extreme left edge level with Maud's elbow, and several touches of blue chalk unrelated to the study appear in the upper left corner.

Figure 263.1.
Harmony in Pink and Grey: Portrait of Lady Meux,
1881–1882, oil on canvas.
Copyright the Frick
collection, New York.

Plate 264.
A Yellow Note

1880–1890s
fabricated chalks on brown paper
28.0 × 18.5 cm.

The Yellow Note may be a work which Whistler drew much earlier than he colored it. The theme of a model lifting her draperies reappears often in Whistler's work (Fig. 264.1). This particular drawing is close to the work of Albert Moore, and may deserve further investigation for a connection with that artist.

Figure 264.1.
Nude Girl Standing with
Raised Arms Removing a
Black Robe, pastel on
brown paper. Hunterian
Art Gallery, University of
Glasgow, Birnie Philip
Bequest.

Plate 266.
Seated Figure

1870s–1880s
fabricated chalks on brown paper
20.1–20.3 × 18.0–18.2 cm.
Inscription: butterfly.

A number of Whistler's lithographs of the
1890s were spoiled when the image drawn
with lithographic crayon on thin paper was
transferred to a stone for printing. One of
these was *Model Seated on a Floor*.[1] Although
the lithograph was unsuccessful, virtually the
same image survives as a pastel on heavy
brown paper, and *Seated Figure* may have been
drawn at the time Whistler was working on the
lithograph. However, Whistler studied the
crouching pose from another angle in a much
earlier black chalk drawing which he signed
with a geometric butterfly (Fig. 266.1). It is not
outside the realm of possibility that Plate 266
is an early drawing to which Whistler later
added color before signing with a butterfly in
the 1890s.

Figure 266.1.
Nude Girl Seated on the
Floor, black crayon,
touched with blue pastel, on
brown paper. Hunterian
Art Gallery, University of
Glasgow, Birnie Philip
Bequest.

Plate 265.
Little Nude

1870s ff.
fabricated chalks on brown paper
26.0 × 13.5 cm.
Inscription: (r) butterfly.

Thomas R. Way gave this account of the *Little
Nude*: "Following the manner of Watteau,
[Whistler] used [pastel] always as a drawing.
Sometimes he blended the backgrounds of his
figure-studies, rubbing them with his finger-
tips, but even when he did so there is very little
chalk upon them. My father used to have,
hanging in his office, a pastel of a little nude
figure, which he had bought from Whistler
many years before. . . . One day Whistler had
it out of its frame, and borrowing my pocket-
box of pastels he spent nearly the whole of a
day in retouching it, and raised its key of tone
amazingly, adding the red background it now
has."[1] The *Little Nude* documents the pit-
falls of assigning dates to the artist's figure
drawings.

Plate 267.
The Purple Cap

1870s, reworked ca. 1885
fabricated chalks on brown paper
27.7 × 16.4 cm.
Inscription: butterfly.

An infrared photograph reveals that Whistler reused a previous drawing. We may speculate that at some time in the 1880s, he chose to color a black and white drawing from the 1870s. The earlier geometric butterfly is visible at the upper left, parallel with the model's shoulder (Fig. 267.1). The old butterfly was covered with a cloud of pale blue. Whistler's new butterfly, richly colored in gray-pink and periwinkle blue, serves to balance the model's voluptuous pale green and brilliant blue draperies. Those draperies hang, for the most part, behind her. This pastel may have been exhibited in 1885–1886 as *Note in Green and Violet*. Both colors appear in the drawing. One of the Royal Academicians, J. C. Horsley, had just read a paper at a church conference, attacking the use of the live model:

> *If those who talk and write so glibly as to the desirability of artists devoting themselves to the representation of the naked human form, only knew a tithe of the degradation enacted before the model is sufficiently hardened to her shameful calling, they would forever hold their tongues and pens in supporting the practice. Is not clothedness a distinct type and feature of our Christian faith? All art representations of nakedness are out of harmony with it.*[1]

Perhaps Horsley's reference to harmony set Whistler off. He was unable to resist making a label for *Green and Violet*, on view at the Society of British Artists' Suffolk Street galleries. The label read, "Horsley soit qui mal y pense."[2] Naturally, Whistler's clever pun did not go unnoticed, and the artist brought his name once again to the attention of the public.

Plate 268.
Harmony in Blue and Violet

late 1880s
fabricated chalks on brown paper
27.5 × 17.9 cm.
Inscription: (r) butterfly; (v) "Harmony in Blue and Violet," butterfly, "J. McNeill Whistler," artist's hand.

Whistler sold this sheet directly to Freer, probably soon after he had made it. *Harmony in Blue and Violet* was one of the first drawings by Whistler to enter the Freer collection. The artist continued to sketch adolescent figures in diaphanous gowns through the 1880s and 1890s, sustaining an interest in figure drawing that began during the 1860s. The pose, with the girl coyly resting her chin on her hand, is familiar from earlier works. Whistler was quite fond of his youthful models, and called them "my little pretties."

Figure 267.1.
The Purple Cap, infrared photograph.

Plate 269.
A Violet Note

ca. 1885
fabricated chalks on gray-brown paper
27.4–27.6 × 17.8–18.0 cm.
Inscription: butterfly.

Application of relatively opaque areas of pastel on this sheet was governed partially by the artist's desire to cover an earlier nude study, visible in an infrared photograph (Fig. 269.1). Not only the sheet but also the pose is reused. Variants begin with the figure at the left of *The White Symphony* from the "Six Projects," and they recur in later works in various media.[1] Whistler painted a close variant in 1892 (Fig. 269.2).

Figure 269.1.
A Violet Note, infrared photograph.

Figure 269.2.
Nude Girl with a Bowl, oil on panel. Hunterian Art Gallery, University of Glasgow, Birnie Philip Bequest.

Plate 270.
Writing on the Wall

1890–1902
fabricated chalks on brown paper
27.5 × 17.8–17.9 cm.
Inscription: butterfly.

This figure drawing is another variant on the stooping young girl from *The White Symphony*. Whistler's handling of the figure has not changed substantially from drawings of the 1860s (Fig. 270.1). It is difficult to say exactly when Whistler drew this figure, since we know he sometimes colored old drawings at a later date. Whistler probably did add color to this drawing in 1902. Freer's memorandum of payments to the artist noted that *Writing on the Wall* and two other pastels were "Left with Mr. Whistler to work on."[1] The sheet has been laid down on cardboard that bears an English frame maker's stamp.[2]

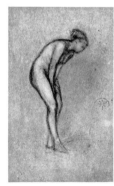

Figure 270.1.
Nude Study, black and white crayon on brown paper. Hunterian Art Gallery, University of Glasgow, Birnie Philip Bequest.

Plate 271.
Pour le Pastel: Rose and Opal

ca. 1885–1895
fabricated chalks on brown paper
14.8–15.0 × 24.5–24.6 cm.
Inscription: butterfly.

The stiff, brittle quality of *Pour le Pastel* may
be explained by the composite nature of the
drawing. As a sort of memory piece, it embodies multiple images by Whistler, along with resonances from past tradition.[1] The long,
stretched-out figure recalls earlier nudes, such
as *The Rokeby Venus* by Velásquez, as well as
modern ones, like Manet's *Olympia*. But rich
surface patterning brings to mind Whistler's
association with Albert Moore (Fig. 271.1).
Despite the title, *Pour le Pastel: Rose and Opal*
is dominated by strident hues of blue-violet
and orange, a reminder that strong color op-
posites were already interesting the artistic circles to which Whistler belonged.

Figure 271.1.
Albert Moore, study for
Reading Aloud, oil on glass.
Hunterian Art Gallery,
University of Glasgow.

Plate 272.
Sleeping

1880s–1902
fabricated chalks on gray-brown paper
17.6 × 25.5 cm.
Inscription: (r) butterfly;[1] (v) "Paris," artist's hand
    "Newman" (stamped on matboard backing).

The awkward pose of this model, as well as the
arrangement of drapery across her thigh, is derived from turning a figure from Tintoretto's
Birth of the Milky Way on its side. Whistler
kept a large photograph of the Tintoretto
painting in his studio.[2] *Sleeping* was reworked
in 1902. Freer "left [it] with Mr. Whistler to
add some orange."[3] The drawing is obviously
related to the figure of a woman and child
purchased by Freer two years after he bought
this work.

Plates 273–277.
Figures of Women with Children

273. Mother and Child: The Pearl

1880s–1890s
18.2–18.5 × 27.5–27.9 cm.

274. Rose and Red: The Little Pink Cap

1890s
27.9 × 18.3 cm.

275. The Purple Cap

1890s
27.5 × 18.0–18.1 cm.

276. The Green Cap

1890s–1902
17.9–18.0 × 27.4–27.6 cm.

277. The Shell

1890s

18.4 × 27.8–27.9 cm.
fabricated chalks on gray-brown paper.
Inscription: **273**, (r) butterfly, (v) "Frederick H. Grau . . .st
in Furniture . . ."; **274**, (r) butterfly, (v) "Rose and Red,
The Little Pink Cap," butterfly, artist's hand (on wood
backing); **275**, (r) butterfly, (v) "No. 35" on backing;
276, butterfly; **277**, butterfly.

Whistler's series of women and children are as
complicated and self-referential as Degas's
pastel drawings of ballet dancers, with which
they are contemporary. In each case, the works
were done in the studio, where the artist could
control and manipulate his imagery at will
(Figs. 273-277.1 and 273-277.2). Like Degas,
Whistler was completely devoted to the reuse
of standard poses explored in seemingly endless variations. *Mother and Child: The Pearl* is
a case in point. An infrared photograph reveals
an earlier black chalk drawing of a standing
figure with a pot of flowers, probably related
to the "Six Projects" (Fig. 273-277.3). The artist's first attempt at a new drawing was obliterated by the drawing as we see it now. The
reclining model was once farther to the right,
and we can still see her lower leg, reworked
into a swag of drapery. In general, the composition is closely related to *Sleeping* (Plate
272), with the pose derived from Tintoretto. A
watercolor, probably made at about the same
time, shows a composite image with one figure
layered atop another (Fig. 273-277.4).

The seated woman in *The Purple Cap* corresponds so closely in size and pose to a related
figure in reverse that one cannot discount the
possibility that Whistler used some sort of
tracing to transfer the image from one sheet to
the next (Fig. 273-277.5). Given Whistler's
working methods, the sequence for the drawings is unclear.

The series embraces an innocent look at
mothers and children, a theme prevalent in
eighteenth-century rococo art, and one still
popular in European painting a hundred years
later.[1] Titles like *Mother and Child: The Pearl*

273

274

Figure 273–277.1.
Whistler's studio,
photograph by George
Jacomb-Hood, ca. 1890.
Courtesy of the Library of
Congress, Pennell
collection.

Figure 273–277.2.
Whistler's studio,
photograph. University of
Glasgow Library, special
collections.

Figure 273–277.3.
*Mother and Child: The
Pearl*, Infrared photograph.

Figure 273–277.4.
Composite image, *Mother
and Child*, watercolor.
Hunterian Art Gallery,
University of Glasgow,
Birnie Philip Bequest.

275

Figure 273–277.5.
*A Seated Girl Holding a
Baby (a Pettigrew Model)*,
pastel on brown paper.
Hunterian Art Gallery,
University of Glasgow,
Birnie Philip Bequest.

Figure 273–277.6.
Baby Pettigrew, etching,
K341. Freer Gallery.

as well as sweetly posed compositions such as *Rose and Red: The Little Pink Cap* reflect this facet of the artist's interests. One or more of the Pettigrew sisters, three well-known models of the 1880s and 1890s, probably sat for these drawings. In 1895 the artist worked on several compositions using Lily Pettigrew as his model. Whistler made an etching, entitled *Baby Pettigrew* at about the same time (Fig. 273-277.6). Undoubtedly the same baby appears in the drawings.[2]

The drawings are not entirely innocent, however. The Pettigrew sisters were described as "three little gypsies," and Whistler allowed himself a certain abandon in depicting them. Whistler was hardly captivated by bourgeois motherhood.[3] A combination of nudity and filmy drapery provides a sexual undercurrent that flows outside the boundaries of the more conventional mother-and-child theme as seen in the work of his fellow expatriate Mary Cassatt. Whistler's unorthodox pair cuddle in *Mother and Child: The Pearl. The Shell* is particularly charged with sexuality. The dominant colors include hot pinks and peaches, forming a warm, womblike curve in which the two figures are supported. The woman's pink cap is like a breast, while the child is posed in an indecorous sprawl with its little draperies suggestively lifted. In *The Green Cap*, it is not a child, but a doll with which the model, now a child-woman, plays.

The drawings gain much of their impact through Whistler's sensitive application of color. Such colors look fresh no matter when the artist applies them, making pastel the ideal medium for this convoluted series. In a number of cases, color was added to a drawing after Freer decided to acquire it.[4] I have already discussed the lessons Whistler learned from Tanagra statuettes, with bits of dusty color clinging to their crumbly surfaces, but it is worth repeating that Tanagra groups of Venus and Cupid are directly paralleled by Whistler's pastels on tinted paper, and he created such figures in other media as well (Figs. 273-277.7 and 273-277.8).[5]

Whistler's series falls into the context of the late nineteenth century. Artists, ranging from Bougereau to MacMonnies, created ostensibly mythological images with thinly veiled sexual overtones (Figs. 273-277.9 and 273-277.10). But Whistler turned to veils of color, whose shimmering beauty is meant less to reveal carnality than to cloak mortals in the ethereal splendor of the gods.

276

277

Figure 273–277.7.
Venus and Cupid, Tanagra figurine. From *Collection Julien Greau: Terres Cuites Greques—Vases Peints et Marbres Antiques* (Paris, 1903), pl. xxiii.

Figure 273–277.8.
Venus and Cupid, 1890s, watercolor. Freer Gallery.

Figure 273–277.9.
William Adolphe Bougereau, *Venus and Cupid*, ca. 1877. Musées Nationaux de France.

Figure 273–277.10.
Frederick MacMonnies, *Bacchante and Infant Faun*, 1894, bronze. Philadelphia Museum of Art, gift of Mr. and Mrs. Clarence E. Hall.

275

Plate 278.
Standing Figure

ca. 1890
lithographic crayon on transfer paper
24.5 × 15.9 cm.
Inscription: butterfly.

Whistler was almost fifty when he finally married in 1888. His new wife, Beatrix Godwin Whistler, helped to foster the artist's interest in lithography during the early 1890s. Whistler captured this puckish figure on transfer paper with a lithographic crayon, and perhaps he intended to print it eventually. Even though he did not do so, the model is closely related to one from his lithographed series of dancing girls (Fig. 278.1). The happiness Whistler found with Trixie is in part translated to this sprightly little dancer.

Figure 278.1.
Dancing Girl, 1890,
lithograph, K30. Freer
Gallery.

Plate 279.
A Study in Red

1890s
fabricated chalks on brown paper
27.8 × 18.3 cm.
Inscription: (r) butterfly; (v) "123.B" (white linen label),
  "W. 13.16."

Color plays an important role in this drawing. Whistler delineated the human form, yet softened and slightly obscured it with a range of pinks and reds carefully related to the tones of flesh itself. Color helps to generalize the figure while lending movement to her sprightly pose. The drawing was once exhibited as *Danseuse Athenienne*, a reminder of the continuity in Whistler's work over several decades.[1] *Study in Red* was probably drawn at around the same time the artist executed a number of lithographs of young girls dancing.[2]

Plate 280.
Blue and Rose: the Open Fan

1890s
fabricated chalks on brown paper
27.7 × 17.5 cm.
Inscription: butterfly.

Faint traces under the finished drawing indicate that the model was once farther to the right. An infrared photograph clarifies the earlier drawing to some extent, revealing a right heel as well as the curving lines of drapery (Fig. 280.1). Whistler later incorporated the heel and instep into a base that supports the round jar with flowers. Once he had determined the placement of his figure on the sheet, Whistler caught her moving swiftly through a shimmer of electric blues and hot pinks. Blue ribbons trail from her fan, while long strokes of pink help define the diaphanous draperies. Whistler seldom achieved a more beautiful fusion of line and color.

Figure 280.1.
Blue and Rose, the Open
Fan, infrared photograph.

Plate 281.
Venus Astarte

1890s
fabricated chalks on brown paper
27.4–27.6 × 18.4–18.5 cm.
Inscription: butterfly.

Whistler's ability to mine his own imagery successfully was made possible in part by fresh nuances he introduced to old themes. *Venus Astarte* presents Whistler's familiar muse in the context of a fertility goddess. But we also see the impact of the American dancer Loie Fuller. Her exotic performances with silken scarves and electric lights, accompanied by avant-garde music, fascinated the European public as the epitome of the sensuous, dangerous *femme fatale* of the *fin de siècle*. Whistler could have seen Fuller as early as 1890 at the Gaiety Theatre in London, or after 1892 at the Follies Bergère in Paris (Fig. 281.1).[1] Whistler might also have become aware of the dancer through his friend, the poet Stéphane Mallarmé.[2] By 1893, Fuller was the subject of myriad posters and statuettes, some of them by well-recognized French artists including Jules Cheret and Henri Toulouse-Lautrec.

Figure 281.1.
Loie Fuller in Serpentine Dance. From Loie Fuller, *Fifteen Years of a Dancer's Life* (New York: Barrie & Jenkins, 1913), opp. p. 28

Whistler and Fuller shared a strong sense of showmanship, and each had a nose for publicity.[3] Moreover, each artist was interested in the conflation of abstract art and music. In her most sophisticated dances, like the "Fire Dance" of 1895, Fuller confined her movements to a small part of the stage, moving vast yards of shimmering silken fabrics to the music as colored lights played over her in a kinetic design—she was a fire, a butterfly, or a lily.[4] In a like vein, *Venus Astarte* was called "exquisite as a flower in its abstract, impersonal grace."[5] Describing an early dance in which she lifted her draperies as Whistler's *Venus Astarte* is doing (Fig. 281.2), Fuller wrote, "[I] raised my arms aloft, all the while that I continued to flit around the stage like a winged spirit. There was a sudden exclamation from the house: It's a butterfly! A butterfly!"[6] Whistler has captured this quality in his pen-and-ink sketch of the dancer (Fig. 281.3). Its similarity to his own butterfly signatures is unmistakable.

Figure 281.2.
Fuller as butterfly. Frontispiece from *Fifteen Years of a Dancer's Life.*

Venus Astarte raises her drapery in the static manner seen in many of the popular Fuller statuettes. Although Whistler has probably used a piece of matting for a backdrop, its bands of checkered decoration abstractly suggest a theater interior. More lively draped figures in other lithographs and related drawings attest to Whistler's interest in Fuller. However, the static quality of this particular pastel reminds us that the artist has combined his observations of Fuller with his Venus figures of the 1860s and 1870s. The title has double significance. *Venus Astarte* was all-consuming and dangerous, like Fuller's sensuous "Fire Dance." Yet like Loie Fuller, she resembles an alluring butterfly, "spreading the mirror of [its] ocellate wings."[7]

Figure 281.3.
Loie Fuller, 1890s, pen. Hunterian Art Gallery, University of Glasgow, Birnie Philip Bequest.

Plate 282.
Portrait of
Miss Emily Tuckerman

1898
fabricated chalks on brown paper
23.2 × 17.3–17.5 cm.
Inscription: butterfly.[1]

Emily Tuckerman was the daughter of Lucius
Tuckerman and Elizabeth W. Gibbs; the family
resided for many years at 1600 I Street in
Washington, D.C. Although she never married, Miss Tuckerman appeared regularly in
the pages of various social registers in both
Washington and New York. She was a member
of the Riding Club, the Colony Club and the
Colonial Dames of America. She maintained
her own Washington residence at 1712 H
Street NW from 1909 until 1911. Thereafter,
she is usually found either under "Diliatory
Domiciles" or else abroad. Among her various
addresses are "Old Place" in Stockbridge,
Massachusetts (1912), and three Park Avenue
addresses from 1918 until 1923. Miss Tuckerman served with the American Ambulance
Corps in Paris in 1917. She went abroad again
in 1923, and she died in 1925. A label once
attached to the back of the frame states that
Whistler drew Miss Tuckerman in London, in
August, 1898.

Plates 283–293.
Illustrations for **The Gentle Art of Making Enemies**

ca. 1890.
283. 19.3 × 12.9 cm.
284. 28.6 × 22.3 cm.
285. 18.2 × 10.5 cm.
286. 11.6 × 11.3 cm.
287. 19.3 × 12.9 cm.
288. 21.5 × 16.4 cm.
289. 16.8 × 11.4 cm.
290. 13.0 × 16.2 cm.
291. 28.6 × 22.2 cm.
292. 28.5 × 22.2 cm.
293. 25.3 × 23.1 cm.
283, pencil; 284, pencil with white gouache; 285, pencil on cardboard; 286 and 289, pencil on cardboard with white gouache; 287, 288, 290, crayon on transfer paper with white gouache; 291 and 292, crayon; 293, crayon with white gouache

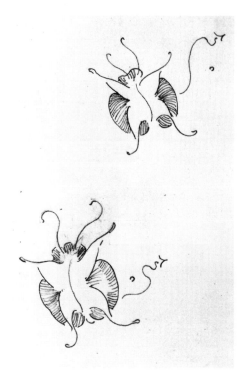

The Gentle Art of Making Enemies crystallized Whistler's already considerable reputation as a witty, if wicked, man of letters. First published in 1890, the book contains Whistler's carefully constructed versions of disputes that had engaged his attentions during the preceding three decades.[1] The *mise-en-page* featured tiny print surrounded by large white spaces, embellished with marginal comments and expressive images of butterflies. Whistler had used varying versions of the butterfly as his signature since the late 1860s.

The Gentle Art, an eccentric publication, may also bear the stamp of an earlier book. Ellen Moers has stressed the influence of Jules Amédée Barbey d'Aurevilly's book, *Du Dandyisme et de Georges Brummel* (1845), upon the dandies of Second Empire Paris. The book was characterized by an obscure epigraph and an unconventional cover design. Barbey decorated the pages with "an overlay of digressive notes" which he "delighted in, regarding them as an embroidered fringe of commentary."[2] Whistler's marginal asides, as well as his finicky and precious style, are notably similar.[3]

The concept of the butterfly embraced several facets of Whistler's era—modern theater, Japanese art, and the revival of interest in eighteenth-century France. In 1860, a comic ballet entitled *Le Papillon* was first performed in Paris.[4] The heroine was transformed into a butterfly twice before the play was brought to happy conclusion. *Le Papillon* was created as a signature role for the actress Emma Livry. An avid theatergoer, Whistler developed his own "signature role," using the butterfly in a flamboyant and theatrical manner to help establish himself as a star in the art firmament.

Whistler's butterfly signatures began to appear as geometric blocks on japonesque paintings by 1869. At first he imitated signatures and seals on Japanese woodblock prints. Eventually, the butterflies evolved into more naturalistic creatures, yet Whistler usually placed them asymmetrically, recalling Japanese art. Butterflies on the pages of *The Gentle Art* balance the text, often on a diagonal. On his drawings and paintings, Whistler used butterfly signatures as decorative accents of color to balance other shapes.

Interested in both modern letters and the art of eighteenth-century France,[5] Whistler would have enjoyed Baudelaire's poem, "Les Phares," which connected the rococo artist Watteau with the evanescent butterfly:

> *Watteau, ce carnaval où bien des coeurs illustres*
> *Comme des papillons, errent en flamboyant,*
> *Décors frais et légers éclaires par des lustres*
> *Qui versent la folie à ce bal tournoyant.*[6]

As in Baudelaire's poem, Whistler's butterflies reveal human folly, at least as the artist perceived it. Their stagey anthropomorphic poses recall his many contemporary drawings of lightly draped dancers, and there is a direct connection between the butterflies and the dances of Loie Fuller. But for all their grace, the butterflies' long barbed tails add a visual counterpoint to the book's sharply worded text. With word and image Whistler pilloried his victims, only to flit away and ask mockingly of some critic-victim stung into lugubrious response, "Who breaks a butterfly upon a wheel?"

Plate 283

Plate 283: From "The Gentle Art," pp. 183 (top), 172 (bottom). Haughty and defiant, the top butterfly accompanies a letter entitled "The Opportunity Neglected." Whistler disliked having his work reproduced in journals. When the prestigious *Gazette des Beaux-Arts* asked to reproduce an etching, he demanded a fee of about two thousand francs. The surprised director demurred, noting that such a fee was not customary. Whistler replied sarcastically that he would have to struggle along as an undiscovered artist since he couldn't afford to appear in the pages of the *Gazette*.

The bottom butterfly decorates a letter addressed to a critic who defended a retiring member of the Royal Academy. Whistler called the defense "cheap companionship of senility." Erasures to the head indicate changes that finally resulted in an unusually large butterfly with a puffed out chest and flaring wings. Whistler's image embodies the confidence of youth and the sense of challenge with which young modernists of the period confronted the art establishment. The butterfly's proud stance visually replicates the title of the letter, "Nous avons changé tout cela!"

Plate 284

Plate 284: From "The Gentle Art," pp. 191 (recto bottom), 225 (verso bottom left). "Autre Temps autre Moeurs" was written when Whistler was the embattled head of the Society of British Artists. He responded to an anonymous accusation that the society's hanging committee was biased, dismissing the charge with contempt. His butterfly (recto bottom) seems to have just sent a repugnant object off into the distance with a good swift kick. The top butterfly on this sheet recalls several in the book (pp. 125, 225) but does not correspond specifically to any. Whistler used white gouache on this and other drawings in the collection to cover parts he wished to change.

The bottom-left butterfly (verso) decorated "Aussi que diable allait-il faire dans cette galère?" Pugnacious as a victorious prize fighter, the butterfly seems to repeat the letter text, "I shall be justified, and it will be boldly denied by some dainty student that the delicate butterfly was *ever* 'soiled' in Suffolk Street." The butterfly next to this one is nearly identical but lacks the characteristic dot near the tail. The top-right drawing relates to the butterfly on the title page, and to others on pages 172 and 235. It seems to project the attitude of moving away from something distasteful. The top-left butterfly on the verso is unfinished but relates to the last butterfly in the book (see Plate 293).

284v

Plate 285

Plate 285: From "The Gentle Art," p. 60. This drawing embellished "The Painter-Etcher Papers," which set forth an early imbroglio. Seymour Haden, along with Messrs. Hamilton and LeGros, mistook Frank Duveneck's etchings for Whistler's. At the time Whistler was under contract to the Fine Art Society, while Duveneck's prints were exhibitèd at another gallery. There was some innuendo that Whistler was trying to evade the terms of his contract, but, in fact, Haden and his friends had confused the work of the two artists. Whistler did not miss this opportunity to roast his hapless brother-in-law. Above the butterfly Whistler printed, "Vat shall de honest man do in my closet? Dere is no honest man dat shall come in my closet."

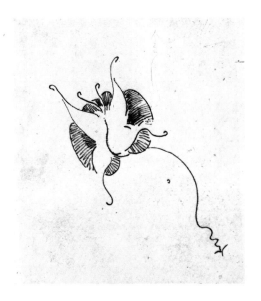

Plate 286

Plate 286: From "The Gentle Art," p. 234. Irritated by a fatuous article about his ideas on house decoration, Whistler responded with "Another Poacher in the Chelsea Preserves," adding a butterfly dancing with rage. Whistler commented, "O, Atlas, they say that I cannot keep a friend—my dear, I cannot afford it." An earlier tail is visible under white gouache, making it apparent how much each butterfly's personality depends upon the location and length of the barbed appendage. Atlas was Whistler's nickname for *The World*, a newspaper that frequently printed his letters.

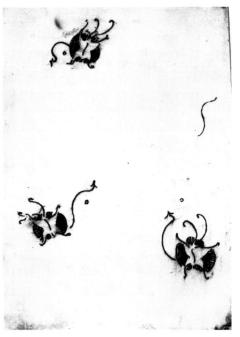

Plate 287

Plate 287: From "The Gentle Art," pp. 71 (top), 283 (middle), 39 (bottom). Never one to admit defeat, Whistler tried to turn the tables even when he was in error. Each of these butterflies illustrates an exchange in which Whistler simply depended upon verbal and visual bravado.

A reader of the *World* presumed to correct titles in Whistler's 1881 exhibition catalogue: "Is the 'Café Orientale' intended to be French or Italian. It has an *e* too many for French, and an *f* too few for Italian." Whistler implied that he was above such picky details: "Atlas . . . you know the story of the witness who, when asked how far he stood from the spot where the deed was done, answered unhesitatingly 'Sixty-three feet seven inches!' When asked how he could be so accurate the man replied, 'You see I thought some d——d fool would be sure to ask me, and so I measured.' " The top butterfly reinforces this attitude with a defiant stance.

The middle butterfly seems to be laughing at an insult Whistler claimed not to have intended to make. His apology was as barbed as the insect's tail. "Who, in Heaven's name, ever dreamed of you as an actual person?—or one whom one would mean to insult?"

The lower right figure decorates a brief note to the art critic Tom Taylor, who had relegated both Whistler's art and writing to "the region of chaff." Whistler rejoined that he had never been serious with Taylor in the first place: "With ages at your disposal, [the] truth will dimly dawn upon you; and as you look back upon this life, perchance many situations that you took *au serieux* (art-critic, who knows? expounder of Velásquez and what not) will explain themselves sadly—chaff!" Even when he had no rational riposte Whistler always tried to have the last word.

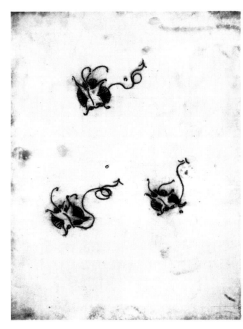

Plate 288

Plate 288: From "The Gentle Art," pp. 114 (top), 165 (bottom left). The upper butterfly raises its tail in pointed derision at "The Easy Expert." Whistler was ridiculing the art critic Harry Quilter for his inability to distinguish one medium from another. The lower-left butterfly decorates Whistler's caustic response to the aesthete Oscar Wilde, who was notorious for plagiarizing Whistler's ideas. "Prettily spurred on to unseemliness and indiscretion" as the book's subtitle put it, Wilde wrote, "With our James vulgarity begins at home, and should be allowed to stay there." Whistler promptly retorted, "A poor thing, Oscar!— but, for once I suppose 'your own.' "

Although the third butterfly does not correspond exactly to any in the book, all three were edited with opaque white pigment. This sheet and the next two are slick transfer paper, and show evidence of smearing. They may have been used in printing the book, whose illustrations are lithographed. There is a purple oval inked stamp, "Gilby & Herrmann, 8/11 Garrick St. London," on the verso of this sheet.

Plate 290

Plate 290: From "The Gentle Art," pp. 243 (top), 108 (bottom). The upper-left image embellished "Just Indignation." Whistler's target was again Oscar Wilde. Extremely careful about his own appearance, Whistler attacked Wilde for wearing an overly artistic costume. The barbed tail of the butterfly points to a marginal note, implying that Whistler was moved to write after "perceiving the Poet, in Polish cap and green overcoat, befrogged and wonderfully befurred." The butterfly also resembles others in the *Gentle Art*, suggesting that Whistler reused parts of his composition.[8]

The lower-right butterfly was reproduced at the end of "An Apology." Frederick Wedmore, an art critic, accused Whistler of misquoting him by changing "understate" to "understand." Tongue in cheek, Whistler apologized cheerfully, adding, "With Mr. Wedmore . . . it is always a matter of understating, and not at all one of understanding." The line marked "base" under the figure indicates that Whistler wanted this butterfly placed at a sharp angle to the edge of the page. The drawing is somewhat smeared, and Whistler edited the insect on the right. He abandoned the third butterfly on this sheet.

Plate 289

Plate 289: From "The Gentle Art," p. 204. Whistler reproduced this drawing at the end of "A Played-out Policy." In 1886 the *London Times* unfavorably reviewed an exhibition installation at the Society of British Artists. As president, Whistler replied sharply, but the *Times* chose not to publish his whole letter. Whistler then sent the entire correspondence to a rival paper, *The Pall Mall Gazette*, along with additional sarcasms aimed at the *Times*. Whistler's butterfly, with its tail repositioned, seems to dance in triumph at having gotten round the editor of London's most august newspaper.

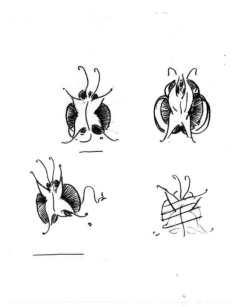

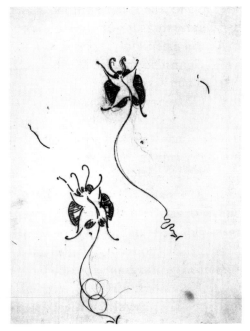

Plate 293

Plate 291

Plate 291: From "The Gentle Art," p. 261 (top left), title page (bottom left). The top-left butterfly looks defiant and self-righteous. He was placed at the end of "Et Tu Brute," Whistler's angry response to his former friend, the poet Algernon Swinburne, who dared to criticize inconsistencies in the *Ten o'Clock Lecture.* The top-right butterfly, with its gladiatorial stance, is similar to several illustrations but does not correspond to a published insect. The bottom-left butterfly appears on the title page of *The Gentle Art.* He is self-assured and entirely pleased with himself, setting the tone for the pages that will follow. Although the last figure on this sheet was abandoned, it relates to the butterfly diagonally opposite and may be an initial sketch.

Plate 292

Plate 292: From "The Gentle Art," pp. 73 (top), 112 (bottom). The top butterfly mocks another art critic, Harry Quilter. Clad in an "amazing 'arrangement' in strong mustard-and-cress with bird's-eye belcher of Reckitt's blue," the critic stood in front of a delicate Whistler painting at the Grosvenor Gallery. According to Whistler, the critic's *outré* costume completely destroyed the subtle harmonies of the painting. The butterfly seems to raise its wings to heaven as the artist cries, "Atlas, shall these things be?" Meanwhile, its long tail is suggestive of a beautiful orchestration of color gone down the drain.

The bottom insect again attacks Quilter. This butterfly's insouciant stance responds to a rubric printed by the *World.* It was suggested that Whistler was going to annoy Quilter, who purchased the White House when the artist went bankrupt in 1879. A "crafty 'arrangement' of reflectors" would enable Whistler to "display in his own studio . . . 'Arry at the White House' under all the appropriate circumstances that might be expected of a 'Celebrity at Home.' "

Each butterfly shows signs of reworking. The additional single lines appear to be experimental feelers.

Plate 293: From "The Gentle Art," p. 335. Having done its mischievous work, Whistler's butterfly turns its back upon "Messieurs les Ennemis" and flits off into the clouds on the final page of *The Gentle Art of Making Enemies.* Whistler concluded the 1892 edition of his book with one last written jibe at his victims: "It was our amusement to convict—they thought we cared to convince. *Allons!* They have served our wicked purpose—Atlas, we 'collect' no more."

But in only a few years, Charles Lang Freer collected this and the preceding butterfly drawings, delighted by the evidence of Whistler's unshakable bravado, as well as his saucy disrespect for the ill-advised pomposity of others.

Plate 295.
Illustrated Letter

Whistler to Thomas R. Way, Jr.
6 March 1892
33 Rue de Tournon, Paris

Whistler's instructions were given to Way in regard to his designs for an invitation card and poster for a forthcoming exhibition at the Goupil Gallery in London. Typically, Whistler's instructions have to do with aesthetic adjustments. By making the printing smaller or increasing the margins, Whistler achieved a lighter look for the poster. He told Way, "You will understand the corrections— would like the whole thing to look whiter." The exhibition, "Nocturnes, Marines and Chevalet Pieces," opened on March 19, 1892, and was a success.

Plate 294.
Illustrated Letter

Whistler to Thomas R. Way, Jr.
7 January 1892
21 Cheyne Walk, Chelsea

In this brief note Whistler ordered additional proofs from his printer, Thomas R. Way: "Among them I would like four more of the Chelsea Embankment shops: like this: on old Dutch." Whistler included a thumbnail sketch of the lithograph *Chelsea Shops* (Fig. 294.1), which was drawn on the stone in 1888. The image captures the little shopfronts in Stanhope Street.[1]

Figure 294.1.
Chelsea Shops, lithograph,
K20. Freer Gallery.

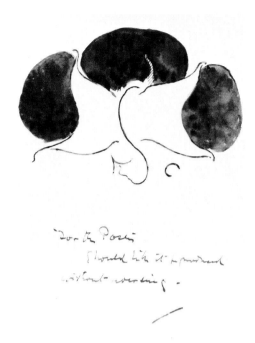

Plate 296.
Illustrated Letter

Whistler to Thomas R. Way, Jr.
6 March 1892
33 Rue de Tournon, Paris

This sketch is an enlargement of the butterfly that decorated Whistler's poster for the exhibition "Nocturnes, Marines and Chevalet Pieces." Whistler requested that Way reproduce the butterfly without reversing it. (Many of Whistler's prints are reversed images of what he saw and drew directly onto the plate or stone.)

Plate 297.
Illustrated Letter

Whistler to Thomas R. Way, Jr.
12 December 1893
110 Rue de Bac, Paris

Whistler discussed both etchings and lithographs in this letter. He was pleased with "the Brittany proofs" but suggested that Way not use any sheets of old paper that were "too spotted with mildew—or wormeaten." Conservative with his supply of old paper, Whistler planned to use the defective sheets for smaller etchings. He noted that a sample sheet Way had sent for examination was "a little too coloured—too dark." Whistler told Way that Gleason White could publish "the second drawing I did from my sister-in-law" (lithograph, *Gants de Suede*, K26) in *The Studio*. He recalled that he had destroyed several stones, but asked "Did I destroy a little draped figure of a girl standing reading a letter? I rather hope not—for I have a proof that I *now* think well of." Whistler included a sketch of *The Novel—Girl Reading* to refresh Way's memory and requested twelve proofs if the stone was still extant (Fig. 297.1). He ordered other proofs as well in this letter, and gave Way the following advice: "The pretty size [of paper] is the smaller Dutch—and print always a *little* higher up in the paper than down—among the lying down figures of the last is one with rather more margin at the bottom than the others—and you have no idea how much daintier she looks! Another little thing to notice is that when the sheet has a cut edge and a rough one, I would always put the straight cut edge at the top." Whistler included a tiny sketch, probably of the etching *Nude Figure Reclining* (K343).

Figure 297.1.
The Novel—Girl Reading,
lithograph, K33. Freer
Gallery.

Plate 298.
Illustrated Letter

Whistler to Thomas R. Way, Jr.
9 July 1894
110 Rue de Bac, Paris

With the aid of tracing paper, Whistler was able to edit his prints, even from a distance. He included this tracing in a long letter to his printmaker. Whistler ended the letter with the following instructions: "I don't think I would use any more of the *thin* Chinese paper. The Japanese is perfect. Tracing enclosed indicates the little line to be scratched off the stone in 'Long Balcony' [Fig. 298.1]—you see it goes through one of the parasols. I have marked it in *red* ink—the tiny portion that passes through the shadowed part of the parasol would of course have to be *picked across* only *very delicately*." The proof in the Freer collection must have been made after Way had edited the stone.

Figure 298.1.
Long Balcony, lithograph,
K49. Freer Gallery.

Plate 299.
Illustrated Letter

Whistler to Thomas R. Way, Jr.
25 October 1895
Royal Lion Hotel, Lyme Regis, Dorsetshire

In this letter Whistler suggested to his printer a system of registers for lithographic stones: "Print me a common proof on the ordinary white printing paper of the Sunny Smithy—The Father & Son—and the Two Brothers. The single figure of the Blacksmith, one of the last set, and mark upon the stone four points, top and bottom, and one upon each side, like this X. and we will have a second stone for each!! to be printed with the same ink—or perhaps even in another tone—and then we shall see something perhaps remarkable! . . . You see then with my proof I can work on my transparent paper over it and making the same marks you can fit the second stone—let us try this *at once*."

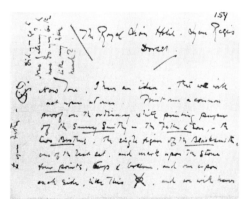

Plate 300.
Illustrated Letter

Whistler to Thomas R. Way, Jr.
25 October 1895
Royal Lion Hotel, Lyme Regis, Dorsetshire

Whistler continued his communications with
Way, telling him that he would have "another
half dozen" drawings ready soon. Whistler
promised to write "good" in pencil or ink on
the chalked side of the paper to help avoid
confusion, for Way was intended to transfer
the drawings to lithographic stones. Whistler
included seven numbered sketches with titles.
The thumbnail sketches give only a general
idea of each composition, but the images are
recognizable and all were printed in 1895.
They include *The Good Shoe* (K86), *The
Sunny Smithy* (K85), *The Master Smith* (K84),
Father and Son (K87), *The Strong Arm* (K89),
The Little Doorway, Lyme Regis (K83), and
The Smith's Yard (K88).

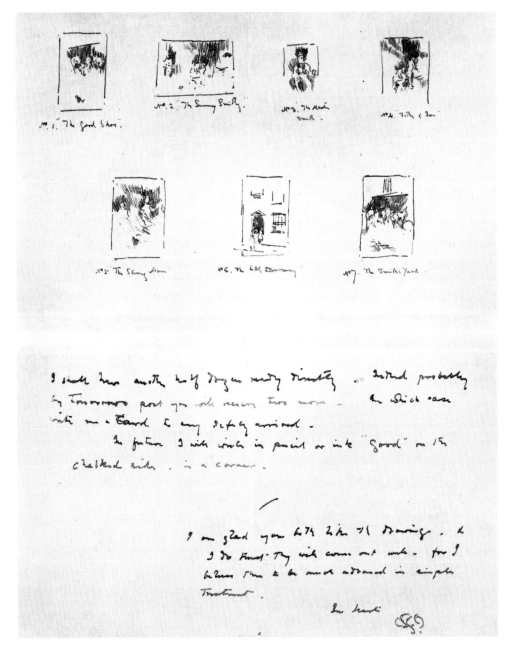

Plate 301.
Illustrated Letter

Whistler to Gleason White
22 July 1894
110 Rue du Bac, Paris

In London, Gleason White edited the *Studio*,
one of the most prominent art magazines of
the late nineteenth century. In a long letter
Whistler chastised White for preferring "the
Bébés of the Luxembourg" to others which
Whistler wanted to have printed in the magazine. Although his titles are unclear, Whistler
probably meant the lithograph now titled
Bonnes du Luxembourg, which was published
in the *Art Journal*. In the letter, Whistler
warned White that "you are not the only one
who has preferred it." One alternative that
Whistler suggested was the "Retameur" of
which he included a small sketch. This must be
The Whitesmiths—Impasse des Carmélites
(Fig. 301.1), which Whistler drew in 1894, possibly at about the same time he wrote to
White.[1]

Figure 301.1.
The Whitesmiths—Impasse
des Carmélites, 1894,
lithograph, K53. Freer
Gallery.

WITH LITTLE SKETCH.   185

WHISTLER (James McNeill). *Painter and Etcher.*
A magnificent **A.L.S.** (signed twice) to Mr. Gleeson White. 4 pp., sm. 4to,
Paris, 22 July, 1894. With addressed envelope.

An unusually interesting letter concerning his work, containing a little sketch in
text and signed with his butterfly signature as well as his ordinary signature. In the
letter he mentions Leighton, Richmond, and Burne-Jones; also refers to Sir Alma-
Tadema as "*Alma the Classic.*"

"I cannot make out what possesses you all. That lithograph of the *Bébés of the Luxembourg* is all very well, but really not to be compared with the others of which I gave you the
choice, and you are not the only one who has preferred it.

"Indeed, at the present moment I could do nothing about it with you and Mr. Holmes
until it is decided elsewhere—the hitch being a question of printing—and I refuse to have my
work printed in London by anybody but Mr. Way.

"If this be not yielded, you shall have the '*Bébés*'

"But if you will listen to me, go and see other new things that Way is proving for me
now—and I give you a fresh chance.

"Among them are several beauties. I wonder what you would think of the '*Retameur*
Impasse des.'

"Then if the Luxembourg Gardens fascinate you, there is the '*Terrace*'—one of the
latest—far away brighter, more sunny and more coloured than the *Bébés*, which was done
with a German chalk that always remains cold and grey, and gave me no chance. I know
better now; besides I am, of course, doing better work.

"I think you might have a swell number by-and-bye, and announce it—with Leighton,
and Richmond, and B. Jones—and I would contribute, if you said nothing until we were
all in.

"Don't you think it would pay?

"But if in the mean time you drop it the thing would drop out—as far as they are
concerned, and it would be difficult to begin again. Of course I shall go on whether or no.
I always do, and I am only at the very beginning.

"Why don't you get all the St. John Wood lot? Why not '*Alma the Classic*'?

"You seem to me to have no serious sense of fun, and to be willing to give up just at
the very moment you have every reason to go on." Etc.

Provenance, Exhibition History, Literature

Plate 1.
Portrait of Whistler with a Hat
1857–1858

Provenance:
Whistler to Ernest Delannoy by 1865, through Hôtel des Ventes, Paris, to H. Valentin, to S. P. Avery, 1871, to Freer, 1906.

Exhibition:
1874, New York, Met, no. 36, as *Head of a Young Man.*
1876, Baltimore, as *Portrait of the Artist by Himself.*
1878, New York.
1881, New York, Met, no. 55, as *Portrait of Himself.*
1881, New York, Union, as *Self Portrait* (uncertain).
1885–1886, New York, Met, no. 99, as *Portrait of Whistler.*
1898–1899, New York, no. 253, as *The Artist.*
1904, Boston, Copley, no. 55, as *Portrait of Whistler with a Hat.*
1905, Paris, Memorial, no. I.
1918–1919, New York.

Literature:
Gallatin, 1913, II, repr. p. 153.
Gallatin, 1918, pp. 6, 25, repr. pl. 1.
Hartmann, 1910, pp. 219–220.
Pennell, J., 1912, repr. p. 25.
Pennell, E., 1921, repr. opp. p. 29.
Sutton, 1966, p. 8, repr. pl. 1.
Young *et al.*, 1980, I, no. 23, pp. 7–8; repr. II, pl. 8.

Plate 2.
Portrait of Major Whistler
1857–1859

Provenance:
Emma W. Palmer to Freer, 1905.

Exhibition:
1904–1905, Pittsburgh, no. 308, as *Portrait of Major George W. Whistler.*

Literature:
Bloor, 1906, repr. p. 131.
Lane, 1942, repr. p. 109.
Young *et al.*, 1980, I, no. 29, p. 11; repr. II, pl. 11.

Plate 3.
Harmony in Green and Rose: The Music Room
1860–1861

Provenance:
Whistler to Anna McNeill Whistler, ca. 1861, to Julia Whistler (second wife of George W. Whistler), to daughter Julia, auctioned London, Christie, 10 February 1894, lot 69, to Collin or Collard; to Colnaghi, London dealers; to F. J. Hecker by 1899, to Freer, 1917.

Exhibition:
1876, Baltimore, as *Portrait of a Lady and Child.*
1892, London, Goupil, no. 12, as *Harmony in Green and Rose: The Music Room.*
1899, Philadelphia, no. 72.
1899, New York, no. 335.
1901, Buffalo, no. 102.
1904, Boston, Copley, no. 15.
1904, New York, Comparative, no. 182.
1905, Paris, Memorial, no. 7.
1910, New York, Met, no. 1.

Literature:
Becker, 1959, pl. 30.
Caffin, 1907, p. 301.
Caffin, 1913, p. 44, repr. p. 46.
Cox, 1905, p. 239.
Dreyfus, 1907, repr. p. 203.

Hartmann, 1910, p. 44.
Laver, 1930, p. 86.
Meyer, 1927, repr. opp. p. 63.
Pennell, 1921, pp. 10, 129.
Pousette-Dart, 1924, repr. pl. 3.
Reff, 1976, pp. 26–28, repr. p. 27.
Sutton, 1964, fig. 3.
Sutton, 1966, pl. 9.
Taylor, 1978, pl. 3.
Young *et al.*, 1980, I, no. 34, p. 13; repr. II, pl. 19.

Plate 4.
Caprice in Purple and Gold: The Golden Screen
1864

Provenance:
Whistler to Cyril Flower by 1892, through W. S. Marchant, London dealers, to Freer, 1904.

Exhibition:
1865, London, RA, no. 90, as *The Golden Screen.*
1873, London, SFA, no. 109, as *The Golden Screen—Harmony in Purple and Gold* (No. 2).
1892, London, Goupil, no. 14, as *Caprice in Purple and Gold: The Golden Screen.*
1904, Edinburgh, RSA, no. 256.
1905, Paris, Memorial, no. 8.
1910, New York, Met, no. 5, as *Harmony in Purple and Gold.*

Literature:
Benedite, 1905, repr. p. 147.
Berger, 1980, pl. II.
Chisaburo, 1980, pp. 47, 62.
Hayward, 1979, fig. 5.
Horowitz, 1979–1980, pp. 124–131.
Johnson, 1981, fig. 4.
Lancaster, 1963, repr. pl. 2 opp. p. 37.
Mechlin, 1907, repr. p. 363.
Meier-Graefe, 1908, II, repr. opp. p. 207.
Pousette-Dart, 1927, repr. pl. 15.
Sweet, 1968, p. 22.
Young *et al.*, 1980, I, no. 60, p. 34; repr. II, pl. 17.

Plate 5.
La Princesse du Pays de la Porcelaine
1863–1864

Provenance:
F. R. Leyland by 1872, auctioned, London, Christie, 28 May 1892, lot 39, to A. Reid, Glasgow dealer, to William Burrell, Glasgow, ca. 1894–1895, to Freer, 1903.

Exhibition:
1865, Paris, Salon, no. 2220, as *La Princesse du Pays de la Porcelaine.*
1872, London, Int. Exh.
1875, Brighton, no. 156, as *Arrangement in Flesh Colour and Grey—La Princesse du Pays de la Porcelaine.*
1892, London, SPP, no. 113, as *Harmony in Flesh-Colour and Grey, La Princesse du Pays de la Porcelaine.*
1893, Chicago, no. 636.
1893–1894, Philadelphia, no. 32.
1896, Glasgow, no. 129.
1898, London, ISSPG, no. 180, as *Rose and Silver: La Princesse du Pays de la Porcelaine.*
1899, Venice, no. 58.
1901, Glasgow, no. 505.
1903, Edinburgh, RSA, no. 29.
1904, Boston, Copley, no. 32.
1905, Paris, Memorial, no. 9.

Literature:
Becker, 1982, pl. 12.

Chisaburo, 1980, pp. 47, 63.
Dewhurst, 1904, repr. opp. p. 91.
Dreyfus, 1907, p. 213.
Eddy, 1903, pp. 58, 128, 130, 210.
Hartmann, 1910, repr. opp. p. 50.
Honeyman, 1951, p. 7.
Honour, 1961, fig. 143.
Horowitz, 1979–1980, pp. 124–131.
Kessler, 1905, p. 458.
Lancaster, 1952, p. 300.
Laver, 1930, pp. 107–108, repr. opp. p. 217.
Matsuki, 1903, pp. 7, 9.
Mauclair, 1905, p. 314.
Pousette-Dart, 1927, repr. pl. 5.
Sickert, B., 1908, no. 18, p. 152.
Sickert, O., 1903, repr. p. 2.
Sweet, 1968, p. 25.
Young *et al.*, 1980, I, no. 50, pp. 26–27; repr. II, pl. 34.

Plate 6.
Variations in Flesh Colour and Green: The Balcony
1864 ff.

Provenance:
Whistler to G. J. Cavafy, London, by 1870, to E. G. Kennedy, New York dealers, 1892, to Freer, 1892.

Exhibition:
1870, London, RA, no. 468, as *The Balcony.*
1873, Paris, Durand-Ruel.
1878, London, Grosvenor, no. 54, as *Variations in Flesh Color and Green.*
1878, London, Ruskin trial.
1889, Paris, Exp. Univ., no. 166.
1892, London, Goupil, no. 40.
1897–1898, Pittsburgh, no. 236.
1901, Buffalo, no. 100.
1903, New York, SAA.
1904, Boston, Copley, no. 37.
1905, Paris, Memorial, no. 12.
1910, Berlin.
1912, Washington.

Literature:
Brinton, 1910, pl. 53.
Caffin, 1913, repr. opp. p. 45.
Chisaburo, 1980, pl. 1.
Clark, 1979, repr. fig. 11.
Cox, 1905, pp. 237–240.
Dreyfus, 1907, repr. p. 205.
Gray, 1965, p. 324.
Hartmann, 1910, p. 54.
Hobbs, 1977, p. 91.
Hobbs, 1981, pp. 1195, 1197.
Laver, 1930, p. 114.
Matsuki, 1903, frontispiece.
Pousette-Dart, 1924, pl. 13.
Reff, 1976, p. 28.
Rossetti, 1903, pp. 228–229.
Sickert, B., 1908, no. 30, p. 154.
Wisberg, 1975, p. 123.
Young *et al.*, 1980, I, no. 56, pp. 30–32; repr. II, pl. 52.

Plates 7–12.
"The Six Projects"
ca. 1868

Provenance:
The White Symphony: Three Girls—Whistler to Thomas R. Way, 1879, Thomas R. Way, Jr. to Freer, 1902. *Others*—Rosalind Birnie Philip to Freer, 1903.

Exhibition:
1874, London: *Blue and Pink* (11); *Blue and Green* (12); *White Symphony* (13).
1887, London, RBA: *White Symphony*.
1899, Paris, Petit: *Blue and Pink; Blue and Green*.
1904, Boston, Copley: *White Symphony* (19); *White and Red* (20); *Venus* (21); *Green and Violet* (22); *Blue and Pink* (23); *Blue and Green* (24).
1905, Paris, Memorial: *White Symphony* (11); *Venus* (12); *Green and Violet* (13); *White and Red* (14); *Blue and Green* (15); *Blue and Pink* (16).
1915, San Francisco: *Blue and Pink* (263); *White and Red* (264); *Blue and Green* (265); *White Symphony* (266); *Venus* (267).

Literature:
Chisaburo, 1980, pp. 67–69.
Hobbs, 1977, p. 90.
Matsuki, 1903, p. 9.
Prideaux, 1970, pp. 96–97.
Staley, 1971, p. 14.
Sutton, 1966, pls. 42, 43.
Taylor, 1978, pls. 31, 32, 33.
Young *et al.*, 1980, I, nos. 82–87, pp. 47–50; repr. II, pls. 47–50, 62, 66.

Plate 13.
Venus Rising from the Sea
ca. 1869–1870

Provenance:
Thomas R. Way, Jr. to Freer, 1903.

Exhibition:
1915, San Francisco, no. 262.

Literature:
Sutton, 1966, pl. 49.
Young *et al.*, 1980, I, no. 93, p. 55; repr. II, pl. 66.

Plate 14.
Self-Portrait
1870–1875

Provenance:
Mrs. Eason to Obach, London dealers, to Freer, 1904.

Exhibition:
1910, New York, Montross, repr. as *Sketch of Mr. Whistler*.
1915, Rochester, no. 26.
1918–1919, New York.

Literature:
Gallatin, 1913, I, p. 18; repr. after p. 24.
Gallatin, 1918, pp. 6, 26; repr. pl. 3.
Hartmann, 1910, p. 8.

Plate 15.
Arrangement in Black: Portrait of F. R. Leyland
1870–1873

Provenance:
Whistler to Leyland, to Mrs. Val Prinsep (daughter), 1892; W. S. Marchant, London dealers, through R. A. Canfield to Freer, 1905.

Exhibition:
1874, London, no. 1, as *Portrait, Arrangement in Black*.
1905, London, Memorial, no. 100.
1910, New York, Met, no. 11.
1912, Washington, no. 21.

Literature:
Dreyfus, 1907, repr. p. 218.
Hartmann, 1910, repr. p. 22.
Hobbs, 1977, p. 98.
Hobbs, 1981, repr. p. 1198.
Mechlin, 1907, repr. p. 364.
Pousette-Dart, 1924, repr. pl. 27.
Sickert, 1908, no. 42, p. 156.
Young *et al.*, 1980, I, no. 97, pp. 56–67; repr. II, pl. 104.

Plates 16 and 17.
The Blue Girl, fragments
1872–1874

Provenance:
Thomas R. Way to Freer, 1907.

Literature:
Caffin, 1909, p. 37.
Lane, 1942, repr. p. 76.
Young *et al.*, 1980, I, no. 111, pp. 66–67; repr. II, pls. 393, 394.

Plate 18.
Portrait Sketch of a Lady
mid-1870s

Provenance:
Thomas R. Way to Freer, 1905.

Literature:
Sutton, 1966, pl. 125.
Young *et al.*, 1980, I, no. 184, p. 108; repr. II, pl. 125.

Plate 19.
Arrangement in White and Black
ca. 1876

Provenance:
H. O. Meithke to Colnaghi, London dealers, 1876, to Dr. Linde, Lubeck, 1897, through Theodore Duret and Bernheim, Paris dealers, to Freer, 1904.

Exhibition:
1878, London, Grosvenor, no. 55, as *Arrangement in White and Black*.
1900, Berlin, no. 343, as *Damenbildness*.
1904, New York, Comparative, no. 175.
1905, Venice.
1912, Washington, no. 20.

Literature:
Hartmann, 1910, p. 263.
Heilbut, 1903, repr. p. 19.
Pennell, 1921, sketch repr. p. 163.
Pousette-Dart, 1924, repr. pl. 48.
Sickert, B., 1908, no. 64, p. 159.
Sutton, 1964, fig. 33.
Sutton, 1966, pl. 62.
Young *et al.*, 1980, I, no. 185, p. 108; repr. II, pl. 154.

Plate 20.
The Thames in Ice
1860

Provenance:
Whistler to Seymour Haden, London, to A. Reid, Glasgow dealer, to J. J. Cowan, Edinburgh, 1897, to Freer, 1901.

Exhibition:
1862, London, RA, no. 114, as *The Twenty-fifth of December, 1860, on the Thames*.
1867, Paris, Salon, no. 1562, as *Sur la Tamise; l'Hiver*.
1898, London, ISSPG, no. 175, as *Thames in Ice*.
1899, Edinburgh, RSA, no. 209.
1901, Glasgow, no. 500.
1904, Boston, Copley, no. 31.
1905, Paris, Memorial, no. 57.

Literature:
Bell, 1905, repr. p. 28.
Benedite, 1905, repr. p. 501.
Born, 1948, fig. 102.
Dreyfus, 1907, repr. p. 217.
Lane, 1942, p. 87.
Matsuki, 1903, p. 9.
Pousette-Dart, 1924, repr. pl. 9.
Sickert, B., 1908, p. 150.
Sutton, 1964, repr. fig. 4.
Sutton, 1966, pl. 13.
Way and Dennis, 1903, repr. p. 56.
Young *et al.*, 1980, I, no. 36, pp. 15–16; repr. II, pl. 24.

Plate 21.
Blue and Silver: Trouville
1865

Provenance:
J. J. Shannon, London, through Goupil, London dealers, to James Staats Forbes, London, 1895, through Agnew, London dealers, to Cottier, New York dealers, 1902, to Freer, 1902.

Exhibition:
1883, Paris, Petit, no. 4, as *Harmonie en Bleu et Argent* (possible).
1892, London, Goupil, no. 37, as *Blue and Silver* (possible).
1893, Chicago, no. 768, as *Harmony in Blue and Silver*.
1899, London, ISSPG, no. 135, as *Blue and Silver, Trouville*.
1904, Boston, Copley, no. 51.
1905, Paris, Memorial, no. 60.
1910, Ann Arbor, no. 74.
1912, Washington, no. 17.

Literature:
Matsuki, 1903, p. 9.
Young *et al.*, 1980, I, no. 66, p. 39; repr. II, pl. 39.

Plate 22.
Nocturne: Blue and Gold—Valparaiso
1866

Provenance:
Henry Hill, Brighton by 1875, auctioned London, Christie, 25 May 1889, lot 80, to Alexander Ionides, London, to Sir John Day, London, 1892, to G. McCulloch, London, to his widow 1907; Wallis & Son, London dealers, through D. C. Thompson to Freer, 1909.

Exhibition:
1875, Brighton, no. 158, as *Nocturne in Blue and Silver*.
1887, London, RBA, no. 156, as *Nocturne in Blue and Gold, Valparaiso Bay*.
1890, Paris, Salon, no. 2439, as *Nocturne en Bleu et Argent*.
1892, London, Goupil, no. 28, as *Nocturne: Blue and Gold—Valparaiso*.
1893, Chicago, no. 787, as *Nocturne, Valparaiso*.
1898, London, Goupil, no. 21, as *Nocturne—Valparaiso*.
1898, London, ISSPG, no. 183, as *Blue and Gold, Valparaiso Nocturne*.
1904, Edinburgh, RSA, no. 294, as *Nocturne Valparaiso*.
1905, London, Memorial, no. 16, as *Blue and Gold: Valparaiso, Nocturne*.
1909, London, RA, no. 249, as *Valparaiso*.
1910, New York, Met, no. 7, as *Nocturne, Blue and Gold, Valparaiso*.
1912, Washington, no. 23, as *Blue and Gold, Valparaiso*.

Literature:
du Maurier, 1969, p. 277.
Holden, 1969, pl. 5, p. 31.
Johnson, 1981, I, fig. 7.
Mauclair, 1905, p. 314.
Pousette-Dart, 1924, repr. pl. 17.
Starr, 1908, pp. 528–537.
Sutton, 1966, pl. 37.
Sweet, 1968, p. 64.
Way, 1912, p. 62.
Young *et al.*, 1980, I, no. 76, pp. 44–45; repr. II, pl. 59.

Plate 23.
Symphony in Grey: Early Morning, Thames
1871

Provenance:
Mrs. Armitage collection; W. S. Marchant, London dealers, to Freer, 1904.

Exhibition:
1872, London, SFA, no. 122, as *Harmony in Grey* (probable).

1901, London, ISSPG, no. 152a, as *Symphony in Grey*.
1905, Buffalo, no. 166, as *Symphony in Grey: Early Morning, Thames*.

Literature:
Matsuki, 1903.
Young *et al.*, 1980, I, no. 98, p. 58; repr. II, pl. 45.

Plate 24.
Variations in Pink and Grey: Chelsea
1871–1872

Provenance:
Whistler to Louis Huth, London 1873, through D. C. Thompson, London dealer, to Cyril Flower (later Lord Battersea), through Agnew, London dealers, to J. J. Cowan, Edinburgh, 1899, through W. S. Marchant, London dealer, to Freer, 1902.

Exhibition:
1873, London, Dudley Gallery, no. 193.
1892, London, Goupil, no. 27.
1901, Edinburgh, RSA, no. 346.
1904, Boston, Copley, no. 57.
1905, Paris, Memorial, no. 63 *bis*.
1910, New York, Montross, no. 19.

Literature:
Holden, 1969, p. 33, pl. 6.
Matsuki, 1903, p. 9.
Pennell, 1921, repr. opp. p. 59.
Sutton, 1964, fig. 24.
Taylor, 1978, pl. 76.
Way, 1912, repr. p. 58.
Young *et al.*, 1980, I, no. 105, pp. 64–65; repr. II, pl. 108.

Plate 25.
Nocturne: Blue and Silver—Battersea Reach
1870–1875

Provenance:
Possibly C. A. Howell collection, London; W. G. Rawlinson by 1887, through W. S. Marchant, London dealers, to Freer, 1902.

Exhibition:
1872, London, Dudley Gallery, no. 237, as *Nocturne, in Blue and Silver* (possible).
1875, Brighton, no. 98, as *Nocturne in Blue and Gold* (possible).
1878, London, Whistler-Ruskin trial (possible).
1892, London, Goupil, no. 17, as *Nocturne. Blue and Silver—Battersea Reach*.
1899, London, Goupil, no. 31.
1904, Boston, Copley, no. 63.
1904, New York, Comparative, no. 177.
1905, Paris, Memorial, no. 70.
1910, New York, Met, no. 16.
1912, Washington, no. 24.

Literature:
Hartmann, 1910, p. 265.
Holden, 1969, pl. 8, p. 37.
Matsuki, 1903, p. 9.
Sickert, B., 1908, no. 80, p. 162.
Young *et al.*, 1980, I, no. 119, pp. 72–73; repr. II, pl. 75.

Plate 26.
Nocturne: Blue and Silver—Bognor
1871–1876

Provenance:
Alfred Chapman, Liverpool, by 1883, to Freer, 1895.[4]

Exhibition:
1883, London, Grosvenor, no. 111, as *Nocturne in Blue and Silver*.
1888, Paris, Durand-Ruel, no. 39 or 42, as *Nocturne en Bleu et Argent*.
1892, London, Goupil, no. 24, as *Nocturne, Blue and Silver—Bognor*.
1892, Paris, Soc. Nat., no. 1067.

1892, Munich, no. 1950b, as *Symphonie in Silber* (possible).
1901, Buffalo, no. 96, as *Bognor—Nocturne*.
1904, Boston, Copley, no. 65.
1904, New York, Comparative, no. 176.
1905, Paris, Memorial, no. 68.
1910, New York, Met, no. 9.
1912, Washington, no. 22.

Literature:
Fenollosa, 1903, repr. opp. p. 14.
Gallatin, 1904, p. 43.
Gallatin, 1907, p. 34.
Hartmann, 1910, p. 265.
Matsuki, 1903, pp. 8–9.
Sickert, B., 1908, no. 63, p. 159.
Young *et al.*, 1980, I, no. 100, pp. 58–59; repr. II, pl. 56.

Plate 27.
Nocturne in Black and Gold: Entrance to Southampton Water
ca. 1875–1876

Provenance:
Whistler to Freer, 1897.

Exhibition:
1876, London, SFA, no. 150, as *Nocturne, in Black and Gold* (possible).
1882, London, Grosvenor, no. 106, as *Nocturne in Black and Gold. Entrance to Southampton Water*.
1892, London, Goupil, no. 32, as *Nocturne. Black and Gold* (possible).
1897–1898, Pittsburgh, no. 237, as *Southampton Harbor*.
1901, Buffalo, no. 101, as *Southampton—Nocturne*.

Literature:
Young *et al.*, 1980, I, no. 179, pp. 104–5; repr. II, pl. 95.

Plate 28.
Nocturne: Cremorne Gardens, No. 3
1872–1877

Provenance:
Charles Conder collection; Percy Moore Turner, London, to Freer, 1919.

Exhibition:
1888, Munich, as *Nachtstuck in Schwartz und Gold: Cremorne* (possible).
1905, London, Memorial, no. 50, as *Nocturne, Cremorne Gardens, No. 3*.
1912, London, Tate, no. 4.

Literature:
Holden, 1969, pl. 11, p. 43.
Sickert, B. 1908, no. 53, p. 157.
Sutton, 1966, pl. 81.
Young *et al.*, 1980, I, no. 165, p. 94; repr. II, pl. 91.

Plate 29.
Nocturne: Trafalgar Square, Chelsea—Snow
ca. 1875–1877

Provenance:
Whistler to Albert Moore; to A. Reid, Glasgow dealer, 1892, to Arthur Kay, Glasgow, by 1893; to Duncan McCorkindale, Glasgow, by 1901; to Theodore Duret, through Agnew, London dealers, to J. Martin White, London, 1902, to Freer, 1908.

Exhibition:
1892, London, Goupil, no. 6, as *Nocturne: Trafalgar Square, Snow*.
1892, Paris, Soc. Nat., no. 1070.
1904, Edinburgh, RSA, no. 255, as *Trafalgar Square, Chelsea*.
1905, London, Memorial, no. 33.
1910, Ann Arbor, no. 75.
1912, Washington, no. 16.
1912, Toledo, no. 107.

Literature:
Holden, 1969. 12, p. 45.
Meier-Graefe, 1908, repr. p. 52.

Pennell, 1908, II, repr. p. 116.
Pousette-Dart, 1924, repr. pl. 43.
Sickert, B., 1908, no. 97, p. 164.
Young *et al.*, 1980, I, no. 173, p. 100; repr. II, pl. 93.

Plate 30.
Nocturne: Grey and Silver—Chelsea Embankment, Winter
1879

Provenance:
A. B. Stewart, Glasgow, 1879, auctioned London, Christie, 9 May 1881, lot 140, to J. G. Orchar, Dundee; G. N. Stevens, Virginia Water, through W. S. Marchant, London dealers, to Freer, 1902.

Exhibition:
1879, Glasgow, White.
1879, Glasgow, GIFA, no. 419, as *A Nocturne in Snow and Silver*.
1889, New York, Wunderlich, no. 6.
1892, London, Goupil, no. 1, as *Nocturne. Grey and Silver—Chelsea Embankment—Winter*.
1904, Boston, Copley, no. 61.
1905, Paris, Memorial, no. 73.
1912, Toledo, no. 106.

Literature:
Hayward, 1979, fig. 6.
Matsuki, 1903, p. 9.
Young *et al.*, 1980, I, no. 205, p. 119; repr. II, pl. 137.

Plate 31.
Nocturne: Silver and Opal—Chelsea
early 1880s

Provenance:
Through Dowdeswell, London dealers, to H. S. Theobald, London, 1884, to Freer, 1902.

Exhibition:
1884, London, Dowdeswell, no. 25, as *Nocturne: Silver and Opal—Chelsea*.
1887, Paris, Petit, no. 165.
1892, London, Goupil, no. 11.
1904, Boston, Copley, no. 68, as *Nocturne—Opal and Silver*.
1905, Paris, Memorial, no. 75.

Literature:
Sickert, B., 1908, no. 149, p. 170.
Young *et al.*, 1980, I, no. 309, pp. 152–153; repr. II, pl. 182.

Plate 32.
Chelsea Shops
early 1880s

Provenance:
H. S. Theobald, London, to Freer, 1902.

Exhibition:
1884, London, Dowdeswell, no. 23 (possible).[3]
1887, Paris, Petit, no. 208, as *Rose et Brun: Les Boutiques de Chelsea*.
1912, Washington, no. 12.

Literature:
Holden, 1969, pl. 24, p. 69.
Sutton, 1966, pl. 103.
Young *et al.*, 1980, I, no. 246, p. 136; repr. II, pl. 222.

Plate 33.
Red and Blue: Lindsey Houses
ca. 1882–1884

Provenance:
H. S. Theobald, London, to Freer, 1902.

Exhibition:
1884, London, Dowdeswell, no. 4, as *Red and Blue—Lindsey Houses*.

1904, Boston, Copley, no. 11, as *A Note in Red*.
1912, Washington, no. 5.

Literature:
Young *et al.*, 1980, I, no. 306, p. 152; repr. II, pl.
194.

Plate 34.
Harmony in Brown and Gold: Old Chelsea Church
ca. 1884

Provenance:
H. S. Theobald, London, to Freer, 1902.

Exhibition:
1884, London, Dowdeswell, no. 44.
1884, Dublin, no. 247.
1912, Washington, no. 2.

Literature:
Young *et al.*, 1980, I, no. 305, pp. 151–152; repr. II,
pl. 217.

Plate 35.
An Orange Note: Sweet Shop
1884

Provenance:
Whistler to Wickham Flower, 1884, auctioned
London, Christie, 17 December 1904, lot 39, to
Colnaghi, London dealers, to Freer, 1905.

Exhibition:
1884, London, Dowdeswell, no. 38, as *An Orange
Note—Sweet Shop*.
1905, Paris, Memorial, no. 84.
1912, Washington, no. 6.

Literature:
Duret, 1904, repr. p. 177.
Sickert, B., 1908, no. 158, p. 172.
Young *et al.*, 1980, I, no. 264, pp. 142–143; repr. II,
pl. 162.

Plate 36.
Black and Emerald: Coal Mine
1883–1884

Provenance:
H. S. Theobald, London, to Freer, 1902.

Exhibition:
1884, London, Dowdeswell, no. 59.
1884, Dublin, no. 248, as *Black and Emerald—Coal
Mine*.
1887, Paris, Petit, no. 174, as *Vert et Noir: La Mine
Abandonnée*.

Literature:
Newton and MacDonald, 1978, p. 156; repr. p. 155.
Young *et al.*, 1980, I, no. 302, p. 151; repr. II, pl. 216.

Plate 37.
Note in green: Wortley
ca. 1884

Provenance:
H. S. Theobald, London, to Freer, 1902.

Exhibition:
1884, London, Dowdeswell, no. 34, as *Wortley:
Note in Green*.
1887, Paris, Petit, no. 163, as *Note en vert: Le village
de Wortley*.
1904, Boston, Copley, no. 81.
1905, Buffalo, no. 167.
1910, New York, Montross, no. 21.
1912, Washington, no. 14.
1915, San Francisco, no. 261.

Literature:
Young *et al.*, 1980, I, no. 303, p. 151; repr. II, pl. 215.

Plate 38.
Note in Blue and Opal: The Sun Cloud
1884

Provenance:
Wickham Flower collection; through Christie's,
London, to Colnaghi, London dealers, 1904, to
Freer, 1905.

Exhibition:
1884, London, Dowdeswell, no. 52.
1905, Paris, Memorial, no. 79.
1912, Washington, no. 10.
1912, Toledo, no. 108.

Literature:
Holden, 1969, pl. 19, p. 59.
Hoopes, 1972, pl. 4, p. 26.
Sickert, B., 1908, no. 153, p. 171.
Young *et al.*, 1980, I, no. 271, pp. 144–145; repr. II,
pl. 184.

Plate 39.
Green and Silver: The Devonshire Cottages
1884

Provenance:
Dr. W. Whistler, through the artist to Goupil,
London dealers, 1895; Alexander Young collec-
tion, London, by 1902; Obach, London dealers, to
Freer, 1906.

Exhibition:
1905, London, Memorial, no. 86, as *Landscape*.

Literature:
Lane, 1942, repr. p. 64.
Pennell, 1908, II, repr. opp. p. 162.
Prideaux, 1970, pp. 182–183.
Young *et al.*, 1980, I, no. 266, pp. 143–144; repr. II,
pl. 180.

Plate 40.
The White House
ca. 1884–1885

Provenance:
H. S. Theobald, London, to Freer, 1902.

Exhibition:
1884 or 1886, London, Dowdeswell (possible).[1]
1910, New York, Montross, no. 20.
1915, San Francisco, no. 260.

Literature:
Young *et al.*, 1980, I, no. 289, p. 148; repr. II, pl.
213.

Plate 41.
Low Tide
ca. 1883–1884

Provenance:
H. S. Theobald, London, to Freer, 1902.

Exhibition:
1884, London, Dowdeswell (possible).
1912, Washington, no. 7.

Literature:
Young *et al.*, 1980, I, no. 280, p. 146; repr. II, pl.
212.

Plate 42.
Blue and Grey: Unloading
ca. 1883–1884

Provenance:
H. S. Theobald, London, to Freer, 1902.

Exhibition:
1884, London, Dowdeswell, no. 56, as *Blue and
Grey—Unloading*.
1887, Paris, Petit, no. 171.
1912, Washington, no. 4.

Literature:
Young *et al.*, 1980, I, no. 296, p. 150; repr. II, pl.
210.

Plate 43.
Grey and Silver: Mist—Life Boat
1884

Provenance:
Whistler to Otto Goldschmidt by 1892, Mrs. Gold-
schmidt to Knoedler, New York dealers, 1913, to
Freer, 1914.

Exhibition:
1884, London, Dowdeswell, no. 54, as *Grey and
Silver Mist—Life Boat*.
1884, Dublin, no. 246.
1887, Paris, Petit, no. 199, as *Gris et Argent: Mer et
Pluie. Bateau de Sauvetage*.
1888, Munich, no. 60, as *Grau und Silber* (probable).
1889, New York, Wunderlich, no. 29, as *A Grey
Note—The Life Boat*.
1890, Brussels, no. 843, as *Le Bateau de Sauvetage*.
1915, San Francisco, no. 257.

Literature:
Young *et al.*, 1980, I, no. 287, p. 148; repr. II, pl.
162.

Plate 44.
The Angry Sea
1884

Provenance:
Goupil, London dealers, to J. J. Cowan, Edinburgh,
ca. 1901, through W. S. Marchant, London dealers, to Freer, 1904.

Exhibition:
1884, London, Dowdeswell, no. 2, as *The Angry
Sea*.
1904, Edinburgh, RSA, no. 314.
1905, Buffalo, no. 164.

Literature:
Hobbs, 1977, p. 96.
Holden, 1969, pl. 18, p. 57.
Lane, 1942, repr. p. 58.
Menpes, 1904, repr. opp. p. 116.
Sickert, O., 1903, repr. p. 14.
Sutton, 1964, fig. 50.
Sutton, 1966, pl. 82.
Taylor, 1978, pl. 22.
Young *et al.*, 1980, I, no. 146, p. 147; repr. II, pl. 189.

Plate 45.
The Sea and Sand
1884

Provenance:
H. S. Theobald to Freer, 1902.

Exhibition:
1884, London, Dowdeswell, no. 36, as *Sea and
Storm: Grey and Green*, or no. 45, as *Sands: Blue
Note*.
1904, Boston, Copley, no. 82, as *The Sea and Sand*.
1905, Buffalo, no. 168.

Literature:
Young *et al.*, 1980, I, no. 188, p. 148; repr. II, pl. 191.

Plate 46.
Violet and Silver: The Great Sea
ca. 1884

Provenance:
H. S. Theobald, London, to Freer, 1902.

Exhibition:
1884, London, Dowdeswell, no. 33, as *Violet and
Silver. The Great Sea*.
1887, Paris, Petit, no. 168, as *Bleu et Argent: La
Grande Mer* (possible).
1902, Paris, Soc. Nat., no. 1192 (possible).
1903, Phildelphia.
1904, Boston, Copley, no. 5, as *Green and Gold—
the Great Sea*.

1905, Paris, Memorial, no. 103.
1912, Washington, no. 11.
1912, Toledo, no. 109.

Literature:
Young *et al.*, I, no. 298, p. 150; repr. II, pl. 193.

Plate 47.
Grey and Brown: The Sad Sea Shore
1885

Provenance:
Possibly C. A. Miller collection, possibly Forbes collection. Knoedler, New York dealers, to Freer, 1914.

Exhibition:
1886, London, Dowdeswell, no. 43, as *Grey and Brown—the Sad Sea Shore.*
1887, Paris, Petit, no. 184 (possible).
1888, Munich, no. 63, as *Grau und Brun. Ruhige See.*
1889, New York, Wunderlich, no. 27, as *Grey and Brown—the Sad Sea—Dieppe.*

Literature:
Taylor, 1978, pl. 96.
Young *et al.*, 1980, I, no. 330, p. 160; repr. II, pl. 221.

Plate 48.
The Summer Sea
1880s

Provenance:
J. J. Cowan, Edinburgh, through W. S. Marchant, London dealers, to Freer, 1904.

Exhibition:
1904, Edinburgh, RSA, no. 309, as *The Summer Sea.*
1905, Buffalo, no. 163.
1912, Washington, no. 3.

Literature:
Taylor, 1978, repr. p. 140.

Plate 49.
Red and Pink: La Petite Mephisto
early 1880s

Provenance:
H. S. Theobald, London, to Freer, 1902.

Exhibition:
1884, London, Dowdeswell, no. 51, as *Red and Pink: La Petite Mephisto.*
1884, Dublin, no. 238.
1887, Paris, Petit, no. 164, as *Note en Rouge: La Petite Mephisto.*
1904, Boston, Copley, no. 14, as *Petite Mephiste.*
1905, Paris, Memorial, no. 52, as *Petite Mephisto . . . Esquisse.*

Literature:
Sickert, B., 1908, no. 145, p. 170.
Young *et al.*, 1980, I, no. 255, p. 140; repr. II, pl. 173.

Plate 50.
Note en Rouge: L'Eventail
ca. 1884

Provenance:
H. Cust Collection by 1905, to Dr. Hogarth, Oxford, ca. 1913, to Freer, 1913.

Exhibition:
1884, London Dowdeswell, no. 6, as *Violet and Red* (possible).
1887, Paris, Petit, no. 170, as *Note en Rouge: L'Eventail.*
1905, Paris, Memorial, no. 54, as *The Little Red Note.*

Literature:
Young *et al.*, 1980, I, no. 256, p. 141; repr. II, pl. 175.

Plate 51.
Arrangement in Grey: Portrait of Master Stephen Manuel
ca. 1885

Provenance:
Whistler to Mrs. M. B. Manuel to sitter to Freer, 1908.

Exhibition:
1885, London, SBA, no. 45, as *Arrangement in Grey: Portrait of Master Stephen Manuel.*
1905, London, Memorial, no. 51.

Literature:
Pennell, 1908, II, repr. p. 196.
Sutton, 1964, fig. 48.
Young *et al.*, 1980, I, no. 321, p. 157; repr. II, pl. 206.

Plate 52.
The Butcher's Shop
late 1880s

Provenance:
Whistler to Freer, 1903.

Exhibition:
1904, Boston, Copley, no. 6.

Literature:
Young *et al.*, 1980, I, no. 383, pp. 171–172; repr. II, pl. 226.

Plate 53.
The Grey House
1889

Provenance:
Whistler to Freer, 1903.

Exhibition:
1904, Boston, Copley, no. 4.

Literature:
Young *et al.*, 1980, I, no. 385, p. 172; repr. II, pl. 226.

Plate 54.
Gold and Orange: The Neighbors
ca. 1894–1895

Provenance:
Whistler through Mrs. E. K. Johnson to John Balli, Paris, February 1903, auctioned Paris, Petit, 22 May 1913, to Albert Rouillier, Chicago dealer, to Freer, 1913.

Exhibition:
1901, London, ISSPG, no. 34, as *Gold and Orange— the Neighbours.*
1902, Paris, Soc. Nat., no. 1196, as *Rose et Or: Les Voisines.*
1903, London, McLean, no. 32, as *Neighbours.*

Literature:
Sutton, 1966, pl. 101.
Young *et al.*, 1980, I, no. 423, pp. 188–189; repr. II, pl. 260.

Plate 55.
The Little Nurse
1895

Provenance:
A. Reid, Glasgow dealer, to J. J. Cowan, Edinburgh, through W. S. Marchant, London dealers, to Freer, 1904.

Exhibition:
1904, Edinburgh, RSA, no. 313.

Literature:
Menpes, 1904, repr. opp. p. 140.
Sickert, O., 1903, repr. p. 16.
Young *et al.*, 1980, I, no. 443, p. 197; repr. II, pl. 290.

Plate 56.
Vert et Or: Le Raconteur
1896–1900

Provenance:
Rosalind Birnie Philip to Freer, 1905.

Exhibition:
1910, New York, Met, no. 40.
1912, Toledo, no. 102.

Literature:
Young *et al.*, 1980, I, no. 513, pp. 218–219; repr. II, pl. 328.

Plate 57.
The Little Faustina
1896–1900

Provenance:
Rosalind Birnie Philip to Freer, 1909.

Exhibition:
1905, Paris, Memorial, no. 43.
1910, New York, Met, no. 44.
1912, Toledo, No. 105.

Literature:
Young *et al.*, 1980, I, no. 510, pp. 217–218; repr. II, pl. 325.

Plate 58.
Green and Gold: The Little Green Cap
1896–1901

Provenance:
Rosalind Birnie Philip to Freer, 1907.

Exhibition:
1909, Buffalo, no. 186.
1910, New York, Met, no. 43.
1912, Toledo, no. 104.
1912, Washington, no. 13.

Literature:
Sutton, 1966, pl. 111.
Young *et al.*, 1980, I, no. 467, p. 204; repr. II, pl. 300.

Plate 59.
The Little Red Glove
1896–1902

Provenance:
Whistler to Freer, 1903.

Exhibition:
1904, Boston, Copley, no. 41.
1904, New York, Comparative, no. 181.
1905, Paris, Memorial, no. 39.

Literature:
Gallatin, 1904, p. 42.
Gallatin, 1907, p. 33.
Matsuki, 1903, p. 9.
Sickert, B., 1908, no. 134, p. 169.
Young *et al.*, 1980, I, no. 468, p. 204; repr. II, pl. 343.

Plate 60.
Rose and Gold: The Little Lady Sophie of Soho
1898–1899

Provenance:
Whistler to Freer, 1900.[5]

Exhibition:
1899, London, ISSPG, no. 138.
1901, Munich, no. 1833a.
1901, Paris, Petit.
1903, Philadelphia, no. 3.
1904, Boston, Copley, no. 83.
1905, Paris, Memorial, no. 37.
1910, New York, Met, no. 41.
1912, Toledo, no. 103.

Literature:
Gallatin, 1904, p. 42.
Gallatin, 1907, p. 33.
Laver, 1930, p. 276.
Matsuki, 1903, pp. 8–9.
Pousette-Dart, 1927, repr. pl. 41.
Sickert, B., 1908, no. 118, p. 167.
Young *et al.*, 1980, I, no. 504, pp. 215–216; repr. II, pl. 324.

Plate 61.
Harmony in Blue and Gold: The Little Blue Girl
1894–1903

Provenance:
Rosalind Birnie Philip to Freer, 1903.[1]

Exhibition:
1904, Boston, Copley, no. 26, as *The Little Blue and Gold Girl*.
1904, New York, Comparative, no. 178.
1905, Paris, Memorial, no. 48.

Literature:
Hobbs, 1977, p. 96.
Laver, 1951, p. 129.
Matsuki, 1903, p. 9.
Sickert, B., 1908, no. 122, p. 167.
Young *et al.*, 1980, I, no. 421, p. 188; repr. II, pls. 278, 426, 427.

Plate 62.
Purple and Gold: Phryne the Superb!—Builder of Temples
1898 ff.

Provenance:
Whistler to Freer, 1902.[4]

Exhibition:
1901, London, ISSPG, no. 37, as *Purple and Gold—Phryne the Superb!—Builder of Temples*
1902, Paris, Soc. Nat., no. 1194.
1903, Venice, no. 39.
1904, Edinburgh, RSA, no. 328.
1905, Buffalo, no. 165.
1912, Washington, no. 9.

Literature:
Hobbs, 1977, p. 96.
Sutton, 1966, pl. 115.
Young, *et al.*, 1980, I, no. 490, p. 211; repr. II, pl. 316.

Plate 63.
Rose and Brown: La Cigale
1899

Provenance:
Whistler to Freer, 1899.[6]

Exhibition:
1899, London, ISSPG, no. 137.
1903, Philadelphia.
1904, Boston, Copley, no. 79.

Literature:
Sickert, B., 1908, no. 117, p. 167.
Young *et al.*, 1980, I, no. 495, p. 213; repr. II, pl. 319.

Plate 64.
Grey and Gold: High Tide at Pourville
1899

Provenance:
J. Staats Forbes collection; Obach, London dealers, to Freer, 1904.

Literature:
Young *et al.*, 1980, I, no. 523, p. 222; repr. II, pl. 334.

Plate 65.
Blue and Silver: Boat Entering Pourville
1899

Provenance:
J. Staats Forbes collection; Obach, London dealers, to Freer, 1904.

Literature:
Lane, 1942, repr. p. 92.
Young *et al.*, 1980, I, no. 524, p. 222; repr. II, pl. 336.

Plate 66.
Portrait of Charles Lang Freer
1902–1903

Provenance:
Rosalind Birnie Philip to Freer, 1903.

Literature:
Hobbs, 1981, repr. p. 1193.
Prideaux, 1970, p. 171.
Taylor, 1978, pl. 23.
Young *et al.*, 1980, I, no. 550, p. 228; repr. II, pl. 354.

Plate 67.
Frame for Caprice in Purple and Gold: The Golden Screen
ca. 1864

Provenance:
Acquired with *Portrait of a Lady* (Plate 18).

Literature:
Horowitz, 1979–1980, Fig. 2, p. 125.

Plate 68.
Frame for La Princesse du Pays de la Porcelaine
1864

Provenance:
Acquired with painting but not given accession number, 1903.

Literature:
Horowitz, 1979–1980, Fig. 3, p. 126.

Plate 69.
Frame for Variations in Pink and Grey: Chelsea
ca. 1871–1872

Provenance:
Acquired with painting in 1902 but given no accession number.

Plate 70.
Frame for Arrangement in White and Black
ca. 1876

Provenance:
Acquired with painting in 1904 but given no accession number.

Plate 71.
Frame for Harmony in Blue and Gold: The Little Blue Girl
1894–1903

Provenance:
Acquired with painting, 1903.

Plate 72.
Staircase dado panels for entrance hall, 49 Prince's Gate
1876

Provenance:
Whistler to F. R. Leyland 1876; to Mrs. Watney 1897 (*in situ*), through Brown and Phillips, London dealers, to Obach, London dealers, to Freer, 1904.

Exhibition:
1904, London, Obach.

Literature:
Young *et al.*, 1980, I, no. 175, p. 101; repr. II, pls. 121–123.

Plate 73.
Portrait of Whistler
1845

Provenance:
Haden collection; H. Wunderlich, New York dealers, to Freer, 1898.

Plate 74.
(r) A Fire at Pomfret and (v) building plan, fragment.
ca. 1850.

Provenance:
Thomas R. Way to Freer, 1905.

Literature:
Pressley, 1972, no. 12, p. 150.
Sandburg, 1966, repr. fig. 8.

Plate 75.
Woman with a Dog and Bird
ca. 1850–1851

Provenance:
Mrs. E. W. Hall to Freer, 1904.

Literature:
Pressley, 1972, p. 151, no. 40.

Plate 76.
Two Lovers and an Old Woman, leaf from the *Album of Archie Gracie*
ca. 1852

Provenance:
Whistler to Archie Gracie, to Gracie's daughter, to David Bendann, to Freer, 1908.

Literature:
Pressley, 1972, pp. 131–132, 142; repr. p. 130.

Plate 77.
The Cobbler
1854–1855

Provenance:
Whistler to Mr. Martin, Washington; Thomas R. Way to Freer, 1905.

Literature:
Pennell, 1908, I, repr. opp. p. 36.
Pressley, 1972, no. 79, p. 154.
Way and Dennis, 1903, repr. opp. p. 96.

Plate 78.
A Street at Saverne
1858

Provenance:
Haden collection; H. Wunderlich, New York dealers, to Freer, 1898.

Plate 79.
Boutique de Boucher—Saverne
1858

Provenance:
Haden collection; H. Wunderlich, New York dealers, to Freer, 1898.

Plate 80.
The Kitchen
1858

Provenance:
Haden collection; H. Wunderlich, New York dealers, to Freer, 1898.

Figure 80.1.
A Kitchen at Lutzelbourg
1858

Provenance:
Haden Collection; H. Wunderlich, New York dealers, to Freer, 1898.

Plate 81.
The Kitchen
1858

Provenance:
Haden collection; H. Wunderlich, New York dealers, to Freer, 1898.

Figure 81.1.
Cuisine at Lutzelbourg
1858

Provenance:
Haden Collection; H. Wunderlich, New York dealers, to Freer, 1898.

Plates 82–89.
Illustrations for **A Catalogue of Blue and White Nankin Porcelain**
1876–1877

Provenance:
No. 82: Whistler to Murray Marks, Max Williams to Freer, 1893; no. 83: Whistler to Marks, F. Keppel, New York dealer, to Freer, 1898; nos. 84–89: Whistler to Marks, Obach, London dealers, to Freer, 1907.

Literature:
Gallatin, 1907, (Plate 84), p. 39.
Lane, 1942, (Plate 87), p. 46, repr. 07.177.
MacDonald, 1978, (Plate 83), repr. 98.154.
Thompson, 1878, repr. all.

Plate 90.
Dragonflies and Butterflies
1870s

Provenance:
Thomas R. Way to Freer, 1905.

Plate 91.
Venice Harbor
1879–1880

Provenance:
Thomas R. Way to Freer, 1905.

Plate 92.
Design for the Coloring of a Room
1870s–1880s

Provenance:
F. Keppel, New York, to Freer, 1901.

Plate 93.
(r) **Study for the Tall Flower** and (v) **Design for a Wall Decoration**
1880s

Provenance:
Obach, London dealers, to Freer, 1904.

Plate 94.
Standing Nude (destroyed)
1880s

Provenance:
Whistler to Freer, 1902.

Plate 95.
Miss Alexander
1870s

Provenance:
F. Keppel, New York dealers, to Freer, 1899.

Literature:
Kennedy, 1910, no. 139.

Plate 96.
Grey and Silver: The Mersey
1880s

Provenance:
H. Wunderlich, New York dealers, to Freer, 1889.

Exhibition:
1901, Buffalo, no. 98.
1904, Boston, Copley, no. 107, p. 14.
1905, Paris, Memorial, no. 113, p. 61.
1915, San Francisco, no. 271.

Literature:
Cary, 1907, p. 174.
Clark, 1979, repr. fig. 7.
Fenollosa, 1907, repr. fol. p. 62.

Plate 97.
London Bridge
1880s

Provenance:
Thomas R. Way to Freer, 1905.

Literature:
Getscher, 1970, pl. 42.
Holden, 1969, pl. 27, p. 75.
Way and Dennis, 1903, repr. p. 96.

Plate 98.
Opal Beach
early 1880s

Provenance:
H. S. Theobald, London, to Freer, 1902.

Exhibition:
1884, London, Dowdeswell, no. 67.
1905, Paris, Memorial, no. 105.

Plate 99.
Note in Blue and Opal: Jersey
1881

Provenance:
Thomas R. Way to Freer, 1904.

Exhibition:
1905, Paris, Memorial, no. 102.
1912, Washington, no. 10.

Plate 100.
The Mouth of the River
early 1880s

Provenance:
H. S. Theobald, London, to Freer, 1902.

Plate 101.
The Bathers
early 1880s

Provenance:
H. S. Theobald, London, to Freer, 1902.

Plate 102.
The Anchorage
early 1880s

Provenance:
H. S. Theobald, London, to Freer, 1902.

Plate 103.
Southend: The Pleasure Yacht
early 1880s

Provenance:
Thomas R. Way to Freer, 1905.

Literature:
Way and Dennis, 1903, repr. fol. p. 96.

Plate 104.
Grey and Silver: Pier, Southend
early 1880s

Provenance:
H. S. Theobald, London, to Freer, 1902.

Exhibition:
1884, London, Dowdeswell, no. 62.
1904, Boston, Copley, no. 135.
1905, Paris, Memorial, no. 109.

Literature:
Cary, 1907, no. 132, p. 178.

Plate 105.
Southend Pier
1880s

Provenance:
Thomas R. Way to Freer, 1904.

Literature:
Cary, 1907, no. 245, p. 195.
Lane, 1942, repr. p. 36.
Sutton, 1966, pl. 105.

Plate 106.
Southend: Sunset
1880s

Provenance:
Thomas R. Way to Freer, 1905.

Plate 107.
The Thames near Erith
early 1880s

Provenance:
Company of the Butterfly to Freer, 1902.

Plate 108.
Erith: Evening
ca. 1883

Provenance:
H. S. Theobald, London, to Freer, 1902.

Plate 109.
A Little Red Note: Dordrecht
1883–1884

Provenance:
W. Bryant collection; H. Wunderlich, New York dealers, to Freer, 1908.

Exhibition:
1884–1885, London, SBA.
1905, London, Memorial, p. 119, no. 112.

Literature:
Pennell, 1921, repr. opp. p. 167, as *The Dyke at Domburg.*

Plate 110.
St. Ives, Cornwall
1883

Provenance:
Thomas R. Way to Freer, 1905.

Exhibition:
1905, London, Memorial, no. 121, repr. p. 124, as *St. Ives, Cornwall.*

Literature:
Pennell, J. 1912, repr. p. 38, as *St. Ives, Cornwall.*
Pennell, 1921, repr. p. 55, as *Lyme Regis.*
Way and Dennis, 1903, repr. frontispiece, as *St. Ives.*

Plate 111.
St. Ives: Sunset
1883

Provenance:
Thomas R. Way to Freer, 1905.

Exhibition:
1905, London, Memorial, no. 130, as *A Marine Sunset.*

Plate 112.
The Ocean Wave
ca. 1883

Provenance:
Obach, London dealers, to Freer, 1906.

Plate 113.
The Sea Shore
1883–1885

Provenance:
W. S. Marchant, London dealers, to Freer, 1902.

Exhibition:
1904, Boston, Copley, no. 147.
1905, Paris, Memorial, no. 104.

Literature:
Cary, 1907, no. 144, p. 180.

Plates 114–117.
"Amsterdam Nocturnes"
1883–1884

Provenance:
Nos. 114–116: H. S. Theobald, London, to Freer, 1902; no. 117: J. J. Cowan, Edinburgh, to Freer, 1904.

Exhibition:
1884, London, Dowdeswell, *Nocturne: Black and Red* as no. 53; *Nocturne, Grey and Gold* as no. 3; *Nocturne: Grand Canal* as no. 18; *Nocturne: Amsterdam in Winter* as no. 49 (uncertain—as *Nocturne: Black & Gold—Winter, Amsterdam*).
1889, New York, Wunderlich: *Nocturne: Grey and Gold,* as no. 12.
1904, Boston, Copley: *Nocturne: Black and Red* as no. 101; *Nocturne: Grey and Gold* as no. 102; *Nocturne: Grand Canal* as no. 106.
1904, Edinburgh, RSA: *Nocturne: Amsterdam in Winter* as no. 75.
1905, Paris, Memorial: *Nocturne: Black and Red* as no. 121; *Nocturne: Grey and Gold* as no. 119; *Nocturne: Grand Canal* as no. 122; *Nocturne: Amsterdam in Winter* as no. 120.

Literature:
Holden, 1969, pl. 22 (*Nocturne: Grand Canal*), p. 65.

Plate 118.
Reach in Upper Thames
1880s

Provenance:
Thomas R. Way to Freer, 1905.

Plate 119.
The Rows, Chester
mid-1880s

Provenance:
Obach, London dealers, to Freer, 1904.

Plate 120.
Chelsea Shops
mid-1880s

Provenance:
J. J. Cowan, Edinburgh, to Freer, 1904.[2]

Exhibition:
1904, Boston, Copley, no. 3, as *Chelsea Shops.*

Literature:
Menpes, 1904, repr. p. 112, as *Chelsea Shops.*
Way, 1903, repr. p. 98, as *Chelsea Shops.*

Plate 121.
Chelsea Children
mid-1880s

Provenance:
Company of the Butterfly to Freer, 1900.[3]

Exhibition:
1905, Paris, Memorial, no. 97.

Literature:
Cary, 1907, no. 236, p. 194.

Plate 122.
Flower Market: Dieppe
1885

Provenance:
Sickert collection; Obach, London dealers, to Freer, 1907.

Plate 123.
Green and Silver: Beaulieu, Touraine
ca. 1888

Provenance:
Goupil, London dealers, to Freer, 1899.

Exhibition:
1904, Boston, Copley, no. 90.
1915, San Francisco, no. 269.

Literature:
Cary, 1907, no. 87, p. 170.

Plate 124.
Breakfast in the Garden
1880s

Provenance:
Thomas R. Way to Freer, 1905.

Literature:
Sutton, 1966, pl. 106.

Plate 125.
Bravura in Brown
early 1880s

Provenance:
H. S. Theobald, London, to Freer, 1902.

Exhibition:
1884, London, Dowdeswell, no. 66.
1905, Paris, Memorial, no. 91.

Plate 126.
Note in Opal: Breakfast
early 1880s

Provenance:
H. S. Theobald, London, to Freer, 1902.

Exhibition:
1884, London, Dowdeswell, no. 13.
1904, Boston, Copley, no. 105.

Literature:
Lane, 1942, repr. p. 83.

Plate 127.
Pink Note: The Novelette
early 1880s

Provenance:
H. S. Theobald, London, to Freer, 1902.

Exhibition:
1884, London, Dowdeswell, no. 16.

Literature:
Lane, 1942, repr. p. 82.

Plate 128.
Resting in Bed
early 1880s

Provenance:
Obach, London dealers, to Freer, 1907.

Plate 129.
Moreby Hall
early 1880s

Provenance:
J. J. Cowan, Edinburgh, to Freer, 1904.

Exhibition:
1884, London, Dowdeswell, no. 28.
1904, Edinburgh, RSA, no. 80.
1905, Paris, Memorial, no. 100.

Literature:
Cary, 1907, no. 253, p. 196.
Menpes, 1904, p. 54.
Pennell, 1908, II, repr. opp. p. 82, as *Interior of Hall.*

Plate 130.
Pink Note: Shelling Peas
early 1880s

Provenance:
H. S. Theobald, London, to Freer, 1902.

Exhibition:
1884, London, Dowdeswell, no. 20.

Literature:
Lane, 1942, repr. p. 41.

Plate 131.
Note in Pink and Purple: The Studio
early 1880s

Provenance:
H. S. Theobald, London, to Freer, 1902.

Exhibition:
1884, London, Dowdeswell, no. 27.
1904, Boston, Copley, no. 137.

Literature:
Cary, 1907, no. 134, p. 179.

Plate 132.
Milly Finch
early 1880s

Provenance:
Whistler to Walter Sickert by 1884,[3] to Obach, London dealers, to Freer, 1907.

Plate 133.
Harmony in Violet and Amber
1881–1884

Provenance:
H. S. Theobald, London, to Freer, 1902.

Exhibition:
1884, London, Dowdeswell, no. 19.
1905, Paris, Memorial, no. 88.

Literature:
Cary, 1907, no. 229, p. 193.

Plate 134.
A Note In Green
1881–1884

Provenance:
H. S. Theobald, London, to Freer, 1902.

Exhibition:
1904, Boston, Copley, no. 100.
1905, Paris, Memorial, no. 89.

Literature:
Cary, 1907, no. 97, p. 172.

Plate 135.
Blue and Silver: The Chopping Channel
1890s

Provenance:
Goupil, London dealers, to Freer, 1899.

Exhibition:
1901, Buffalo, no. 97.

Literature:
Cary, 1907, no. 96, p. 172.
Holden, 1969, pl. 30, p. 81.

Plate 136.
Rose and Silver: Portrait of Mrs. Whibley
early 1890s

Provenance:
J. J. Cowan, Edinburgh, to Freer, 1901.

Exhibition:
1904, Boston, Copley, no. 103.
1905, Paris, Memorial, no. 86.
1915, San Francisco, no. 270.

Literature:
Hobbs, 1977, p. 96.
Sutton, 1966, pl. 94.

Plate 137.
Blue and Gold: The Rose Azalea
ca. 1890–1895

Provenance:
Whistler to Freer, 1894.

Exhibition:
1903, Philadelphia.
1904, Boston, Copley, no. 111.
1905, Paris, Memorial, no. 138.
1915, San Francisco, no. 268.

Literature:
Cary, 1907, no. 108, p. 174.

Plate 138.
Venus and Cupid
1890s

Provenance:
Collection Mme. la Comtesse de Bearn, Paris; D. C.
    Thompson for French Gallery, London dealers, to
    Freer, 1913.

Exhibition:
1905, London, Memorial, no. 41; repr. opp. p. 56 as
    Nude Figure and Cupid.
1915, San Francisco, no. 272.

Literature:
Pennell, 1908, II, repr. p. 86.

Plate 139.
Design for a Decorated Fan
1895

Provenance:
Whistler to Freer, 1899.

Plate 140.
St. Augustine and Other Figures
ca. 1849–1851

Provenance:
Thomas R. Way to Freer, 1905.

Literature:
Pennell, 1908, I, repr. p. 29.

Plates 141–144.
Leaves from the **Album of Archie Gracie**
ca. 1852

Provenance:
Whistler to Archie Gracie, to Gracie's daughter;
    through David Bendann, Baltimore, to Freer,
    1908.[1]

Literature:
Pressley, 1972, pp. 131–132, 152, no. 47.

Plate 145.
A Group of Figures at West Point
1852–1854

Provenance:
Whistler to Archie Gracie, to Gracie's daughter;
    through David Bendann, Baltimore, to Freer,
    1908.

Plate 146.
Portrait of John Ross Key
1854

Provenance:
Whistler to John Ross Key, to Freer, 1908.

Literature:
Lane, 1942, repr. p. 61.
Pressley, 1972, p. 154, no. 78.

Plate 147.
An Artist in His Studio
ca. 1856

Provenance:
Knoedler, New York dealers, to Freer, 1906.

Plate 148.
Standing Figure
ca. 1855–1858

Provenance:
Haden collection; H. Wunderlich, New York deal-
    ers, to Freer, 1898.

Plate 149.
Standing Figure, Profile
ca. 1855–1858

Provenance:
Haden collection; H. Wunderlich, New York deal-
    ers, to Freer, 1898.

Plate 150.
Profile Sketch of a Child
ca. 1855–1860

Provenance:
Haden collection; H. Wunderlich, New York deal-
    ers, to Freer, 1898.

Plate 151.
Young Man Smoking a Pipe; Bending Figure
ca. 1855–1859

Provenance:
Haden collection; H. Wunderlich, New York deal-
    ers, to Freer, 1898.

Plate 152.
(r) **Head of a Man in a Tall Hat** and (v) **Standing
Figure**
ca. 1855–1859

Provenance:
Haden collection; H. Wunderlich, New York deal-
    ers, to Freer, 1898.

Plate 153.
Heads of Two Men
ca. 1855–1859

Provenance:
Haden collection; H. Wunderlich, New York deal-
    ers, to Freer, 1898.

Plate 154.
(r) **Les Côtes à Dieppe** and (v) **Cliff at Dieppe**
1857

Provenance:
Haden collection; H. Wunderlich, New York deal-
    ers, to Freer, 1898.

Plate 155.
(r) **The Esplanade at Dieppe** and (v) **Studies of a
Young Boy**
1857, 1858–1860

Provenance:
Haden collection; H. Wunderlich, New York deal-
    ers, to Freer, 1898.

Plate 156.
A Bridge
ca. 1858

Provenance:
Haden collection; H. Wunderlich, New York deal-
    ers, to Freer, 1898.

Plate 157.
Whistler Sketching
1858

Provenance:
Haden collection; H. Wunderlich, New York deal-
    ers, to Freer, 1898.

Literature:
Gallatin, 1913, I, no. 20, p. 32.
Gallatin, 1913, II, no. 24, p. 31.

Plate 158.
Seated Man Examining Foot
1858

Provenance:
Haden collection; H. Wunderlich, New York deal-
    ers, to Freer, 1898.

Literature:
Gallatin, 1913, I, no. 17.
Gallatin, 1918, no. 21.

Plate 159.
A Street Scene
1858

Provenance:
Haden collection; H. Wunderlich, New York deal-
    ers, to Freer, 1898.

Plate 160.
Figures by a Fountain
ca. 1858

Provenance:
Haden collection; H. Wunderlich, New York deal-
    ers, to Freer, 1898.

Plate 161.
Three Standing Figures
1858

Provenance:
Haden collection: H. Wunderlich, New York deal-
    ers, to Freer, 1898.

Plate 162.
À La Ferme de Maladrie
1858

Provenance:
Haden collection; H. Wunderlich, New York dealers, to Freer, 1898.

Plate 163.
Chambre à la Ferme de Maladrie
1858

Provenance:
Haden collection; H. Wunderlich, New York dealers, to Freer, 1898.

Plate 164.
(r) Four Men on a Boat and (v) Sailor
1858

Provenance:
Haden collection; H. Wunderlich, New York dealers, to Freer, 1898.

Literature:
Gallatin, 1913, I, no. 18.
Gallatin, 1913, II, no. 22.

Plate 165.
Two Figures
1858

Provenance:
Haden collection; H. Wunderlich, New York dealers, to Freer, 1898.

Plate 166.
Chez George Sauer
1858

Provenance:
Haden collection; H. Wunderlich, New York dealers, to Freer, 1898.

Plate 167.
Le Rhin
1858

Provenance:
Haden collection; H. Wunderlich, New York dealers, to Freer, 1898.

Exhibition:
1905, Paris, Memorial, no. 122, as *Croquis de la Série des Voyages du Rhin.*

Literature:
Cary, 1907 no. 254, p. 196.

Plates 168–171.
"Rhine River Scenes"
1858

Provenance:
Haden collection; H. Wunderlich, New York dealers, to Freer, 1898.

Plate 172.
Man Asleep on a Pile of Luggage
1858

Provenance:
Haden collection; H. Wunderlich, New York dealers, to Freer, 1898.

Plate 173.
(r) Group of Travelers and (v) Man Seated on Bench
1858

Provenance:
Haden collection; H. Wunderlich, New York dealers, to Freer, 1898.

Plate 174.
Barbier à Mayence
1858

Provenance:
Haden collection; H. Wunderlich, New York dealers, to Freer, 1898.

Plate 175.
(r) Brasserie à Mayence and (v) River Steamer, detail
1858

Provenance:
Haden collection; H. Wunderlich, New York dealers, to Freer, 1898.

Plate 176.
Entre sur la Grande Promenade à Baden
1858

Provenance:
Haden collection; H. Wunderlich, New York dealers, to Freer, 1898.

Plate 177.
(r) Baden Baden and (v) Table with Glasses
1858

Provenance:
Haden collection; H. Wunderlich, New York dealers, to Freer, 1898.

Plate 178.
Promenade à Baden
1858

Provenance:
Haden collection; H. Wunderlich, New York dealers, to Freer, 1898.

Plate 179
Group Conversing
1858

Provenance:
Haden Collection; H. Wunderlich, New York dealers, to Freer, 1898.

Plate 180.
Couple Seated at a Table
1858

Provenance:
Haden collection; H. Wunderlich, New York dealers, to Freer, 1898.

Plate 181.
(r) Group of Figures around a Brazier and
(v) Figures in a Chariot
1858

Provenance:
Haden collection; H. Wunderlich, New York dealers, to Freer, 1898.

Plate 182.
(r) Gambling Salon at Baden Baden and
(v) Girl Knitting, Street Scene, Cloaked Figure
1858

Provenance:
Haden Collection; H. Wunderlich, New York dealers, to Freer, 1898.

Plate 183.
La Jeunesse à Coblentz
1858

Provenance:
Haden collection; H. Wunderlich, New York dealers, to Freer, 1898.

Plate 184.
Deux Artistes Celèbres de Paris
1858

Provenance:
Haden collection; H. Wunderlich, New York dealers, to Freer, 1898.

Plate 185.
Blanchissage à Cologne
1858

Provenance:
Haden collection; H. Wunderlich, New York dealers, to Freer, 1898.

Literature:
Gallatin, 1913, I, no. 19.
Gallatin, 1918, no. 23.

Plate 186.
Attendant Que le Linge Séche! Cologne
1858

Provenance:
Haden collection; H. Wunderlich, New York dealers, to Freer, 1898.

Plate 187.
Reclining Figure with Table and Glasses
1858

Provenance:
Haden collection; H. Wunderlich, New York dealers, to Freer, 1898.

Plate 188.
Marchand de Potirons à Cologne
1858

Provenance:
Haden Collection; H. Wunderlich, New York dealers, to Freer, 1898.

Plate 189.
La Marchande de Moutarde
1858

Provenance:
Haden collection; H. Wunderlich, New York dealers, to Freer, 1898.

Plate 190.
Woman Seated at Window
1858

Provenance:
Haden collection; H. Wunderlich, New York dealers, to Freer, 1898.

Plate 191.
Enfant de Choeur de Cologne
1858

Provenance:
Haden collection; H. Wunderlich, New York dealers, to Freer, 1898.

Plate 192.
Succès d'Erneste à Cologne
1858

Provenance:
Haden collection; H. Wunderlich, New York dealers, to Freer, 1898.

Plate 193.
Group of Four Men
1858

Provenance:
Haden collection; H. Wunderlich, New York dealers, to Freer, 1898.

Plate 194.
Whistler with Friends
1859

Provenance:
Haden collection; H. Wunderlich, New York dealers, to Freer, 1898.

Literature:
Gallatin, 1913, I, repr. p. 32.
Gallatin, 1918, repr. p. 31.

Plate 195.
Sir Seymour Haden Playing the Cello
1858–1859

Provenance:
Haden collection; H. Wunderlich, New York dealers, to Freer, 1898.

Plate 196.
(r) Nelly (Helen Ionides) and (v) Peasant Woman
ca. 1858

Provenance:
Haden collection; H. Wunderlich, New York dealers, to Freer, 1898.

Plate 197.
Seated Seamstress with Male Companion
ca. 1855–1859

Provenance:
Haden collection; H. Wunderlich, New York dealers, to Freer, 1898.

Plate 198.
(r) Seated Woman, Smoking and (v) Head
ca. 1858–1859

Provenance:
Haden collection; H. Wunderlich, New York dealers, to Freer, 1898.

Plate 199.
(r) Girl Reclining on a Couch, Reading and (v) Female Head
1858–1860

Provenance:
Haden collection; H. Wunderlich, New York dealers, to Freer, 1898.

Plate 200.
(r) Fumette and (v) Dancing Clowns
ca. 1855–1859

Provenance:
Haden collection; H. Wunderlich, New York dealers, to Freer, 1898.

Plate 201.
Annie Haden
1858–1859

Provenance:
Haden collection; H. Wunderlich, New York dealers, to Freer, 1898.

Plate 202.
Nelly
ca. 1860–1862

Provenance:
Haden collection; H. Wunderlich, New York dealers, to Freer, 1898.

Plate 203.
Self-Portrait
ca. 1860s

Provenance:
Goupil, London dealers, to Freer, 1899.

Literature:
Gallatin, 1913, I, repr. fol. p. 24.
Gallatin, 1918, repr. pl. 10.

Plate 204.
(r) Portrait of the Artist and (v) Partial Figure
ca. 1860s

Provenance:
Thomas R. Way to Freer, 1905.

Exhibition:
1905, London, Memorial, no. 203, p. 71 as *Portrait of the Artist*, repr. opp. p. 24.
1915, Rochester, no. 13, p. 12.

Literature:
Gallatin, 1913, I, no. 26, p. 24.
Gallatin, 1918, no. 11, p. 29.
Pennell, 1908, I, repr. opp. p. 136 as *Portrait of Whistler.*
Pennell, J., 1912, repr. p. 25.
Way and Dennis, 1903, repr. opp. p. 8 as *Portrait Study of the Artist, by Himself.*

Plate 205.
Greek Girl
ca. 1865

Provenance:
Thomas R. Way to Freer, 1905.

Literature:
Mullikin, 1905, facsimile repr., p. 233.

Plate 206.
(r) Female Figure, Seated and (v) Drawing for a Screen
ca. 1865–1870

Provenance:
Forbes collection; W. S. Marchant, London dealers, to Freer, 1905.

Exhibition:
1904–1905, Dublin, no. 252, as *Female Figure Seated.*

Plate 207.
Woman with Parasol
ca. 1868

Provenance:
Forbes collection; W. S. Marchant, London dealers, to Freer, 1905.

Exhibition:
1904, London, Goupil, no. 6.

Plate 208.
Draped Female Figure
ca. 1868–1870

Provenance:
Forbes collection; W. S. Marchant, London dealers, to Freer, 1905.

Plate 209.
(r) Draped Figure Standing and (v) Drapery Study
ca. 1868

Provenance:
Forbes collection; W. S. Marchant, London dealers, to Freer, 1905.

Literature:
Pennell, 1908, I, repr. opp. p. 138, as *Study for the Six Projects.*

Plate 210.
(r) Standing Draped Figure and (v) Standing Nude
ca. 1868

Provenance:
Forbes collection; W. S. Marchant, London dealers, to Freer, 1905.

Literature:
Pennell, 1908, I, repr. opp. p. 138 as *Study for the Six Projects.*

Plate 211.
Standing Nude
ca. 1865–1870

Provenance:
Forbes collection; W. S. Marchant, London dealers, to Freer, 1905.

Literature:
Pennell, 1908, I, repr. opp. p. 138, as *Study for the Six Projects.*

Plate 212.
Draped Figure at a Railing
ca. 1868–1870

Provenance:
Forbes collection; W. S. Marchant, London dealers, to Freer, 1905.

Literature:
Pennell, 1908, I, repr. opp. p. 138, as *Study for the Six Projects.*

Plate 213.
(r) Study for Morning Glories and (v) Standing Nude
ca. 1870

Provenance:
Thomas R. Way to Freer, 1905.

Plate 214.
(r) Morning Glories and (v) Nude Study
ca. 1865–1870

Provenance:
W. Burrell, Glasgow, to Freer, 1903.

Exhibition:
1904, Boston, Copley, no. 114.
1905, Paris, Memorial, no. 136.

Literature:
Cary, 1907, no. 111, p. 175.
Gallatin, 1904, p. 44.
Gallatin, 1907, p. 35.

Plate 215.
Annabel Lee
ca. 1870

Provenance:
Thomas R. Way to Freer, 1905.

Exhibition:
1905, London, Memorial, no. 63, as *Annabel Lee.*
1910, New York, Met, no. 18.

Literature:
Getscher, 1970, pl. 5.
Pennell, 1908, II, repr. opp. p. 92.
Sutton, 1966, pl. 39.

Plate 216.
Venus
1869

Provenance:
La Société des Beaux-Arts, Glasgow, to Freer, 1904.

Literature:
Duret, 1917, repr. p. 66.

Plate 217.
(r) **Nude Study** and (v) **Standing Nude**
ca. 1868–1875

Provenance:
Thomas R. Way to Freer, 1902.

Plate 218.
The Purple Iris
ca. 1870

Provenance:
William Burrell, Glasgow, to Freer, 1904.

Exhibition:
1905, Paris, Memorial, no. 137.

Literature:
Cary, 1907, no. 267, p. 197.

Plate 219.
Japanese Figure, Seated
ca. 1870–1875

Provenance:
Forbes collection; W. S. Marchant, London dealers, to Freer, 1905.

Exhibition:
1904, Dublin, no. 259, as *A Model of Japan*.
1905, London, Memorial, no. 389, as *Japanese Figure, Seated*.

Plate 220.
(r) **Nocturne: Battersea Bridge** and
(v) **Standing Female Nude**
ca. 1872

Provenance:
Colnaghi, London dealers, to Freer, 1904.

Literature:
Getscher, 1970, pl. 8.
Young *et al.*, 1980, I, no. 139, p. 85.

Plate 221.
Two Sketches for Furniture
1870s

Provenance:
Thomas R. Way, London, to Freer, 1905.

Plates 222–223.
Portrait Sketches of Thomas Carlyle
1872

Provenance:
222: Thomas R. Way to Freer, 1905.
223: W. S. Marchant, London dealers, to Freer, 1905.

Exhibition:
222: 1905, London, Memorial, no. 185.
1904, Dublin, no. 258.
223: 1904, London, Goupil, no. 5.

Literature:
Pennell, 1908, Plate 222 repr. I, opp. p. 170.
Pennell, 1921, Plate 222 repr. opp. p. 174.
Sellin, 1976, repr. figs. 91, 92.
Young *et al.*, 1980, I, no. 137, pp. 82–84.

Plate 224.
Sketch of F. R. Leyland and Daughter
ca. 1869–1874

Provenance:
Thomas R. Way to Freer, 1905.

Plate 225.
The Leyland Girls
ca. 1872–1874

Provenance:
Obach, London dealers, to Freer, 1908.

Plate 226.
Baby Leyland, Reading
ca. 1872–1874

Provenance:
Thomas R. Way to Freer, 1905.

Exhibition:
1905, London, Memorial, no. 111.

Plate 227.
Portrait of Baby Leyland
ca. 1872–1874

Provenance:
Thomas R. Way to Freer, 1905.

Literature:
Sickert, O., 1903, repr. opp. p. 4 as *A Study in Black and White*; repr. *International Studio* (November 1903), p. 5, as *Baby Leyland*.
Way and Dennis, 1903, repr. p. 46.

Plate 228.
(r) **The Blue Girl** and (v) **Study for a Portière**
1872–1874

Provenance:
Thomas R. Way to Freer, 1905.

Literature:
Maus, 1904, repr. opp. p. 7.
Studio Portfolio, 1905, pl. 8.
Way and Dennis, 1903, repr. p. 90.

Plates 229–234.
Studies for **Symphony in Flesh Colour and Pink**
1871 ff.

Provenance:
229: H. Wunderlich, New York dealers, to Freer, 1892.
231, 233: Thomas R. Way to Freer, 1905.
230, 232, 234: Obach, London dealers, to Freer, 1908.

Exhibition:
233: 1905, London, Memorial, no. 47.

Literature:
233: Way and Dennis, 1903, p. 90, repr. p. 22.

Plate 235.
Young Girl Standing
ca. 1870–1875

Provenance:
Forbes collection; W. S. Marchant, London dealers, to Freer, 1905.

Literature:
Pennell, 1908, II, repr. p. 260 as *Figure with Fan*.

Plate 236.
Standing Figure with Fan
ca. 1870–1875

Provenance:
Forbes collection; W. S. Marchant, London dealers, to Freer, 1905.

Plate 237.
The Lady with the Fan
ca. 1870–1875

Provenance:
Forbes collection; W. S. Marchant, London dealers, to Freer, 1905.

Exhibition:
1904, Dublin, no. 253, as *The Lady with the Fan*.

Plate 238.
(r) **Resting** and (v) **Sketch of Standing Figure**
ca. 1870–1875

Provenance:
H. S. Theobald, London, to Freer, 1902.

Plate 239.
Seated Figure
1870s

Provenance:
Thomas R. Way to Freer, 1905.

Literature:
Baldry, 1903, repr. opp. p. 238, as *Seated Figure of a Woman Wearing a Long Full-Skirted Dress and a Hat*.

Plate 240.
Study in Grey and Pink
ca. 1872–1874

Provenance:
Thomas R. Way to Freer, 1905.

Literature:
Way, 1912, repr. p. 138.
Way and Dennis, 1903, repr. p. 26, as *Study for a White Girl*.

Plate 241.
Standing Woman in Flounced Dress
ca. 1870–1875

Provenance:
Forbes collection; W. S. Marchant, London dealers, to Freer, 1905.

Plate 242.
Standing Figure in Fur Jacket
1870–1875

Provenance:
Forbes collection; W. S. Marchant, London dealers, to Freer, 1905.

Exhibition:
1904, Dublin, no. 256, as *The Sable Jacket*.

Plate 243.
Maud, Reading
ca. 1878

Provenance:
Thomas R. Way to Freer, 1905.

Plate 244.
Venice Bay
1879

Provenance:
Thomas R. Way to Freer, 1905.

Literature:
Getscher, 1970, pl. 19.

Plate 245.
The Grand Canal, Venice
1879

Provenance:
Obach, London dealers, to Freer, 1904.

Exhibition:
1905, Paris, Memorial, no. 153, as *Le Grand Canal à Venise.*

Literature:
Baldry, 1903, repr. opp. p. 246, as *On a Venetian Canal.*

Plate 246.
(r) Venice: Sunrise on the Rialto and
(v) Venetian Scene
1879–1880

Provenance:
Thomas R. Way to Freer, 1905.

Literature:
Getscher, 1970, pl. 17.

Plate 247.
Venice: Sunset on Harbour
1879–1880

Provenance:
Thomas R. Way, London, to Freer, 1905.

Literature:
Getscher, 1970, pl. 18.

Plate 248.
Venice
1879–1889

Provenance:
H. Wunderlich, New York dealers, to Freer, 1893.

Literature:
Getscher, 1970, pl. 16.

Plate 249.
Nocturne: San Giorgio
1879–1880

Provenance:
Whistler to Mrs. H. O. Havemeyer, to Freer, 1917.

Exhibition:
1881, London, no. 18.

Literature:
Getscher, 1970, pl. 26.
Havemeyer, 1923, p. 534.
Way, 1912, repr. fol. p. 52, no. 18.

Plate 250.
The Steps
1879–1880

Provenance:
Whistler to Mrs. H. O. Havemeyer, to Freer, 1917.

Exhibition:
1881, London, no. 23.

Literature:
Havemeyer, 1923, p. 534.
Way, 1912, repr. fol. p. 52, no. 23.

Plate 251.
San Giovanni Apostolo et Evangelistae
1879–1880

Provenance:
William Burrell, Glasgow, to Freer, 1902.

Exhibition:
1881, London, no. 12.
1904, Boston, Copley, no. 112.
1905, Paris, Memorial, no. 165.

Literature:
Getscher, 1970, pl. 23.
Way, 1912, repr. fol. p. 52, no. 12.

Plate 252.
The Staircase: Note in Red
1879–1880

Provenance:
H. S. Theobald, London, to Freer, 1902.

Exhibition:
1881, London, no. 35, as *The Staircase: Note in Red.*
1904, Boston, Copley, no. 93, as *Venetian Courtyard.*
1905, Paris, Memorial, no. 163, as *Venetian Courtyard.*

Literature:
Getscher, 1970, pl. 36.
Way, 1912, repr. fol. p. 52, no. 35.

Plate 253.
The Marble Palace
1879–1880

Provenance:
Thomas R. Way to Freer, 1905.

Exhibition:
1881, London, no. 22.
1905, London, Memorial, no. 54.

Literature:
Getscher, 1970, pl. 28.
Horowitz, 1979–1980, fig. 6.
Pennell, 1908, I, repr. p. 278.
Way and Dennis, 1903, repr. after p. 92.

Plate 254.
Quiet Canal
1879–1880

Provenance:
Thomas R. Way to Freer, 1905.

Plate 255.
Bead-Stringers
1879–1880

Provenance:
Thomas R. Way to Freer, 1905.

Exhibition:
1881, London, no. 45, as *Bead Stringers.*
1905, London, Memorial, no. 52, as *Bead Stringers, Venice.*

Literature:
Maus, 1904, repr. p. 9.
Pennell, 1921, repr. fol. p. 182.
Way, 1912, repr. fol. p. 52, no. 45.
Way and Dennis, 1903, repr. p. 92.

Plate 256.
A Street in Venice
1879–1880

Provenance:
Colnaghi, London dealers, to Freer, 1904.

Exhibition:
1905, Paris, Memorial, no. 160, as *A Street in Venice.*

Plate 257.
The Beggars—Winter
ca. 1880

Provenance:
H. S. Theobald, London, to Freer, 1902 (as *The Doorway*).

Exhibition:
1881, London, no. 32, as *The Beggars—Winter.*
1905, Paris, Memorial, no. 167.

Literature:
Getscher, 1970, pl. 34.
Way, 1912, repr. fol. p. 52, no. 32.

Plate 258.
Winter Evening
1880

Provenance:
Whistler to Mrs. H. O. Havemeyer, to Freer, 1917.

Exhibition:
1881, London, no. 50.

Literature:
Getscher, 1970, pl. 39.
Havemeyer, 1923, p. 534.
Way, 1912, repr. fol. p. 52, no. 50.

Plate 259.
Sunset in Red and Brown
1879–1880

Provenance:
Whistler to Mrs. H. O. Havemeyer, to Freer, 1917.

Exhibition:
1881, London, no. 25.

Literature:
Getscher, 1970, pl. 30.
Havemeyer, 1923, p. 534.
Way, 1912, repr. fol. p. 52, no. 25.

Plate 260.
Campo S. Marta: Winter Evening
1880

Provenance:
Whistler to Mrs. H. O. Havemeyer, to Freer, 1917.

Exhibition:
1881, London, no. 51.

Literature:
Getscher, 1970, pl. 40.
Havemeyer, 1923, p. 534.
Way, 1912, repr. fol. p. 52, no. 51.

Plate 261.
The Isles of Venice
1880

Provenance:
Mr. Scroones through W. S. Marchant, London dealers, to Freer, 1905.

Exhibition:
1884, London, Dowdeswell, no. 50 (possible).
1905, London, Memorial, no. 92.
1910, New York, Met, no. 27.
1912, Washington, no. 1.

Literature:
Getscher, 1970, pl. 20.

Plate 262.
(r) Seven Sketches of Heads and (v) Chart
ca. 1880

Provenance:
E. Gottschalk to Freer, 1908.

Plate 263.
Maud Standing
ca. 1881

Provenance:
Thomas R. Way to Freer, 1905.

Exhibition:
1905, London, Memorial, no. 172.

Plate 264.
A Yellow Note
1880–1890s

Provenance:
Obach, London dealers, to Freer, 1902.[1]

Plate 265.
Little Nude
1870s ff.

Provenance:
Thomas R. Way to Freer, 1905.

Exhibition:
1905, London, Memorial, no. 70.

Literature:
Duret, 1904, repr. btwn. pp. 138 and 139.
Hartmann, 1910, repr. p. 178.
Way and Dennis, 1903, repr. fol. p. 94.

Plate 266.
Seated Figure
1870s–1880s

Provenance:
Thomas R. Way to Freer, 1905.

Exhibition:
1905, London, Memorial, no. 99 as *Seated Figure;*
   repr. p. 110.

Literature:
Pennell, 1911, repr. p. 388.

Plate 267.
The Purple Cap
1870s, reworked ca. 1885

Provenance:
Thomas R. Way to Freer, 1905.

Exhibition:
1885–1886, London, SBA, as *Note in Green and
   Violet.*
1905, London, Memorial, no. 73, as *The Purple
   Cap.*

Literature:
Pennell, 1921, repr. opp. p. 78 as *The Purple Cap.*
Scott, 1903, repr. p. 108.
Studio Portfolio, 1905, repr. pl. 3

Plate 268.
Harmony in Blue and Violet
late 1880s

Provenance:
Whistler to Freer, 1890.

Exhibition:
1889, New York, Wunderlich, no. 57.
1905, Buffalo, no. 162.

Literature:
Clark, 1979, repr. fig. 8.
Gallatin, 1904, p. 44.
Gallatin, 1907, p. 35.

Plate 269.
A Violet Note
ca. 1885

Provenance:
Whistler to Freer, 1894.

Exhibition:
1886, London, Dowdeswell, no. 37.
1889, New York, Wunderlich, no. 56.
1901, London, ISSPG, no. 33.
1904, Boston, Copley, no. 133.

Plate 270.
Writing on the Wall
1890–1902

Provenance:
Whistler to Freer, 1902.

Exhibition:
1904, Boston, Copley, no. 128.
1905, Paris, Memorial, no. 131.
1914, Minneapolis.

Plate 271.
Pour le Pastel: Rose and Opal
ca. 1885–1895

Provenance:
Alexander Reid, Edinburgh, to Freer, 1902.

Literature:
Lane, 1942, repr. p. 88.

Plate 272.
Sleeping
1880s–1902

Provenance:
Whistler to Freer, 1902.

Exhibition:
1904, Boston, Copley, no. 120.

Plates 273–277.
Figures of Women with Children

Plate 273. Mother and Child: The Pearl
1880s–1890s

Exhibition:
1884, London, Dowdeswell, no. 54.
1904. Boston, Copley, no. 126.

Literature:
Cary, 1907, no. 123, p. 177.
Gallatin, 1904, p. 44.
Gallatin, 1907, p. 35.

Plate 274.
Rose and Red: The Little Pink Cap
1890s

Provenance:
Whistler to Freer, 1894.

Exhibition:
1889, London, NEAC.
1903, Philadelphia.
1904, Boston, Copley, no. 130.
1905, Paris, Memorial, no. 144.
1910, New York, Met, no. 36.
1912, Washington, no. 19.
1914, Minneapolis.

Literature:
Cary, 1907, no. 127, p. 178.

Plate 275.
The Purple Cap
1890s

Provenance:
Whistler to Freer, 1902.

Exhibition:
1904, Boston, Copley, no. 121.
1905, Paris, Memorial, no. 146.

Literature:
Cary, 1907, no. 118, p. 176.
Gallatin, 1904, p. 44.
Gallatin, 1907, p. 35.

Plate 276.
The Green Cap
1890s–1902

Provenance:
Whistler to Freer, 1902.

Exhibition:
1904, Boston, Copley, no. 131.
1905, Buffalo, no. 169.

Literature:
Cary, 1907, no. 128, p. 178.

Plate 277.
The Shell
1890s

Provenance:
W. S. Marchant, London dealers, to Freer, 1905.

Exhibition:
1905, Paris, Memorial, no. 148.

Literature:
Cary, 1907, no. 273, p. 198.
Way and Dennis, 1903, repr. p. 94.

Plate 278.
Standing Figure
ca. 1890

Provenance:
Obach, London dealers, to Freer, 1904.

Plate 279.
A Study in Red
1890s

Provenance:
Wallis and Son, London dealers, to Freer, 1909.

Exhibition:
1903, Paris, Petit, as *Danseuse Athenienne.*
1910, New York, Met, no. 34.

Literature:
Forthuny, 1903, repr. p. 385.

Plate 280.
Blue and Rose, the Open Fan
1890s

Provenance:
Wallis and Son, London dealers, to Freer, 1909.

Exhibition:
1903, Paris, Petit, pl. 3, as *La Femme à L'Eventail.*
1910, New York, Met, no. 35.

Plate 281.
Venus Astarte
1890s

Provenance:
J. G. Arthur collection; La Société des Beaux-Arts,
   Glasgow, to Freer, 1904.

Exhibition:
1905, Paris, Memorial, no. 132.
1910, New York, Met, no. 28.
1912, Washington, no. 15.

Literature:
Sickert, O., 1903, repr. p. 15.
Sutton, 1966, repr. pl. 118.

Plate 282.
Portrait of Miss Emily Tuckerman
1898

Provenance:
Miss Emily Tuckerman through Mrs. George Draper
   (Miss Tuckerman's niece), to Charles Adams Platt,
   to Freer Gallery of Art.[2]

Plates 283–293.
Illustrations for **The Gentle Art of Making Enemies**
ca. 1890

Provenance:
Obach, London dealers, to Freer, 1904 and 1905.

Plates 294–301.
Illustrated letters
1892–1895

Provenance:
Unrecorded.

Notes

A note on notes: Although notes in the plates section are indicated by superscripted (raised) numbers, the text of the notes in this section are arranged according to plate number (the first number) and note number (the second number). Thus, 3.8 here means Plate 3, note 8. References to K. refer to Kennedy publications history in the bibliography.

1.1 Duret, 1904, quoted in Young et al., 1980 I, no. 23, p. 8. Rembrandt reproduced in Bredius, *The Paintings of Rembrandt* (London, 1937), no. 292.

1.2 Cox, 1905, p. 231.

1.3 Hobbs, 1981, p. 1195, pl. II.

2.1 Young et al., 1980, cite this problem as evidence for doubting the portrait. They also point out that Whistler's "copy" for Palmer in 1857 could easily have been a European painting at the Louvre. See I, no. 29, p. 11.

2.2 "I am trying to make a portrait of Father for George [brother] from a lithograph he sent me—this is very difficult, but with the aid of a glass and a friend who has promised to sit for me, and who is like Father in color, I hope to succeed." Whistler to Deborah Haden, January 1859, quoted *ibid*. The lithograph may have been the one by C. G. Crehen, which was published by Thomas Larcombe in about 1848.

2.3 I am grateful to Leah Lipton for sharing her work on Harding with me.

3.1 See Young et al., 1980, I, no. 34, p. 13. The identification of Miss Boott was made by Fleming.

3.2 The painting may have originally been entitled *The Morning Call. Ibid.*

3.3 See Sandberg, 1964, p. 503.

3.4 Theodore Reff has pointed out that Whistler's painting precedes spatially complex interior views done by Degas in the late 1860s. See Reff, 1976, p. 27.

3.5 "Vous ne sauriez, Madame, apporter trop de soin à tous les détails de votre vêtement, afin de n'être pas gênée dans vos mouvements et de ne pas vous écarter des règles de l'étiquette, qui est ici très stricte." F. Musany goes on to describe the costume at length. See *L'Amazone: au ménage—à la promenade. Traite de l'Équitation des dames* (Paris, 1888), pp. 17–18.

3.6 "Le tricorne eut longtemps—pendant plus de cent ans—la préférence des cavalières. Il fut détrône par le haut de forme mais ne disparaitra jamais entièrement des ménages et des allées cavalières." Émile Toebosch, *Amazones, cavalières et femmes à cheval* (Brussels, 1968), p. 54.

3.7 See Hanson, *Manet and the Modern Tradition* (New Haven, 1977), p. 86, for discussion.

3.8 Whistler to Fantin-Latour, 3 February 1864, Glasgow University archives. I do not mean to suggest that Miss Boott was a courtesan. As a matter of fact she was the niece of the founder of Lowell, Massachusetts. Her oldest sister was married to Haden's younger brother, and Whistler's younger brother Kirk also had the name Boott. See Young et al., 1980, I, no. 34, p. 13. The point is that Whistler was painting a type.

3.9 Charles Baudelaire, *The Painter of Modern Life*, ed. Sydney J. Freedberg (New York, 1979), p. 1.

5.1 See Hartmann, 1910, p. 50. The painting's debt to French chinoiserie is discussed in "Artist and Architect."

5.2 Pennell, 1908, I, pp. 24–25. A large cartoon of Venus, now in the Freer collection (Plate 216), bears one of Whistler's earliest known cyphers. The work was made in 1869. The idea for a cypher could have

been suggested by Rossetti, whose initials appear in a cartouche on a portrait of Murray Marks's wife painted in 1868. I am grateful to Susan Hobbs for this information.

6.1 The painting was originally inscribed "Whistler 1865."

6.2 For a thorough discussion of the various states of the painting, see Young et al., 1980, I, no. 56, pp. 30–32. In addition to the watercolor, related works include a preliminary pen drawing, ca. 1864, Avery Collection, New York Public Library; and a photograph when the signature was still "Whistler, 1865" in Lucas collection, Baltimore Museum of Art. Whistler made a pencil sketch after *The Balcony* in about 1886, now at Glasgow; and a pen drawing in 1892, now at the New York Public Library. By 1879 the painting may have had a frame decorated by Whistler, although its current whereabouts are unknown. See letter, Whistler to Cavafy, n.d., quoted in Young et al., 1980, I, no. 56, p. 32.

6.3 See Young et al., 1980, I, no. 57, p. 57; repr. II, pl. 53. The sketch dates from about 1867–1870 and is almost exactly the same size as the Freer oil.

6.4 Quoted in Young et al., 1980, I, no. 56, p. 32.

6.5 For possible woodblock prints with a direct influence upon the painting, see the discussion in Young et al., I, p. 32.

6.6 Theodore Child, "American Artists at the Paris Exhibition," *Harper's Magazine* 79 (September 1889):492. I am grateful to Susan Hobbs for this reference.

6.7 See "Artist and Site."

6.8 Mrs. Anna McNeill Whistler to Gamble, 10–11 February 1864, quoted in Young et al., 1980, I, no. 56, p. 31.

6.9 William Michael Rossetti objected to the "unmitigated tint" of the flooring, but Whistler ignored his suggestion to change it. *Rossetti Papers* (London, 1903), p. 229.

7-12.1 See discussion, and working figure drawing for the *The White Symphony*, in "Artist and Model." Whistler's colors in the projects are built up in layers of relatively thick impasto. The complicated brush work in the draperies of the woman at the far right of *Symphony in Blue and Pink* gives some idea of the painstaking accretion of tiny color strokes.

7-12.2 See Deborah Gribbon, "Whistler's Sketch of an Unfinished Symphony," *Fenway Court* (Boston: Isabella Stewart Gardner Museum, 1980):26–33.

7-12.3 A. G. Swinburne, "Notes on Some Pictures of 1868," in *Essays and Studies* (London, 1875), pp. 372–73.

7-12.4 See *Girl with Cherry Blossom* in Young et al., 1980, I, no. 90, p. 53.

7-12.5 See Young et al., 1980, I, no. 82, p. 48.

7-12.6 Illustrated Pennell, 1908, II, opp. p. 144.

7-12.7 It was one of the "Six Projects," the *Symphony in Blue and Pink*, that prompted Whistler's anguish over the possibility that his work and Albert Moore's looked too much alike. See Young et al., 1980, I, no. 86, p. 49. For a discussion of the Moore-Whistler relationship, see John Sandberg, "Whistler Studies," *Art Bulletin* 50 (March 1968):59–64.

7-12.8 See Maenad from Benghazi, third century B.C., no. 1856. 10.1.35. See also nos. 1863.7-28.412, an Aphrodite and Eros from Sicily, and 1868.7.5.13. All are in the collection of the British Museum.

7-12.9 Now at Hunterian Art Gallery, University of Glasgow.

7-12.10 Diaries, Book 12, Freer Archive.

7-12.11 Discussed in "Artist and Model."

7-12.12 The "Six Projects" have not been consistently exhibited in any particular order. In some cases, only a few of the paintings were shown. Once Freer owned the paintings, he lent them to memorial exhibitions in Boston, 1904, and Paris, 1905. As the exhibition history for this entry indicates, the paintings were catalogued in a different order each time.

7-12.13 See "Artist and Model," for a fuller discussion.

7-12.14 See Fenollosa, 1907, 57–66. Reproduced opp. p. 58.

7-12.15 Swinburne, pp. 373–374.

14.1 Anonymous, "The Whistler Exhibition at the Metropolitan Museum of Art," *Academy Notes* 5, 2 (April 1910):1.

14.2 See Pennell, 1911, p. 57. Mrs. Pennell published the oil as "attributed to Whistler" in Pennell, 1921, repr. opp. p. 25.

15.1 Pennell, 1908, I, p. 50.

15.2 Two oil sketches precede the work. See Young et al., 1980, I, nos. 95, 96, p. 56. In order to depict Leyland's legs correctly, Whistler hired a model to pose nude. Whistler etched the model as well. See Whistler's etching, *Fosco*, K99. Whistler later made an etched version of the Leyland portrait, giving the stiffly posed subject almost feminine curves. See K102, discussed in MacDonald, 1976, p. 37. For a discussion of Whistler's methods in portraiture, see Duret, 1917, pp. 69–72, and Pennell, 1911, p. 212.

18.1 According to Thomas R. Way, Whistler "more or less destroyed" some of his canvases, including a number of portraits, before giving them to the auctioneers. Canvases that were rejected by the auctioneers were acquired shortly thereafter by Way's father. See Young et al., 1980, I, no. 74, p. 43. This particular work does not show much evidence of willful defacement, but in its unfinished state would not have been very attractive to most buyers. The canvas was in fragile condition when Freer purchased it and has been relined and resurfaced since.

18.2 See Young et al., 1980, I, no. 184, p. 108. Whistler's technique in this thinly painted portrait is compared to a work from the mid-1870s, *Arrangement in Yellow and Grey: Effie Deans*. See I, no. 183, pp. 107–108.

18.3 For drawing see Way, 1912, repr. opp. p. 36. *The Gold Scab* is in the frame originally decorated to hold *The Three Girls*. Young et al., 1980, I, no. 208, pp. 120–121.

19.1 Located at the level just below Maud's protuberant knee, on the extreme right edge of the canvas as the viewer faces the painting, the butterfly is painted in dark reddish-brown pigment. It has become almost invisible over the years.

19.2 "Artist and Patron."

19.3 Another full-length oil that resembles the photograph is *Arrangement in Black and Brown: The Fur Jacket*, 1876, at the Worcester Art Museum. Repr. Young et al., 1980, II, pl. 124.

19.4 Henry James, *Democracy* (New York, 1981), pp. 194–195.

19.5 See Young et al., 1980, I, no. 186, p. 108. The art critic Duret is credited with this information. The subject was considered to be an American when Freer bought the picture.

20.1 Meier-Graefe, 1908, II, p. 206: Meier-Graefe found that Whistler easily handled "a multitude of straight, thin lines: to depict the ships' rigging, but his color was less choice." Young et al., 1980, I, no.

36, p. 16: the authors of the *catalogue raisonné* wrote that the rigging was "done with a certain lack of confidence" while "the strength of the painting lies in its colour."

20.2 The painter Augustus Egg and the novelist Charles Dickens were among them. The quarter developed around the wet docks along the Thames River during the late eighteenth and early nineteenth centuries. For information on the Thames I am most grateful to the Museum of the City of London.

20.3 *Illustrated London News* (19 January 1861), p. 1063.

21.1 See Young *et al.*, I, 1980, I, nos. 64, 65, 66, 67, pp. 37–39.

23.1 James McNeill Whistler, *Ten o'Clock Lecture* (London, 1888), p. 25.

23.2 Fenollosa, 1907, p. 62.

24.1 Whistler's japonesque paintings of the 1860s include Oriental art used as exotic props. See *The Golden Screen*, Plate 4, and *La Princesse du Pays de la Porcelaine*, Plate 5.

24.2 Freer noted that the view was taken from Whistler's studio in Lindsey Houses. Folder sheet, Freer curatorial records.

24.3 Whistler's use of the flag bearing his butterfly signature also recalls French modernists—in this case, Manet. The flag is supposed to be in the middle distance, but by placing it at the edge of the frame, Whistler creates surface tension that denies spatial recession. See Anne Coffin Hanson, "A Group of Marine Paintings by Manet," *Art Bulletin* 44 (1962):336.

25.1 See Young *et al.*, 1980, I, no. 119, pp. 72–73, for discussion.

25.2 See technical laboratory notes, folder sheet 02.97. At some point the painting was retouched with zinc white (zinc oxide). The retouches had whitened considerably by 1965, at which time the painting was cleaned, revarnished, restretched onto a new stretcher, filled, and inpainted before a protective varnish was applied.

25.3 Quoted in Philippe Jullian, *La Belle Epoque*, (exh. cat.) (New York: Metropolitan Museum of Art, 1982), p. 11.

26.1 At various times he called it "one of my finest, perhaps the most brilliant," and "surely one of the most important of the whole collection of pictures" (shown at Goupil in 1892). See Young *et al.*, 1980, I, no. 100, pp. 58–59.

26.2 *The Academy* (19 February 1876), quoted *ibid.*, p. 59.

26.3 Degas to Tissot, 19 November 1872, quoted in *Edgar Germain Hilaire Degas. Letters*, ed. Marcel Guerin (Oxford, 1948), p. 19. I am grateful to George T. M. Shackelford for this quotation and for many other helpful suggestions in the catalogue.

26.4 The misleading accession number would have been assigned as Freer began to inventory his collection for the eventual transfer to the Smithsonian Institution.

27.1 *The Atheneum* (1882), quoted in Young *et al.*, 1980, I, no. 179, p. 105.

27.2 Folder sheet, 97.21, Freer Archive. Thompson was a restorer who had relined and resurfaced the painting by 1925. It was again cleaned in 1965. At that time a "very thick-toned varnish" was removed.

28.1 See "Artist and Site."

28.2 See "Artist and Site." Figure 209, map of Cremorne Gardens.

29.1 The site's name was changed to Chelsea Square on 21 June 1937, probably to reduce confusion at the post office. See letter, John F. C. Phillips, Greater London Council Director-General's Department, the County Hall, London; to Miss Faul, 11 July 1977, curatorial file 08.169, Freer Archive.

29.2 *Bradshaw's Illustrated Tourist Handbook* (London, 1867).

29.3 A related pastel was auctioned by Galerie Wolfgang Ketterer in Munich. See their sales catalogue *14. Auktion 19. und 20. Jahrhundert*, 20–25 May 1975, no. 2020, repr.

30.1 *The Times*, London, quoted in Young *et al.*, 1980, I, no. 205, p. 119.

30.2 For a concise discussion of the painting's qualities, both veristic and decorative, see Young *et al., loc. cit.*

30.3 Jacques-Émile Blanche, *Essais et portraits* (Paris, 1912), p. 81. George Shackelford kindly brought this book to my attention.

31.1 The bridge was replaced in 1934. See Young *et al.*, 1980, I, no. 309, p. 152.

31.2 Quoted *ibid.*

32.1 See argument in Young *et al.*, 1980, I, no. 246, p. 136. Whistler offers a tantalizing glimpse of the address of the shop with the opened awning. One can make out "85 Bu . . . & Cro . . ." Further research may identify this shop.

31.2 Holden, 1969, p. 68. Holden notes that Whistler divided the panel into two horizontal rectangles of about equal size. The bottom one was left empty, but the top half was divided into four sections. Each of the four was then further divided.

32.3 No. 23 was described in a newspaper review as "more elaborate than the others." The amount of detail in *Chelsea Shops*, when compared to related works, has been the basis for believing it to be no. 23 at the Dowdeswell exhibition. The title of no. 23 was *Pink Note—Chelsea*. Rose reds dominate the two shops at the left of the Freer painting. There is a pink stripe on the awning of the third shop, and a bar of reddish pink along the top of the fourth.

33.1 See Peter Kroyer, *The Story of Lindsey House, Chelsea* (London, 1956).

33.2 Before he actually lived in the house, he lived next door at 7 Lindsey Row. Young *et al.*, 1980, I, no. 306, p. 152.

33.3 For a map pinpointing the location, see William Gaunt, *Chelsea* (London, 1954), p. 14.

34.1 Tom Pocock, *By Chelsea Reach* (London, 1970), p. 16.

34.2 *The Adam and Eve, Old Chelsea*, etching, K175. Perhaps Whistler etched directly onto the plate, for the scene appears in reverse.

34.3 Pocock, pp. 90–91.

35.1 Several of these are included in Young *et al.*, 1980, I, no. 264, pp. 142–143.

35.2 According to a note by Freer, the work was painted at St. Ives from January to March 1884. Curatorial file 04.315, Freer Archive.

35.3 See *Blue and Orange: Sweet Shop*, repr. in Young *et al.*, 1980, II, pl. 161.

36.1 Visual hymns to honest labor are typified by Ford Madox Brown's *Work*, painted in 1862–1865, repr. in Linda Nochlin, *Realism* (London, 1972), no. 69. For coal miners, see William Bell Scott's *Iron and Coal*, 1861, repr. Nochlin, fig. 114.

36.2 See Nochlin, "Hail the Worker-Hero," in *Realism*, pp. 111–137, for a discussion.

36.3 *Ibid.*, p. 157.

36.4 *Ibid.*, p. 139.

36.5 For the distinction, see *ibid.*

36.6 The oils were so quickly brushed on that the colors blended while still wet. Some of the abandoned mine's struts were created by washing oil pigment away. Whistler was greatly interested in watercolor at this time, and the technique resembles that of a watercolorist. Perhaps Whistler hoped that viewers unable to accept sketchy images might at least recognize the oil sketch as the honest artist's tool, just as the pick and shovel are the coal miner's.

37.1 On the Freer Gallery folder sheet, Susan Hobbs notes that Whistler wrote a letter from Wortley Hall. B/P II G 20, Birnie Philip collection, University of Glasgow.

37.2 Wortley was the seat of Lord Wharncliffe. Whistler could have been acquainted with the family. See Young *et al.*, 1980, I, no. 303, p. 151.

38.1 Holden, 1969, p. 58; James McNeill Whistler, *Ten o'Clock Lecture* (London, 1888), p. 14.

39.1 See Young *et al.*, 1980, I, no. 266, p. 143, for Whistler's letter to the dealer D. C. Thompson.

39.2 *Ibid.*

40.1 The painting cannot be identified by title in either exhibition.

42.1 For example, etchings *Limehouse*, K40, and *The Pool*, K43.

43.1 The frame originally bore a label written by the artist. It read "Gris et Argent—Le Bateau de Sauvetage" along with Whistler's signature and the address 21 Cheyne Walk, Chelsea, London.

43.2 Begun in 1881, the painting was reworked in Homer's studio in 1907, the year before Freer purchased it. Homer changed the setting from Tynemouth to the coast of New England.

43.3 Whistler to *The World* (22 May 1878). Quoted in Young *et al.*, 1980, I, p. lxiii.

44.1 See Young *et al.*, 1980, I, no. 282, p. 147.

46.1 It is difficult to know how the painting could ever have been labeled with the title *Green and Gold*.

46.2 See Young *et al.*, 1980, I, no. 298, p. 150.

47.1 See Young *et al.*, 1980, I, no. 330, p. 160.

48.1 This is the only oil in the Freer Gallery's Whistler collection that is not included in Young *et al.*, 1980.

48.2 Menpes served as a sort of whipping boy during Whistler's Holland trip in the company of William Merritt Chase. See Menpes, 1904, pp. 139–153.

49.1 The watercolor is actually brought to a greater state of finish than the oil. *La Petite Mephisto*, like the *Milly Finch*, is related to Manet's work. See discussion Plate 132.

49.2 The producer Hollingshead described the play as "one of our best short burlesques." John Hollingshead, *Gaiety Chronicles* (London, 1898), p. 376. Several productions at the Gaiety involved devil themes. *Robert the Devil*, starring Miss Faren, was the theater's first attempt at burlesque, shortly after the theater opened in the 1860s. Hollingshead, pp. 39–40; see also W. J. Macqueen-Pope, *Gaiety: Theatre of Enchantment* (London, 1949), p. 128. The Gaiety presented *Faust up to Date* beginning on 30 October 1888, although Nellie Farren was not in the cast. See Macqueen-Pope, pp. 265 ff. Whistler first expressed a desire to paint Miss Farren on 2 January 1878. Letter to T. Watts-Dunton, noted in Young *et al*, 1980, I, no. 196, p. 114. Several pen drawings of *Little Dr. Faust* were made by Whistler in October 1877.

49.3 Henry Morley, in *The Examiner*, quoted in Macqueen-Pope, p. 70.

49.4 Charles Baudelaire, "Women and Prostitutes," from *The Painter of Modern Life and Other Essays*, trans. Jonathan Mayne (London, 1964), p. 36.

50.1 An open fan signaled "I will wait for you," according to *The Mysteries of Love and Courtship Explained* (New York, 1890). I am grateful to George Shackelford for this information.

51.1 His aunt, Nelly Ionides, married Whistler's brother.

52.1 Young *et al.* point out that Whistler was in Dieppe in 1885 but made subsequent trips. They suggest a date of 1888 or 1889 for the painting on the basis of its rich palette. See Young *et al.*, 1980, I, no. 383, pp. 171–172.

52.2 Other butcher-shop images by Whistler include his early watercolor *Boutique de Boucher, Savergne* (Plate 79) and an etching, *Butcher's Shop, Sandwich*, K308.

54.1 See list of exhibitions above. Balli purchased the piece as *Brown and Gold: the Neighbours*.

55.1 Young *et al.*, 1980, suggest that the label may indicate Goupil purchased the painting directly from Whistler. See I, no. 443, p. 197.

55.2 *Ibid.*

57.1 For a discussion, see Young *et al.*, 1980, I, nos. 510–514, pp. 217–219.

57.2 Freer Diaries, Book 13, Freer Archive.

57.3 Faustina was the wife of the Roman emperor Marcus Aurelius, who ruled from A.D. 161 to 180. Although he was traditionally a paragon of morality, his empress was supposedly licentious. As a subject, Faustina appeared in Victorian poetry at the outset of Whistler's career. See, for example, "Faustine," in Algernon Swinburne, *Poems and Ballads* (Indianapolis, 1970), pp. 108–114.

59.1 For others, see Young *et al.*, 1980, I, nos. 463–466, 469–471a, b, c; pp. 203–205.

59.2 The photograph remained in his studio at the time of his death.

59.3 Freer Diaries, Book 12, Freer Archive.

60.1 See Young *et al.*, 1980, I, no. 504, pp. 215–216.

60.2 Freer to Agnes Meyer, 14 February 1910, Freer Archive, letter book vol. 29, no. 260.

60.3 "Whistler Exhibition: the Metropolitan Museum of Art," *Academy Notes* 5, no. 2 (April 1910). For somewhat more purple prose in the same vein, see Caffin, 1907, pp. 299–300.

60.4 The painting even inspired a fatuous romance by Mary Wagnalls, "The Little Lady Sophia of Soho," *Criterion* 4, no. 11 (February 1904): 25–27. The story ends, "I tell you we both saw it—saw the *Little Lady Sophia* smile."

60.5 Whistler sold the painting to Freer in 1899 but kept it for some time thereafter. By December 1900 the painting was in Detroit, but Freer did not actually pay for the painting until 1902.

61.1 Freer actually purchased the work on 23 November 1894, long before it was finished. The work was originally entitled *Harmony in Blue and Gold: The Little Blue Girl*.

62.1 The issue of Whistler's interest in Tanagra figurines may also have played a role. See Young *et al.*, 1980, I, no. 490, pp. 211–212.

62.2 *Ibid.*

62.3 See letter from Whistler to Heinemann, ca. 1898, quoted *ibid.*

62.4 Paid for in 1902, but not delivered until after the artist's death.

63.1 For a lengthy description, see W. J. Macqueen-Pope, *Gaiety: Theatre of Enchantment* (London, 1949), pp. 357–363.

63.2 The name of the model is not known, but Whistler wrote to Freer, "I am glad you have the little 'Cigale'—she is one of my latest pets—and of a rare type of beauty—the child herself I mean." Letter from Whistler to Freer, 29 July 1899, Freer Archive.

63.3 The English burlesque was written by John Hollingshead, proprietor of the Gaiety Theater in London. See Hollingshead, *Gaiety Chronicles* (London, 1898), pp. 376–377. The original play was by Meilhac and Halévy. For publicity purposes, Hollingshead deliberately put "the names of the French authors prominently in the bills, and [kept] my own name, as the journeyman-tinker, in the background."

63.4 His theater tickets and a copy of the play are in University of Glasgow Library, special collections.

63.5 Hollingshead later noted, "I was accused of bad taste in exhibiting caricatures of living people, as if no such thing existed as caricature journalism!" But Whistler had given his permission for the caricature, and Hollingshead later published Whistler's letter. Whistler, like Hollingshead, had a good nose for publicity.

63.6 Although Freer secured the work in 1899, he did not actually pay for *Rose and Brown* until May 1902.

64.1 Young *et al.*, 1980, I, p. lxix.

66.1 Freer Diaries, Book 12, Freer Archive.

66.2 The Arts Council of Great Britain, *James McNeill Whistler* (Ipswich, Suffolk, 1960), pp. 29–30.

66.3 Whistler's other major patron, Frederick Richards Leyland, had described the painting of his portrait as "my own martyrdom."

66.4 Freer to Frank J. Hecker, 13 June 1902, Box V, Freer Archive.

69.1 Horowitz, 1979–1980, p. 126.

72.1 The following are the dimensions for each dado panel, listed by acquisition number: 04.458, 58.0 × 26.5 cm.; 04.459, 50.5 × 32.7 cm.; 04.460, 50.5 × 32.8 cm.; 04.461. 58.5 × 42.6 cm.; 04.462, 49.7 × 32.8 cm.; 04.463, 51.5 × 37.0 cm.; 04.464, 51.1 × 37.0 cm.; 04.465, 50.8 × 36.8 cm.; 04.466, 51.1 × 36.8 cm.; 04.467, 51.1 × 36.8 cm.; 04.468, 51.1 × 36.8 cm.; 04.469, 51.1 × 36.8 cm.; 04.470, 43.3 × 25.0 cm.; 04.471, 43.8 × 37.2 cm.; 04.472, 51.1 × 36.8 cm.; 04.473, 51.5 × 36.8 cm.; 04.474, 44.8 × 36.8 cm.

72.2 Freer to Gustav Mayer at Obach and Company, London, 23 June 1904, Freer Archives. Freer bought the panels for £300. Besides Freer's seventeen panels, there are four in the collection of the Victoria and Albert Museum, London. However, only two are completed.

72.3 In a letter to his friend Charles C. Coleman, Freer described the Dutch metal process at length. He had learned it from a New York gilder and frame maker named Le Brocq: "First, prepare the ceiling with sufficient coats of paint mixed in oil to bring a smooth surface, using either white or any neutral tint most convenient, making the last coat a flat color, that is, using all turpentine. After the paint has become dry, apply one coat of size, use the French size if it is obtainable. Reduce the size with benzene; turpentine may be used, but benzene is far better. Let the size dry twelve hours; then apply the Dutch metal leaf, forcing the leaf into the crevices with a stiff brush. After all of the space has been covered with the leaf, apply one coat of lacquer made of one-third orange shellac and two-thirds grain alcohol. After the lacquer has dried, apply one or two coats of glazing to suit your taste. Let the glazing consist of low tone bitumen and Italian pink of quantities to suit, to which add one-third Japan dryer or any *siccative* and turpentine. You may find that one coat of glazing will be sufficient. Possibly two will look better, but of this you can judge best yourself. Of course, the quantity of bitumen to use in the glazing will be controlled largely by the amount of light you have in your room, and the quantity of brightness you wish the ceiling to have." Freer to Coleman, 12 December 1900, Freer Archives (FLB no. 106, vol. 7). A letter from Leyland to Whistler suggested the use of Dutch metal "like the hall dado" in the Peacock Room. Leyland to Whistler, 26 April 1876.

72.4 Freer to Coleman, 12 December 1900, Freer Archives.

72.5 Whistler moved to 2 Lindsey Row, now called 96 Cheyne Walk, in February 1867. He lived there for the next eleven years. See Young *et al.*, 1980, I, p. lxi.

72.6 Although the staircase drawing is inscribed "Layland House, Prince's Gate," the staircase does not conform to the configuration of the sweeping main stair at 49 Prince's Gate, nor does it indicate individual moldings that punctuate the dado in the Leyland design. Leyland's name is not even correctly spelled. The inscription was probably added later by Harold Wright, Rosalind Birnie Philip's adviser at Colnaghi, London dealers.

72.7 Owen Jones, "Proposition 10," in *The Grammer of Ornament* (London, 1868), p. 6.

72.8 Theodore Child, "A Pre-Raphaelite Mansion," *Harper's New Monthly Magazine* 82 (December 1890): 82.

72.9 The popular green and yellow color scheme was satirized in the operetta *Patience* by Gilbert and Sullivan: "A pallid and thin young man, A haggard and lank young man, A greenery-yallery, Grosvenor Gallery, Foot-in-the-grave young man." See Elizabeth Aslin, *The Aesthetic Movement: Prelude to Art Nouveau* (New York, 1981), p. 126.

72.10 The advertisement went on to mention "others a yard wide Embossed-work in imitation of Gilded Leather." This can be recognized as an important impetus for the use of leather hangings in the Peacock Room. Advertisement from *The Postman*, 1703, quoted in Alan V. Sugden and John L. Edmondson, *A History of British Wallpaper: 1509–1914* (London, ca. 1926), p. 40.

72.11 Jones, p. 8: "Imitations, such as the graining of woods, and of the various coloured marbles, allowable only when the employment of the thing imitated would not have been inconsistent."

72.12 Nancy McClelland, *Historic Wall-Papers. From Their Inception to the Introduction of Machinery* (Philadelphia, 1927), p. 29. "Dominotiers" began to paste book-size sheets of end paper into larger pieces to sell as wallpaper after the guild of booksellers and printers tried to limit their bookbinding activities.

72.13 *Ibid.*, p. 26.

72.14 Bacher, 1908, pp. 122 ff.

72.15 Child, 82.

72.16 *Ibid.* Child described the hall fully: "The first thing that strikes you when you enter the vast entrance hall, lighted by ample windows in the daytime and by electric lamps, distributed over the ceiling, at night, is the staircase, with its fine balustrade of gilt bronze. . . . The pillar from which the handrail starts is surmounted by two crowned female figures, one of which waves a long oriflamme. This group of gilt wood in all probability adorned originally the prow of a Venetian galley, and Sansovino may have designed it. The tonality of the hall and of the staircase, from the foot to the top of the house, is green. The whole is panelled in shades of willow. The dado of the darker shades is enriched with panels imitating aventurine lacquer, decorated with delicate sprigs of pale rose and white flowers in the Japanese taste. . . . On the walls of the staircase are hung Burne-Jones's *Circe*, Rossetti's *Loving-Cup*, Alphonse Legros' *Rehearsal*, while on the walls of the hall itself are placed the *Sea Spell*, the *Dis Manibus*, and *La Pia*, by Rossetti; *Cupid reviving Psyche*, by Burne-Jones; and a portrait of Rossetti by G. F. Watts, which give the key-note of Mr. Leyland's tastes. The place of honor in this house we shall find is divided between Dante Gabriel Rossetti and Sandro Botticelli. The furniture of the hall is effective and discretely rich. The mosaic floor is partly covered with Oriental rugs, and dotted here and there with gigantic vases of cloisonné enamel. In the centre is a circular divan, and around the walls gilt Venetian seventeenth-century chairs."

72.17 Jun'ichiro Tanizaki, *In Praise of Shadows*, trans. Thomas J. Harper and Edward G. Seidensticker (New Haven, 1977), p. 22.

73.1 See Plates 74, 77. Sam Weller drawing, Pomfret drawing.

73.2 See Gallatin, I, 1913, p. 23. Repeated verbatim in Gallatin, 1918, pp. 30–31. See also Lane, 1942, p. 81.

75.1 Reproduced in Pressley, 1972, p. 128.

77.1 John Ross Key believed the drawing was made during Whistler's sojourn at the Coast Survey in Washington, 1854–1855. It impressed Key as "the only drawing that I ever saw Whistler make at that time which could be called a picture." See Key, 1908, p. 929. For a related drawing, probably made at Westpoint, see *Sam Weller and Mary Fold a Carpet*, Pressley, 1972, no. 58, p. 153.

77.2 Charles Dickens, *The Pickwick Papers* (London, 1947), pp. 618–619. In the novel, the cobbler is bald and bearded.

77.3 Joseph Grego, *Pictorial Pickwickiana: Charles Dickens and His Illustrators*, 2 vols. (London, 1899), records only one illustration of the cobbler, by Alfred Crowquill, a pseudonym for Alfred Henry Forrester (vol. I, p. 347). Whistler might have seen it.

77.4 Dickens quoted in Way and Dennis, 1903, pp. 95–96.

78.1 Pennell, 1908, I, p. 72. Working from memory was one of the lessons absorbed by Whistler and others in Gleyre's studio.

82–89.1 The full title of the publication is *A Catalogue of Blue and White Nankin Porcelain Forming the Collection of Sir Henry Thompson, Illustrated by the Autotype Process from Drawings by James Whistler, Esq., and Sir Henry Thompson* (London, 1878). The book was published in an edition of 220 copies with a gold cover bearing a stamped prunus design.

82–89.2 Marks wrote, "The choice collections of Mr. Whistler, Mr. D. G. Rossetti, Mr. Louis Huth, and later, that of Sir Henry Thompson, have given an impulse to that appreciation for this branch of decorative art." Thompson, 1878, p. vi. Both Whistler's and Thompson's collections were sold at auction in 1880.

82–89.3 See MacDonald, 1978, p. 295.

82–89.4 Gabriel P. Weisberg, "Félix Bracquemond and Japanese Influence in Ceramic Decoration," *The Art Bulletin* 51 (1969):277–280. Other painters who designed ceramics include Monet, Gauguin, the Left-Bank Cubists, and Picasso.

82–89.5 See, for example, Alan S. Cole's diary entry for 16 November 1875: "Dined with Jimmy; Tissot, A. Moore and Captain Crabb. Lovely blue and white China—and capital small dinner. General conversation and ideas on art unfettered by principles. Lovely Japanese lacquer." Quoted Pennell, 1908, I, p. 189.

82–89.6 Anonymous quote, from C. G. Williamson, *Murray Marks and His Friends: A Tribute of Regard* (London and New York, 1919), p. 46.

82–89.7 Whistler to Fantin-Latour, 3 February 1864, Pennell collection, Library of Congress, quoted in MacDonald, 1978, p. 291.

82–89.8 I am grateful to Mrs. Josephine Knapp for this insight and for her help in analyzing the porcelain depicted in Whistler's illustrations.

82–89.9 Whistler to Marks, 29 December 1876. Facsimile reproduction, Williamson, opp. p. 48. Williamson erroneously dated the letter 1873.

82–89.10 MacDonald, 1978, pp. 292–293.

82–89.11 Whistler to Marks, 29 December 1876. Williamson commented, "The water-colour drawings passed out of Marks' possession into the hands of a well-known collector, and realized a very high figure. So high a price was, in fact, offered for them that Marks felt he was unable, with any ideas of economy, to retain them in his own hands" (p. 44).

90.1 A drawing on the recto of this sheet is discussed in the drawings section, plate 239.

90.2 By 1869, the artist had developed a monogram from the initials J. W. The monogram underwent various changes. See Young *et al.*, 1980, I, pp. xvii–xviii.

91.1 Otto Bacher did mention that Whistler used watercolor to correct or change proofs of some of his Venetian etchings. See Bacher, 1908, p. 115.

93.1 See *Rose and Brown, La Cigale*, Plate 63, and *Rose et Vert: Une Etude*, repr. Young *et al.*, 1980, II, pl. 315.

93.2 See Figure 72.2.

97.1 Young *et al.*, 1980, I, no. 5, p. 2. Neither the subject nor the whereabouts of the copy is known at present.

97.2 See Pennell, 1921, p. 120. Pennell's source was Walter Greaves, and the interview was conducted in about 1900. Asked to give an opinion whether a particular painting was a real Turner or a sham, Whistler is said to have replied, "Quite impossible, my dear Lady Eden, but, after all, isn't the distinction a very subtle one?" *Ibid.*, p. 228. For Whistler's comparison of Turner and Claude, see Pennell, 1908, II, p. 178.

98.1 MacDonald, 1976, p. 4.

99.1 Young *et al.*, 1980, I, p. lxiii.

109.1 Young *et al.*, 1980, I, p. lxiv. According to the Freer Gallery's curatorial records, the back of the frame once bore a label with an inscription in Whistler's hand reading "A little red note—Dordrecht. JH. McNeill Whistler" as well as a butterfly. This note has been removed since.

109.2 Young *et al.*, 1980, I, p. lxiv.

109.3 Newspaper cuttings pasted upon the verso include *Daily News*, n.d., and *The Academy*, 6 December 1884.

110.1 *Bradshaw's Handbook for Tourists in Great Britain and Ireland*, II (London, 1867), p. 37. St. Ives had both an old church and castle. There seems to be some confusion about the location depicted in this watercolor. The Pennells published the site as St. Ives in 1912, but as Lyme Regis in the *Whistler Journal* (1921). A list of "Studies by J. Mc N. Whistler" accompanied Freer's major purchases in 1905. In the margin of the entry "St. Ives" Freer wrote "Penzance curved." Folder 279, Whistleriana, Freer Archive. Until I manage a visit to these sites, however, I will accept the earliest location mentioned in the literature—that is, St. Ives.

110.2 The same composition is used for a watercolor, *Waterloo Bridge from the Savoy*, repr. Pennell, J., 1912, p. 38.

114–117.1 For a discussion, see "Artist and Site."

114–117.2 MacDonald, 1976, p. 48.

114–117.3 The etching was probably made in 1889. See *ibid.*, nos. 113–114, pp. 51–52.

119.1 Leon Seltzer, ed., *Columbia Lippincott Gazatteer of the World* (New York, 1952), p. 387.

120.1 Now at the Boston Museum of Fine Arts. Reprinted in Young *et al.*, 1980, II, no. 166.

120.2 Freer records suggests that *Chelsea Shops* might have been exhibited in 1904 as *Onstead, Surrey*. No. 81, entitled *Onstead, Surrey*, was owned by J. J. Cowan, who exhibited it in Edinburgh in 1904. Cowan sold *Chelsea Shops* to Freer in the same year. Perhaps this coincidence resulted in a confusion of titles.

121.1 Young *et al.*, 1980, I, p. lxviii. The company was not successful. It was in operation from about 1898 to 1901.

121.2 The Pennells later noted, "The Company of the Butterfly was to be his own incubator for his own golden eggs, but [it] succeeded chiefly in proving to him that dealers have their use. It was a nuisance to him almost to the end of his life, his landlord pursuing him to Corsica with bills for rent and complaints of the condition of the outside doorplate—the scheme perfect in theory, he thought, but the trouble was, he had no time for it." Pennell, 1921, p. 15. His other business venture, the Academie Carmen, was also unsuccessful. See also Pennell, 1908, II, pp. 199–200.

121.3 The reason for assigning the object a 1902 accession number is not clear.

122.1 These numbers probably indicate framing instructions.

122.2 "The two other watercolors I know to be by Whistler. I have had them since about 1884–85. One represents Maud in bed in 448 Fulham Road. The other is a French scene painted when he was staying with me in Dieppe in 1885." Sickert to Obach, undated, Xerox copy of letter in Curatorial File, 07.171, Freer Archive.

122.3 James McNeill Whistler, *Ten o'Clock Lecture* (London, 1888), p. 23.

123.1 *Baedeker's Northern France*, 3d ed. (Leipzig and London, 1899), pp. 286–287. See also Hachette, *Les Guides bleus: Val de Loire* (Paris, 1970), p. 447. For related etchings, see Kennedy, 1910, nos. 382–392.

124.1 Pencil sketches for two cabinets appear on the verso of this sheet and are discussed in the drawings section of the catalogue, Plate 221.

124.2 See Way's list, "Studies by J. McN Whistler," folder 279, Whistleriana, Freer Archive.

124.3 Gladys Taylor, *Old London Gardens* (London, 1953), pp. 126–127.

124.4 The chair upon which Maud sits is not typical of Victorian garden furniture. Rather, it resembles the stick chairs that are visible in photographs of Whistler's studios. The small table at the left seems to be a folding table, but the large table is hidden under a voluminous cloth.

124.5 Way's list "Studies by J. McN. Whistler." Freer's annotation reads, "Maud Seated, Breakfast in the garden of the Vale, Chelsea." For Whistler's residence, see Young *et al.*, 1980, I, p. lxiv.

124.6 Taylor, p. 127.

127.1 Duret also holds a red fan of the type seen in *Pink Note*. For the oil portrait of Théodore Duret, *Arrangement en coleur chair et noire*, 1883–1884, see Young *et al.*, 1980, II, pl. 159.

128.1 The work is entitled *The Convalescent*. It cannot be fully interpreted until we know Maud's malady, which could be anything from a cold to a pregnancy.

129.1 The house was designed by Salvin. See Nikolaus Pevsner, *The Buildings of England: Yorkshire: York and the East Riding* (Harmondsworth, 1972), pp. 41, 313.

130.1 *Pink Note* was exhibited in 1884. Two years later, a remarkably similar photograph was made by P. H. Emerson. Even if there is no specific link between the two, Emerson's work suggests the standardization of artistic response to a particular theme. His photograph, called *A Spring Idyl*, is illustrated in Helmut Gernsheim, *Masterpieces of Victorian Photography* (London, 1951), no. 60.

131.1 The couch is a modern form, the meridienne, which was developed during the Second Empire. It probably had casters and was movable. A similar folding table appears in Whistler's watercolor *Breakfast in the Garden*, Plate 124.

132.1 Compare also Manet's *Jeune Femme en costume espagnol*, 1862, and *Portrait of Nina de Callias (La Dame aux eventails)* ca. 1873, repr. in Anne Coffin Hanson, *Manet and the Modern Tradition* (New Haven, 1977), pl. III and fig. 60, respectively.

132.2 For related Whistler oils, see Plates 49 and 50.

132.3 See letter, Sickert to Obach, Xerox copy in Freer Object File, 07.170: "I have much pleasure in stating that the 2 watercolours shown me are by Whistler who gave them to me about 1884. Milly Finch on a sofa and a little Chelsea shop with a child."

134.1 See *Portrait of Miss Florence Leyland*, first state, repr. Young *et al.*, 1980, II, pl. 388.

134.2 Reproduced *ibid.*, pl. 72.

134.3 See oil paintings, Plates 15 and 19.

134.4 See Young *et al.*, 1980, I, no. 96, p. 107. The artist reduced the prominent flounce on the skirt and softened the almost angular *contrapposto* of the figure. However, as far as portraiture is concerned, Miss Leyland's face became comingled with that of Maud, who posed for the reworking of the portrait.

134.5 Quoted in Theodore Reff, "To Make Sculpture Modern," in *Degas: The Artist's Mind* (New York, 1976), pp. 239.

134.6 Quoted *ibid.*

134.7 Gauguin also made a sculpture that year. See Reff's discussion in *ibid.*

134.8 Letter from Henry Sandon, curator, Dyson Perrins Museum Trust, to author, 31 January 1983. I am extremely grateful to Mr. Sandon, and also to Ros Savill of the Wallace Collection, for helping me assess the statuette. The importance of the statuette in Whistler's mind at the time is suggested by its prominent placement in the photograph. The large bowl that also appears was another favorite prop of the artist. He used it in numerous compositions over a twenty-year period.

134.9 See Young *et al.*, 1980, I, no. 324, p. 158.

134.10 *Ibid.* At the time Blanchet owned a portrait of Henry E. Dixey, an American stage actor. See *ibid.*, no. 356, p. 165.

134.11 Whistler's reuse of imagery is further substantiated by a destroyed variant of *The Convalescent*, which can be found on the verso of *A Note in Green*. For the *The Convalescent*, see Figure 128.3.

135.1 See Albert Boime, *The Academy and French Painting in the Nineteenth Century* (London, 1971).

136.1 See Young *et al.*, 1980, I, nos. 378, 417–419.

136.2 See Rosalind Birnie Philip writing for Whistler to Freer, 25 October 1901, no. 50, Freer Archive.

136.3 These include paintings, watercolors, drawings, and prints. See Burns A. Stubbs, *Paintings, Pastels, Drawings, Prints, and Copper Plates by and Attributed to American and European Artists, Together with a list of Original Whistleriana, in the Freer Gallery of Art*, rev. ed. (Washington, D.C.: Smithsonian Institution, 1967).

137.1 Gustave Geffroy noted, "Les tableaux de ses formats restreints mettent aussi en scène des figurines précises, délicates, sveltes comme des statuettes colorées de Tanagra." In *La Vie artistique*, typewritten excerpt, 1891, Freer Library, p. 266. See typescript in Freer Library. He may have been making reference to a pastel. Whistler made more pastels than watercolors with Tanagralike surfaces.

138.1 See Plate 273 for further discussion.

139.1 Neither the original owner of the fan nor its current whereabouts are known at present.

140.1 For the Freer drawing, see Pressley, 1972, no. 41, p. 151. See also a related drawing, no. 34, p. 151.

140.2 Pressley suggests that this drawing might have been exhibited at the Copley Society's memorial exhibition in 1904 under the title *Benedictine Monks*. However, that drawing was lent by Mrs. W. McNeill Whistler, while the Freer records indicate that the drawing was purchased from Thomas Way in 1905. Perhaps Mrs. Whistler disposed of the drawing through Way.

141–144.1 For a related watercolor, see Plate 76.

145.1 Pressley, 1972, pp. 131–132, 152, no. 47.

146.1 John Ross Key, "Recollections of Whistler While in the Office of the United States Coast Survey," *Century Magazine* (April 1908), p. 929.

147.1 Young *et al.*, 1980, I, p. lviii.

147.2 Pressley, 1972, p. 139. The Freer drawing is reproduced as fig. 33, p. 146.

154.1 John Murray, *Handbook for Travellers in France* (London, 1854), p. 26.

154.2 See Young *et al.*, 1980, II, pls. 203, 207, 209, 239, 304, 321.

156.1 Compare, for example, J. B. Oudry's *Stone Bridge with a Mill*, a drawing now in the Louvre. Illustrated in Hal Opperman, *Jean-Baptiste Oudry*, 2 vols. (New York, 1977), II, fig. 27.

156.2 See Plate 220.

157.1 Quoted in Fleming, 1978, p. 142.

157.2 See *Whistler Sketching*, K25 1/2. Freer did not own a copy of this print.

158.1 Fleming, 1978, p. 142.

163.1 Frederick Wedmore, *Whistler's Etchings: A Study and a Catalogue*, 2d ed., rev. and enl. (London, 1899), no. 65.

163.2 Fleming, 1978, p. 142.

164.1 Gustave Flaubert, *The Sentimental Education* (Paris, 1869), p. 7.

164.2 Typed manuscript from Whistler's notebook, 1896, University of Glasgow Library, special collections.

165.1 Gustave Flaubert, *The Sentimental Education* (Paris, 1869), p. 8.

166.1 Fleming, 1978, p. 142.

167.1 Gustave Flaubert, *The Sentimental Education* (Paris, 1869), pp. 9–10.

168–171.1 Karl Baedeker, *The Rhine, Including the Black Forest and the Vosges*, 17th rev. ed. (Leipzig, 1911), p. 235. The building was erected by Lewis the Bavarian.

168–171.2 It is not clear whether Whistler's view looks north or south, which makes it difficult to identify the larger building.

172.1 Pennell, 1908, I, pp. 62–63.

176.1 George Alexander Cooke, *Cooke's Geography* (London, 1813), II, p. 573.

176.2 Élisée Reclus, *Nouvelle Geographie universelle: La Terre et les Hommes* (Paris, 1878), III, p. 573.

176.3 Pennell, 1908, I, pp. 61–64.

178.1 Élisée Reclus, *Nouvelle Geographie universelle: La Terre et les Hommes* (Paris, 1878), III, p. 573.

183.1 Fleming, 1978, pp. 41–42.

184.1 Whistler's reference to "la cave" probably means the boot of a coach, a joking reference to hitchhiking.

184.2 Fleming, 1978, p. 142, n. 51.

185.1 Quoted in Fleming, 1978, p. 129.

187.1 Quoted in Fleming, 1978, p. 142. The Freer accession sheet describes this drawing as "a man reclining on a bed, leaning against an upturned chair."

188–189.1 Pierre Larousse, *Grand Dictionnaire Universel du XIXe Siècle*, XII (Paris, 1874).

188–189.2 Both drawings in the Freer collection were originally given the title *La Marchande de Moutarde*, despite Whistler's own inscription on Plate 188. The mount of Plate 189 originally bore the inscription "S.H. 1858," but this was later erased.

190.1 Pennell, 1908, I, p. 62.

192.1 I am grateful to Margaret MacDonald for pointing out this information.

193.1 Pennell, 1908, I, p. 64.

195.1 Now at the Metropolitan Museum of Art. See Pressley's (1972) comparison, p. 147, figs. 36, 37.

196.1 Young *et al.*, 1980, I, p. 75.

199.1 Young *et al.*, 1980, I, no. 61, pp. 34–36.

200.1 Pennell, 1908, I, p. 56.

200.2 The etching was published in the fourth state as no. 11 of *Twelve Etchings from Nature (The French Set)*, 1859. Besides K13, there are two more etchings of Fumette, K56 and K57.

200.3 Pennell, 1908, I, p. 56.

200.4 From *Impressions de Ménage*, 2d series, No. 24, 1847. Reproduced in "Artist and Model," Fig. 66.

201.1 The subject is Annie Haden. Her father wrote on the drawing's mount "S.H. Drawing for At the Piano 1858 or 9." This inscription was erased on June 16, 1925. For a reproduction of the painting, see "Artist and Patron," Fig. 16.

201.2 For the history of the painting, see Young *et al.*, 1980, I, no. 24, pp. 8–9.

201.3 See "Artist and Patron," Fig. 16, and discussion.

204.1 Whistler to Thomas Way, 31 October 1893, letter no. 103, Freer Archive.

207.1 For rococo French image, see "Artist and Model," Fig. 80.

207.2 Kenneth L. Ames, "Oriental Forms and the Shape of Western Decorative Arts," *Journal of the Society of Architectural Historians* 35, no. 4 (December 1976):300.

213.1 Way's list "Studies by J. McN. Whistler," Folder 279, Whistleriana, Freer Archive.

215.1 See list, "Studies by J. McN Whistler," which accompanied Freer's acquisitions of 1905 from Thomas Way. Next to Way's entry "Niobe" Freer wrote in the margin "Pastel, Annabel Lee." Freer

Archive, folder 279, Whistleriana. The drawing has been called *Annabel Lee* since its exhibition in 1905.

215.2 Ronald Gotlesman *et al.*, *The Norton Anthology of American Literature*, 2 vols. (New York, 1979), p. 1226. Oil images entitled *Annabel Lee* are frontal views of a figure by a railing. In them, the figure looks a bit lively for a ghost. See Young *et al.*, 1980, I, nos. 79, 80, pp. 46–47.

215.3 James McNeill Whistler, *Ten o'Clock Lecture* (London, 1888), p. 18.

216.1 Another pounced cartoon, this one for the Peacock Room, survives at the University of Glasgow.

216.2 Young *et al.*, 1980, cite a letter ca. 1869 from Whistler to Thomas Winans, an American patron, with the comment "I send you a small photograph of the cartoon for the one of the pictures I am engaged upon. The figure itself is about small life size and will when painted be clad in thin transparent drapery, a lot of flowers and very light bright colour go to make up the picture." See I, no. 92, p. 55.

216.3 See Mary Frances Williams, *Catalogue of the Collection of American Art at Randolph-Macon Woman's College* (Charlottesville, 1977), pp. 168–169. Pounced cartoon repr. fig. 182c.

216.4 The oil sketch probably served the same purpose as any one of the "Six Projects," that is, it is intended to establish the composition and general color harmonies.

216.5 Another drawing with slightly different details is in the collection of Wesleyan University.

216.6 The letter was written in late April 1873. Whistler continued, "If you will have it sent for and put at once in hand, I will myself attend and assist all the next day when by Monday night it will be doubtless ready for hanging. If it be impossible to work at the photography on Sunday next, I can only say that you shall have the cartoon and canvas on the Monday, and my pupils shall work upon it during my absence, and I engage myself to return it to you coloured and ready to hang on the 1st of May." Whistler to Henry Cole, Box 1, Alan Cole letters, Pennell collection, Library of Congress.

216.7 Discussed in Young *et al.*, 1980, I, no. 92, p. 55.

216.8 Now in the collections of Johannisburg Art Gallery and City of York Art Gallery, respectively. The relation between Moore's *Venus*, which once belonged to F. R. Leyland, and Whistler's version is discussed in Spencer, 1972, p. 42. See also *Figure Cartoon for Battledore*, dated 1869. This drawing in black chalk on brown paper is a full-sized study of a female nude picked for transfer to canvas. No. 29, in *Albert Moore and His Contemporaries*, (exh. cat., Laing Art Gallery) (New Castle, 1972). I am grateful to Susan Hobbs for this information.

216.9 Whistler to Fantin, ca. 1868, copy of a letter once owned by Mary Cassatt, no. 263, Freer Archive.

217.1 See the discussion in Young *et al.*, 1980, I, no. 88, pp. 50–52.

217.2 See Plate 216. At an early stage of his work on the large picture for Leyland, Whistler is said to have used a pounced cartoon. The source was Pennell. See Young *et al.*, 1980, I, p. 50.

217.3 For a color illustration, see Young *et al.*, 1980, II, pl. 64.

218.1 One of the models for the painting was Marie Spartali, sister to Christine, who posed for Whistler's *La Princesse du Pays de la Porcelaine*. See sales catalogue, Sotheby's Belgravia, 6 October 1980, no. 24. The lot was a drawing for a female attendant in *Dante's Dream*, 1871. The painting is now at Walker Art Gallery, Liverpool.

220.1 See also photograph, in "Artist and Site," Figure 179.

220.2 The bridge would have looked highest at low tide.

220.3 Discussed in Young *et al.*, 1980, I, no. 139, p. 85.

221.1 The recto is a watercolor, *Breakfast in the Garden* (Plate 124).

222–223.1 The house itself had been opened as a public museum by 1895, only four years after the *Carlyle* was one of the first Whistler paintings to be acquired by a large public institution.

222–223.2 See "Artist and Site," Fig. 175.

222–223.3 The problem of ink sketches executed before or after paintings is vexing in Whistler's work. Sellin published the Freer ink drawing as a composition study *for* the oil, and I am inclined to agree. Sellin, 1976, pp. 64–65. In 1921 Elizabeth Pennell published the drawing as a sketch *after* the drawing, but she thought it belonged to Alan S. Cole, which was impossible since Freer acquired it in 1905. See Pennell, 1921, opp. p. 174. For a discussion of Whistler's many changes to the oil itself, see Young *et al.*, 1980, I, no. 137, p. 84.

222–223.4 She went on, "True, he does you no injustice, and, with his admirable penetration sees the disclaimer in your mind, so that you are not morally delinquent; but it is not pleasant to be unable to utter it." Edith Sitwell, *English Eccentrics* (Harmondsworth, 1971), pp. 163–164.

222–223.5 Quoted in Young *et al.*, 1980, I, no. 137, p. 82.

225.1 Young *et al.*, 1980, I, no. 110, p. 68; no. 107, pp. 66–67; no. 111, pp. 68–69.

225.2 *Ibid.*, pp. lxi–lxii.

227.1 Reproduced in Young *et al.*, 1980, II, no. 391.

228.1 See Young *et al.*, 1980, I, no. 111, pp. 68–69.

228.2 For a discussion of a copy possibly by Manet, see Theodore Reff, *Manet and Modern Paris: One Hundred Paintings, Drawings, Prints and Photographs by Manet and His Contemporaries* (exh. cat.) (Washington, National Gallery of Art, 1982), no. 31, p. 106. Reff also discusses the importance of the then-accepted idea that Velásquez had painted an actor.

228.3 Examples of portraits by Whistler that incorporate the pose of the arms, or the legs, or both included in Young *et al.*, II, nos. 128, 143, 178, 200, 218, 280.

228.4 Quoted *ibid.*, I, no. 111, p. 69.

229–234.1 Illustrated in "Artist and Model," Fig. 89. For history, see Young *et al.*, I, 1980, no. 106, p. 66. Whistler designed costumes for other sitters as well.

229–234.2 "Fashion represents nothing more than one of the many forms of life by the aid of which we seek to combine in uniform spheres of activity the tendency towards social equalization with the desire for individual differentiation and change." From Georg Simmel, "Fashion," in Donald N. Levine, ed. *On Individuality and Social Forms* (Chicago and London, 1971), p. 296. See also pp. 294–323.

229–234.3 *The Red Rag*, in Sutton, 1966, p. 58.

229–234.4 Baron Haussmann in *Confession d'un Lion Devenu Vieux*; quoted in Walter Benjamin, *Reflections, Essays, Aphorisms, Autobiographical Writings*, trans. Edmund Jephcott (New York and London, 1978), p. 159.

237.1 This drawing came from the Forbes collection, as did the drawings that may depict Fanny Leyland.

238.1 Bacher, 1908, p. 81.

239.1 A watercolor on the verso of this sheet is discussed in the watercolor section of the catalogue, Plate 90.

239.2 *Sketch of a Lady, Seated*, in Way, 1912, repr. opp. p. 96.

239.3 See *Reading*, repr. no. 9 in Susan Hobbs and Nesta Spink, *Lithographs of James McNeill Whistler from the Collection of Stephen Louis Block* (exh. cat.) (Washington, 1982), p. 45. Although drawing and lithograph do not correspond exactly, the composition is the reverse of *Seated Figure*, and both are drawn with the same vigorous, scribbling line.

240.1 Executed 1872–1873. For a discussion, see Young *et al.*, 1980, I, no. 129, pp. 78–79. A number of other related drawings are cited.

240.2 Young *et al.*, 1980, I, no. 131, pp. 79–80. The painting has also been associated with Whistler's series of "White Girls" and is catalogued at the Fogg Art Museum, its present owner, as *The White Girl No. IV.*

243.1. The figure in the lithograph appears in a flat profile view.

244.1 Getscher, 1970, pp. 105–106.

245.1 The *Studio* reproduction is somewhat misleading. It loses much of the bright red-orange that relates the central figure in the gondola to several roofs at the right. The blues are much brighter than the reproduction would suggest.

245.2 The gouache was given to the Art Institute of Chicago in 1933 by Walter S. Brewster, a collector of Whistleriana.

246.1 As Getscher has pointed out, the appearance of buildings in reverse suggests that Whistler was making his etchings directly onto the copper plates.

246.2 Bacher, 1908, pp. 76–77.

247.1 See Getscher, 1970, pp. 105–106.

248.1 The difference between the recto and verso of this sheet indicates the extent to which some of Whistler's paper supports have changed color in about one century's time.

248.2 See discussion of *The Doorway* (Fig. 251.1).

248.3 Getscher, 1970, p. 137.

248.4 Whistler press cuttings, *The Whitehall Review*, vol. 4, p. 57, quoted *ibid.*, p. 128.

249.1 Originally dark brown, the paper (site) has faded unevenly toward gray.

249.2 Originally, the backing of the frame had a label inscribed "Nocturne: San Giorgio" in the artist's hand, along with a butterfly.

249.3 She later wrote of Whistler's having "selected for me the pastels I gave you [Freer] for the museum." See Havemeyer, 1923. Others in the group include Plates 250, 258–260.

250.1 Originally, the backing of the frame had a label inscribed "The Steps" in Whistler's hand, along with a butterfly.

250.2 There is probably a different drawing underneath the present one, but the composition is difficult to make out. Nonetheless, Whistler's application of chalks is dictated to some degree by his desire to cover the earlier lines.

250.3 Whistler to his mother, undated, autograph letter, Freer Archive, no. 176. Quoted Getscher, 1970, p. 118.

251.1 Whistler made a similar decision for *The Garden*, one of the Venetian etchings (K210). One of two boys on the steps was replaced by a cat. See Getscher, 1970, pp. 89–90.

251.2 The pastel was another of the most expensive in the 1881 exhibition. It was priced at forty guineas. Apparently it did not immediately find a buyer. See Getscher, 1970, p. 285.

252.1 It was noted in *The Whitehall Review* that the drawing was one of several that "mar the general excellence." Whistler press cuttings, vol. IV, p. 57, quoted Getscher, 1970, p. 128. It would have stood out from the others, and it was expensive, priced at forty guineas. The drawing remained unsold at the end of the exhibition. See Getscher, p. 286.

253.1 The sheet is unevenly faded.

254.1 An etching, also called *Quiet Canal*, is similar in general composition, but it is a daylight scene, filled with detail. The architecture in the etching does not exactly match that seen in the drawing. See K214.

255.1 The narrow passage, the doorway at the end, and the vertical format are all familiar design elements in Whistler's series of Venetian views.

255.2 Priced at forty guineas and sold out of the exhibition, *Bead-Stringers* was one of the more elaborate pastels shown at the Fine Art Society in 1881. See Getscher, 1970, Appendix II, p. 287, based on Joseph Pennell's catalogue of the exhibition, with notes made by the dealer D. C. Thompson.

256.1 See, for example, *The White Symphony: Three Girls* (Plate 11).

256.2 Harry Quilter, quoted by Whistler in *Mr. Whistler and His Critics*, exhibition catalogue, reprinted *The Gentle Art of Making Enemies* (1892; reprinted New York, 1967), p. 98.

256.3 See Way, 1903, thumbnail sketches following p. 52; no. 8, *Little Calle in San Barnaba: Gold and Brown*; and no. 41, *Note in Flesh Colour and Red*. Unfortunately Way's reproductions are not in color, but the pinks and blues of this drawing do not seem to fit with either title.

258.1 The support is no longer evenly colored.

258.2 Originally, the backing of the frame had a label inscribed "Winter Evening" in the artist's hand, along with a butterfly.

258.3 Bacher, 1908, pp. 75–76.

258.4 See Getscher, 1970, pp. 120–121.

259.1 Originally the backing of the frame had a label inscribed "Sunset in red and brown—" in the artist's hand, along with a butterfly.

259.2 Getscher, 1970, discusses Whistler's use of the sheet to deal with different problems (pp. 95–96).

259.3 For example, the buildings are found in the background of two etchings of *The Riva*, K192 and K206. Getscher discusses this issue (*ibid.*, pp. 96–97). It is important to add that Whistler brought the practice of reused motifs with him to Venice, having already based many of his figure drawings around stock poses from the "Six Projects." At least one figure in a Venice etching is plucked out of the "Six Projects" and rendered in miniature. The stooping woman in *The Doorway*, K188, also seen in the etching *Tillie a Model*, K117, is derived from the figure on the left in *The White Symphony: Three Girls*.

259.4 Priced at twenty guineas, *Sunset* was one of the least expensive drawings in the exhibition. The drawing remained unsold but eventually was chosen by Whistler himself for Mrs. Havemeyer's collection.

259.5 Further evidence of experimentation is offered by the Freer Gallery's copy of the related etching, *The Balcony*, upon which the artist drew in ink, darkening the spaces between the volutes that support the balcony.

260.1 Robert Getscher has argued that this drawing was executed just before Whistler left Venice for London in November 1880. See Getscher, 1970, pp. 120–121. The basis for his argument is the drawing's refined balance between black line, color, and empty brown paper.

260.2 Originally, the backing of the frame had a label inscribed "Campo S. Marta—Winter evening—" in the artist's hand, along with a butterfly.

261.1 Whistler to his mother, undated, autograph letter, no. 176, Freer Archive. Quoted in Getscher, 1970, p. 118.

263.1 See Young *et al.*, 1980, I, no. 229, p. 129.

264.1 According to the curatorial sheet (which cites the "Original Whistler List"), this drawing was previously part of the Ionides and Samura collections.

265.1 Way also noted, "It is now in Mr. Freer's collection, and I made a lithograph of it in colour for M. Duret's *Life*." Way, 1912, pp. 55–56.

266.1 Reproduced Levy, 1975, no. 57. The image is quite smudged. It was not recorded by Thomas Way in his list of lithographs, and Freer did not bother to acquire a print for his collection. The Kennedy number is 163.

267.1 Pennell, 1908, II, p. 57.

267.2 According to a note in the Freer curatorial file, this was the drawing exhibited.

269.1 An etching similar to this figure was made around 1873. See *Tillie a Model*, K147. A male figure takes the same pose at the left of *The Little Forge*, K117. The figures from *The White Symphony* reappear in *Pink and Grey: Three Figures*, 1879. This is typical of Whistler's reemployment of standard poses with slight variations, such as the reversal of the figure's direction or the turning of a head.

270.1 "Memorandum of Payments Made to J. McNeill Whistler, June 16th, 1902," typescript, dated Detroit, 25 August 1902. Freer Archive.

270.2 In an oval cartouche: "W. Holland, Frame Maker and Mount Cutter, 12 Sherwood St., Golden Square, W."

271.1 For related etchings, see K121 and K343.

272.1 For watercolor on verso of Plate 271 see Plate 94. Whistler has incorporated a lobed form on the left arm of the sofa. Two of the lobes are colored green—it is not a distinct butterfly signature but could be interpreted as such. There is no question of the work's authenticity.

272.2 Illustrated in "Artist and Model," Figure 102.

272.3 "Memorandum of Payments Made to J. McNeill Whistler, June 16th, 1902," typescript, dated Detroit, 25 August 1902, Freer Archive. The pastel is referred to as "A Woman lying on a sofa with her head low down."

273–277.1 Carol Duncan, "Happy Mothers and Other New Ideas in French Art," *Art Bulletin* 55 (December 1973):570–583.

273–277.2 See Young *et al.*, 1980, I, nos. 434, 435, 491, 496. Lily was born in about 1874 and was the middle child. Brought to London around 1884, Lily and her two sisters Hetty and Rose posed for many artists, including Poynter, Leighton, Val Prinsep, and Sargent. See *ibid.*, no. 434, p. 192. Whistler painted an oil portrait of Lily in about 1895.

273–277.3 All of his offspring were illegitimate.

273–277.4 See "Memorandum of Payments Made to J. McNeill Whistler, June 16th, 1902." "A young girl seated on a sofa, holding a doll," erroneously entitled *The Violet Cap* was "Left with Mr. Whistler to work on." This must have been *The Green Cap* (Plate 276). In addition, "A woman lying on a sofa with her head low down" was "Left with Mr.

Whistler to add some orange." This was *Sleeping* (Plate 272). Typed manuscript, Detroit, 25 August 1902, Freer Archive. Another drawing left behind for color work was *Writing on the Wall* (Plate 270).

273–277.5 In the case of the mother-and-child drawings, the color of the paper support is fairly uniform, a warm gray-brown. However, the papers are not identical, and they vary considerably in roughness of surface. For printed images related to the drawings, see etchings K347 and K348, and lithographs K80, K102, K134, K135, and K136.

279.1 Compare with *Greek Girl*, Plate 205.

279.2 See lithographs, K30 and K161.

281.1 Fuller made her debut there on 5 November 1892. Eventually her stage devices included a patented glass stage, surrounded by black fabric, and colored gels through which electric light was projected. See Margaret Haile Harris, *Loie Fuller, Magician of Light*, exh. cat. (Richmond Museum of Art, 1979), p. 16.

281.2 Mallarmé published an essay on Fuller in the *National Observer* on 13 March 1893.

281.3 Harris (p. 15) describes Fuller as an unreliable source of information about herself, prone to embroidering the truth: "Recognizing the importance of publicity, she would, when public interest subsided, instigate a lawsuit or announce a dramatic illness." The parallel with Whistler's quarrelsome public behavior is striking.

281.4 *Ibid.*

281.5 Charles Henry Caffin, "The Art of James McNeill Whistler: A Lecture . . . at the Detroit Museum of Art, Friday, April 23rd, 1908," p. 34. Ms., Freer Archive.

281.6 From Loie Fuller, *Fifteen Years of a Dancer's Life* (Boston, 1913), quoted Harris, p. 28. For a gilt bronze of Miss Fuller that closely resembles the pose of *Venus Astarte*, see Harris, no. 51.

281.7 Roger Marx on Fuller, quoted in Harris, p. 18.

282.1 The back of the frame originally bore a label "Portrait of Emily Tuckerman by J. McN. Whistler—LONDON, Aug. 1898. *Pastel*, should not be shaken or jarred" (not in the artist's hand).

282.2 The drawing was actually bequeathed to the gallery by Miss Tuckerman. But in order to adhere to the provisions of the Freer will, the drawing was passed through Mrs. Draper and Platt.

283–293.1 The one exception is the Whistler-Leyland quarrel of spring 1877, which is not included in the book. Perhaps Whistler soft-pedaled this dispute because of his friendship with the Leyland children and the estranged wife of his former patron.

283–293.2 Ellen Moers, *The Dandy: Brummell to Beerbohm* (New York, 1960), p. 261.

283–293.3 Ivor Guest, *The Ballet of the Second Empire*, vol. II, pp. 19–21. Whistler was an avid theatergoer, beginning as a student.

283–293.4 Baudelaire, "Les Phares," p. 354, written ca. 1845–1846; first published 1855.

283–293.5 See *Venus Astarte*, Plate 281.

283–293.6 See James McNeill Whistler, *The Gentle Art of Making Enemies* (1892; reprinted New York, 1967), pp. 11, 20, 183. The butterfly on page 201 is the same as that on page 11.

294.1 See lithographs, K20, for the Stanhope reference. There is also a photograph of this letter in the Pennell collection at the Library of Congress.

301.1 See lithographs, K53.

Bibliography

Bacher, 1908. Otto Bacher, *With Whistler in Venice* (New York, 1908).

Baldry, 1903. A. L. Baldry, "James McNeill Whistler: His Art and Influence," *The Studio* 39 (October, 1903):237–245.

Becker, 1959. Eugene Matthew Becker, *Whistler and the Aesthetic Movement* (Ph.D. diss., Princeton University, 1959); Ann Arbor: University Microfilms, 1981.

Bell, 1905. Nancy R. E. Bell, *James McNeill Whistler* (London, 1905).

Bénédite, 1905. Leonce Benedite, "Artistes contemporains: Whistler," *Gazette des Beaux-Arts* 33 (1905):403–410, 496–511; 34 (1905):142–158, 231–246.

Berger, 1980. Klaus Berger, *Japonismus in der westlichen Malerei* (Munich, 1980).

Bloor, 1906. Alfred Janson Bloor, "The Beginnings of James McNeill Whistler," *Critic* 48, no. 2 (February 1906):123–135.

Born, 1948. Wolfgang Born, *American Landscape Painting: An Interpretation* (New Haven, 1948).

Brinton, 1910. Christian Brinton, *Masterpieces of American Painting: A Selection of Photogravures after Paintings Exhibited at the Royal Academy of Arts, Berlin, 1910* (New York, 1910).

Caffin, 1907. Charles H. Caffin, *The Story of American Painting* (New York, 1907).

Caffin, 1913. Charles H. Caffin, *American Masters of Painting* (New York, 1913).

Cary, 1907. Elizabeth Luther Cary, *The Works of James McNeill Whistler: A Study, with a Tentative List of the Artist's Works* (New York, 1907).

Chisaburo, 1980. Yamada Chisaburo, ed., *Japonisme in Art: An International Symposium* (Tokyo: Committee for the Year 2001, 1980).

Clark, 1979. Henry N. B. Clark, "Charles Lang Freer: An Aesthete in the Gilded Era," *American Art Journal* 11, no. 4 (October, 1979):54–68.

Cox, 1905. Kenyon Cox, *Old Masters and New* (Freeport, N.Y., 1905).

Curry, 1983. David Park Curry, "Charles Lang Freer and American Art," *Apollo* 118, no. 258 (August 1983):164–179.

Dewhurst, 1904. W. Dewhurst, *Impressionist Painting* (London, 1904).

Dreyfus, 1907. Albert Dreyfus, "James Abbott McNeill Whistler," *Kunst für Alle* 22 (February, 1907):201–220.

Du Maurier, 1969. Daphne du Maurier, ed. *The Young George du Maurier: A Selection of His Letters, 1860–67* (Westport, Conn. 1969).

Duret, 1904. Theodore Duret, *Histoire de J. McN. Whistler et de son oeuvre* (Paris, 1904).

Duret, 1917. *Whistler*, trans. Frank Rutter (London and Philadelphia, 1917).

Eddy, 1903. Arthur J. Eddy, *Recollections and Impressions of James A. McNeill Whistler* (Philadelphia and London, 1903).

Fenollosa, 1903. Ernest F. Fenollosa, "The Place in History of Mr. Whistler's Art," *Lotus: In Memoriam: James A. McNeill Whistler* (Special Holiday Number, December 1903):14–17.

Fleming, 1978. Gordon Fleming, *The Young Whistler* (London, 1978).

Forthuny, 1903. Pascal Forthuny, "Notes sur James Whistler," *Gazette des Beaux-Arts* 30 (November, 1903):381–390.

Gallatin, 1904. A. E. Gallatin, *Whistler's Art Dicta and Other Essays* (Boston, 1904).

Gallatin, 1907. A. E. Gallatin, *Whistler: Notes and Footnotes and Other Memoranda* (New York, 1907).

Gallatin, 1913, I. A. E. Gallatin, *Portraits and Caricatures of James McNeill Whistler, an Iconography* (London, New York, and Toronto, 1913).

Gallatin, 1913, II. "Whistler: The Self-Portraits in Oil," *Art in America* 1 (July 1913):151–158.

Gallatin, 1918. A. E. Gallatin, *Portraits of Whistler: A Critical Study and an Iconography* (New York, 1918).

Getscher, 1970. Robert Getscher, *Whistler and Venice* (Ph.D. diss., Case Western Reserve University, 1970); Ann Arbor: University Microfilms, 1971.

Gray, 1965. Basil Gray, "Japonisme and Whistler," *Burlington Magazine* 107 (June 1965):324.

Hartmann, 1910. Sadakichi Hartmann, *The Whistler Book* (Boston, 1910).

Havemeyer, 1923. Louisine Havemeyer, "The Freer Museum of Oriental Art," *Scribner's* 73, no. 5 (May 1923): 529–540.

Hayward, 1979. Mary E. Hayward, "The Influence of the Classical Oriental Tradition," *Winterthur Portfolio* 14, no. 2 (Summer 1979):107–142.

Heilbut, 1903. *Emil Heilbut*, "Die Sammlung Linde in Lübeck," *Kunst und Kunstler* 2, no. 1 (October 1903): 19.

Hobbs, 1977. Susan Hobbs, "A Connoisseur's Vision: The American Collection of Charles Lang Freer," *American Art Review* 4 (August 1977):76–101.

Hobbs, 1981. Susan Hobbs, "Whistler at the Freer Gallery of Art," *Antiques* (November, 1981):1192 ff.

Holden, 1969. Donald Holden, *Whistler Landscapes and Seascapes* (New York, 1969).

Honeyman, 1951. T. J. Honeyman, *Whistler: Arrangements in Grey and Black* (exh. cat.) (Glasgow: Corporation of the City of Glasgow, Glasgow Art Gallery, 1951).

Honour, 1961. Hugh Honour, *Chinoiserie: The Vision of Cathay* (London, 1961).

Hoopes, 1972. Donelson F. Hoopes, *The American Impressionists* (New York, 1972).

Horowitz, 1979–1980. Ira Horowitz, "Whistler's Frames," *Art Journal* 39, no. 2 (Winter 1979–1980):124–131.

Johnson, 1981. Ron Johnson, "Whistler's Musical Modes: Symbolist Symphonies, Numinous Nocturnes," *Arts Magazine* 55, no. 8 (April 1981):164–176.

Kennedy, 1910. Edward G. Kennedy, *The Etched Work of Whistler, Illustrated by Reproductions in Collotype of the Different States of the Plates* (1910; New York, 1914; reprinted San Francisco, 1978).

Kennedy, 1914. *The Lithograph by Whistler.* Illustrated by reproductions in photogravure and lithograph, arranged according to the catalogue by Thomas R. Way with additional subjects not before recorded. (New York, 1914).

Lancaster, 1952. Clay Lancaster, "Oriental Contributions to Art Nouveau," *Art Bulletin* 34, no. 4 (1952):297–310.

Lancaster, 1963. Clay Lancaster, *The Japanese Influence in America* (New York, 1963).

Lane, 1942. James Warren Lane, *Whistler* (New York, 1942).

Laver, 1930. James Laver, *Whistler* (London, 1930).

Laver, 1951. James Laver, *Whistler*, 2d ed. rev. (London, 1951).

Levy, 1975. Mervyn Levy, *Whistler Lithographs: A Catalogue Raisonné* (London, 1975).

MacDonald, 1976. Margaret MacDonald, *Whistler, the Graphic Work: Amsterdam, Liverpool, London, Venice* (exh. cat.) (London: The Arts Council of Great Britain, 1976).

MacDonald, 1978. Margaret MacDonald, "Whistler's Designs for a Catalogue of Blue and White Nankin Porcelain," *Connoisseur* 198 (August 1978):290–295.

Matsuki, 1903. B. Matsuki, ed. "Whistler Memorial Exhibition," *Lotus: In Memoriam: James A. McNeill Whistler* Special Holiday Issue (1903):7–9.

Mauclair, 1905. Camille Mauclair, *DeWatteau à Whistler* (Paris, 1905).

Maus, 1904. Octave Maus, "Whistler in Belgium," *Studio* 32, no. 135 (July 1904):7–10.

Mechlin, 1907. Leila Mechlin, "The Freer Collection of Art," *Century Illustrated Monthly Magazine* 73, no. 3 (January 1907):357–370.

Meier-Graefe, 1908. Julius Meier-Graefe, *Modern Art*, trans. F. Simmonds and G. W. Chrystal, 2 vols. (London and New York, 1908).

Menpes, 1904. Mortimer Menpes, *Whistler As I Knew Him* (London, 1904).

Meyer, 1927. Agnes E. Meyer, "The Charles L. Freer Collection," *Arts* 12, no. 2 (August 1927):65–82.

Mullikin, 1905. Mary Augusta Mullikin, "The International Society's Whistler Exhibition" and "Reminiscences of the Whistler Academy," *Studio* 34 (April–May 1905):223–233, 237–239.

Newton and MacDonald, 1978. Joy Newton and Margaret F. MacDonald, "Search for a European Reputation," *Zeitschrift für Kunstgeschichte* 41 (1978):148–159.

Pennell, 1908. Elizabeth Robins Pennell and Joseph Pennell, *The Life of James McNeill Whistler*, 2 vols. (London and Philadelphia, 1908).

Pennell, 1911. Elizabeth Robins Pennell and Joseph Pennell, *The Life of James McNeill Whistler*, 5th ed. rev. (Philadelphia, 1911).

Pennell, E., 1912. E. R. Pennell, "Whistler as a Decorator," *Century Magazine* 73 (February, 1912):500–513.

Pennell, J., 1912. Joseph Pennell, "The Triumph of Whistler," *Bookman* 43, no. 253 (October, 1912):19–30.

Pennell, 1921. E. R. Pennell, *The Whistler Journal* (Philadelphia, 1921).

Pousette-Dart, 1924. Nathaniel Pousette-Dart, *James McNeill Whistler* (New York, 1924).

Pressley, 1972. Nancy D. Pressley, "Whistler in America: An Album of Early Drawings," *Metropolitan Museum Journal* 5 (1972):125–154.

Prideaux, 1970. Tom Prideaux, *The World of Whistler* (New York, 1970).

Reff, 1976. Theodore Reff, "The Butterfly and the Old Ox," in *Degas: The Artist's Mind* (New York, 1976), pp. 15–36.

Rossetti, 1903. William M. Rossetti, ed., *Rossetti Papers, 1862–1870* (London, 1903).

Sandburg, 1964. John Sandburg, "Japonisme and Whistler," *Burlington Magazine* 106 (November, 1964):500–507.

Sandburg, 1966. John Sandburg, "Whistler's Early Work in America, 1834–1855," *Art Quarterly* 29, no. 1 (1966):46–59.

Sandburg, 1968. "Whistler Studies," *Art Bulletin* 50 (March 1968):59–64.

Scott, 1903. William Scott, "Reminiscences of Whistler, Some Venice Recollections," *Studio* 30 (November, 1903):97–107.

Sellin, 1976. David Sellin, *American Art in the Making: Preparatory Studies for Masterpieces of American Painting, 1800–1900* (exh. cat.) (Washington, D.C.: Smithsonian Institution, 1976).

Sickert, B., 1908. Bernhard Sickert, *Whistler* (London and New York, 1908).

Sickert, O., 1903. Oswald Sickert, "The Oil Paintings of James McNeill Whistler," *Studio* 30 (October, 1903):3–10.

Spencer, 1972. Robin Spencer, *The Aesthetic Movement* (London and New York, 1972).

Staley, 1971. Alan Staley, ed., *From Realism to Symbolism: Whistler and His World* (exh. cat.) (New York: Columbia University Press, 1971).

Starr, 1908. Sidney Starr, "Personal Recollections of Whistler," *Atlantic Monthly* 101 (April, 1908):528–537.

Studio Portfolio, 1905. *The Studio Whistler Portfolio* (London, 1905).

Sutton, 1964. Denys Sutton, *Nocturne: The Art of James McNeill Whistler* (Philadelphia and New York, 1964).

Sutton, 1965. Denys Sutton, "Proust and His World," *Apollo* 82 (August 1965):118–127.

Sutton, 1966. Denys Sutton, James McNeill Whistler: Paintings, Etchings, Pastels and Watercolours (London, 1966).

Sweet, 1968. Frederick A. Sweet, *James McNeill Whistler* (exh. cat.) (Chicago: Art Institute of Chicago, 1968).

Taylor, 1978. Hilary Taylor, *James McNeill Whistler* (London, 1978).

Thompson, 1878. *A Catalogue of Blue and White Nankin Porcelain Forming the Collection of Sir Henry Thompson, Illustrated by the Autotype Process from Drawings by James Whistler, Esq., and Sir Henry Thompson* (London, 1878).

Way, 1903. T. R. Way, Jr., "Mr. Whistler as a Lithographer," *Studio* 30 (December, 1903):10–21.

Way, 1912. T. R. Way, Jr., *Memories of James McNeill Whistler, the Artist* (London and New York, 1912).

Way and Dennis, 1903. T. R. Way and G. R. Dennis, *The Art of James McNeill Whistler: An Appreciation* (London, 1903).

Weisberg, 1975. Gabriel P. Weisberg *et al.*, *Japonisme: Japanese Influence on French Art, 1854–1910* (exh. cat.) (Cleveland: Cleveland Museum of Art, 1975).

Young *et al.*, 1980. Andrew McLaren Young, Margaret MacDonald, Robin Spencer, and Hamish Miles, *The Paintings of James McNeill Whistler*, 2 vols. (New Haven and London, 1980).

Exhibition List

1862. London. RA. *94th Exhibition of the Royal Academy of Arts.*

1865. Paris. Salon. *83d Exhibition, Oeuvrages de peinture, sculpture, architecture, gravure et lithographie des artists vivants,* Palais des Champs-Elysées, 1 May–20 June.

1865. London. RA. *97th Exhibition of the Royal Academy of Arts.*

1867. Paris. Salon. *85th Exhibition,* 15 April–5 June.

1870. London. RA. *102nd Exhibition of the Royal Academy of Arts.*

1872. London. SFA. Society of French Artists, *5th Exhibition,* Deschamps Gallery, 168 New Bond Street, opened 4 November.

1872. London. Int. Exh. *International Exhibition.* Fine Art Department, South Kensington Museum.

1872. London. Dudley Gallery. *6th Winter Exhibition of Cabinet Pictures in Oil,* Egyptian Hall, Piccadilly.

1873. London. Dudley Gallery. *7th Winter Exhibition of Cabinet Pictures in Oil,* Egyptian Hall, Piccadilly.

1873. London. SFA. Society of French Artists, *6th Exhibition,* opened 21 April.

1873. Paris. Durand-Ruel. Galerie Durand-Ruel, January (catalogue untraced).

1874. New York. Met. *Loan Exhibition of Paintings,* Metropolitan Museum of Art, March.

1874. London. *Mr. Whistler's Exhibition,* Flemish Gallery, 48 Pall Mall, opened 8 June (Whistler's first one-man show).

1875. Brighton. *Second Annual Exhibition of Modern Pictures,* Corporation of Brighton, Royal Pavilion Gallery, opened 9 September.

1876. Baltimore. *Academy Charity Exhibition,* Academy of Music, 16–30 March (catalogue untraced).

1876. London. SFA. Society of French Artists, *12th Exhibition,* Deschamps Gallery, 168 New Bond Street, spring.

1878. New York. Lotos Club (catalogue untraced).

1878. London. Grosvenor. Grosvenor Gallery, *II Summer Exhibition,* 1 May–5 August.

1879. Glasgow. White. Mr. White's North British Galleries, January (catalogue untraced).

1879. Glasgow. GIFA. *18th Exhibition of Works of Modern Artists,* Glasgow Institute of the Fine Arts, February–April.

1881. New York. Met. *Loan Collection of Paintings,* Metropolitan Museum of Art, May–October.

1881. New York. Union. The Union League Club, October (catalogue untraced).

1881. London. Fine Art Society, private view of fifty-three Venice pastels, 29 January.

1882. London. Grosvenor. Grosvenor Gallery. *VI Summer Exhibition,* 1 May–31 July.

1883. London. Grosvenor. Grosvenor Gallery. *VII Summer Exhibition,* 1 May–30 July.

1883. Paris. Petit. *Exposition Internationale de Peinture,* Deuxième année, Galerie Georges Petit, 8 Rue de Sèze, 11 May–10 June.

1884. London, Dowdeswell. *'Notes'—'Harmonies'—'Nocturnes,'* Messrs. Dowdeswell, 133 New Bond Street, May (catalogue designed by Whistler).

1884. Dublin. *Annual Exhibition of Sketches, Pictures and Photography,* Dublin Sketching Club, Leinster Hall, 35 Molesworth Street, opened 1 December.

1884–1885. London. SBA. *Winter Exhibition,* Society of British Artists, Suffolk Street, Pall Mall East, November–February.

1885. London. SBA. *62nd Annual Exhibition,* Society of British Artists, Suffolk Street, Pall Mall East, March–August.

1885–1886. New York. Met. *Loan Collection of Paintings and Sculpture,* Metropolitan Museum of Art, November 1885–April 1886.

1885–1886. London. SBA. *Winter Exhibition,* Society of British Artists, Suffolk Street, Pall Mall East, November–February.

1886. London. Dowdeswell. *'Notes'—'Harmonies'—'Nocturnes,'* Second Series, May (catalogue designed by Whistler).

1887. London. RBA. *64th Annual Exhibition,* Royal Society of British Artists, Suffolk Street, Pall Mall East, March–August (catalogue designed by Whistler).

1887. Paris. Petit. *Exposition Internationale de Peinture et de Sculpture, Sixième année,* Galerie Georges Petit, 8 rue de Seze, 8 May–8 June.

1888. Paris. Durand-Ruel. *Exposition,* Galerie Durand-Ruel, 11 rue Le Pèletier, 25 May–25 June.

1888. Munich. *III Internationale Kunst—Austellung (Munchener Jubilaums—Austellung),* Königlichen Glaspalast.

1889. Paris. Exp. Univ. *Universal Exhibition,* British Fine Art Section.

1889. London, NEAC. New English Art Club at Dudley Gallery, Egyptian Hall Piccadilly.

1889. New York. Wunderlich. *'Notes'—'Harmonies'—'Nocturnes,'* H. Wunderlich & Co., March.

1890. Brussels. *Exposition Générale des Beaux-Arts,* May–June.

1890. Paris. Salon. 105th Exhibition, *Oeuvrages de peinture, sculpture, architecture, gravure et lithographie des artists vivants,* Palais des Champs-Elysées, opened 1 May.

1892. London. Goupil. *Nocturnes, Marines and Chevalet Pieces,* Boussod, Valadon & Cie., Goupil Gallery, 116–17 New Bond Street, March–April (retrospective, catalogue designed by Whistler).

1892. Paris. Soc. Nat. 2d Exhibition, Société Nationale des Beaux-Arts, Champs de Mars, opened 7 May.

1892. Munich. VI International Kunst—Austellung, 1 June–end of October.

1892. London. SPP. 2d Exhibition, Society of Portrait Painters, at Royal Institute of Painters in Watercolours, Piccadilly.

1893. Chicago. *World's Columbian Exposition,* Department of Fine Arts.

1893–1894. Philadelphia. *63d Annual Exhibition,* Pennsylvania Academy of the Fine Arts, 18 December–24 February.

1896. Glasgow. *35th Exhibition of Works of Modern Artists,* Glasgow Institute of the Fine Arts, 3 February–May.

1897–1898. Pittsburgh. *2d Annual Exhibition,* Carnegie Institute, 4 November–1 January.

1898. London. Goupil. Goupil Gallery, *A Collection of Selected Works by Painters of the English, French and Dutch Schools,* opened 5 March.

1898. London, ISSPG. *Exhibition of International Art,* International Society of Sculptors, Painters and Gravers, Knightsbridge, May.

1898–1899. New York. *Loan Exhibition of Portraits for the Benefit of the Orthopaedic Hospital,* National Academy of Design, 14 December–14 January.

1899. Philadelphia. *68th Annual Exhibition,* Pennsylvania Academy of the Fine Arts, 16 January–23 February.

1899. London. Goupil. Goupil Gallery, *Spring Exhibition of pictures, and objects of Art,* March.

1899. New York. SAA. *21st Annual Exhibition,* Society of American Artists, American Fine Arts Society Galleries, 25 March–29 April.

1899. Venice. *III Esposizione Internazionale d'Arte della Città di Venezia,* 22 April–31 October.

1899. London. ISSPG. International Society of Sculptors, Painters and Gravers, *2d Exhibition, Pictures, Drawings, Prints and Sculptures,* Knightsbridge, May–July (catalogue designed by Whistler).

1899. Paris. Petit. *Exposition Internationale de Peinture et de Sculpture,* Galerie Georges Petit, December (catalogue untraced).

1899. Edinburgh. RSA. *73d Exhibition of the Royal Scottish Academy of Painting, Sculpture and Architecture,* Royal Scottish Academy.

1900. Berlin. *II Kunstaustellung der Berliner Sezession,* Kantstrasse 12, Spring.

1901. Glasgow. *International Exhibition,* Fine Art Section, Glasgow Art Galleries, May–October.

1901. Munich. *VIII Internationale Kunst—Austellung,* Königlichen Glaspalast, 1 June–end October.

1901. London. ISSPG. *3d Exhibition,* International Society of Sculptors, Painters and Gravers, at the Galleries of the Royal Institute, 191 Piccadilly, 7 October–10 December.

1901. Paris. Petit. *Exposition Internationale de Peinture et de Sculpture,* Galerie Georges Petit, 6–31 December (catalogue untraced).

1901. Edinburgh. RSA. *75th Exhibition of the Royal Scottish Academy of Painting, Sculpture and Architecture,* Royal Scottish Academy.

1901. Buffalo. *Pan-American Exposition,* Fine Arts Section.

1902. Paris. Soc. Nat. *12th Exhibition, Société Nationale des Beaux-Arts, Ouvrages de Peintures, Sculpture, Dessin, Gravure, Architecture et Objets d'Art,* Grand Palais, avenue d'Antoin, 20 April–30 June.

1903. Philadelphia. *72d Annual Exhibition,* Pennsylvania Academy of the Fine Arts, 19 January–28 February.

1903. London. McLean. *39th Annual Exhibition of Oil Paintings,* Thomas McLean's Gallery, 7 Haymarket, April.

1903. Venice. *V Esposizione Internazionale d'Arte della Città di Venezia,* 22 April–31 October.

1903. **Edinburgh. RSA.** *77th Exhibition of the Royal Scottish Academy of Painting, Sculpture and Architecture*, Royal Scottish Academy.

1903. **New York. SAA.** *25th Annual Exhibition*, Society of American Artists.

1903. **Paris, Petit.** Georges Petit, *Catalogue des Tableaux, Pastels, Dessins, Pointes Sèches*, Hôtel Drouot, 24–25 November.

1904. **London. Goupil.** *Watercolors, Pastels, Drawings in Black and White, Sculptures and Bronzes by British and Foreign Artists, Including . . . a Collection of Pastels, Etchings and Lithographs by the Late James McNeill Whistler*, William Marchant and Company, at Goupil Gallery, January.

1904. **Boston. Copley.** *Oil Paintings, Water Colors, Pastels and Drawings: Memorial Exhibition of the Works of Mr. J. McNeill Whistler*, Copley Society, Copley Hall, February.

1904. **London. Obach.** *The Peacock Room painted for Mr. F. R. Leyland by James McNeil Whistler, Removed in Its Entirety from the Late Owner's Residence and Exhibited at Messrs. Obach's Galleries*, 168 New Bond Street, June.

1904. **New York.** *Comparative Exhibition of Native and Foreign Art under the Auspices of the Society of Art Collectors*, 15 November–11 December.

1904. **Edinburgh. RSA.** *78th Exhibition of the Royal Scottish Academy of Painting, Sculpture and Architecture*, Royal Scottish Academy.

1904–1905. **Pittsburgh.** *9th Annual Exhibition*, Carnegie Institute, 3 November–1 January.

1904. **Dublin.** *Pictures Presented to the City of Dublin to Form the Nucleus of a Gallery of Modern Art, Also Pictures Lent by the Executors of the Late James Staats Forbes and Others*, Royal Hibernian Academy, December.

1905. **Venice.** *VI Esposizione Internazionale d'Arte della Città di Venezia.*

1905. **Buffalo.** *The Inaugural Loan Collection of Paintings*, Buffalo Fine Arts Academy, Albright Art Gallery, 31 May–1 July.

1905. **London. Memorial.** *Memorial Exhibition of the Works of the Late James McNeill Whistler, First President of the International Society of Sculptors, Painters and Gravers*, New Gallery, Regent Street, 22 February–15 April.

1905. **Paris. Memorial.** *Oeuvres de James McNeill Whistler*, Palais de L'Ecole des Beaux-Arts, Quai Malaquais, May.

1907. **Chicago.** Art Institute of Chicago, *Catalogue of the 28th Annual Exhibition of Oil Paintings and Sculpture by American Artists*, 22 October–1 December.

1909. **Buffalo.** *4th Annual Exhibition of Selected Paintings by American Artists*, Buffalo Fine Arts Academy, Albright Art Gallery, 5 May–29 August.

1909. **London. RA.** Royal Academy of Arts, *Exhibition of Modern Works in Painting and Sculpture Forming the Collection of the Late George M. McCulloch, Esq., Winter Exhibition 40th Year.*

1910. **New York. Montross.** *Loan Exhibition of Pictures by T. W. Dewing, A. H. Thayer, D. W. Tryon, J. A. McN. Whistler*, Montross Gallery, 10–26 February.

1910. **Berlin.** *Austellung Amerikanischer Kunst*, Königliche Academie der Kunste, March–April.

1910. **New York. Met.** *Paintings in Oil and Pastel by James McNeill Whistler*, Metropolitan Museum of Art, 15 March–31 May.

1910. **Ann Arbor.** Exhibition of Oriental and American Art, under the joint auspices of the Alumni Memorial Committee and the Ann Arbor Art Association. Alumni Memorial Hall, University of Michigan, 11–30 May.

1912. **Washington.** *Selection of Art Objects from the Freer Collection*, National Museum, Washington, D.C., 15 April–15 June.

1912. **London. Tate.** *Loan Collection of Works by James McNeill Whistler*, National Gallery of British Art, Room V, July–October.

1912. **Toldeo.** Toledo Museum of Art, *Catalogue of the Inaugural Exhibition*, 17 January–12 February.

1914. **Minneapolis.** Institute of Arts.

1915. **Rochester.** *Rochester Memorial Art Gallery. Catalogue of an Exhibition of Portraitures of James McNeill Whistler*, 9–27 April.

1915. **San Francisco.** *Panama-Pacific International Exposition*, Department of Fine Arts, Summer.

1918–1919. **New York.** *Portraits of Whistler and Other Whistleriana*, loan collection, Arden Gallery, 6 December–6 January.

Index of Pictures